ZAGATSURVEY®

2007

AMERICA'S TOP RESTAURANTS

Editors: Shelley Gallagher
and Robert Seixas

Published and distributed by
ZAGAT SURVEY, LLC
4 Columbus Circle
New York, New York 10019
Tel: 212 977 6000
E-mail: americastop@zagat.com
Web site: www.zagat.com

Acknowledgments

Our special thanks to the thousands of surveyors who have shared their views with us and made this nationwide *Survey* possible, as well as our editors and coordinators in each city: Claudia Alarcón, Alicia Arter, Ron Bechtol, Olga Boikess, Amanda Boyd, Lauren Chapin, Suzi Forbes Chase, Ann Christenson, Elaine T. Cicora, Andrea Clurfeld, Gabrielle Cosgriff, Camas Davis, Jackie Dishner, Victoria Elliott, Jeanette Foster, Lorraine Gengo, Rona Gindin, Sharon Gintzler, Teresa Gubbins, Meesha Halm, Lynn Hazlewood, Edie Jarolim, Lena Katz, Marty Katz, Michael Klein, Marilyn Kleinberg, Rochelle S. Koff, Gretchen Kurz, Sharon Litwin, Lori Midson, Maryanne Muller, David Nelson, Jan Norris, Angela Pettera, Ann Lemons Pollack, Joe Pollack, Virginia Rainey, Mimi Read, Laura E. Reiley, Heidi Knapp Rinella, Shelley Skiles Sawyer, Helen Schwab, Merrill Shindler, Jane Slaughter, Ruth Tobias, John Bruno Turiano, Jill Van Cleave, Alice Van Housen, Carla Waldemar and Kay Winzenried. We are also grateful to Victoria Elmacioglu (assistant editor) and Kelly Stewart (editorial assistant), as well as the following members of our staff: Sean Beachell, Maryanne Bertollo, Catherine Bigwood, Reni Chin, Larry Cohn, Carol Diuguid, Andrew Eng, Jeff Freier, Curt Gathje, Randi Gollin, Jessica Grose, Karen Hudes, Roy Jacob, Natalie Lebert, Mike Liao, Dave Makulec, Rachel McConlogue, Emily Parsons, Andre Pilette, Josh Rogers, Becky Ruthenburg, Thomas Sheehan, Carla Spartos, Kilolo Strobert, Donna Marino Wilkins, Yoji Yamaguchi, Sharon Yates and Kyle Zolner.

Contents

About This Survey   4
What's New   5
Ratings & Symbols   6
Top Food Rankings by Area.   7
Most Popular by Area 10
RESTAURANT DIRECTORY
  Names, Addresses, Phone Numbers,
  Web Sites, Ratings and Reviews
    • Atlanta. 14
    • Atlantic City 23
    • Austin 25
    • Baltimore/Annapolis 30
    • Boston. 35
    • Charlotte. 44
    • Chicago. 49
    • Cincinnati 59
    • Cleveland 64
    • Connecticut. 69
    • Dallas/Ft. Worth 77
    • Denver/Mtn. Resorts 87
    • Detroit. 96
    • Ft. Lauderdale. 101
    • Honolulu 105
    • Houston 110
    • Kansas City. 119
    • Las Vegas 124
    • Long Island. 134
    • Los Angeles 143
    • Miami 153
    • Milwaukee 161
    • Minneapolis/St. Paul 166
    • New Jersey. 171
    • New Orleans. 179
    • New York City 188
    • Orange County, CA 198
    • Orlando. 203
    • Palm Beach. 212
    • Philadelphia 217
    • Phoenix/Scottsdale 225
    • Portland, OR. 230
    • Salt Lake City/Mtn. Resorts 234
    • San Antonio 239
    • San Diego. 244
    • San Francisco Bay Area. 248
    • Seattle. 258
    • St. Louis 266
    • Tampa/Sarasota 271
    • Tucson. 276
    • Washington, DC 281
    • Westchester/HRV 290
Cuisines by Area Index 300
Alphabetical Page Index 321
Wine Chart. 332

About This Survey

Here are the results of our *2007 America's Top Restaurants Survey,* covering 1,389 restaurants across the country. This guide's coverage of the top restaurants in the 42 major markets contained herein demonstrates the fact that dining throughout America just keeps getting better and better.

This marks the 28th year that Zagat Survey has reported on the shared experiences of diners like you. What started in 1979 as a hobby involving 200 of our friends rating NYC restaurants has come a long way. Today we have over 250,000 active surveyors and now cover dining, entertaining, golf, hotels, movies, music, nightlife, resorts, shopping, spas, theater and tourist attractions around the world. All of these guides are based on consumer surveys. They are also available by subscription at zagat.com, and for use on BlackBerry, Palm, Windows Mobile devices and mobile phones.

By regularly surveying large numbers of avid customers, we hope to have achieved a uniquely current and reliable series of guides. More than a quarter-century of experience has verified this. In effect, these guides are the restaurant industry's report card, since each place's ratings and review are really a free market study of its own consumers.

Over 123,000 restaurant-goers contributed to this book. Of these surveyors, 47% are women, 53% men; the breakdown by age is 12% in their 20s; 26%, 30s; 22%, 40s; 23%, 50s; and 17%, 60s or above. While these people are a diverse group, they share one thing in common – they are all restaurant lovers. Our editors have done their best to synopsize these surveyors' opinions, with their direct comments shown in quotation marks. We sincerely thank each of these people; this book is really "theirs."

While all the restaurants in this guide were chosen for their high quality, we have prepared two separate lists to facilitate your search: see Top Food Rankings by Area (pages 7–9) and Most Popular by Area (pages 10–12). To assist you in finding just what you want when you want it, we have also provided various handy indexes.

Finally, we invite you to join any of our upcoming *Surveys*. To do so, just register at zagat.com, where you can rate and review any restaurant at any time during the year. Each participant will receive a free copy of the resulting guide when it is published. Your comments and even criticisms of this guide are also solicited. There is always room for improvement with your help. You can contact us at americastop@zagat.com.

New York, NY
October 26, 2006

Nina and Tim Zagat

What's New

Good Times: Nowadays, it's hard to find a U.S. city that doesn't have a healthy fine-dining scene. In nearly all locales, significant openings are outpacing closings. And there's more good news: our surveys show that the rise in the average cost of a meal over the last year has been limited to 2.8% nationally. In comparison, the Consumer Price Index (the most widely used measure of inflation) rose nearly a third more (4%) during the same period. That means American diners are getting more and more bang for their bucks.

Slighting Service: When asked about what irritates them the most, 72% of our respondents cited service, while all other complaints cumulatively accounted for only 28% of surveyors' grievances nationwide. To be blunt about it, service is the restaurant industry's weak link and it's time something was done to improve it.

One Space, More Choices: Noted restaurateurs are attracting a more diverse clientele by promoting dual dining areas in one location: a formal room with attendant high tabs, and a more casual room at a lower cost. Following the lead of Jean Georges (NYC) are Coi (San Francisco); Primo (Tucson); The Modern (NYC); and Joël Robuchon, with two restaurants in Las Vegas (Joël Robuchon and his L'Atelier).

Stepping Out: The branding of the celebrity chef continues unabated. While there's still plenty of money in Las Vegas, star chefs are now moving into other tourist magnets, such as Atlantic City, Palm Beach and South Beach. While part of the appeal is tourist dollars, these destinations also allow chefs to spread their fame to other parts of the country.

The Resurgence of Hotel Dining: More than ever, top chefs are setting up shop in hotels. The reason: many hotels, in order to improve their reputation (and therefore room rates), are often willing to pay for the costs of building a restaurant while offering extremely favorable rents to gain a marquee name. Based on this premise, Las Vegas has become a major culinary center in the past few years, and the same trend is occurring across the country. Even NYC hotels are importing top talent, to wit, Laurent Tourondel (Ritz-Carlton), Alan Yau (Gramercy Park) and Geoffrey Zakarian (Carlton). And a major debut from Gordon Ramsay is slated for NYC's The London hotel.

New Orleans Update: Despite the devastation caused by Hurricane Katrina, we just surveyed nearly 400 New Orleans restaurants (see 40 top choices on page 179). And with the highly anticipated reopening of Commander's Palace happening as we go to press, it's obvious the Big Easy's dining scene is coming on strong.

New York, NY
October 26, 2006

Nina and Tim Zagat

Ratings & Symbols

Name, Address, Phone Number & Web Site

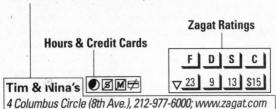

Zagat Ratings

Hours & Credit Cards

Tim & Nina's

4 Columbus Circle (8th Ave.), 212-977-6000; www.zagat.com

"You're the tapas" croon contented connoisseurs of the "cheap" cart-circulated Chinese-Castilian cuisine at this "cramped" concrete-clad Columbus Circle compound; to the contrary, critics claim Tim and Nina "push the concept too far" with dishes such as sweet-and-sour sardines, Szechuan ceviche and Beijing-Barcelona bouillabaisse, with service that comes from Spain in the '30s and China in the '60s.

Review, with surveyors' comments in quotes

Top Spots: Places with the highest overall ratings, popularity and importance are listed in BLOCK CAPITAL LETTERS.

Hours: ◑ serves after 11 PM
⊠ closed on Sunday
Ⓜ closed on Monday

Credit Cards: ⇸ no credit cards accepted

Ratings are on a scale of **0 to 30**.

F Food	D Decor	S Service	C Cost
23	9	13	$15

0–9 poor to fair	**20–25** very good to excellent
10–15 fair to good	**26–30** extraordinary to perfection
16–19 good to very good	▽ low response/less reliable

Cost (C): Reflects our surveyors' average estimate of the price of a dinner with one drink and tip and is a benchmark only. Lunch is usually 25% less.

For newcomers or survey write-ins listed without ratings, the price range is indicated as follows:

I	$25 and below	**E**	$41 to $65
M	$26 to $40	**VE**	$66 or more

Top Food Rankings by Area

Atlanta
29 Bacchanalia
28 Quinones
   Rathbun's
   Ritz Buckhead Din. Rm.
27 Aria

Atlantic City
27 White House
26 Chef Vola's
   Brighton
25 Capriccio
   Suilan

Austin
28 Vespaio
   Wink
   Hudson's
27 Jeffrey's
   Musashino Sushi

Baltimore/Annapolis
28 Sushi Sono
   Joss Cafe
27 Charleston
   Samos
   Hampton's

Boston
28 Oishii
   L'Espalier
   Aujourd'hui
27 No. 9 Park
   Hamersley's Bistro

Charlotte
29 Barrington's
28 Volare
27 McIntosh's
   Sullivan's
26 Nikko

Chicago
29 Carlos'
28 Le Français
   Les Nomades
   Tru
   Alinea

Cincinnati
29 Jean-Robert at Pigall's
28 Daveed's at 934
27 Boca
   BonBonerie
   Palace, The

Cleveland
28 Johnny's Bar
27 Chez François
   Phnom Penh
   Lolita
   Blue Point Grille

Connecticut
28 Thomas Henkelmann
   Le Petit Cafe
27 Ibiza
   Jeffrey's
   Jean-Louis

Dallas/Ft. Worth
29 French Room
28 York Street
   Abacus
   Aurora
   Lola

Denver/Mtn. Resorts
28 Mizuna
27 Highland's Garden
   Del Frisco's
   L'Atelier
   Sweet Basil

Detroit
28 Rugby Grille
   Lark, The
27 Zingerman's
   Tribute
   Bacco

Ft. Lauderdale
28 Sunfish Grill
27 La Brochette
   Cafe Maxx
26 Canyon
   Cafe Martorano

Top Food

Honolulu
28 Alan Wong's
27 La Mer
26 Hoku's
    Roy's
    Chef Mavro

Houston
28 Mark's American
27 Da Marco
    Brennan's
    Bistro Moderne
    Pappas Bros.

Kansas City
27 Bluestem
26 Stroud's
    Oklahoma Joe's
    Le Fou Frog
    American Rest.

Las Vegas
28 Rosemary's
    Lotus of Siam
27 Nobu
    Picasso
    Michael Mina

Long Island
28 Kotobuki
    Polo
27 Kitchen à Bistro
    Peter Luger
    Mill River Inn

Los Angeles
28 Matsuhisa
27 Mélisse
    Sushi Nozawa
    Leila's
    Saddle Peak

Miami
28 Francesco
27 Romeo's Cafe
    Nobu Miami Beach
    Chef Allen's
    Matsuri

Milwaukee
29 Sanford
26 Eddie Martini's
    5 O'Clock Club
    Immigrant Room
    Bacchus

Minneapolis/St. Paul
28 Bayport Cookery
    La Belle Vie
27 D'Amico Cucina
    Vincent
    Manny's

New Jersey
28 Nicholas
    Ryland Inn
27 DeLorenzo's
    Cafe Panache
    Cafe Matisse

New Orleans
28 August
    Brigtsen's
    Bayona
    Stella!
    Alberta

New York City
28 Le Bernardin
    Daniel
    Sushi Yasuda
    per se
    Peter Luger

Orange County, CA
27 Hobbit, The
    Basilic
    Tabu Grill
    Ramos House
26 Pinot Provence

Orlando
27 Le Coq au Vin
    Victoria & Albert's
    Chatham's Place
    Del Frisco's
    Taquitos Jalisco

Palm Beach
27 11 Maple Street
    Chez Jean-Pierre
    Four Seasons
    Little Moirs
26 Kathy's Gazebo

Philadelphia
28 Fountain
    Le Bar Lyonnais
    Birchrunville Store
    Le Bec-Fin
    Vetri

Phoenix/Scottsdale
28 Pizzeria Bianco
    Sea Saw
27 Marquesa
    Binkley's
    Barrio Café

Portland, OR
27 Paley's Place
    Genoa
    Apizza Scholls
26 Higgins
    Heathman

Salt Lake City/Mtn. Resorts
27 Tree Room
    Red Iguana
    Mariposa
26 Michelangelo
    Seafood Buffet

San Antonio
28 Le Rêve
27 Lodge Rest.
26 Korean BBQ House
    Biga on the Banks
    Bistro Vatel

San Diego
27 WineSellar & Brasserie
    Sushi Ota
    Pamplemousse Grille
    Arterra
    A.R. Valentien

San Francisco Bay Area
29 Gary Danko
    French Laundry
28 Cyrus
    Marinus
    Chez Panisse

Seattle
28 Herbfarm
    Nishino
    Lampreia
    Rover's
    Mistral

St. Louis
28 Sidney St. Cafe
    Paul Manno's
27 Tony's
    Trattoria Marcella
    Niche

Tampa/Sarasota
28 Cafe Ponte
27 Restaurant B.T.
    Beach Bistro
    SideBern's
26 Mise en Place

Tucson
28 Dish
26 Vivace
    Grill at Hacienda del Sol
    Le Rendez-Vous
    Cafe Poca Cosa

Washington, DC
29 Inn at Little Washington
28 Makoto
    Maestro
    Citronelle
    Marcel's

Westchester/HRV
29 Freelance Café
    Xaviar's at Piermont
27 Rest. X & Bully Boy Bar
    Blue Hill/Stone Barns
    Buffet de la Gare

Most Popular by Area

Atlanta
1. Bacchanalia
2. Rathbun's
3. Bone's
4. Chops/Lobster Bar
5. Aria

Atlantic City
1. P.F. Chang's
2. Chef Vola's
3. White House
4. Dock's Oyster
5. Ombra
6. Suilan*

Austin
1. Chuy's
2. Salt Lick
3. Eddie V's
4. Vespaio
5. Uchi

Baltimore/Annapolis
1. Clyde's
2. Ruth's Chris
3. Prime Rib
4. Charleston
5. McCormick & Schmick's

Boston
1. Legal Sea Foods
2. Blue Ginger
3. No. 9 Park
4. L'Espalier
5. Hamersley's

Charlotte
1. Barrington's
2. Upstream
3. Mickey & Mooch
4. Bonterra
5. Palm

Chicago
1. Charlie Trotter's
2. Tru
3. Frontera Grill
4. Wildfire
5. Morton's

Cincinnati
1. Jean-Robert at Pigall's
2. Montgomery Inn
3. Palomino
4. Jeff Ruby's
5. Precinct

Cleveland
1. Blue Point Grille
2. Lolita
3. Johnny's Bar
4. Hyde Park Prime
5. Baricelli Inn

Connecticut
1. Thomas Henkelmann
2. Union League
3. Barcelona
4. City Limits Diner
5. Jean-Louis
6. Rebeccas*

Dallas/Ft. Worth
1. Abacus
2. Del Frisco's
3. Mi Cocina
4. Mansion on Turtle Creek
5. Café Pacific

Denver/Mtn. Resorts
1. Sweet Basil
2. Flagstaff House
3. Mizuna
4. Del Frisco's
5. 240 Union

Detroit
1. Lark
2. Tribute
3. Zingerman's
4. Common Grill
5. Opus One

Ft. Lauderdale
1. Cheesecake Factory
2. Houston's
3. Mark's Las Olas
4. Casa D'Angelo
5. Ruth's Chris

---

* Indicates a tie with restaurant above

Honolulu
1. Alan Wong's
2. Roy's
3. Hoku's
4. La Mer
5. Duke's Canoe Club

Houston
1. Mark's American
2. Cafe Annie
3. Carrabba's
4. Pappas Bros.
5. Brennan's

Kansas City
1. McCormick & Schmick's
2. Fiorella's Jack Stack
3. Plaza III
4. Lidia's
5. Grand St. Cafe

Las Vegas
1. Picasso
2. Aureole
3. Delmonico
4. Buffet at Bellagio
5. Prime Steak

Long Island
1. Peter Luger
2. Cheesecake Factory
3. Coolfish
4. Bryant/Cooper
5. Mill River Inn

Los Angeles
1. Cheesecake Factory
2. A.O.C.
3. Spago
4. Café Bizou
5. Campanile

Miami
1. Joe's Stone Crab
2. Cheesecake Factory
3. Nobu Miami Beach
4. Houston's
5. Norman's

Milwaukee
1. Maggiano's
2. P.F. Chang's
3. Sanford
4. Lake Park Bistro
5. Potbelly Sandwich*

Minneapolis/St. Paul
1. Oceanaire
2. Manny's
3. Vincent
4. Zelo
5. St. Paul Grill

New Jersey
1. Ryland Inn
2. Scalini Fedeli
3. Bernards Inn
4. Frog & Peach
5. Amanda's

New Orleans
1. Galatoire's
2. Bayona
3. NOLA
4. Emeril's
5. Brennan's

New York City
1. Gramercy Tavern
2. Union Sq. Cafe
3. Le Bernardin
4. Babbo
5. Peter Luger

Orange County, CA
1. Cheesecake Factory
2. Roy's
3. Ruth's Chris
4. Houston's
5. P.F. Chang's

Orlando
1. California Grill
2. Emeril's Orlando
3. Seasons 52
4. Victoria & Albert's
5. Wolfgang Puck Cafe

Palm Beach
1. Cheesecake Factory
2. Houston's
3. Kee Grill
4. P.F. Chang's
5. Café L'Europe

Philadelphia
1. Buddakan
2. Le Bec-Fin
3. Fountain
4. Lacroix/Rittenhouse
5. Brasserie Perrier

By Popularity Rank

Phoenix/Scottsdale
1. T. Cook's
2. Roy's
3. P.F. Chang's
4. Mary Elaine's
5. Mastro's

Portland, OR
1. Higgins
2. Andina
3. Paley's Place
4. Wildwood
5. Bluehour

Salt Lake City/Mtn. Resorts
1. Market St. Grill
2. New Yorker Club
3. Wahso
4. Chimayo
5. Red Iguana

San Antonio
1. Paesanos
2. Le Rêve
3. Biga on the Banks
4. Boudro's/Riverwalk
5. P.F. Chang's

San Diego
1. George's at the Cove
2. Pamplemousse Grille
3. Marine Room
4. Roppongi
5. Ruth's Chris

San Francisco Bay Area
1. Gary Danko
2. Boulevard
3. Slanted Door
4. French Laundry
5. Michael Mina

Seattle
1. Wild Ginger
2. Dahlia Lounge
3. Metropolitan Grill
4. Canlis
5. Cafe Juanita

St. Louis
1. Sidney St. Cafe
2. Annie Gunn's
3. 1111 Mississippi
4. Trattoria Marcella
5. Tony's

Tampa/Sarasota
1. Bern's
2. Columbia
3. Roy's
4. SideBern's
5. Bijou Café

Tucson
1. Cafe Poca Cosa
2. Grill at Hacienda del Sol
3. Terra Cotta
4. Wildflower
5. Janos

Washington, DC
1. Kinkead's
2. Citronelle
3. Jaleo
4. Zaytinya
5. TenPenh

Westchester/HRV
1. Crabtree's Kittle House
2. Xaviar's at Piermont
3. Harvest on Hudson
4. La Panetière
5. Blue Hill/Stone Barns

Restaurant Directory

Atlanta

TOP FOOD RANKING

	Restaurant	Cuisine
29	Bacchanalia	New American
28	Quinones Room	New American
	Rathbun's	New American
	Ritz Buckhead Din. Rm.	Med./New French
27	Aria	New American
	Bone's	Steakhouse
	Tamarind	Thai
	Park 75	New American
	di Paolo	Northern Italian
	Seeger's	European
26	Floataway Cafe	French/Italian
	MF Sushibar	Japanese
	McKendrick's	Steakhouse
	Taka	Japanese
	Nan Thai	Thai
	Chops/Lobster Bar	Seafood/Steakhouse
	Joël	French
	La Grotta	Northern Italian
	Madras Saravana	Indian/Vegetarian
	New York Prime	Steakhouse

OTHER NOTEWORTHY PLACES

Atlanta Fish Market	Seafood
BluePointe	New American
Canoe	New American
dick and harry's	New Amer./Seafood
Ecco	Continental
Hashiguchi	Japanese
Kyma	Greek
La Tavola	Italian
Muss & Turner's	Deli/New American
Nam	Vietnamese
Nava	Southwestern
Pano's & Paul's	Continental
Restaurant Eugene	New American
Sia's	Asian/Southwestern
Sotto Sotto	Northern Italian
South City Kitchen	Southern
Tierra	Pan-Latin
Watershed	Southern
Wisteria	Southern
Woodfire Grill	Californian

subscribe to zagat.com

ARIA ☒
27 25 25 $51

490 E. Paces Ferry Rd. (Maple Dr.), 404-233-7673; www.aria-atl.com
"Gerry Klaskala continues to be at the top of his game" at this
Buckhead "beauty", creating "amazing" New American cuisine
"with a soul", while pastry chef Kathryn King's desserts are some
of the "best in town"; the "gorgeous" space includes a "cool"
bar, "romantic" wine cellar for private dining and "cozy" patio,
and though the scene can get "way too loud", "superb" service
makes "you feel like a million bucks"; it's "expensive" too, but
"you get what you pay for."

Atlanta Fish Market
23 19 20 $38

*265 Pharr Rd. (bet. Peachtree St. & Piedmont Rd.), 404-262-3165;
www.buckheadrestaurants.com*
"If it swims, you can get it" at this "seafood lover's paradise" from
the Buckhead Life Group, where an "unrivaled selection" of
"schools upon schools" of "fabulous fish" flown in fresh three
times daily is prepared "any way imaginable"; you can almost
"feel the ocean breezes" in the "welcoming" "nautical" setting,
though "even with reservations" it can be a "two-glasses-of-
wine wait" when it's packed with as "many tourists" as on a
"Carnival Cruise"; regulars recommend this one primarily for
"business" or "group" dining.

BACCHANALIA ☒
29 25 28 $77

*Westside Mktpl., 1198 Howell Mill Rd. (bet. 14th St. & Huff Rd.),
404-365-0410; www.starprovisions.com*
"Any conversation about Atlanta's best" must include this
"seamless" New American on the Westside, voted the city's
Most Popular and No. 1 for Food, with a "big time wow factor"
that "could make a rainy Tuesday seem like a special occasion";
"husband-and-wife team" Anne Quatrano and Clifford Harrison's
"focused" cuisine guarantees "gastronomic ecstasy" that's a
"true bargain despite the price", and "sublime" service is "choreographed like a ballet" in the "refined" warehouse space with
a "laid-back" vibe in spite of its "top-tier status."

BluePointe
24 26 21 $47

*3455 Peachtree Rd. (Lenox Rd.), 404-237-9070;
www.buckheadrestaurants.com*
Everything about this New American "marvel" on the "ground floor
of a Buckhead high-rise" is "gorgeous", from the "sleek" and
"modern" dining room with a lofty "ceiling in the clouds", to the
"pure artistry" of the "Asian-inflected", "fish-heavy" cuisine that
"hits the right note", to the "electric" lounge scene crackling with
"celebrities", "VIPs" and "beautiful women"; despite grumbles
about servers with "attitude" and "gold diggers" "hoarding the
bar", it's still a "shining star" on the city's "glitterati" dining scene.

BONE'S RESTAURANT
27 22 26 $55

*3130 Piedmont Rd. (Peachtree Rd.), 404-237-2663;
www.bonesrestaurant.com*
"Impeccable" right "down to the bone", this "carnivore central"
in Buckhead delivers "time and again" with "classic" steaks that
"Fred Flintstone would die for", plus "generous sides", "big, cold
drinks" and a "phone book" of a wine list; "polished" servers and
"fabulous bartenders" "take excellent care" of the requisite "old
money", "serious business-lunchers" and "power players" in a

"plush red", "old-world" setting that's "drenched in testosterone" as well as "tremendous history and personality"; in short, this "local legend lives on."

Canoe | 25 | 26 | 24 | $46 |

Vinings on the River, 4199 Paces Ferry Rd. (I-75), 770-432-2663;
www.canoeatl.com

In a "beautifully landscaped" setting "on the banks of the Chattahoochee River", the "ambiance" of this "fairy-tale" "favorite" in Vinings "goes on for days" while "adventuresome" chef Carvel Grant Gould "successfully navigates" the dining scene with her "stunning" New American cuisine that's heavy on "Southern hunter's fare" ("if you can shoot it in the woods" it's "on the menu"); "impeccable" service adds to an experience so "romantic" that dating doyens declare "if you don't get lucky after going here, then it's time to end the relationship."

CHOPS/LOBSTER BAR | 26 | 24 | 24 | $55 |

Buckhead Plaza, 70 W. Paces Ferry Rd. (Peachtree Rd.), 404-262-2675;
www.buckheadrestaurants.com

A "bit of heaven on earth" for "carnivores and their fish-loving brethren", this "consistently spectacular" Buckhead Life production offers "exemplary" steaks and "unbeatable seafood", paired with a "phenomenal wine list" and "pampering" service that "makes you feel like royalty"; there's a "good bar scene" peopled by the "'in' crowd" in the "elegant", "man's man" chophouse upstairs, while the "dungeon of deliciousness" below boasts an awesome" "Grand Central Station"–inspired look.

dick and harry's ⊠ | 25 | 19 | 23 | $40 |

Holcomb Woods Village, 1570 Holcomb Bridge Rd. (½ mi. east of
GA 400), Roswell, 770-641-8757; www.dickandharrys.com

An "old standby" that "gets better with age", this Roswell New American "consistently" serves "exceptional" seafood-centric cuisine "so fresh" some finatics order "clams for dessert", while "crab-cake snobs" deem its version among the "best in town"; though it's "strangely located" in a "bland" strip mall, "accommodating" service (some find it "snooty") and an "elegant", "upscale" setting help make it a "hot" spot to "celebrate any event."

di Paolo Ⓜ | 27 | 21 | 25 | $37 |

Rivermont Sq., 8560 Holcomb Bridge Rd. (Nesbitt Ferry Rd.),
Alpharetta, 770-587-1051; www.dipaolorestaurant.com

The "magnificent obsession" of a "loyal army of regulars", this restaurant is "worth the drive to the end of the earth" (i.e. Alpharetta) for "superb" Northern Italian creations from an open kitchen that'll "knock your socks off" and "impeccable" service; there's a "surprise with every detail" in the "quaint", "relaxing" dining room, and though the "old strip-mall location doesn't do it justice", for many it's the "perfect choice for any occasion."

Ecco | – | – | – | M |

40 Seventh St. NE (Cypress St.), 404-347-9555; www.fifthgroup.com

The Fifth Group (its restaurants include South City Kitchen and La Tavola) offers a fresh take on the neighborhood restaurant with this casual Continental housed in a former fencing club in Midtown; chef Micah Willix's simple, seasonal cuisine and small plates are served in a Johnson Studio–designed space that combines modern and old world with a blend of marble, leather and dark walnut, and includes large dining areas, an expansive lounge and an outdoor patio.

Floataway Cafe ⚄Ⓜ　　　　　　26 | 22 | 24 | $43
Floataway Bldg., 1123 Zonolite Rd. NE (bet. Briarcliff & Johnson Rds.), 404-892-1414; www.starprovisions.com
Intowners "never tire of" this "foodies' delight", the "more informal" sibling of Bacchanalia and Quinones that wins props for "deceptively simple" and "stunning" French-Italian cuisine emphasizing "local organic produce", an "eclectic" wine list and "gracious" service; nestled in an "oasis of artists' studios" amid an "industrial wasteland" near Emory, the "sleek" space with "ethereal curtains" cultivates an "energetic" vibe – if they could "just get rid of the noise", it "would be the perfect place."

Hashiguchi ❶⚄　　　　　　25 | 15 | 19 | $28
Shops Around Lenox, 3400 Woodale Dr. NE (Peachtree St.), 404-841-9229
The Terrace, 3000 Windy Hill Rd. SE (Powers Ferry Rd.), Marietta, 770-955-2337
"Countless regulars" count on these "consistent" Japanese twins in Buckhead and Marietta for "excellent" eats at "fair prices", including "quality" sushi and a "great variety" of "authentic cooked" offerings, served by a "friendly", "caring" staff; "not many know about" the "hidden" Lenox location, making it a more "intimate" setting, but either venue is a "wonderful" choice for a "quiet business gathering" or a "lively ladies' night."

Joël ⚄　　　　　　26 | 26 | 24 | $58
The Forum, 3290 Northside Pkwy. NW (W. Paces Ferry Rd.), 404-233-3500; www.joelrestaurant.com
Joël Antunes is a "true artist" creating "brilliant" French cuisine in the "lavishly appointed kitchen" of his Buckhead establishment, while sommelier Philippe Buttin is in "a class of his own" selecting a "formidable" wine list; the "stunning" space boasts "high ceilings" and an "exquisite bar", and while the service strikes a few as "snooty", most find it "superb"; "perfection" may not be "for the faint of pocketbook", but many still keep this "standout" "high on their list for special occasions."

Kyma ⚄　　　　　　25 | 24 | 23 | $47
3085 Piedmont Rd. NE (E. Paces Ferry Rd.), 404-262-0702; www.buckheadrestaurants.com
"I didn't know Atlanta was on the coast" gush groupies about this "brilliant conceptualization" of an "upscale Greek taverna" from the Buckhead Life Group, where "simple preparations" of the "freshest fish" "allow" the "flavors to shine", and an "amazing wine program" complements "marvelous meze"; a "polished" staff delivers "wonderful" service in the "gorgeous" space, and while the experience may max out your "expense account", for most it's "worth every penny."

La Grotta ⚄　　　　　　26 | 22 | 25 | $49
Crowne Plaza Ravinia Hotel, 4355 Ashford Dunwoody Rd. (Hammond Dr.), 770-395-9925
2637 Peachtree Rd. NE (bet. Lindbergh Dr. & Wesley Rd.), 404-231-1368 www.lagrottaatlanta.com
"La Grade A" is what aficionados call this "anniversary-worthy" Northern Italian duo where "fabulous" cuisine that "never disap-

points" and "exemplary" service from a "professional" staff represent "fine dining at its very best"; fans of the Buckhead original, including an "older, affluent crowd", are unfazed by the "strange basement location" and enjoy a "sense of calm" and "great acoustics", while the Dunwoody location offers an "elegant", "plush" space that overlooks a garden and waterfalls.

La Tavola

23 | 20 | 22 | $32

992 Virginia Ave. NE (N. Highland Ave.), 404-873-5430;
www.latavolatrattoria.com

"Everything has that homemade touch" at this "stylish" Italian in the "heart of Va-Highlands", where chef Craig Richards (ex Felidia in NYC) creates "sophisticated" yet "simple" cuisine that is paired with a "superb" wine list; "attentive" service "makes you feel like a regular" in the "shotgun" space with a "long, gleaming" bar, "romantic" balcony and "intimate" (read: "cramped") dining room; P.S. the "fabulous" Sunday brunch is a "well-kept secret."

Madras Saravana Bhavan

26 | 10 | 14 | $15

North Dekalb Sq., 2179 Lawrenceville Hwy. (N. Druid Hills Rd.),
Decatur, 404-636-4400; www.madrassaravanabhavan.net

Faithful fans wish they had "more arms than Vishnu to shovel in all the wonderful delights" at this "superb" Indian in Decatur offering "incredible", "extremely spicy" vegetarian fare at "affordable prices"; service can be a "crapshoot" and the decor resembles something like "tiki hut meets" the subcontinent, but aficionados just "close their eyes" and "wallow in the smells and tastes" that "take you to India for the price of three coffees from Starbucks."

McKendrick's Steak House

26 | 21 | 25 | $52

Park Place Shopping Ctr., 4505 Ashford Dunwoody Rd. NE
(bet. Hammond Dr. & Perimeter Ctr.), 770-512-8888;
www.mckendricks.com

This "high-end" "power" spot in Dunwoody "competes with the best of Buckhead" via "fabulous" steaks that are "worth the cholesterol", "huge", "tasty sides", an "impressive wine list" and "wonderful" "old-fashioned" service that "makes you feel special"; the atmosphere is "vibrant" (and a "little noisy") in "quintessential" steakhouse digs of "dark oak" and "white tablecloths" – just be sure to "bring lots of money" because "everything's à la carte."

MF Sushibar

26 | 23 | 21 | $39

265 Ponce de Leon Ave. (Penn St.), 404-815-8844; www.mfsushibar.com

At this Midtown Japanese, the "lovingly prepared" offerings of "amazingly fresh" sushi are "literally art" and the "fresh wasabi" is "not to be missed"; the "cool factor is high" in the "modern" space located in a "wonderfully renovated section" of Ponce that attracts an "eye-appealing" "hip" crowd, so "make reservations" and be prepared to "pay extra" or "forget about eating here."

Muss & Turner's ⊠

25 | 19 | 23 | $17

1675 Cumberland Pkwy. (Atlanta Rd.), Smyrna, 770-434-1114;
www.mussandturners.com

"These guys know their stuff" gush groupies of this "gourmet" deli/restaurant in Smyrna; during the day, it dishes out "amazing" (albeit "pricey") sandwiches that "always hit the spot" and has arguably the "coolest takeaway", but it goes full-service in the evenings, when a menu of New American small plates and entrees is offered; "witty" descriptions of the "creative" selections can "make deciding difficult" for some, but the "helpful" "owners and employees love their work" "and it shows."

Nam 🗷   26 | 23 | 22 | $33

Midtown Promenade, 931 Monroe Dr. NE (Ponce de Leon Ave.), 404-541-9997; www.namrestaurant.com

"It's not every day you get to gnaw on sugarcane at the table", but this "stellar" Midtown sibling of MF Sushibar has certainly "upped the ante" when it comes to "exotic", "delicious" Vietnamese eats that are a "visual feast" (the "shaking beef is one of the wonders of the world"); the "stylish" and "elegant" environs make you "forget you're in a strip mall in dire need of renovation", while the "impeccable" service and "sexy" vibe add to the "wow factor."

Nan Thai Fine Dining   26 | 27 | 24 | $41

1350 Spring St. NW (17th St.), 404-870-9933; www.nanfinedining.com

This "smoothly sexy" "high-end" Midtown Thai (and Tamarind sibling) is "like a trip to Bangkok without the airfare" thanks to a "dazzlingly dramatic" Johnson Studio—designed space that "gushes Asian sophistication and charm" ("even the restroom is gorgeous"); the cuisine is "art on your plate" that's delivered with "impeccable" grace by a "gorgeous" staff, making it "an experience you don't want to miss" and the "best place" to "impress your friends, clients, or in-laws."

Nava   24 | 24 | 22 | $40

Buckhead Plaza, 3060 Peachtree Rd. NE (W. Paces Ferry Rd.), 404-240-1984; www.buckheadrestaurants.com

Even those who "don't like Southwestern" may have a "change of mind" at this "upscale" "Santa Fe"—inspired Buckhead Life Group production serving a menu of "spectacular" "fresh flavors" that are a "fiesta for the taste buds" and "flavorful drinks", including "perfect" margaritas that are "worth the trip" alone; a "steady" staff "aims to please" in the "fabulous" "multi-tiered room" or on the "fantastic patio" and outdoor bar area.

New York Prime   26 | 22 | 24 | $57

Monarch Tower, 3424 Peachtree Rd. NE (Lenox Rd.), 404-846-0644; www.centraarchy.com

"Oh yeah, baby" crow carnivores who "rejoice" over this "prime" Buckhead link in a national chain that's "rising in the ranks" with "perfect" steaks that "melt in your mouth", side dishes "to die for" and a "phenomenal" wine list that come together for a "special occasion"– and "expense account"–worthy experience; the staff of "real pros" is praised for their "attention to detail" in the "masculine" space where there's "always a happening happy hour" ("better not mind cigar smoke").

Pano's & Paul's 🗷   26 | 23 | 25 | $55

West Paces Ferry Shopping Ctr., 1232 W. Paces Ferry Rd. (Northside Pkwy.), 404-261-3662; www.buckheadrestaurants.com

At this Buckhead "pinnacle of old-style dining", a "deep wine list" matches the "elegant" Continental menu, and "immaculate" dishes arrive "hot and timely" thanks to "crazy perfect" service; the "expense-account crowd" and "comb-over and trophy-wife" types alike celebrate "special occasions" in the "opulent" "early '20s" setting, and while a few feel it's "lost its moorings", defenders insist "Pano's flagship is still sailing" smoothly "after all these years."

Park 75
| 27 | 25 | 28 | $60 |

Four Seasons Atlanta, 75 14th St. (bet. Peachtree & W. Peachtree Sts.), 404-253-3840; www.fourseasons.com

The "elegant" Four Seasons "lives up to its image" with this "flawless" New American showcasing the "extraordinary flavors" of chef Robert Gerstenecker's "sublime" cuisine, including a "beyond-belief brunch"; the service is "off the charts", mapping "power meals" for "neighborhood lawyers, bankers, headhunters" and other "who's who" guests who gather for "white-tablecloth dining" in the "handsomely appointed" room; P.S. the "divine" chef's table in the kitchen is a "fantastic experience."

QUINONES ROOM AT BACCHANALIA ⑤ Ⓜ
| 28 | 27 | 28 | $122 |

Courtyard of Bacchanalia, 1198 Howell Mill Rd. NW (bet. 14th & Huff Sts.), 404-365-0410; www.starprovisions.com

Bacchanalia may have "one-upped" itself with this "truly remarkable" New American prix fixe–only "experience" in the same Westside complex; "every bite" offers an "unforgettably superb taste" and "fantastic wine pairings" "won't disappoint", while "impeccable", "synchronized" service and a "gorgeous", "intimate" room with "wonderful linens" add to a "$$$'s no object special-occasion" experience that's "worth every penny"; in short, it should be on everyone's "once-before-I-die list."

RATHBUN'S ⑤
| 28 | 25 | 25 | $45 |

Stove Works, 112 Krog St. NE (bet. Edgewood Ave. & Irwin St.), 404-524-8280; www.rathbunsrestaurant.com

This "trendy but not pretentious" New American in a "refurbished industrial area" of Inman Park "leaves the hip pretenders in the dust" thanks to Kevin Rathbun's "spectacular", "visually appealing" "creations" from daily "hand-scrawled" menus that offer "something for everyone" and "every budget", topped off with "small and perfect" desserts; "homey" "greetings from the man himself" are part of the "charming" service, and the "beautiful" "rehabbed stove plant" resonates with a "lively" vibe (but "bad acoustics") that "makes life seem glam and fun."

Restaurant Eugene
| 26 | 25 | 24 | $56 |

The Aramore, 2277 Peachtree Rd. (Peachtree Memorial Dr.), 404-355-0321; www.restauranteugene.com

"Tradition and innovation pat each other on the back" in the kitchen of this "first-class" New American in South Buckhead, where the "husband-and-wife duo has got it going on" with a "constantly changing menu" of "fresh", Southern-accented fare emphasizing "local" ingredients and an "impressive boutique wine list"; "impeccable" service "makes everyone feel special and welcome" in the "beautiful" "quiet" room, and satisfied surveyors go so far as to say it's "a pleasure to pay the bill."

RITZ-CARLTON BUCKHEAD DINING ROOM ⑤ Ⓜ
| 28 | 27 | 28 | $82 |

Ritz-Carlton Buckhead, 3434 Peachtree Rd. NE (Lenox Rd.), 404-237-2700; www.ritzcarlton.com

Near "perfect from beginning to end", this "elegant", upscale "grande dame" boasts a "kind" and "impeccable" staff that "makes all diners feel special", a "knowledgeable" sommelier who is "helpful" with her "wine novella" and "the best maitre d' in town"; chef Arnaud Berthelier's New French–Med cuisine "holds a universe of remarkable flavors" that are "unforgettable" and the green damask setting with "cozy" booths "makes you feel like a Rockefeller"; N.B. jackets required.

Seeger's ⊠   27 25 26 $101

111 W. Paces Ferry Rd. (E. Andrews Dr.), 404-846-9779;
www.seegers.com

"Like being in Europe without having to clear customs", this Buckhead contemporary European is a "foodies' paradise" thanks to "genius" chef-owner Guenter Seeger, whose "love affair with food" shows up in "every luminous dish"; a "professional" staff delivers just the "right balance of attention and privacy" and the "stunning decor" of the cozy house "envelops you" "like a dream"; a few wags rename it "Meagers" for the "small", "expensive" portions, but most laud it as an "elegant" "gift" that "could stand up anywhere in the world."

Sia's ⊠   26 22 24 $45

10305 Medlock Bridge Rd. (Wilson Rd.), Duluth, 770-497-9727;
www.siasrestaurant.com

For "cutting-edge" cuisine "without the drive to Buckhead", aficionados recommend Sia Moshk's "wonderfully inventive" Asian-Southwestern in Duluth, an oasis of "flair and finesse" "in the midst of the big box chains" that delivers a "little spice" to the 'burbs; a "friendly" staff provides "consistent" service in an "attractive" "art deco"–inspired room; in short, they "do it all well."

Sotto Sotto ⊠   26 19 21 $37

313 N. Highland Ave. NE (Elizabeth St.), 404-523-6678;
www.sottosottorestaurant.com

"Riccardo Ullio continues to set the bar" high for "elegant" Northern Italian cuisine with "dazzling performances in the kitchen" of his "super trattoria" that's the "highlight of Inman Park", where "heavenly" dishes are paired with a "well-chosen" wine list; the "courteous" service "seduces with small touches", "acoustical ceiling tiles" have "improved the din" in the "cozy" space and a "nifty little" patio offers a respite for "claustrophobics."

South City Kitchen   24 20 21 $35

1144 Crescent Ave. NE (14th St.), 404-873-7358
1675 Cumberland Pkwy. (Atlanta Rd. SE), Smyrna, 770-435-0700
www.southcitykitchen.com

"Dixie meets Manhattan" at this "upscale" Midtown venue by the Fifth Group (of Ecco and La Tavola), a "long-term member of the can't-miss club" for fans of its "magnificent" "eclectic" Southern cuisine with a "new accent" brought to table by a "knowledgeable" staff; the renovated "old house" with a "trendy urban groove" can get "crowded" and "loud", but it's "worth enduring for the food"; N.B. the Smyrna location opened post-*Survey*.

Taka ⊠   26 14 21 $38

375 Pharr Rd. NE (Grandview Ave.), 404-869-2802; www.taka-atlanta.com

"Insiders" are tickled by the "hilarious" e-mails they receive from chef Taka Moriuchi, an "absolute delight" who turns out "artistic" sushi and "sashimi that will make your head swim" at his Buckhead Japanese; even the "waiters are a joy" in the "small" venue that's "never crowded"; boosters say it's one of the "best in town – without the attitude."

Tamarind
27 | 19 | 23 | $32

*80 14th St. NW (bet. Spring & Williams Sts.), 404-873-4888;
www.nanfinedining.com*
"As genuine as the best in Bangkok", this "off-the-charts"
Midtown Thai (and elder sibling of Nan) serves "perfect" "beautifully presented" cuisine that's "worth every penny", and an "impeccable staff" delivers "tip-top" service; the "unassuming
exterior" in a challenging location "right off the highway" masks
an "upscale" yet "relaxed" setting where you can "see famous
golfers" – "it's a favorite of past Masters champions."

Tierra ⊠ Ⓜ
25 | 18 | 25 | $34

*1425B Piedmont Ave. NE (Westminster Dr.), 404-874-5951;
www.tierrarestaurant.com*
Take a "superb" "culinary tour of South America" at this Midtown
Pan-Latin where "knowledgeable and passionate owners" Ticha
and Dan Krinsky "carefully" craft an "ever-changing seasonal
menu" of "superb" dishes "with great integrity" that's matched with
an "intriguing" wine list, while the signature tres leches cake is "to
die for"; the "itty-bitty" space near the Botanical Garden is un-
imposing from the outside, but the "pleasant bistro atmosphere"
and "great" outdoor patio are "conducive to a comfy evening."

Watershed
25 | 19 | 21 | $30

*406 W. Ponce de Leon Ave. (Commerce Dr.), Decatur, 404-378-4900;
www.watershedrestaurant.com*
"Superb hardly sums up" chef Scott Peacock's "whimsical, chic
and nostalgic" "interpretations of Southern fare" at this "asset to
Atlanta's dining scene" in Decatur, where cognoscenti caution
"stay out of our way" on Tuesday nights, the only time the "best
fried chicken in town" is served; a "great staff" serves a "diverse
clientele" in the "minimalist" (some say "cold") converted gas
station space, and while wags dub the "pricey" affair "'Wallet-
shed'", most agree it "never disappoints."

Wisteria
24 | 20 | 22 | $37

*471 N. Highland Ave. NE (bet. Colquitt Ave. & Freedom Pkwy.),
404-525-3363*
"They provide relaxation at no extra charge" at this "hip but laid-
back" "high-caliber hideaway" in Inman Park that's the "dining
room away from home" for fans of chef Jason Hill's "fantastic"
"Southern fare with a modern twist" that's paired with "varied and
well-priced wines by the glass", and served by a "top-notch" staff;
the "cozy" (but "loud") "urban" space in a century-old building has
a "romantic" feel that makes it a "great first-date place", especially
on a "weeknight" when it's relatively less "packed."

Woodfire Grill
24 | 21 | 22 | $41

*1782 Cheshire Bridge Rd. NE (Piedmont Ave.), 404-347-9055;
www.woodfiregrill.com*
This Cheshire Bridge "altar to fresh food" is a "foodie's paradise"
where chef Michael Tuohy's "outstanding" "homage to Californian
cuisine", including a "tremendous cheese plate" and a "delectable
wine list" that's "half price on Sundays", is served by an "attentive" staff in a "softly lit" space redolent with the "lovely smell of a
wood fire"; while some smolder over "expensive" "small portions",
most agree this "crowd-pleaser" is "burning up the competition";
P.S. the "casual" cafe is "quite a bargain."

TOP FOOD RANKING

Restaurant	Cuisine
27 White House	Sandwich Shop
26 Chef Vola's	Italian
Brighton	Steakhouse
25 Capriccio	Italian
Suilan	Chinese/French

OTHER NOTEWORTHY PLACES

Bobby Flay Steak	Steakhouse
Dock's Oyster House	Seafood
Mia	Italian/Med.
Ombra	Italian
P.F. Chang's	Chinese

F	D	S	C
–	–	–	E

Bobby Flay Steak
Borgata Hotel, Casino & Spa, 1 Borgata Way (Atlantic City Expwy., exit 1), 609-317-1000; www.theborgata.com
The eponymous celebrity chef (of NYC's Mesa Grill, Bolo and Bar Americain, and Las Vegas' Mesa Grill) has gone sleek and sexy for this upscale meatery in the Borgata; the kitchen turns out an updated chophouse menu with nods to Jersey produce, while über-designer David Rockwell has fitted out the interior with natural materials (check out the red leather entryway).

BRIGHTON STEAKHOUSE | 26 | 24 | 24 | $55 |
Sands Hotel & Casino, 136 S. Kentucky Ave. (Pacific Ave.), 609-441-4300; www.acsands.com
If you like odds that are stacked in your favor, find your way to this slabhouse in the Sands serving some of the "best steaks in AC"; fans take comfort in the "excellent" service and "fabulous" decor, but they also pray that someone else picks up the bill, because the beef isn't the only thing that's "premium" here.

CAPRICCIO | 25 | 25 | 25 | $64 |
Resorts Atlantic City Casino & Hotel, 1133 Boardwalk (North Carolina Ave.), 609-340-6789
Consider playing the slots to pay for a meal at this "pretty" Italian in the Resorts, where fans say you've "hit the jackpot" since the food is "superb", the staff is "excellent" and the big bonus is the "ocean view" (though "not visible at night"); "even if you're not comped", it's "worth every poker chip" in your pocket.

CHEF VOLA'S Ⓜ⌿ | 26 | 10 | 22 | $44 |
111 S. Albion Pl. (Pacific Ave.), 609-345-2022
You may just have to "know the right people" to get in to this reservations-only "find" in an AC "basement", "one of the more original places around" that delivers with "sensational" Italian fare, "incredible hospitality" and a "quirky" "non-decor" that's

"part of the charm"; P.S. "bring cash", and don't forget a bottle, since it's BYO.

DOCK'S OYSTER HOUSE   24 | 19 | 22 | $47

2405 Atlantic Ave. (Georgia Ave.), 609-345-0092;
www.docksoysterhouse.com

Those who like to "escape the casinos" for a while and feast on "delicious" seafood recommend this "tried and true" AC "institution" (100 years+) known for its "fabulous assortment of pristine oysters" and "outstanding" service; though you may have to "wait" for a table, it's still "hard to beat", especially with "free parking."

Mia Ⓜ   – | – | – | E

Caesars on the Boardwalk, 2100 Pacific Ave. (S. Arkansas Ave.),
609-441-2345; www.miaac.com

Philly celeb chefs Georges Perrier (Le Bec-Fin, Brasserie Perrier, Georges') and Chris Scarduzio (Brasserie Perrier) have set up shop in AC with this romantic, Italo-centric Med bistro and lounge off the Caesars lobby; the white-tablecloth venue is set in a high-ceilinged, Roman-columned space, and a wide wine-by-the-glass selection suits late-night guests grooving to the DJ.

OMBRA Ⓢ Ⓜ   24 | 26 | 23 | $50

Borgata Hotel, Casino & Spa, 1 Borgata Way (Atlantic City Expwy.,
exit 1), 866-692-6742; www.theborgata.com

"Don't be surprised" if you spot "superstars from sports and entertainment" tuning into chef Luke Palladino's "marvelous" cooking at this "classy", "grottolike" Italian in the Borgata; the decor makes you "feel like you're in a cellar" since "bottles surround you" (literally), so try a "terrific" wine flight paired with a "nice cheese selection" – and try not to take umbrage at the "high" tabs.

P.F. CHANG'S CHINA BISTRO ◑   22 | 22 | 20 | $28

The Quarter at the Tropicana, 2801 N. Pacific Ave. (Iowa Ave.),
609-348-4600; www.pfchangs.com

"Chain dining at its best", this "high-decibel" Chinese, AC's Most Popular eatery, offers "delicious" food and "reasonable prices" that ensure fans leave "shaking heads" and "wondering how they pull it off"; the few who quip about "Americanized" "fast food in disguise" are overruled.

SUILAN   25 | 26 | 24 | $61

Borgata Hotel, Casino & Spa, 1 Borgata Way (Atlantic City Expwy.,
exit 1), 609-317-7725; www.theborgata.com

Susanna Foo brings her trademark Chinese-French fusion fare to AC in the form of this "spectacular", "very upscale" entry in the Borgata's all-star lineup; "from potstickers to complex preparations of fresh fish", "you'll be in for the experience of a lifetime" and be "doted on" by the staff amid "soothing" surroundings.

WHITE HOUSE ⊭   27 | 8 | 15 | $12

2301 Arctic Ave. (Mississippi Ave.), 609-345-1564

"Hail to the chief!" of cheese steaks, hoagies, subs – whatever you want to call them, since this "landmark", AC's No. 1 for Food, is known to have patrons who've "driven the 100-mile round-trip on many occasions" just to pick up the "best sandwiches on earth"; but note: there's "no decor except the wall-to-wall pictures of famous clientele", and ya bettah unnerstan' you can't reserve a table even "if you're Jerry Vale."

TOP FOOD RANKING

Restaurant	Cuisine
28 Vespaio	Italian
Wink	New American
Hudson's on the Bend	New American
27 Jeffrey's	New American
Musashino Sushi	Japanese
Aquarelle	French
Café/Four Seasons	New American
Mirabelle	New American
Fonda San Miguel	Mexican
Driskill Grill	New American

OTHER NOTEWORTHY PLACES

Bistro 88	Euro-Asian
Chuy's	Tex-Mex
Eddie V's	Seafood/Steakhouse
Fino	Mediterranean
La Traviata	Italian
Salt Lick	Barbecue
Siena	Northern Italian
Starlite	New American
Uchi	Japanese
Zoot	New American

F	D	S	C

Aquarelle ⌷Ⓜ | 27 | 26 | 26 | $54 |
606 Rio Grande St. (W. 6th St.), 512-479-8117;
www.aquarellerestaurant.com
"Enjoy a leisurely dinner" of "exquisite", "expensive" fare "with layer upon layer of flavor" at this "romantic" "French gem" set in a "beautiful" "old Downtown Austin home"; not only does the "authentic" Classic and Provençal cuisine attain a "wonderful" "level of refinement", but the "attentive", "knowledgeable" staff provides "outstanding service" and "will offer sublime pairing suggestions" from the "excellent wine list", making it "the place to go to celebrate special occasions" – or to "take your future parents-in-law."

Bistro 88 | 26 | 19 | 23 | $36 |
2712 Bee Cave Rd. (Dellana Ln.), 512-328-8888;
www.bistro88.com
Exemplifying "fusion at its best", "chef Jeff Liu creates beautiful, exquisite" Euro-Asian cuisine that's "wonderful every time" at this "real jewel" in West Lake Hills; the staff is "friendly and knowledgeable about the dishes", and while "the decor could be more hip", "the unique menu pairings have enough style to make up for it" – plus a "quiet" setting contributes to the "nice atmosphere."

Café at the Four Seasons   27 | 26 | 26 | $46
Four Seasons Hotel, 98 San Jacinto Blvd. (Cesar Chavez St. E.),
512-685-8300; www.fourseasons.com
"One of Austin's finest dining destinations", this "classy" "favorite"
in Downtown's Four Seasons Hotel boasts chef Elmar Prambs'
"reliably inventive" New American fare, "distinctively presented" by an "exceptional" staff within a "romantic", "lovely
setting"; whether "inside or out on the patio", you'll also enjoy "a
gorgeous view of Town Lake" – plus the nightly winged "exodus
from the Congress Avenue bridge", reportedly home to the "largest
urban bat colony" in America; P.S. the "Sunday brunch buffet is
a special treat."

CHUY'S   21 | 21 | 19 | $16
1728 Barton Springs Rd. (S. Lamar Blvd.), 512-474-4452
10520 N. Lamar Blvd. (Meadows Dr. N.), 512-836-3218
11680 Research Blvd. (Thunder Creek Rd.), 512-342-0011
www.chuys.com
"Elvis meets Tex-Mex" – "emphasis on the Tex" – at this chain of
"green-chile" meccas rated Most Popular among Austin restaurants; it "always hits the spot" with the "young crowd", which
willingly "endures long waits" to revel in its "raucous" atmosphere amid "kitschy decor" while downing "delicious margaritas"; speaking of those "strong" libations, it's also "notable" for
the "international fame" it achieved when "the Bush twins were
busted for underage drinking" at the flagship in Zilker.

Driskill Grill ⊠ Ⓜ   27 | 26 | 26 | $52
Driskill Hotel, 604 Brazos St. (6th St.), 512-391-7162; www.driskillgrill.com
Supporters "love everything about" this "upscale classic" nestled within a "Texas landmark", Downtown's "historic Driskill
Hotel"; "renowned chef" David Bull "does wonders", "combining
beautiful presentations and amazing flavors in every course" of
his "exquisite" New American cuisine, which is "impeccably
served" by a "top-notch" staff in an "elegant" room "decorated
with no-holds-barred Western-luxury style"; sure, it's "expensive, but it's worth it" "when it's time to splurge" on a "magnificent experience" that's "sublime from start to end."

EDDIE V'S EDGEWATER GRILLE   25 | 24 | 24 | $42
9400 Arboretum Blvd. (N. Capital of Texas Hwy.), 512-342-2642
301 E. Fifth St. (San Jacinto Blvd.), 512-472-1860
www.eddiev.com
"Though primarily seafood" focused, the "extensive menu" of
"consistently" "delicious" fare at this pair of "upscale (but not
uptight)" "high-end winners" sports "great steaks too"; the
Downtown location is "dark, jazzy and intimate", while the
Arboretum outpost boasts "great views", but both offer "outstanding service" and an "excellent wine list" – plus one of "the
best happy-hour deals in town", with "half-priced appetizers"
like the "sinful crab cakes."

Fino ⊠   23 | 25 | 23 | $36
2905 San Gabriel St. (29th St.), 512-474-2905
"Modern, minimalist decor" that's both "casual and chic" makes
for a "welcoming atmosphere" at this "hip" Mediterranean
within "the West Campus cuisine scene"; also "inviting" is the
"inventive" menu featuring "fresh ingredients in simple, flavorful

dishes", which are served with "interesting mixed drinks" and a "wonderful wine list" by a "personable staff"; P.S. "when the temperature dips below 100 degrees, the outdoor seating" "is hard to beat."

Fonda San Miguel   27 | 27 | 24 | $34
2330 W. North Loop Blvd. (Hancock Dr.), 512-459-4121; www.fondasanmiguel.com

"The huge antique wooden doors signal you're entering another world" at this "charming", "upscale" Highland Park "landmark" known for "divine" regional cuisine featuring "authentic dishes from all parts of Mexico"; set in "a building resembling a hacienda", with a "lovely bar and inside courtyard", it all adds up to a "stunning and dramatic yet festive and relaxed" atmosphere; P.S. though pricey, its "legendary" Sunday brunch makes for "an exceptional end to a visit by out-of-towners."

HUDSON'S ON THE BEND   28 | 23 | 25 | $44
3509 Ranch Rd. 620 N. (Texas St.), Lakeway, 512-266-1369; www.hudsonsonthebend.com

"All of God's creatures have a place on this earth, and if Hudson's had its way, it would be next to the mashed potatoes" claim carnivores who crow about this "upscale" New American in Lakeway (about a 30-minute drive from Austin), a bastion of "inventive" "Hill Country haute cuisine" that's known as the "best destination for wild game" around; "expect excellence" in all aspects, including "a unique setting" with "rustic" "country" decor and a patio that's "a divine place to dine under the Texas sky"; P.S. "bring friends, family and a fat wallet."

JEFFREY'S   27 | 23 | 27 | $51
1204 W. Lynn St. (12th St.), 512-477-5584; www.jeffreysofaustin.com

For "a really special night out", this "cozy culinary haven" in Clarksville is a "perennial" "fine-dining" "favorite", with a "friendly staff" that delivers "impeccable service"; its "take on Texas cuisine" renders "palate-pleasing presentations" of near-"flawless" New American fare ("the tasting menu is not to be missed"), enhanced by "excellent wine" pairings and a "casual setting" that's both "intimate and romantic."

La Traviata ⧄   25 | 21 | 22 | $31
314 Congress Ave. (3rd St.), 512-479-8131

"Just the right match" of "delightful Italian" food and an "urban neighborhood" feel distinguishes this "warm, bustling" Downtown venue, an "authentic trattoria" right on Congress Avenue whose "interesting adaptations" of "hearty" "old favorites" are not only "consistently delicious" but "affordable" to Boot; the "fun wine list" and "informed, attentive staff" also make it "great for lunch or a lovely dinner", more than compensating for the sometimes "cramped" and "noisy" atmosphere.

Mirabelle ⧄   27 | 21 | 24 | $32
8127 Mesa Dr. (bet. Spicewood Springs Rd. & Steck Ave.), 512-346-7900; www.mirabellerestaurant.com

Located "in a strip mall" in Northwest Hills, this New American is "a true treasure" thanks to "plentiful portions" from an "amazingly creative", "chef-driven" seasonal menu and "generous pours" "at very reasonable prices", plus "unique pairings" that provide "the average person" a chance to "try new things and learn about wines"; the "cool, arty decor" "defines casual elegance", and the "knowledgeable staff" adds to the "well-crafted dining experience", making it "a great alternative to Downtown."

MUSASHINO SUSHI DOKORO Ⓜ   27 | 18 | 19 | $32 |
3407 Greystone Dr. (Mo-Pac Expwy.), 512-795-8593;
www.musashinosushi.com
"Tucked away on the first floor" of a Northwest Hills building, this Japanese establishment is "one of the best" spots for sushi in Austin, known for "fantastic" preparations of "fresh fish"; the "talented chefs" will make you feel like you've "stepped into Japan" thanks to their "unique" offerings, "incredible rolls" and "off-the-menu specials", although some are "rankled" by the "hostile staff", quipping they've "met friendlier kamikaze pilots."

SALT LICK 360   25 | 20 | 20 | $19 |
Davenport Village, 3801 N. Capital of Texas Hwy. (Westlake Dr.),
512-328-4957
"Even a New Yorker will feel like a cowboy" at this "classic" West Lake Hills meat mecca that's "a real experience for out-of-towners"; it offers "inventive" cuisine that's "as close to upscale BBQ as it gets", plus a "nice wine list", either in a high-ceilinged interior or out on a glass-enclosed patio; P.S. it's the spinoff of the Hill Country original (a Driftwood "tradition" since 1969, with a more "casual" vibe).

Siena   24 | 27 | 22 | $36 |
6203 N. Capital Of Texas Hwy. (2222 Rd.), 512-349-7667;
www.sienarestaurant.com
"You'll be transported to Tuscany when you step inside" the "romantic setting" of this "great special-event place" set in a "stone building" amid "beautiful surroundings" in Northwest Hills; its Northern Italian cuisine is "hearty and wonderful", the "wine selection is outstanding" and the "service never disappoints" – plus "the daily four-course menu is a good value" and the "happy hour with half-price appetizers" lets you indulge "without breaking the bank."

Starlite   25 | 25 | 23 | $38 |
407 Colorado St. (4th St.), 512-374-9012; www.starliteaustin.net
"Starlite, star bright, eat and drink your fill tonight" muse surveyors about this "sophisticated" eatery in the Warehouse District, where the New American "cuisine is divine" and the chef has an enviable "sensibility for food, flavor and matching ingredients"; you can also "trust your server and your bartender to delight you" with their "excellent" ministrations, which include suggestions on choosing from the selection of "unique drinks."

UCHI   26 | 27 | 24 | $40 |
801 S. Lamar Blvd. (Barton Springs Rd.), 512-916-4808;
www.uchiaustin.com
"Superlatives don't do justice" to the "amazing fusion of flavors" featured in the "inventive" Japanese cuisine at this "mecca for foodies" in Zilker; it's an "oasis of culinary fun and adventure" that's "outstanding in every way" thanks to the "creative genius" of "soon-to-be celebrity chef Tyson Cole", whose "always-fresh" dishes "truly are art", as well as a "sumptuous", "chic" interior that's a "nice mix of formal and casual"; yes, it's "expensive, but it's really worth" it for such a "world-class sushi experience."

VESPAIO Ⓜ 28 | 23 | 25 | $36

1610 S. Congress Ave. (Monroe St.), 512-441-6100
"Believe the buzz" about this "hip" "but unpretentious" South Congress Italian ranked No. 1 for Food in Austin thanks to a "creative" kitchen that "expertly prepares" "sublime", "complex" creations ("amazing daily specials", "tempting antipasti"), which are served in a "small, romantic setting" by "attentive staffers" who are "knowledgeable about the incredible food selection" and "extensive wine list"; its "popularity" can mean "long waits" and a "noisy dining room", "but who cares" when there's so much to "be dazzled" by?

WINK Ⓩ 28 | 21 | 26 | $44

1014 N. Lamar Blvd. (11th St.), 512-482-8868; www.winkrestaurant.com
"Hidden in a strip mall" in Old West Austin is this "boutique" "gourmet gem" (with "adjoining wine bar") whose "amazing, interesting menu" changes "every day depending on" "the local fresh offerings", rendering "exquisitely well-prepared" and "impeccably served" French-inspired New American dishes of "jaw-dropping quality"; some "can't overcome" the "overpriced, under-filled plates", while others say that "noise is an issue" "when a big crowd" is crammed into the "too-close-together tables"; all agree, however, that "the food is above reproach."

Zoot Ⓜ 26 | 22 | 26 | $43

509 Hearn St. (Lake Austin Blvd.), 512-477-6535; www.zootrestaurant.com
Partisans praise this stylish Old West Austin New American both for its "exquisitely prepared" menu ("complemented by a thoughtfully selected wine list") and the "mature, traditional service" offered by its "intelligent, unpretentious" staff; also appreciated is the "romantic setting" of its "quiet, elegant" interior in a "charming" old home, which cements its status as the "place for a serious date"; P.S. "the chef's tasting menu with wine pairings is a special-occasion treat for the fat-wallet crowd."

Baltimore/Annapolis

TOP FOOD RANKING

Restaurant	Cuisine
28 Sushi Sono	Japanese
Joss Cafe	Japanese
27 Charleston	New American
Samos	Greek
Hampton's	New American
Peter's Inn	New American
Prime Rib	Steakhouse
Lemongrass	Thai
Tersiguel's	French
Mari Luna	Mexican

OTHER NOTEWORTHY PLACES

Boccaccio	Northern Italian
Clyde's	American
Corks	New American
Helmand	Afghan
Lewnes'	Steakhouse
Linwoods	New American
McCormick & Schmick's	Seafood
Paul's Homewood	Greek
Ruth's Chris	Steakhouse
Saffron	New American

F	D	S	C

Boccaccio   25 | 21 | 23 | $53
925 Eastern Ave. (bet. Exeter & High Sts.), Baltimore, 410-234-1322; www.boccaccio-restaurant.com
Catch this "solid performer" on "a good night" and the "flavorful" Northern Italian cuisine "will be the best you ever had", as will the "professional" service; with "tables far apart", it lends itself to "romance or closing the big deal", so while the unimpressed gripe about "mega bills", the majority agrees it's "a cut above the other Little Italy restaurants" and "worth it."

CHARLESTON ⑤   27 | 26 | 27 | $74
1000 Lancaster St. (S. Exeter St.), Baltimore, 410-332-7373; www.charlestonrestaurant.com
"One of Baltimore's best" is "even better" thanks to a "strikingly elegant" makeover and a relatively new set-price format that lets diners "try more" of chef/co-owner Cindy Wolf's "cutting-edge", "Southern-style" New American small plates offered in three-, five- and six-course "create-your-own tasting menus"; though a few are perturbed about the now-"tiny portions", the "celestial" tabs at this Harbor East experience are justified by the "exceptional service" and an "exquisite wine list" from co-owner Tony Foreman.

CLYDE'S
18 | 21 | 19 | $30

10221 Wincopin Circle (Little Patuxent Pkwy.), Columbia, 410-730-2829; www.clydes.com

While this "original" American "dining saloon" "has created a vast legion of copycats", it remains a "staple" that's "always good, year after year" (it's the Most Popular restaurant in the Baltimore area); with "fresh" oysters, "delicious" crab cakes, "the best" burgers and other "bar food, par excellence" served in a "brash" setting amid "nostalgic decor", it proves a "reliable" choice.

Corks
25 | 19 | 23 | $51

1026 S. Charles St. (bet. Cross & Hamburg Sts.), Baltimore, 410-752-3810; www.corksrestaurant.com

This "hidden gem" in a South Baltimore row house keeps the "passionate" oenophile "in mind", pairing its "sublime", seasonally changing New American menu with an "outstanding" "all-American wine list" featuring "little-known vineyards"; "attentive, knowledgeable servers" help compensate for the "intimate (read: small, but nice)" space and "costly" tabs; N.B. dinner only.

HAMPTON'S Ⓜ
27 | 28 | 28 | $67

InterContinental Harbor Court Hotel, 550 Light St. (bet. Conway & Lee Sts.), Baltimore, 410-347-9744; www.harborcourt.com

"For a special occasion or just because you deserve it", "break out the pearls" and "bathe in the ambiance" of this "elegant" hotel restaurant; the "sumptuous" French-influenced New American cuisine is served with "focused attention" by an "impeccable" staff, and though a minority views the atmosphere as "a bit stuffy", they don't complain about the "top-notch view of the Inner Harbor."

Helmand
26 | 20 | 23 | $28

806 N. Charles St. (bet. Madison & Read Sts.), Baltimore, 410-752-0311; www.helmand.com

At this dinner-only "institution" in Mt. Vernon, "your taste buds will dance" to the "delicious diplomacy" of "complex, eye-opening" Afghan dishes that "go far, far beyond the kebab" "without being offputting" (don't miss the "bliss-on-a-plate pumpkin appetizer"); "vegetarians and meat eaters alike" "may fall in love with" its "exotic character" and "reasonable prices", and if "seating can be crowded", most feel "the food is worth the coziness."

JOSS CAFE & SUSHI BAR
28 | 16 | 23 | $34

195 Main St. (Church Circle), Annapolis, 410-263-4688; www.josscafe-sushibar.com

"You'd have to catch it yourself to get fish any fresher" than at this "adventurous" "source of pride" in Annapolis, where sushi-philes savor "heaven-in-a-wrapper" rolls plus "yummy options that don't involve raw" fin fare; claustrophobes complain it's "cramped" and "crowded" and "doesn't take reservations", but once you're in, expect "efficient" service and "kitschy" if "sparse" decor.

Lemongrass
27 | 19 | 21 | $28

167 West St. (Colonial Ave.), Annapolis, 410-280-0086; www.lemongrassannapolis.com

"Annapolis rejoices!" – "finally, decent Thai" comes to the epicenter of wild West Street's building boom in the guise of this "hip" "oasis for absolutely top-notch" fare "beautifully served" by a "relaxed staff"; the "innovative" dishes are proffered in a setting that's "too damn small" but "lively, noisy and hot" – "both the spices and the clientele" – not to mention "always packed" given "no reservations."

Lewnes' Steakhouse

| 26 | 20 | 24 | $53 |

401 Fourth St. (Severn Ave.), Eastport, 410-263-1617;
www.lewnessteakhouse.com

This "low-key", two-story Eastport chophouse "proves that a local, family-owned restaurant" can "trump" the national chains with "the real thing": "melt-in-your-mouth steaks", "sides without compare" and a "can-do" "staff that knows you by name"; carnivores also give "kudos" to an "intimate" setup with a "separate area where you can enjoy a cigar" and "meet the locals"; N.B. a planned expansion will double their capacity.

Linwoods

| 26 | 25 | 25 | $49 |

25 Crossroads Dr. (bet. McDonogh & Reisterstown Rds.), Owings Mills, 410-356-3030; www.linwoods.com

After nearly 20 years, surveyors can still "count on" this "upscale" Owings Mills "gold standard" "blessed with many" "consistently delicious" "spins on New American fare"; "owner Linwood Dame knows his business well", and his "clubby" restaurant "is all class" "without pretense", with an open kitchen and "professional service" to boot; some note, however, that a meal here can "put a dent in your wallet."

Mari Luna Mexican Grill Ⓜ

| 27 | 13 | 20 | $18 |

102 Reisterstown Rd. (Seven Mile Ln.), Pikesville, 410-486-9910; www.mariluna.com

"Located in a converted Carvel store", this Pikesville "gem" "may not have a ton of curb appeal" according to surveyors, but it does have "authentic" "Mexican (not Tex-Mex)" fare that's "divine"; locals say it's "easy to get hooked on" this "friendly, family-owned" "find" that's both "small" and "popular as all get-out", so be "prepared to fight for a table"; P.S. a BYO policy makes it even more of a "value."

MCCORMICK & SCHMICK'S

| 21 | 20 | 20 | $41 |

Pier 5 Hotel, 711 Eastern Ave. (President St.), Baltimore, 410-234-1300; www.mccormickandschmicks.com

The "daily fresh-catch offering can't be beat" say habitués hooked on this "clubby", "classic" Inner Harbor chain link where the "plethora of choices" "cooked as simply or as complicated as one would like" and "knowledgeable servers" make it "a safe bet for a biz lunch" or "excellent for a family celebration"; though the "disappointed" suggest that the "overpriced", "uninspired" "fish factory" fare is a "let-down", barflies insist that "great specials" during happy hour deliver "real value."

Paul's Homewood Café Ⓩ

| 22 | 14 | 21 | $26 |

919 West St. (Taylor Ave.), Annapolis, 410-267-7891

For "excellent spanakopita" and "can't-beat souvlaki", stop by this "family-run" Annapolis Greek where the food tastes even better thanks to the "warm owners" and "smiley" "server-relatives" who dish it up (there's a selection of "wholesome" New American offerings too); eating here is "like having your best friend make dinner for you", with "size the only problem" – "cozy" equals "crowded" to some – although plans are in place to double their capacity.

Peter's Inn ⊠ Ⓜ   27 | 15 | 20 | $28

504 S. Ann St. (Eastern Ave.), Baltimore, 410-675-7313;
www.petersinn.com

"Defining Baltimore quirkiness" with its "strange collision" of "leather-clad biker" and "gourmet", this "teeny-tiny" Fells Point "hangout" may "look like a dive", but it's "as culinary as places twice as fancy and four times as dull" with a "limited" but "surprisingly ambitious" New American menu that "rotates weekly"; "get there early" since "it can get crowded" and "noisy", though regulars reveal "it's much more pleasant" "now that it's non-smoking"; N.B. dinner only.

PRIME RIB ◑   27 | 24 | 26 | $62

1101 N. Calvert St. (Chase St.), Baltimore, 410-539-1804;
www.theprimerib.com

"Classy, swanky and all dressed up", this black-lacquered "old-fashioned supper club" in Downtown North is the quintessential spot to celebrate anniversaries or the "close of a big deal" over "massive cuts of buttery, beefy, masculine prime rib", the "most succulent" crab and "perfect" martinis brought to table by "impeccable" tuxedoed waiters; although a few find it "ripe for a makeover", it has that "old-school", "sophisticated ambiance" that enables "everyone to pretend they're a powerbroker, bon vivant or participant in a clandestine tryst – and maybe they are."

RUTH'S CHRIS STEAK HOUSE   24 | 21 | 23 | $57

Pier 5 Hotel, 711 Eastern Ave. (S. President St.), Baltimore, 410-230-0033
600 Water St. (bet. Gay St. & Market Pl.), Baltimore, 410-783-0033
301 Severn Ave. (3rd St.), Eastport, 410-990-0033
1777 Reisterstown Rd. (Hooks Ln.), Pikesville, 410-837-0033
www.ruthschris.com

"Everything is big" at these "high-end" "budget-busting" houses of beef – the steaks "sizzling in butter, the sides, the drinks, the bill!" – but "so what?", since you'll "check your diet at the door and rip into" a slab that "melts in your mouth", augmented by a "great bottle of wine"; the "well-timed" service further "pampers" and the dark-wood interiors are just right for business, but some naysayers insist these chainsters are "not as good" as the city's other chophouse options.

Saffron   – | 25 | 21 | $38

802 N. Charles St. (Madison St.), Baltimore, 410-528-1616;
www.saffronbaltimore.com

At this "chic" Mt. Vernon venue, Indian fusion has made way for New American with the post-*Survey* arrival of chef Edward Kim, whose globally tinged menu features dishes like seared tuna in miso; expect the same "warm, friendly" service and "sumptuous" setting, although they've removed a few of the more "opulent" elements; N.B. dinner only, with an omakase chef's tasting menu available for parties of six or more.

SAMOS ⊠ ≢   27 | 12 | 20 | $18

600 S. Oldham St. (Fleet St.), Baltimore, 410-675-5292

Meet the "Greektown family you never knew you had": chef-owner Nick Georgalas, "there every day" with "capable son Michael at his side", along with "hometown waitresses" who "call you 'hon' and mean it" as they bring around "huge portions" of "divinely zesty" "delights"; it's "no-frills" and "doesn't take reservations", but diners have determined it's "far and away" "Baltimore's top Greek", with a "BYO that makes it easy on the wallet" too; P.S. "remember, it's cash-only."

SUSHI SONO ☒ 28 19 24 $34

10215 Wincopin Circle (Little Patuxent Pkwy.), Columbia, 410-997-6131; www.sushisonomd.com

"Lovely views" "overlooking serene Lake Kittamaqundi" "add to the Zen ambiance" at "Columbia's pristine Japanese haven", rated No. 1 for Food in the Baltimore area; "unmatched sushi and sashimi" and a "mouthwatering" "selection of specialty rolls" are "served with grace and charm" by a "kimono-clad" staff that has "a way of making you feel welcome"; "it's like being in another world" (especially after a few cups of sake), but be advised that it can be "quite pricey" and "packed."

Tersiguel's 27 23 26 $51

8293 Main St. (Old Columbia Pike), Ellicott City, 410-465-4004; www.tersiguels.com

"Allow chef/co-owner Michel Tersiguel to take you on a tour" of "fine French country cuisine" at this "first-rate", family-run Gallic "in the heart of Ellicott City"; it "has a following" for its "rich", "fabulous food" (they even "grow their own vegetables"), and the "extensive wine" list and "wonderful service" help ensure it's "perfect for a special occasion"; a "whopping bill" doesn't deter fans who note they've "paid three times as much for offerings that don't compare."

TOP FOOD RANKING

28	Oishii	Japanese
	L'Espalier	New French
	Aujourd'hui	New French
27	No. 9 Park	French/Italian
	Hamersley's Bistro	French/New Amer.
	Blue Ginger	Asian Fusion
	Mistral	French/Med.
	Icarus	New American
	Il Capriccio	Northern Italian
	Oleana	Mediterranean
	Clio	New French
	Carmen	Italian
	Rialto	Mediterranean
	Coriander	French Bistro
	Craigie St. Bistrot	French Bistro
26	Sage	Northern Italian
	Helmand	Afghan
	Salts	New American
	Saporito's	Northern Italian
	Radius	New French

OTHER NOTEWORTHY PLACES

B&G Oysters	Seafood
Dalí	Spanish/Tapas
East Coast Grill	Barbecue/Seafood
EVOO	Eclectic
Franklin Café	New American
Grotto	Italian
Harvest	New American
Legal Sea Foods	Seafood
Locke-Ober	Continental
Meritage	New American
Neptune Oyster	Seafood
Petit Robert Bistro	French Bistro
Pigalle	French Bistro
Rendezvous	Mediterranean
Restaurant L	Asian Fusion
Tamarind Bay	Indian
Taranta	Peruvian/S. Italian
Toro	Spanish/Tapas
Troquet	French/New Amer.
UpStairs on the Square	New American

AUJOURD'HUI
28 | 27 | 28 | $72

Four Seasons Hotel, 200 Boylston St. (bet. Arlington & Charles Sts.), 617-351-2037; www.fourseasons.com

As "the gold standard" for "special occasions", this New French destination in the Back Bay's "outstanding Four Seasons" Hotel is itself "cause for celebration": it features a staff that "takes attentive to a whole new level", making you "feel like royalty" as you dine on "superlative" cuisine "cooked to perfection" and proffered against a renovated backdrop of "elegance layered upon elegance" – so "book a windowside table, order some bubbly and let someone else pick up the tab."

B&G Oysters
26 | 22 | 23 | $40

550 Tremont St. (Waltham St.), 617-423-0550; www.bandgoysters.com

"Truly a pearl", this "sleek, smart" South End raw bar from No. 9 Park's Barbara Lynch showcases the "aphrodisiac" effects of "innumerable varieties" of "fantastically fresh" (if "pricey") oysters, paired with "sublime wines by the glass" and rounded out by a "limited" but "innovative" seafood menu; it's "popular", so there's "not always a table", but you can "sit at the bar and watch the open kitchen" as you glean "vast knowledge" from your savvy server.

BLUE GINGER ⊠
27 | 22 | 24 | $49

583 Washington St. (Rte. 16), Wellesley, 781-283-5790; www.ming.com

"The culmination of Ming Tsai's quest for the perfect balance of East meets West", this Wellesley "perennial" arguably serves the "best Asian fusion in the country", as the celebrity chef-owner "transcends the sometimes pretentious nature of the genre" with his "brilliant" culinary creations; a handful – perceiving "occasional lapses" in the "crisp, professional service" and decrying the "spare" interior as "ordinary" – conclude it's "coasting on its reputation", although most insist "Ming's still got zing", retorting with "just one word: go!"

Carmen Ⓜ
27 | 22 | 22 | $39

33 North Sq. (Richmond St.), 617-742-6421

"Defying clichés" and space constraints alike, this North End neighbor to Paul Revere's house "is a special place" whose "cubicle-sized kitchen turns out" "innovative", "sophisticated" – heck, "fantastic" – Italian dishes like "delicious" crespelle Bolognese; though you'd best "forget privacy", remember that "rubbing shoulders with your neighbors" "is sometimes comforting", sometimes even "sexy" (just "don't tell the tourists").

Clio/Uni
27 | 25 | 25 | $68

Eliot Suite Hotel, 370A Commonwealth Ave. (Mass. Ave.), 617-536-7200; www.cliorestaurant.com

With "a genius" and "madman" like Ken Oringer in the kitchen, this Back Bay "showstopper" "continues to reign" "supreme", converting most critics of "la-di-da dining" via "wonderfully strange" New French "masterpieces" showcased against an "understated" backdrop; still, the remaining skeptics – who "leave having experienced food but actually eaten very little" – complain that their "wishes come second" to the chef's "ideas", a "risky" state of affairs "given the price tag"; P.S. adjoining sashimi bar Uni "rocks the palates" of piscivores.

Coriander Bistro 🅂 Ⓜ   27 | 22 | 26 | $48

5 Post Office Sq. (bet. Billings & S. Main Sts.), Sharon, 781-784-5450;
www.corianderbistro.com

Urbanites whose culinary expectations head south when they do
are downright "shocked" to discover Sharon's French "star";
owners Kevin and Jill Crawley have "put their hearts into this bistro,
and it shows in every way", from the "all-around excellent"
"gourmet" meals sprinkled with "elegant little extras" to an "engaging" "attention to service"; *c'est cher, naturellement,* but "for
a special occasion", it "ranks up there with the best in Boston."

Craigie Street Bistrot Ⓜ   27 | 20 | 25 | $46

5 Craigie Circle (bet. Brattle St. & Concord Ave.), Cambridge,
617-497-5511; www.craigiestreetbistrot.com

"Chef-on-the-rise" Tony Maws' "mission and talent are pure" to
the many "serious foodies" who have made this French bistro
"sleeper" "in the basement of an apartment building" outside
Harvard Square their "teeny-tiny" "home away from home";
"sparkling flavors" distinguish "one tantalizing dish after another" on the "constantly changing menu", and the "educated,
eager" "staff thoroughly spoils" you with "spot-on advice about
wine pairings"; no wonder a majority calls its kitchen "the little
engine that could"; N.B. closed Mondays and Tuesdays.

Dalí Restaurant & Tapas Bar   25 | 25 | 23 | $32

415 Washington St. (Beacon St.), Somerville, 617-661-3254;
www.dalirestaurant.com

"Baroque", "electric" and "magical", this "perpetually crowded"
Spanish "restaurant that put Somerville on the map" still treats its
customers to "an event, not just a meal" – "teasing all of their
senses" with "rich, delectable tapas" and "fruity sangria" served
"in a kaleidoscope" of rooms by an "effervescent" staff "that
seems to love the place too"; no wonder only a small minority
sniffs they're "frankly over it."

East Coast Grill & Raw Bar   26 | 18 | 21 | $35

1271 Cambridge St. (Prospect St.), Cambridge, 617-491-6568;
www.eastcoastgrill.net

"There's nobody quite like [chef-owner] Chris Schlesinger", whose
"energy" imbues every inch of this "jumping" joint in Inman
Square, "assuring great food is the focus" – namely, "spicy, smoky,
adventurous" seafood and BBQ that skew tropical to match
"flaming cocktails" from the in-house tiki lounge; meanwhile, the
servers remain "professionals" no matter how "crowded" the place
gets, even during its celebrated Sunday "brunch with a punch" and
on notorious Hell Nights (when chile-chompers test their mettle).

Evoo 🅂   26 | 20 | 23 | $45

118 Beacon St. (Washington St.), Somerville, 617-661-3866;
www.evoorestaurant.com

"Duck, oxtail, rabbit – the zoo was never this much fun" joke otherwise "serious" gourmands about this "exemplary" Eclectic
bistro in Somerville that has "firmly established itself" in their es-
teem: now "rich", now "ethereal", chef Peter McCarthy's "seasonal menu" "just gets better and more interesting", while his
wife, Colleen, oversees a "well-informed" and "extremely nice"
staff in a "casual", "comfy setting"; perhaps, then, the 'E' is not
only for 'extra' (as in 'extra virgin olive oil') but also "for 'excellent.'"

Franklin Café ◕
25 | 18 | 20 | $32

278 Shawmut Ave. (Hanson St.), 617-350-0010;
www.franklincafe.com
An "all-time favorite" among South Enders, this "dimly lit",
"rollicking" joint "fires on all cylinders" with a "limited" and
"understated" (but "ravishing") New American menu that's
"much better than many that are twice as expensive"; it's always
"filled to the brim", so expect "a two- or three-martini wait" and
a "noise level" that can be "too much to take" – indeed, it only
"gets louder as it gets later", since the "kitchen's open late", a
"rare find" in Boston.

Grotto
25 | 18 | 22 | $37

37 Bowdoin St. (bet. Beacon & Cambridge Sts.), 617-227-3434;
www.grottorestaurant.com
A "bit of vintage Greenwich Village" on Beacon Hill, this "inspired",
"subterranean" Italian brooks "no silliness" even as its "fantastic", "monthly changing" menu "riffs on old favorites to create
something entirely new" like "interesting", "delicious spaghetti
and meatballs"; indeed, served by a "gracious" staff, "the food
more than makes up for" a "quirky" space that's "a little uncomfortable" for legroom-lovers (yet plenty "cozy" to "romantics").

HAMERSLEY'S BISTRO
27 | 24 | 25 | $56

553 Tremont St. (Clarendon St.), 617-423-2700;
www.hamersleysbistro.com
"Pioneer" "Gordon Hamersley just keeps on trucking" in "the
open kitchen" of his "bright, airy" "South End classic" – arguably
the "best bistro in New England" according to some – "and all
without putting on airs": the "hearty, harvest-inspired" French–
New American dishes exhibit "dash" but eschew "fads" ("the
usual kudos" go to the "last meal"–worthy roast chicken), and
the staff displays "enduring commitment and energy"; so for each
cynic who spurns the "hype", there is many a satisfied – make
that "spoiled" – "loyalist."

Harvest
25 | 23 | 23 | $46

44 Brattle St. (Church St.), Cambridge, 617-868-2255;
www.harvestcambridge.com
Not only has it "aged gracefully", this Harvard Square "old-timer"
is "still worthy of a magazine spread", sigh the starry-eyed while
seated among "the campus glitterati, waxing eloquent" over
"sensational, seasonal" New American meals; a "reliably excellent feeding place, it's not flashy but respectful" of New England
culinary traditions – "and of you" – as exhibited by the "down-to-
earth staff's" "perfect pacing"; a bit "tweedy" and "faculty loung-
ish" in tone, it's nonetheless "worth smartening yourself up for."

Helmand
26 | 22 | 20 | $29

143 First St. (Bent St.), Cambridge, 617-492-4646;
www.helmandrestaurantcambridge.com
"Bored? – then eat" at this "class act" on "a strip" of "industrial
blight" in East Cambridge, where a simple meal becomes "a pure
delight and an education"; the "exotic yet accessible" Afghan
cuisine "far exceeds expectations" "in a setting with the warmth
and comfort of a living room" – albeit one more evocative of
"Pottery Barn" than Kandahar; while the "prompt" servers are
not themselves so "warm and fuzzy", "the prices are kind."

Icarus
27 | 24 | 25 | $54

3 Appleton St. (bet. Arlington & Berkeley Sts.), 617-426-1790;
www.icarusrestaurant.com

After 25-plus years, Chris Douglass' "subdued", mildly "art deco" supper club in the South End remains the "crème de la crème" of New American "gourmet" dining, "not too nouveau" but plenty "intriguing"; since it "doesn't get overwhelmed by 'in' crowds or tourists", "you're able to talk" or listen to a "delicious" "jazz combo on Friday nights", aided by "unobtrusive" servers that "bring it all together."

Il Capriccio ⌧
27 | 22 | 25 | $52

888 Main St. (Prospect St.), Waltham, 781-894-2234

Showing "originality within the framework" of a Northern Italian menu that's alternately "earthy" and "polished", this "magnifico" Waltham winner is known "among the cognoscenti" for its "sparkling wine list", while "crisp service" from a "personable staff" makes "a special occasion special" – assuming you don't mind "sharing conversations with neighboring tables"; still, scrimpers label the tab "excessive" no matter the event.

LEGAL SEA FOODS
22 | 18 | 20 | $35

Copley Pl., 100 Huntington Ave. (bet. Dartmouth & Exeter Sts.), 617-266-7775
Long Wharf, 255 State St. (Atlantic Ave.), 617-227-3115
26 Park Pl. (Columbus Ave.), 617-426-4444
Prudential Ctr., 800 Boylston St. (Ring Rd.), 617-266-6800
South Shore Plaza, 250 Granite St. (I-95, exit 6), Braintree, 781-356-3070
Burlington Mall, 1131 Middlesex Tpke. (Rte. 128), Burlington, 781-270-9700
5 Cambridge Ctr. (bet. Ames & Main Sts.), Cambridge, 617-864-3400
20 University Rd. (Eliot St.), Cambridge, 617-491-9400
The Mall at Chestnut Hill, 43 Boylston St. (Hammond Pond Pkwy.), Chestnut Hill, 617-277-7300
50-60 Worcester Rd./Rte. 9 (Ring Rd.), Framingham, 508-766-0600
www.legalseafoods.com

"Loyalty" to this "ubiquitous" seafood franchise remains "high" – indeed, it's Boston's Most Popular – because it's a "well-oiled machine" that "manages to maintain its identity" and preserve the "status quo" even as it "keeps reinventing itself" and "revitalizing its menu" (besides, "the clam chowder really is all that"); while the culinary elite may criticize its "vanilla" "cafeteria atmosphere", the vast majority insists its sheer "quality" "will change the way you think about chains."

L'ESPALIER ⌧
28 | 27 | 27 | $84

30 Gloucester St. (bet. Commonwealth Ave. & Newbury St.), 617-262-3023; www.lespalier.com

By most accounts "the only world-class restaurant in Boston", this "favorite" offers a "once-in-a-blue-moon experience" of "unparalleled gustatory extravagance"; an "enchanting" Back Bay townhouse sets the stage for a "succulent" New England–accented "nouveau French" prix fixe menu born of Frank McClelland's "painstaking" technique and brought to table by veritable "mind-readers" who know "royal treatment"; still, it's "not for everyone" according to those who find the "elegant atmosphere" "intimidating" ("be sure to know proper etiquette").

Locke-Ober ⊠   23 24 23 $60
3 Winter Pl. (bet. Tremont & Washington Sts.), 617-542-1340;
www.locke-ober.com
"All spiffy" since Lydia Shire's "redo", this "venerable institution"
in Downtown Crossing remains "a throwback to the days when
fine dining meant fine dining": "the silver gleams, the service cos-
sets" and the "preservation of haute Yankee cuisine" makes for
"signature dishes that mean so much" (like the "divine lobster
stew", JFK's purported fave) – though for hipsters, the
Continental menu's token "innovative" gestures are merely "soul
food for Wasps."

Meritage Ⓜ   26 26 25 $63
Boston Harbor Hotel, 70 Rowes Wharf (Atlantic Ave.), 617-439-3995;
www.meritagetherestaurant.com
"Forget your preconceptions about hotel restaurants" – this
"sleek" "celebration" "does an extraordinary job" with a "brilliant
concept": the "entrancing" "avant-garde" New American
creations from "master" chef Daniel Bruce come in "half or full
portions to allow lots of tastings", for which the highly "wine-
savvy" (but "not condescending") staff provides "dead-on pairing"
picks from an "exquisite", "comprehensive" list; granted, "the
tab can be shocking", but it pales beside the "swoon"-eliciting
experience – complete with "dramatic" waterfront views.

Mistral   27 26 25 $59
223 Columbus Ave. (bet. Berkeley & Clarendon Sts.), 617-867-9300;
www.mistralbistro.com
"Even better than when it opened", this "sexy" South End French-
Med "cultural" "happening" has "matured" into a "classic" that
still hits the "heights of chic" – as the "beautiful people, including
the staff", around the "hot bar" attest; "masterful cooking" and
"hard-to-find gems" by the bottle are the keys to its "success",
though the value-conscious complain about "price-gouging" by a
crew that "takes itself too seriously."

Neptune Oyster   –   –   –   M
63 Salem St. (Cross St.), 617-742-3474;
www.neptuneoyster.com
Say *ciao* to red-sauce kitsch when you enter this tiny but
"cheery" North Ender that houses a clean, spare raw bar with an
old-fashioned feel (think etched glass, subway tiles and a
pressed-tin ceiling); a modern menu puts a "clever" Italian spin
on its featured seafood entrees along with a spectrum of shucked
shellfish; N.B. there's a savvy wine list too.

NO. 9 PARK ⊠   27 24 26 $61
9 Park St. (bet. Beacon & Tremont Sts.), 617-742-9991;
www.no9park.com
"When it really matters", head to Barbara Lynch's "au courant"
"heavy hitter" on Beacon Hill to be "treated like honored guests"
by the "sharp staff" – and to be "left speechless" by the "dynamite" Country French–Italian menu and its "casual yet precise
execution", abetted by "wines chosen for taste, not label"; so
though non-subscribers to the "less is more" philosophy squint at
the "astronomically priced, minuscule portions" that are set
against a "stark" backdrop, converts chant "time and time again,
No. 9 is a 10."

OISHII Ⓜ `28` `11` `19` `$35`

1166 Washington St. (Berkeley St.), 617-482-8868 ☒
612 Hammond St. (Boylston St.), Chestnut Hill, 617-277-7888
*Mill Village, 365 Boston Post Rd./Rte. 20 (Concord Rd.), Sudbury,
978-440-8300*
www.oishiisushi.com

"Proud Bostonians" may debate whether these twin Japanese
"gastro-temples" in Chestnut Hill and Sudbury are simply No. 1
for Food in the Boston area or whether they offer the "best sushi
in New England" – but all agree the "mind-altering" "masterpieces", be they "melt-in-your-mouth maki" or "tender", "thick
slices" of sashimi, trounce the "frustrating" waits for "precious"
seats in the "criminally small" dining rooms amid "insane
crowds"; N.B. a third location opened post-*Survey* in the South End.

Oleana `27` `23` `23` `$43`

*134 Hampshire St. (bet. Columbia & Prospect Sts.), Cambridge,
617-661-0505; www.oleanarestaurant.com*

"Culinary goddess" Ana Sortun's self-described "groupies" "sing
the praises" of her "original" Eastern "Med mecca" near Inman
Square: the "daring" yet "carefully crafted" menu's "execution is
equal to the ideas" it conveys – a "very rare" achievement, whether
relished in the "romantic" if "cramped quarters" or out on the
"pretty, peaceful" "garden patio"; though the "usually" "know-
ing" but occasionally "standoffish waitrons" can be "a tad slow",
"all is forgiven" by the time "you leave, stuffed and in heaven."

Petit Robert Bistro `–` `–` `–` `M`

480 Columbus Ave. (Rutland Sq.), 617-867-0600
468 Commonwealth Ave. (Charlesgate W.), 617-375-0699
www.petitrobertbistro.com

Occupying two floors of a Kenmore Square town house, this classic
French bistro from Jacky Robert (of erstwhile institution Maison
Robert) re-creates the workaday Parisian experience with fairly
priced *plats* like rabbit moutarde; between lunch and dinner, a
pastry bar presents time-honored sweets like profiteroles – but all
the menus contain a nontraditional surprise or two; N.B. a South
End sibling opened post-*Survey* and does not accept reservations.

Pigalle Ⓜ `26` `22` `24` `$53`

*75 Charles St. S. (bet. Stuart St. & Warrenton Pl.), 617-423-4944;
www.pigalleboston.com*

"Serious foodies" agree this "Theater District destination" "richly
deserves the kudos" it receives for "doing everything with quiet
style": you'll watch (and taste) French bistro "classics evolve" into
chef Marc Orfaly's "imaginative" yet "mature" creations, while
manager Kerri Foley and her "sweet" crew – "setting a high
standard" – "make you feel comfortably pampered"; while "low
lighting sets the mood for romance", "perfect pacing" clinches it.

Radius ☒ `26` `25` `25` `$64`

*8 High St. (bet. Federal & Summer Sts.), 617-426-1234;
www.radiusrestaurant.com*

A "serious address" in any gastronome's directory, this New French
"gold" mine still sets the Financial District "buzzing"; Michael
Schlow's "superlative" "art on a plate" "always comes first", but
"gorgeous" servers thrill the "fashion-forward crowd" too;
granted, the indifferent feel a "chill" emanating from the kitchen

(it "sometimes over-emphasizes technique") and the dining room ("too edgy to be completely comfortable"), but most would gladly "refinance their homes" to eat here.

Rendezvous   26 | 17 | 23 | $44 |

502 Mass. Ave. (Brookline St.), Cambridge, 617-576-1900; www.rendezvouscentralsquare.com

"Steve Johnson is back and that's a very good thing" enthuse admirers of the chef's latest venture, a "welcome presence in Central Square" whose "superb kitchen" spins out an "always changing, exciting" Mediterranean dinner menu featuring "clean, direct flavors" from France, Italy and North Africa; "caring servers" are "friendly and professional", but nitpickers note the "sparse decor" "leaves something to be desired" – "please do something so we can't tell we're eating at a former Burger King!"

Restaurant L ∅   23 | 20 | 20 | $47 |

Louis Boston, 234 Berkeley St. (Newbury St.), 617-266-4680; www.louisboston.com

"Cotton candy, Pop Rocks and Kobe beef live in harmony" at Louis Boston's "cutting-edge" in-store bistro in the Back Bay: though "not too many people seem to know about" "superb" "young" "talent" Pino Maffeo, his "tricky" Asian fusion fare tastes "delicious"; still, some (after "leaving hungry, without understanding what they ate") downgrade the "minimalist cool" vibe to "cold."

Rialto   27 | 24 | 24 | $57 |

Charles Hotel, 1 Bennett St. (University Rd.), Cambridge, 617-661-5050; www.rialto-restaurant.com

"Doing for food what Harvard does for education", the Charles Hotel's signature dining room, just over a decade old, remains "a tour de force" of Mediterranean cuisine: "Jody Adams is such a smart and well-traveled chef", and it shows in the "wonders [she] works" with a menu that's "inventive without being unapproachable"; perhaps "the space could use an update – it still feels like a hotel restaurant" – but it's sufficiently "elegant" and "romantic" enough to "cherish" "with your significant other", especially since the staff, though "bright" and "eager", isn't "overbearing."

Sage ∅   26 | 19 | 22 | $43 |

69 Prince St. (Salem St.), 617-248-8814; www.sageboston.com

"Resisting the peer pressure" of nearby "pasta shacks", this North End "must-visit" "continues to turn out fresh", "ethereal" New American–accented renditions of Northern Italian favorites ("no one does rabbit like chef-owner Anthony Susi", whose "gnocchi float" like "clouds"); granted, the mostly "accommodating" staff "couldn't shoehorn one more person" into the "closet" of a dining room, but "the wise know" "size isn't everything."

Salts ∅ Ⓜ   26 | 22 | 25 | $51 |

798 Main St. (Windsor St.), Cambridge, 617-876-8444; www.saltsrestaurant.com

Take this "quiet, romantic" "detour" from the "student-oriented eateries" of Central Square, and you'll have yourself an "unforgettable experience"; while the much-touted "duck for two is divine", "you'll migrate here for the rest" of chef/co-owner Gabriel Bremer's "earthy", "meticulously" "handcrafted" New American dishes as well; true, it's "very small" with "large" prices, but it still feels like a "warm" "home away from home."

Saporito's Ⓜ
| 26 | 19 | 24 | $40 |

11 Rockland Circle (George Washington Blvd.), Hull, 781-925-3023;
www.saporitoscafe.com

At this "quaint" Northern Italian, the food is "fantastic" and the "unpretentious staff" "tries to do everything for its patrons"; occupying a "secluded" "seaside bungalow" in Hull, it may be an "unkept secret", but scoring a reservation is "worth the effort."

Tamarind Bay
| ▽ 26 | 19 | 22 | $26 |

75 Winthrop St. (JFK St.), Cambridge, 617-491-4552;
www.tamarind-bay.com

"Definitely different than any other Indian restaurant you've ever visited", this "phenomenal" Harvard Square spot adds "a whole new dimension of flavor" to the genre via "cooked-to-order" dishes that "delight the palate" with "the complexity of their spicing"; a "courteous" staff oversees the "crowded" but "warm" "basement" space, where a "fun and inexpensive prix fixe menu" replaces the "typical buffet" come lunchtime.

Taranta
| 24 | 21 | 23 | $37 |

210 Hanover St. (Cross St.), 617-720-0052; www.tarantarist.com

An "exciting" "experiment" in the North End, this "modern"-looking "multilevel" "star" shines with the "fusion of Southern Italian" and, "of all things, Peruvian" cuisines, highlighted by uncommon wines; though the "gregarious owner" is usually on hand "to make sure everything works", the staff is equally "informed" and "helpful."

Toro
| ▽ 27 | 19 | 19 | $38 |

1704 Washington St. (W. Springfield St.), 617-536-4300

This "pleasant" South End "surprise" from Clio's Ken Oringer "has hit the ground running" with its "fabulous", "creative" Spanish small plates that "will shock you with the amount of flavor" but are "not overwhelming"; an open kitchen, communal countertop and fireplace add to the "welcoming vibe", as does "great sangria" and an "innovative wine list", but some recommend you "get there early" – a "no-reservations policy" means it's "always crowded."

Troquet Ⓢ Ⓜ
| 26 | 21 | 24 | $54 |

140 Boylston St. (bet. S. Charles & Tremont Sts.), 617-695-9463;
www.troquetboston.com

"It's grown-up time" for the "oenophiles" who take "great joy in this well-run", "informal" yet "serious" Theater District wine bar where a "small" French–New American menu, "glistening" with "simple bistro dishes", brings out the "breadth and depth" of the *carte du vins*; even if it's "no bargain", "what's not to love about a place that serves imported butter by the ice cream scoop?"

UpStairs on the Square
| 24 | 25 | 23 | $51 |

91 Winthrop St. (JFK St.), Cambridge, 617-864-1933;
www.upstairsonthesquare.com

"A worthy successor" to UpStairs at the Pudding, this New American in Harvard Square is "actually two restaurants": the "pink" and "mirrored" Soirée Room, resembling "a life-size jewel box" or "dollhouse", "sparkles" as much as its "magic" menu, while the more casual Monday Club Bar is like *Alice in Wonderland*'s tea party"; expect "over-the-top service upstairs" and "pleasantly brisk service downstairs" (but "stop at the bank first" in either case); N.B. a post-*Survey* chef change may outdate the Food score.

Charlotte

TOP FOOD RANKING

Restaurant	Cuisine
29 Barrington's	New American
28 Volare	Italian
27 McIntosh's	Seafood/Steakhouse
Sullivan's	Steakhouse
26 Nikko	Japanese
Upstream	Seafood
Toscana	Northern Italian
Noble's	Eclectic
Luce	Italian
Carpe Diem	New American

OTHER NOTEWORTHY PLACES

Bonterra	New American
ilios noche	Greek/Italian
Lulu	French/Med.
McNinch House	Continental
Mickey & Mooch	Steakhouse
Palm	Steakhouse
Patou	French
Restaurant i	Japanese
Sonoma Modern	Californian/New Amer.
Zebra Rest.	New French

F	D	S	C

BARRINGTON'S ⓩ 29 | 21 | 25 | $46
FoxCroft Shopping Ctr., 7822 Fairview Rd. (bet. Carmel & Colony Rds.), 704-364-5755; www.barringtonsrestaurant.com
No wonder it can be "impossible to get in to": No. 1 for Food and Popularity in Charlotte, this SouthPark New American "delights" and "surprises" fans with "memorable", "understated" creations from chef-owner Bruce Moffett (who's blessed with the "most sophisticated palate" in the area) and service "as good as it gets"; those who felt the "tiny" space was too "cramped" should note that recent renovations have added a new dining area, a change which may outdate the above Decor score.

BONTERRA DINING & WINE ROOM ⓩ 25 | 25 | 25 | $48
1829 Cleveland Ave. (E. Worthington Ave.), 704-333-9463; www.bonterradining.com
It's "only fitting to be served such heavenly food in a former church" proclaim patrons who sing the praises of this Dilworth New American that's akin to a "religious experience" considering the "imaginative" menu ("amazing" fried lobster tail) and a wine selection with enough "breadth" to "astonish" oenophiles (there's a "superb" by-the-glass lineup); plus, the "considerate", "knowledgeable" staff will "make you want to say 'amen.'"

Carpe Diem 🅢
| 26 | 25 | 24 | $39 |

1535 Elizabeth Ave. (Travis Ave.), 704-377-7976;
www.carpediemrestaurant.com

"Everybody wins" at this New American "staple" in Elizabeth that impresses admirers with its winning combination of "artful", "stellar" food (including a couple of "sophisticated" vegetarian options) and "gorgeous" art nouveau–style decor; further abetting the "wow" factor is an "attentive" staff that adds to the eatery's "eclectic" "charm."

ilios noche 🅢
| 24 | 19 | 21 | $26 |

11508 Providence Rd. (I-485), 704-814-9882; www.iliosnoche.com

"If only they would take reservations" for parties of less than six, moan fans of this "unique" Greek-Italian that "knows what it's doing" in light of its "excellent" Med food that draws an "attractive clientele" to "suburban" Ballantyne; if the "edgy", "funky" quarters don't provide enough entertainment, the "loud, loud, loud" ambiance may do the trick; N.B. the post-*Survey* arrival of chef Joe Morrison (ex NYC's Aureole) may outdate the above Food score.

Luce 🅢
| 26 | 25 | 25 | $45 |

Hearst Tower, 214 N. Tryon St. (bet. 5th & 6th Sts.), 704-344-9222;
www.luceristorante.net

A "Tuscan oasis in a sea of barbecue", this "first-class" Uptown Italian shines with "luscious" food, a "wonderful" Boot-centric wine list and "excellent" service; further enhancing the "rich" experience is "exquisite" decor that features Moreno glass and works by local artist Ben Long; all of the above proves that peripatetic restaurateur Augusto Conte's "done it again!"

Lulu
| – | – | – | M |

1911 Central Ave. (Nandina St.), 704-376-2242

Its seasonally changing menu may intrigue eaters via playful dish names like 'Duck Duck Jus', but this Plaza/Midwood bistro produces comfortable French-Med cuisine that uses a smattering of organic ingredients and focuses on simple, vivid flavors with a Southern twist; true to its unpretentious style, it's located in a renovated '30s-era house and is staffed with servers who stick to a relaxed, amiable approach.

MCINTOSH'S STEAKS & SEAFOOD 🅢
| 27 | 22 | 25 | $53 |

1812 South Blvd. (East Blvd.), 704-342-1088; www.mcintoshs1.com

There's "no better steak in town" crow content constituents who "don't leave a speck of food" on their plates at this "superb", locally owned South End surf 'n' turfer, whose "impeccable" service, dark-wood interior with piano bar (Wednesday–Saturday) and patio with fireplace make it "feel like a private club" – though "not a stuffy" one; it's "just what a steakhouse should be" and "worth every penny" of the price.

McNinch House 🅢 🅜
| 25 | 26 | 27 | $95 |

511 N. Church St. (bet. 8th & 9th Sts.), 704-332-6159;
www.mcninchhouserestaurant.com

Those looking to "score some points with that special somebody" shouldn't overlook this "romantic" Continental that "treats you like royalty"; it's housed in a restored Victorian abode in Uptown, and while the kitchen turns out "wonderful" food, expect a "whopper of a tab" that a few grinches call "overpriced"; N.B. jackets, and reservations, required.

MICKEY & MOOCH
| 23 | 21 | 20 | $33 |

The Arboretum, 8128 Providence Rd. (Hwy. 51), 704-752-8080
9723 Sam Furr Rd. (I-77), Huntersville, 704-895-6654
www.mickeyandmooch.com

"So low-key" yet "so well done", this pair of chophouses off Highway 51 and in Huntersville wins kudos for "mammoth" portions of consistently "excellent" offerings, "from sushi to steak"; the settings, reminiscent of "a '50s New York supper club" (with "Frank playing on the sound system") are "always hopping", so don't be taken aback by the "long waits" for a table or a "noise level [that's] off the charts"; P.S. with "reasonable prices", you won't need to mooch moola from family or friends.

NIKKO
| 26 | 18 | 22 | $30 |

Ballantyne Commons E., 15105 John J. Delaney Dr.
(Ballantyne Commons Pkwy.), 704-341-5550
1300 South Blvd. (Arlington Ave.), 704-370-0100
www.nikkosushibar.net

Charlotte can "thank God" that "superb" sushi's "finally come to town": chef/co-owner Joanna Nix "proves" that "fabulous" raw fare "doesn't require you to be near the water" at her Japanese eateries in Ballantyne and South End; they're "the standard" for "fresh" fish, so don't be surprised if they can get a little "disco"-like on weekend nights (i.e. "loud, like a party's going on").

Noble's ☒
| 26 | 26 | 25 | $45 |

3 Morrocroft Ctr. at SouthPark, 6801 Morrison Blvd.
(Cameron Valley Pkwy.), 704-367-9463;
www.noblesrestaurant.com

A "temple of gastronomic pleasure", this SouthPark "treasure" delivers chef-owner Jim Noble's "spectacular" French-, Italian- and Med-influenced Eclectic creations to fawning fans from far and wide; the "elegant", "Tuscan-retreat" setting gets high marks, while the ministrations of a "superb" floor crew enhance what some deem a "magical" experience – albeit one that may require "saving your pennies" to pay for.

PALM
| 24 | 21 | 24 | $52 |

6705B Phillips Place Ct. (bet. Fairview & Sharon Rds.), 704-552-7256;
www.thepalm.com

In the steak sweepstakes, "consistency" gets you far, decree devotees of this Charlotte member of the national chophouse chain, whose "tried-and-true" formula corrals herds into its SouthPark digs to sample "serious", "well-prepared" cuts; you'll also find caricatures of "local personalities" on the walls and a "buzzy" "banker bar scene" ("why pay the power bill when the noise alone could cook the food?"), but be prepared, since "you'll $$$ dearly" for the experience.

Patou
| 24 | 20 | 22 | $41 |

1315 East Blvd. (Scott Ave.), 704-376-2233; www.patoubistro.com

Don't expect a "see-and-be-seen" vibe at this Dilworth bistro that's as "close to France as Charlotte gets"; diners drop by "to enjoy great cooking" in the form of Classic Gallic specialties that, while "simple", "excel" nonetheless; all in all, it's a "find" that's "quality – all the way."

Restaurant i Ⓜ
— | — | — | E |

1524 East Blvd. (Scott Ave.), 704-333-8118;
www.restaurant-i.com

Its name is a play on the Japanese word for love (*ai*) and the culinary i-fuls at this fusion restaurant set in a tiny Dilworth building come courtesy of chef Masa Kokubu, who relies on the freshest of ingredients and over a decade of experience in French technique; his architectural entrees have equally artistic names (e.g. 'Rhapsody in Blue Ocean'), while the more standard sushi and sashimi selections complement the simple, quiet decor.

Sonoma Modern American Ⓢ
24 | 22 | 23 | $40 |

Founders Hall, 100 N. Tryon St. (Trade St.), 704-332-1132;
www.sonomarestaurants.net

"Feel transported" to NYC at this "hot, hot, hot", "trendy" Uptowner attracting acolytes with its "terrific", "innovative" Cal-New American food and "excellent wine list"; owner Pierre Bader helps deliver a "great experience" to diners, who find the "modern", "minimalist" space either "chic" or "cold"; P.S. checking out the "must-see bathrooms", however, is compulsory.

SULLIVAN'S STEAKHOUSE
27 | 24 | 25 | $48 |

1928 South Blvd. (Tremont Ave.), 704-335-8228;
www.sullivansteakhouse.com

Bring "fellow carnivores" to this "classy" South End steakhouse that proffers "huge portions" ("wear elastic waistbands") of "consistently excellent" slabs of beef and "scrumptious" seafood amid a "swanky", "boxing-themed" setting, and where the "great bar scene" and nightly live jazz pep up the overall "happenin'" vibe; it may be "pricey", but for a "high-end" celebration, it "can't be beat."

Toscana Ⓢ
26 | 23 | 25 | $42 |

Specialty Shops on the Park, 6401 Morrison Blvd. (Roxborough Rd.),
704-367-1808

You just "won't be able to go wrong" at serial restaurateur Augusto Conte's SouthPark standby that "deserves" – and gets – high marks for "insanely good" Northern Italian specialties ("bravo!" to the "wonderful" white bean and olive oil overture) and "cordial", "attentive" service; P.S. opt for the "lovely patio" if weather permits.

UPSTREAM
26 | 25 | 24 | $46 |

Phillips Pl., 6902 Phillips Place Ct. (bet. Colony & Sharon Rds.),
704-556-7730; www.upstreamit.com

Surveyors swim from all corners to sup on "outrageously good" seafood at this "chic" SouthPark eatery where chef Tom Condron's "exotic", "outside-the-box" cooking "amazes", and the "attentive", "enthusiastic" staff "pampers" both the "ladies who lunch and chaps who cut deals"; it manages to be "upscale" and "not uptight", and if some wallet-watchers balk at the prices, far more maintain it's "worth every dime"; N.B. there's also a covered, heated patio.

VOLARE Ⓢ
28 | 22 | 26 | $43 |

545B Providence Rd. (Laurel Ave.), 704-370-0208

Dinner "can qualify as foreplay" at this "very small but very romantic" "hidden" "gem" in Myers Park that scores with "serious", "heavenly" Italian food that's "magic" to the eyes and "perfection" to the palate; "passionate" service and a "charming" owner produce "pampering done right", so "reserve early" and get ready for a "splurge" that's a "must."

Zebra Restaurant & Wine Bar ⑤　　25 | 24 | 22 | $50
4521 Sharon Rd. (bet. Fairview Rd. & Morrison Blvd.), 704-442-9525; www.zebrarestaurant.net
"Attention to detail" abounds at this SouthPark New French, from the "fantastic" fare whose "superb flavors are exceeded by the visual appeal" of the dishes to "unobtrusive" service to an "impressive" 800-label wine list; they keep the "noise level well under control", which suits those interested in business or romance just fine; P.S. "lunch is a steal", but you may wish to "pack your platinum card" for dinner.

Chicago

TOP FOOD RANKING

Restaurant	Cuisine
29 Carlos'	New French
28 Le Français	New French
Les Nomades	New French
Tru	New French
Alinea	New American
Tallgrass	New French
Arun's	Thai
Ambria	New French
27 Topolobampo	Mexican
Charlie Trotter's	New American
Everest	Alsatian/New French
Vie	New American
Spring	New Amer./Seafood
Barrington Bistro	French Bistro
Oceanique	New French/Seafood
Ritz-Carlton Din. Rm.	New French
Blackbird	New American
26 Courtright's	New American
Frontera Grill	Mexican
Spiaggia	Italian

OTHER NOTEWORTHY PLACES

Avec	Mediterranean
Avenues	New French/Seafood
Chicago Chop Hse.	Steakhouse
Gibsons	Steakhouse
Green Zebra	Vegetarian
Heat	Japanese
Japonais	Japanese
Lou Malnati's	Pizza
Mirai Sushi	Japanese
mk	New American
Morton's	Steakhouse
Mulan	Asian
Naha	Med./New American
NoMI	New French
North Pond	New American
one sixtyblue	New French
Schwa	New American
Seasons	New American
Shanghai Terrace	Pan-Asian
Wildfire	American/Steakhouse

ALINEA Ⓜ
| 28 | 27 | 28 | $168 |

1723 N. Halsted St. (bet. North Ave. & Willow St.), 312-867-0110;
www.alinearestaurant.com

Soaring scoring supports the "sheer genius" of chef-owner Grant Achatz and the "astonishing flavors" of his "fabulous" "experimental" New American cuisine at this Lincoln Park "thrill ride" that "engages all of your senses" and "expands your concept of fine dining"; the space is "lovely, understated and serene", the nearly 700-bottle wine list is "superb" and the "polished service" is near "perfect"; be prepared, though, as this "surreal" "journey" will be "loooong" and "ungodly expensive" – though "worth it"; N.B. open Wednesday–Sunday for dinner only.

Ambria Ⓢ
| 28 | 26 | 27 | $79 |

Belden-Stratford Hotel, 2300 N. Lincoln Park W. (Belden Ave.),
773-472-5959; www.leye.com

Lincoln Park's "perennial favorite" "splurge destination" "has had a shot of energy" from "new chef" Christian Eckmann, whose "outstanding" Spanish-tinged New French cuisine exhibits "interesting, well-executed modern twists"; the "expert" staff's "unobtrusive service" includes "outstanding wine pairings" ("personable "sommelier Bob Bansberg is a gift"), and the "dark-wood" paneling, "fresh flowers" and "tuxedos" make for *très romantique* dining – even if the "staid", "civilized" experience spells "stuffy" to some; P.S. "don't forget your jacket or your wallet."

Arun's Ⓜ
| 28 | 24 | 26 | $88 |

4156 N. Kedzie Ave. (bet. Belle Plaine & Berteau Aves.), 773-539-1909;
www.arunsthai.com

Chef-owner Arun Sampanthavivat's "completely inventive", "customized" 12-course tasting-only menu of "transcendental" Thai is tantamount to "edible art", "served with care and courtesy" in a "simply" "elegant gallery" setting with a "great wine cellar"; sure, it's "tucked in an industrial/residential neighborhood" on the Northwest Side, but it's "as good as the best in Thailand" and "a whole lot easier to get to", even if it "can seem wildly expensive"; in other words, "make sure this is on your 'things to do before I die' list."

Avec ●
| 25 | 19 | 22 | $42 |

615 W. Randolph St. (Jefferson St.), 312-377-2002;
www.avecrestaurant.com

"The fabulous people" "squeeze into" this "must-dine" Med small plate specialist for the "incredible flavors" of chef Koren Grieveson's "fantasy" "peasant cuisine", paired with an "eclectic, affordable wine list" and served by a "knowledgeable staff"; its "metrosexual Paul Bunyan", "wood-lined steam-room" setting with "table sharing" and "bench seating" is "not for the anti-social", who lambaste it as "loud" and "wildly uncomfortable", although extroverts enthuse over the "hip" West Loop "scene"; P.S. "if only they took reservations."

Avenues Ⓜ
| 26 | 26 | 26 | $88 |

Peninsula Hotel, 108 E. Superior St. (bet. Michigan Ave. & Rush St.),
312-573-6754; www.peninsula.com

At this "posh", "gracious" River North New French–seafood sophisticate, boulevardiers are buoyed by Graham Elliot Bowles' "amazing tasting menus" and "innovative, avant-garde presentations" – plus the "champagne cart pre-dinner is a nice touch" too; the "well-spaced" tables of its "luxurious" Peninsula Hotel setting provide "beautiful views", and service strikes most as "impeccable" (though a smidge "stuffy" to some); P.S. you might want to "come with an expense account or rich aunt."

Barrington Country Bistro
27 | 21 | 24 | $42

Foundry Shopping Ctr., 700 W. Northwest Hwy. (Hart Rd.), Barrington, 847-842-1300; www.barringtoncountrybistro.com

Toques off to the "top-quality traditional bistro fare" at this "hidden gem" situated in an "inauspicious" Northwest Suburban mall; "excellent service" is provided within a "pleasant country-French setting", and it's all overseen by a particularly "gracious owner"; P.S. "lunch is a special treat", and the Sunday prix fixe is a steal.

Blackbird ⓢ
27 | 20 | 23 | $57

619 W. Randolph St. (bet. Desplaines & Jefferson Sts.), 312-715-0708; www.blackbirdrestaurant.com

Make sure this "fabulously polished" West Loop "classic" is on your list for "pure tastes in a pure space" courtesy of chef Paul "'King' Kahan", whose "exquisite" New American cuisine employing "local, organic and unique ingredients" "makes you proud to be from Chicago"; the setting may be "stark" ("the whole white on white thing"), the "tables cramped" and the "din" "astonishing", but there's "plenty of eye candy", plus "consummately professional" service and "one of the highest-quality wine selections in the city, at all price ranges."

CARLOS'
29 | 25 | 28 | $89

429 Temple Ave. (Waukegan Ave.), Highland Park, 847-432-0770; www.carlos-restaurant.com

A "memorable evening" awaits visitors to this 25-year-old North Shore "treasure", a "fine-dining" "temple on Temple Avenue" that's ranked No. 1 for Food among Chicagoland restaurants on the strength of its "superb", "very creative" New French fare, which is accompanied by a "fantastic wine list" and served by a "staff that knows when to be friendly and when to be reserved"; the feel is "formal yet extremely comfortable, with cozy booths and soft lighting", making it a "great celebration place" – "if you can afford it"; N.B. jackets required.

CHARLIE TROTTER'S ⓢ
27 | 25 | 27 | VE

816 W. Armitage Ave. (Halsted St.), 773-248-6228; www.charlietrotters.com

This "religious experience" in Lincoln Park is "worth a mortgage payment", since it's both the "epitome of [New] American gastronomy" and the Most Popular restaurant in Chicagoland; its customers are "dazzled" by "brilliant" chef Charlie Trotter's daily changing menu (with "fantastic pairings" from an "exceptional wine cellar") and "cosseted" by a "courteous and knowledgeable" staff; and though a few find the "formal" feel "churchlike" and the whole experience "precious", most maintain it's "absolutely sublime"; P.S. "for the ultimate, get a reservation at the kitchen table."

Chicago Chop House
25 | 20 | 22 | $54

60 W. Ontario St. (bet. Clark & Dearborn Sts.), 312-787-7100; www.chicagochophouse.com

"In a city that knows meat", this "quintessential Chicago steak joint" and "ol' boys club" in River North is a "heavy hitter": it's "rich in tradition – and you can taste it in the food" (including "wonderful prime rib") not to mention see it in the "historical" setting with "tin ceilings", "old Chicago photos" and other "memorabilia", as well as a "great bar area with old-time drinks made the way they should be made"; P.S. "men with white collars" like to "expense this one."

Courtright's Ⓜ 26 | 25 | 26 | $58
8989 S. Archer Ave. (Willow Springs Rd.), Willow Springs, 708-839-8000; www.courtrights.com
Excursionists to the Southwest Surburbs eagerly enthuse about this "excellent out-of-the-way" "destination restaurant" where "marvelous", "creative seasonal" New American "meals are carefully planned, expertly prepared and exquisitely presented" in a "classic atmosphere" with "beautiful gardens" ("grazing deer appear magically as if on cue outside the [nearly] floor-to-ceiling windows"); P.S. "the wine alone is worth the trip."

Everest ⑤Ⓜ 27 | 26 | 27 | $91
One Financial Pl., 440 S. LaSalle St. (Congress Pkwy.), 312-663-8920; www.everestrestaurant.com
Financiers feel an affinity for this "romantic", "formal" "expense-account haven", "still at its peak" thanks to chef/co-owner Jean Joho's "delectable" New French–Alsatian cuisine, an "exemplary wine list", "totally professional service" and "a breathtaking view" from "the top of the [Loop] Financial District"; even fans feel the "nouveau riche" "decor is stuck in the '80s", though, and a few revolutionaries report the "attitude is loftier than the location."

FRONTERA GRILL ⑤Ⓜ 26 | 21 | 22 | $39
445 N. Clark St. (bet. Hubbard & Illinois Sts.), 312-661-1434; www.fronterakitchens.com
"Top-of-the-line Mexican [food] with a focus on fresh ingredients" comes courtesy of "culinary hero Rick Bayless" at this River North "treasure" with a "national reputation"; "bold, bright" and "somewhat raucous", it's "less expensive and more casual" than its "refined big brother", Topolobampo, with the same "superb wines" and "great margarita-tequila menu", but some say "service can be spotty when it's busy – which is always"; N.B. reservations accepted for dinner (parties of five or more) and lunch.

Gibsons Steakhouse ❶ 25 | 19 | 23 | $56
1028 N. Rush St. (Bellevue Pl.), 312-266-8999
Doubletree Hotel, 5464 N. River Rd. (bet. Balmoral & Bryn Mawr Aves.), Rosemont, 847-928-9900
www.gibsonssteakhouse.com
Carnivores take an "authentic Chicago power trip" at this Gold Coast "high-roller" haven "where everything is big", including the "excellent cuts of [prime] meat cooked to perfection", "lampshade-sized martinis", the personalities of the "outgoing staff" – and the "big check"; there's a "fantastic" "cigar-friendly" bar scene for those "long, crowded waits", so "make a reservation, arrive early and hope [you get] your table before the seasons change"; P.S. "the Rosemont location is as good – and easier" to navigate.

Green Zebra Ⓜ 25 | 23 | 23 | $51
1460 W. Chicago Ave. (Greenview Ave.), 312-243-7100; www.greenzebrachicago.com
"You don't have to be a tree-hugger to love" this West Town "winner" where Shawn McClain (Spring) "makes you want to eat your

vegetables" with his "phenomenal", "complex" "seasonal" "small plates" ("converts" crow "you'll never miss the meat" – though a few "chicken and fish dishes" are also offered); add "knowledgeable service" and "smart" "Zen" surroundings and you have a "haute" "heaven" – though catty carnivores contend "nothing impresses as much as the prices."

Heat �☒   25 | 21 | 23 | $85

1507 N. Sedgwick St. (North Ave.), 312-397-9818; www.heatsushi.com
Sushi is a life and death matter at this "unique" Old Town Japanese omakase-only outpost offering the "most amazing selections of imported seafoods and sake"; the "live-kill" candidates "swim by your feet at the bar", making for plates of "food so fresh it's still moving" – in other words, it's "not for the faint of heart", or the light of wallet, given that it's "very expensive"; N.B. bringing children is discouraged.

Japonais   24 | 26 | 20 | $58

600 W. Chicago Ave. (Larrabee St.), 312-822-9600;
www.japonaischicago.com
"Toward the top of the list for sushi", this Near West "up-market [Japanese] fusion" "hot" spot dishes out a "remarkable menu" of "innovative cuisine" and "dazzling decor" enhanced by a "very attractive crowd of twenty- to fiftysomething" "eye candy"; ok, it's a "budget buster", "but you're paying for" the "chic, happening ambiance" (and folks "love" the "hoppin' lounge" "on the river"), although classicists who call it "too trendy for its own good" dismiss the "serious attitude."

LE FRANÇAIS ⊠   28 | 25 | 28 | $93

269 S. Milwaukee Ave. (Dundee Rd.), Wheeling, 847-541-7470;
www.lefrancaisrestaurant.com
"Thank you for coming back to us" say surveyors about the return of "masterful" chef Roland Liccioni, who has "re-created the magic" at this "delightful, upscale special-occasion" North Suburban spot after "many ownership changes" with his New French cooking featuring "bold, delicious flavors" and "incredible sauces"; serving the "select clientele" are "helpful" staffers who are "professional" but "not afraid to be human", and the wine list is similarly "outstanding", so few fault it for being "fully priced" – especially given the "reasonable prix fixe lunch"; N.B. jackets are suggested.

LES NOMADES ⊠Ⓜ   28 | 26 | 28 | $90

222 E. Ontario St. (bet. Fairbanks Ct. & St. Clair St.), 312-649-9010;
www.lesnomades.net
"Despite a change in chef", this "refined" former private club in Streeterville "still satisfies": newcomer Chris Nugent "uses generous quantities of luxury ingredients" in his "excellent" New French cuisine, which is backed by a "fine" wine list and "superb service"; the "formal" (some say "stuffy") setting has an "understated", "hushed" tone that befits "a romantic rendezvous" or "an important business dinner" for a "cut-above" clientele that can afford "top-of-the-line prices."

Lou Malnati's Pizzeria   24 | 13 | 17 | $18
439 N. Wells St. (Hubbard St.), 312-828-9800
3859 W. Ogden Ave. (Cermak Rd.), 773-762-0800

(continued)

(continued)
Lou Malnati's Pizzeria
958 W. Wrightwood Ave. (Lincoln Ave.), 773-832-4030
85 S. Buffalo Grove Rd. (Lake Cook Rd.), Buffalo Grove, 847-215-7100
1050 E. Higgins Rd. (bet. Arlington Heights & Busse Rds.),
Elk Grove Village, 847-439-2000
1850 Sherman Ave. (University Pl.), Evanston, 847-328-5400
6649 N. Lincoln Ave. (bet. Devon & Pratt Aves.), Lincolnwood,
847-673-0800
131 W. Jefferson Ave. (Washington St.), Naperville, 630-717-0700
1 S. Roselle Rd. (Schaumburg Rd.), Schaumburg, 847-985-1525
www.loumalnatis.com
Standing "supreme", this "local chain" boasts a "cult following" of "addicts" who relish its "ridiculously good", "real Chicago pizza" – both the "decadent deep-dish" and the "even-better thin-crust" version – and "love the butter crust", "pure, simple sauce" with "chunks of tomato" and "thick cheese"; still, its reign at the top of the pie charts "of the known world" (and the local competition) is "not undisputed", with some citing "inconsistent service" and "cookie-cutter decor" as drawbacks.

Mirai Sushi ⊠   26 | 20 | 20 | $46
2020 W. Division St. (Damen Ave.), 773-862-8500
"In the face of a Chicago sushi explosion", this "hip" Wicker Park Japanese "remains the best" per raters who prefer its "pricey" but "pristine fish" – the "unusual" "maki don't disappoint but the quality of the straight-up sashimi sets this place apart" – or "put themselves in the chef's hands for a sublime omakase dinner"; add in the "divine sake" (over 30 varieties) and the "scene", especially "upstairs" where it's "definitely darker and more swank", and it's no surprise satisfied surveyors make this their "go-to" for raw fin fare.

mk   26 | 24 | 25 | $62
868 N. Franklin St. (bet. Chestnut & Locust Sts.), 312-482-9179;
www.mkchicago.com
Owner Michael "Kornick has turned the toque over to Todd Stein" at this "suave" River North New American, a still-"humming" "hot spot" that's managed to "endure and reinvent itself", where the cooking is "outstanding without being fussy or pretentious", the "bi-level" "loft" interior is "sleek" and the "attentive, accommodating" staffers know the "masterful wine list" and cheeses "like it's their business"; some raters report "rushed service" and "dreadfully noisy" digs, but more maintain it's a "favorite."

MORTON'S, THE STEAKHOUSE   26 | 21 | 24 | $59
65 E. Wacker Pl. (bet. Michigan & Wabash Aves.), 312-201-0410
Newberry Plaza, 1050 N. State St. (Maple St.), 312-266-4820
9525 W. Bryn Mawr Ave. (River Rd.), Rosemont, 847-678-5155
1470 McConnor Pkwy. (Meacham Rd.), Schaumburg, 847-413-8771
1 Westbrook Corporate Ctr. (22nd St.), Westchester, 708-562-7000
www.mortons.com
"Still the standard" for "scrumptious slabs of the best [prime] beef known to man", this "granddaddy" of a steakhouse is a "candy store for carnivores" complete with the "show-and-tell" presentation cart, "huge sides" and "soufflés meant to be shared", a "great wine list" and a "professional staff"; decor at various locations may stray from the "quintessential", "manly"

Gold Coast "mother ship", and some raters reckon it's "resting on its laurels", but a well-fed majority insists this "class act" is "worth" its "break-the-bank prices."

Mulan　　　　　–　–　–　M
Chinatown Sq., 2017 S. Wells St., 2nd fl. (China Pl.), 312-842-8282; www.mulanrestaurant.com
At this ultrachic but moderately priced Chinatown entrant from chef-owner Kee Chan (Heat), each of the avant-garde Asian dishes combine meat and seafood, e.g. duck breast with sea horse; it's hard to know where to look first (the inverted wine decanters on the tables, the plush ultrasuede booths, the aqua wave in the floor), or which vino to order from an extensive list of New World selections; N.B. be sure to enter at the East Gate.

Naha ☒　　　　　26　23　24　$59
500 N. Clark St. (Illinois St.), 312-321-6242; www.naha-chicago.com
Expect "unfussy", "innovative fine dining" at this River North "favorite" that's considered "consistently among the best"; chef/co-owner Carrie Nahabedian's "exciting menu" of "fresh" New American fare with "Mediterranean" flair is paired with a "thoughtful wine list", "seductively served" by a "cool staff" and "shown off" in a "clean-lined", "minimalist" space that "feels like a spa" – in fact, the "excellent" experience is "only marred by the high decibel level" "when it's crowded"; P.S. don't miss "one of the city's best burgers (lunch only)."

NoMI　　　　　26　27　26　$71
Park Hyatt Chicago, 800 N. Michigan Ave. (Chicago Ave.), 312-239-4030; www.nomirestaurant.com
"Ethereal" "zen" environs including "Chihuly chandeliers" and an "unbeatable view" of the Water Tower sets the stage for this Gold Coast "lap-of-luxury" restaurant where the "intriguing flavor combinations" of chef Christophe David's "exquisite" New French cuisine pair with "quality sushi" and an "excellent wine list" to warrant the "special-occasion" "splurge"; additional assets are the "discreet service", "killer Sunday brunch", "lovely outdoor terrace" and "very swishy bar", though you still have a segment that finds the service "stuffy" and doesn't relish "paying for the view."

North Pond Ⓜ　　　　　25　27　23　$59
2610 N. Cannon Dr. (bet. Diversey & Fullerton Pkwys.), 773-477-5845; www.northpondrestaurant.com
The "uncommon combination" of chef/co-owner Bruce Sherman's "wonderfully crafted" "seasonal" cuisine, a "tranquil", "idyllic setting" of "lovely Arts and Crafts rooms" with "great skyline views" and an "excellent wine list" make this New American "on the pond in [Lincoln] Park" "one of Chicago's finest and most unique" places for a "romantic meal or special occasion"; most surveyors "feel transported a million miles away", but others are earthbound by "inconsistent food and service" and "prices that have crept up"; P.S. they serve summer lunch and "delightful Sunday brunch" year-round.

Oceanique ☒　　　　　27　21　24　$52
505 Main St. (bet. Chicago & Hinman Aves.), Evanston, 847-864-3435; www.oceanique.com
"Unpretentious" "fine dining" is the house special at this North Suburban New French "treasure" where chef-owner Mark Grosz

creates "a flawless assortment of beautifully prepared dishes" featuring what may be the "best seafood in the Chicago area", plus "plenty of alternate choices for meat people"; expect an "excellent wine list" and "well-educated staff" in a "pleasant" setting where you can "enjoy the food and your companions without being dressed to the nines" (though luxe-lovers would "upgrade" the atmosphere); P.S. try "the $35 three-course dinner Monday–Friday."

one sixtyblue ⑧   25 | 24 | 23 | $56
1400 W. Randolph St. (Ogden Ave.), 312-850-0303;
www.onesixtyblue.com

"Exciting and adventurous meals" await at this "stylish" New French establishment co-owned by basketball icon Michael Jordan that's "worth the detour" to the fringe of the Market District for "terrific" cuisine "balancing creativity and simplicity" from Martial Noguier, "a chef who cares", plus "a good selection of reasonably priced wines" and a "beautifully designed" room by Adam Tihany; it's a package that leads satisfied respondents to describe it as a "perfect place" "for a romantic dinner" or "before a concert at the United Center."

Ritz-Carlton Dining Room Ⓜ   27 | 27 | 28 | $80
Ritz-Carlton Hotel, 160 E. Pearson St., 12th fl. (Michigan Ave.),
312-573-5223; www.fourseasons.com

"Elegant, excellent" and "expensive", this "epitome of gracious dining" in the Ritz is a Streeterville "culinary oasis" where "top-tier" New French fare meets an 800-bottle wine list that might "make you weep (and Amex jump for joy)"; the "beautiful" setting is "grand" and "romantic", and the "professional staff is extremely helpful", contributing to a "special-event experience extraordinaire"; N.B. rumblings of "inconsistency" reflect a series of chef changes, the latest being the post-*Survey* departure of chef Kevin Hickey for Seasons and promotion of former sous-chef Mark Payne.

Schwa ⑧   ▽ 26 | 14 | 24 | $54
1466 N. Ashland Ave. (LeMoyne St.), 773-252-1466;
www.schwarestaurant.com

Patrons predict chef Michael Carlson "will be a star someday" as they "dream of [their] next meal" of his "spectacular" "seasonal" New American cuisine, "artfully presented" within the "minimalist, unpretentious atmosphere" of "the smallest dining room and kitchen imaginable" on Lincoln Park's western edge; bargain-hunters find it "a bit pricey", but supporters swear this "little-restaurant-that-could" is "a must"; P.S. "plan ahead, given the" space limitations, "and inquire about the daily menu, since it's BYO."

Seasons   26 | 27 | 27 | $78
Four Seasons Hotel, 120 E. Delaware Pl., 7th fl. (bet. Michigan Ave. &
Rush St.), 312-649-2349; www.fourseasons.com

A "classic" "for all seasons", this Gold Coast "formal" "fine-dining" venue treats guests "like royalty", with "pampering" service, a "magnificent", "refined" setting seen as "one of Chicago's prettiest rooms" and "excellent" New American cuisine augmented by an "amazing wine selection"; those who suggest "the food is sometimes a little less than expected for the price" may not have visited since "new chef" Kevin Hickey (ex Ritz-Carlton) "came on board"; P.S. for many, the "out-of-this-world" "Sunday brunch is the reason to head here."

Shanghai Terrace 🍴
24 | 26 | 25 | $57

Peninsula Hotel, 108 E. Superior St., 5th fl. (bet. Michigan Ave. & Rush St.), 312-573-6744; www.chicago.peninsula.com

"Attention to detail and interesting flavors" are hallmarks of this "exceptional", "marvelously appointed temple of outstanding Pan-Asian cuisine" in the Peninsula that "transports" raters with the "refined elegance" of its "gorgeous" River North setting and its "quality service" – whether "for special occasions" or "expense-account" dining; fans also praise its rooftop terrace as the "most beautiful Zen garden in the city" and "the ideal summer date venue", but a minority finds the destination "pricey above its merit."

Spiaggia
26 | 27 | 25 | $80

One Magnificent Mile Bldg., 980 N. Michigan Ave., 2nd fl. (Oak St.), 312-280-2750; www.spiaggiarestaurant.com

Expect a "peak dining experience" at this "honed-to-perfection", "luxury" Gold Coaster boasting a "sumptuous" setting with "spectacular views" of the Michigans (both Lake and Avenue), chef Tony Mantuano's "sublime", "incomparable Italian" cuisine, an "excellent", "extensive wine list" and "superlative service"; most maintain it's "one of the few places where the high price tag is worth it", though a segment of surveyors submits that the staff's "snooty" and the "small portions" are "overpriced" ("lunch is a lot less expensive"); N.B. jackets required.

Spring 🅼
27 | 25 | 25 | $59

2039 W. North Ave. (Damen Ave.), 773-395-7100; www.springrestaurant.net

Shawn McClain's "incredible creations" of "perfectly prepared" New American seafood "with a slight Asian slant" inspire acolytes to inquire "is it impolite to lick the plate?" at this "hip" Wicker Park place that's "as fresh and exciting as the season it's named after"; the "quietly elegant setting" "in a converted bathhouse" is "beautiful and peaceful", the service is "polished but not over-whelming" and there's an "outstanding wine list", all of which adds up to "a wonderful experience" – so if you don't have a "special occasion, just come up with one."

Tallgrass 🅼
28 | 24 | 25 | $69

1006 S. State St. (10th St.), Lockport, 815-838-5566; www.tallgrassrestaurant.com

"Spectacular", "innovative" New French fare and a "deep wine list" (600 labels strong) fuel this "venerable" "foodie's paradise" "in the middle of nowhere" – aka historic Southwest Suburban Lockport – that's "well worth the drive from anywhere"; gourmets gush they "would go broke if they [lived] nearby", returning for chef-partner Robert Burcenski's "fine haute cuisine" with "wonderful presentation" in a "very private", "romantic" space; N.B. jackets are suggested for gentlemen.

Topolobampo 🍴🅼
27 | 23 | 25 | $57

445 N. Clark St. (bet. Hubbard & Illinois Sts.), 312-661-1434; www.fronterakitchens.com

"This is what the food in heaven must taste like" posit praisers of this "pinnacle" of Mexican *alta cucina* in River North, where "every bite" of "creative genius" Rick Bayless' cuisine is "utterly swoon-worthy", the tequila list is "to die for" and the "passionate staff" "pampers" patrons; most feel it's "more elegant than its attached sister restaurant, Frontera Grill", with fare that "really is better", even if a handful of heretics wonder "is it worth the price difference?"; P.S. "book well ahead", as getting "weekend reservations can take forever."

TRU ☒ | 28 | 27 | 28 | $117 |

676 N. St. Clair St. (bet. Erie & Huron Sts.), 312-202-0001;
www.trurestaurant.com

"Art and food meet and really, really like each other" at this Streeterville "temple of excess" where chefs Rick Tramonto ("bravo!") and Gale Gand ("the goddess of the dessert") "amaze" with "progressive, daring" New French plates plus sommelier Scott Tyree's "divinely inspired" 1,400-bottle wine selection, all borne by a virtually "flawless" staff within a "stark, simple" setting sporting an "original Andy Warhol" and "a lovely little tuffet for Madame's handbag"; "sticker shock" aside, it's a "magical experience" that "will become a lasting memory"; N.B. jackets required.

Vie ☒ | 27 | 23 | 23 | $55 |

4471 Lawn Ave. (Burlington Ave.), Western Springs, 708-246-2082;
www.vierestaurant.com

"Wow"-ed West Suburbanites feel "lucky to have" this New American in the "quaint", "sleepy" town of Western Springs, where chef-owner "Paul Virant brings many of his Blackbird sensibilities" to his "haute" "seasonal" "dishes with excellent flavor combinations", paired with a "very interesting wine list"; just "steps from the train station", it's even "worth the reverse commute for adventurous Chicagoans", though some call the "modern, minimalist" decor "cold" and others purport it would be "perfect" "if the service could catch up with the brilliance of the food."

WILDFIRE | 23 | 21 | 21 | $40 |

159 W. Erie St. (bet. LaSalle & Wells Sts.), 312-787-9000
1300 Patriot Blvd. (Lake Ave.), Glenview, 847-657-6363
235 Parkway Dr. (Milwaukee Ave.), Lincolnshire, 847-279-7900
Oakbrook Center Mall, 232 Oakbrook Ctr. (Rte. 83), Oak Brook,
630-586-9000
1250 E. Higgins Rd. (National Pkwy.), Schaumburg, 847-995-0100
www.wildfirerestaurant.com

Spreading like their namesake, this "insanely popular" passel of Traditional American steakhouses from the "Lettuce Entertain You group" keeps carnivores "coming back" with "hearty Midwest-sized portions" from a "crowd-pleasing menu" of "awesome wood-fired" fare ("juicy" steaks and chops), "delicious chopped salad" and "great martini flights" in a "classy", "clubby" "'40s-style" setting; salivating surveyors swear it's "worth the wait" ("even with reservations"), but wet blankets rank these "noisy" "madhouses" "rather ordinary, just on a grand scale."

Cincinnati

TOP FOOD RANKING

	Restaurant	Cuisine
29	Jean-Robert at Pigall's	New French
28	Daveed's at 934	Eclectic
27	Boca	Italian
	BonBonerie	Bakery/Dessert
	Palace, The	Continental/New Amer.
26	Precinct	Steakhouse
	Sturkey's	Eclectic
	Jeff Ruby's	Steakhouse
25	Morton's	Steakhouse
	South Beach Grill	Seafood/Steakhouse

OTHER NOTEWORTHY PLACES

Beluga	Asian Fusion
China Gourmet	Chinese
Cumin	Indian
Dewey's	Pizza
JeanRo	French
Montgomery Inn	Barbecue
Nectar	Eclectic
Nicola's	Northern Italian
Palomino	Med./New American
Pho Paris	French/Vietnamese

	F	D	S	C

Beluga ◐ ⧄   25 | 23 | 20 | $42
3520 Edwards Rd. (Erie Ave.), 513-533-4444
A whale of a nightspot, this "hip-as-it-gets" Asian fusion favorite in monied Hyde Park serves up "amazing sushi" and more during dinner hours, then "shifts into high gear" when the house DJ starts spinning and the martinis begin to flow; a "delightfully meandering floor plan" and "minimalist" white rooms keep the focus on the "gorgeous clientele", while "accommodating" service helps compensate for the Tokyo-esque prices.

BOCA ⧄ Ⓜ   27 | – | 24 | $48
3200 Madison Rd. (bet. Braizee St. & Ridge Rd.), 513-542-2022; www.boca-restaurant.com
An "impassioned local following" heads to this Oakley Italian from gregarious chef/co-owner David Falk, whose "utter devotion to sharp, distinctive flavors" gives rise to "contemporary cuisine" with the "perfect balance of color, taste, and texture"; customized digs bring this "foodie mecca" more attention, as does "excellent" wine pairings on the six-to-eight-course Chef's Grand Tasting Menu; diners find themselves divided on service, though – some call it "superb", while others deem it "spotty."

BONBONERIE 🗷 `27 | 17 | 18 | $14`
2030 Madison Rd. (Grandin Rd.), 513-321-3399; www.thebonbon.com
"They could charge just for the aroma" of the "decadent desserts" at this East Side "sweet-tooth heaven" coo carbophiles who claim the cakes constitute a "reason to look forward to your birthday"; what's more, the bakery's "quirky" tea room offers light breakfasts and lunches, and an "excellent selection" of leaves plus the "world's best scones" make it a "great place to meet a friend" for a cuppa (reserve 24 hours ahead for a full tea service).

China Gourmet 🗷 `24 | 17 | 23 | $37`
3340 Erie Ave. (Marburg Ave.), 513-871-6612
Sino-style specialties (whole steamed fish, "five-spice oysters" in season) are prepared and served "with flair and uncommon elegance" at this Hyde Park "fixture" beloved by an "upscale crowd"; proprietors from the Moy family dynasty "are always present and it shows": "they know you by name" and "make you feel right at home", while the "accommodating" staff "will adapt a dish to any desire"; a small minority calls prices "inscrutably high", but most feel the "total experience justifies the cost."

Cumin `25 | 17 | 19 | $27`
3514 Erie Ave. (Pinehurst St.), 513-871-8714
Cumin and sit down at this "nouveau" Indian bistro in Hyde Park, where "lots of unusual taste mixtures", "creativity and flair" from chef-owner Yajan Upadhyaya go into the "superlative", "cutting-edge" subcontinental fare ("delicious dosas"); with portions "on the small side", you can "try a bit of many things", but the "minimalist, Ikea-like" space is diminutive as well, which makes claustrophobes feel "cramped" and "crowded" and perhaps more likely to notice that the "service needs a bit of help."

DAVEED'S AT 934 🗷 Ⓜ `28 | 20 | 24 | $58`
934 Hatch St. (Louden St.), 513-721-2665
At this "romantic, intimate" 65-seat "hideaway" in trendy Mt. Adams, chef/co-owner David Cook lives up to his name, creating an Asian- and Med-accented Eclectic menu that "mixes the familiar and the innovative" to create an "adventure for the palate"; wife Liz "lovingly" manages the "comfortable", colorful dining rooms, a "delightful back patio under the trees" and a crew of "considerate" servers (a few do find them "condescending" to non-"connoisseurs"); in short, it's a "terrific choice for special occasions."

Dewey's Pizza `23 | 16 | 20 | $17`
265 Hosea Ave. (Clifton Ave.), 513-221-0400
Oakley Sq., 3014 Madison Rd. (bet. Markbreit Ave. & Romana Pl.), 513-731-7755
Newport on the Levee, 1 Levee Way (Monmouth St.), Newport, 859-431-9700
Shops at Harper's Point, 11338 Montgomery Rd. (bet. E Kemper Rd. & Harpers Point Dr.), Symmes, 513-247-9955
www.deweyspizza.com
"Why can't all pizza be this good?" wonder 'za zealots who zip over to this local chain of pie palaces for the "perfect formula" of "great crust", "top-notch toppings and good value" rolled into "exotic", "garlic-laden" combinations (e.g. the "incredible Bronx Bomber"); you can also opt to "build your own" or dig into "excel-

lent", "very shareable salads"; staffers are "friendly" and "lively", and while "kids love watching" the "chefs toss and top" the dough in the open-windowed kitchen, their parents appreciate the "terrific wines" and "good beers on tap."

JeanRo　　　　　　　　　　　　25 | 24 | 23 | $36
413 Vine St. (bet. 4th & 5th Sts.), 513-621-1465;
www.bistrojeanro.com

"Like everything else Jean-Robert de Cavel touches", this Gallic is "golden" report city "power brokers" who peg this "low-cost offspring of [Jean-Robert at] Pigall's" as a Downtown "star"; at the "chummy yet sophisticated" bistro, "casual but not lax" servers proffer "authentic" "French comfort foods" that are "not over-fussy", plus a "wine list full of values"; the deep, narrow room has walls of "Provençal yellow" with "café-style posters", and its copper bar proves ideal for "meeting friends" and pretending "you've escaped" to Paris.

JEAN-ROBERT AT PIGALL'S 🗷Ⓜ　29 | 28 | 29 | $83
127 W. Fourth St. (bet. Elm & Race Sts.), 513-721-1345;
www.jean-robertatpigalls.com

"Alain Ducasse, look out for Jean-Robert" de Cavel, whose Downtown New French has been voted No. 1 for Popularity and Food in Cincinnati; demonstrating "impeccable taste", the maestro's "ethereal" cuisine (offered only as a three-course prix fixe or a five-course tasting menu) "stimulates the eye as much as the palate" against the backdrop of an "elegant but understated" room where the "welcoming" servers "read your mind"; in short, according to the "upper-crust" "society-crowd" clientele, the whole experience is simply "world-class."

JEFF RUBY'S STEAKHOUSE 🗷　　26 | 22 | 24 | $59
700 Walnut St. (7th St.), 513-784-1200; www.jeffruby.com

Living large is the motif at this Downtown chophouse, a "celebrity hot spot" where "everything is supersized" from the "great martinis" and "deep wine list" to the "shrimp on steroids" and "aged-on-the-premises" "roasts disguised as steaks"; meanwhile, the "well-done" art deco–influenced interiors are "flashy" but "not over-the-top gaudy" and servers "never miss a beat"; all agree you'll need a "fat wallet" or an "expense account" to dine here, though the unimpressed couldn't care less: "overrated, overpriced, overdone – I'm over it."

MONTGOMERY INN　　　　　　22 | 19 | 20 | $31
925 Riverside Dr. (Pete Rose Way), 513-721-7427
400 Buttermilk Pike (I-75), Ft. Mitchell, 859-344-5333
9440 Montgomery Rd. (bet. Cooper & Remington Rds.),
Montgomery, 513-791-3482
www.montgomeryinn.com

"I'd like to be committed into this local institution" pun partisans of this "venerable" BBQ trio known for "steamed, not smoked, ribs"; they praise "melt-in-your-mouth" meat ("no gnawing necessary") and "sauce so good you won't mind wearing it" as you perch in the "crowded", "bustling" dining rooms (Downtown's Boathouse location offers sports artifacts and "nice evening views of the Ohio River"); still, the reluctant rib "it's living on its rep" and reject the "factory" feel, the "long waits" and what they consider "fatty, greasy", "heavy and boring" eats.

Morton's, The Steakhouse

| 25 | 20 | 24 | $59 |

Tower Place Mall, 28 W. Fourth St. (Race St.), 513-241-4104;
www.mortons.com

"Expense accounters" know there are "mountains of meat" and
"Paul Bunyanesque" vegetables to be had at this "very reliable"
Downtown chainster, a "traditional steakhouse" that's always
"good for business" dining; the room is "big, open and bright" and
staffers help earn "the Midwest its friendly reputation", but the
restaurants' standard pre-meal display of ingredients leaves some
wondering "who wants to meet their dinner before they eat it?"

Nectar ⊠ Ⓜ

| – | – | – | I |

1000 Delta Ave. (Linwood Ave.), 513-929-0525;
www.thenectarrestaurant.com

Having shuttered her Downtown restaurant, Aioli, chef-owner
Julie Francis has opened this new Eclectic bistro in Mt. Lookout
Square; suburban foodies dig the daily changing menu, which
tempts with local and organic ingredients, yet still retains the
toque's familiar Southwestern and Asian accents; meanwhile, a
black-clad crew covers the narrow, sparsely decorated dining
room where bare tables can make for noisy noshing; N.B. open
for weeknight dinners only.

Nicola's ⊠

| 25 | 21 | 22 | $44 |

1420 Sycamore St. (Liberty St.), 513-721-6200;
www.nicolasrestaurant.com

"You may stay" in "Porkopolis", but "your taste buds leave for
Firenze" when you dine at this Downtown Tuscan offering "expertly crafted food", a "strong" 600-label Italian wine list and
"marvelous sauces" ("you'll never want to touch another jar of
Ragu"), plus tasting menus from chef Christian Pietoso (son of
Nicola) that "add contemporary flair"; meanwhile, the spacious
setting (a "transformed old trolley barn" with a "pleasant patio")
provides a "nice atmosphere", although the "friendly" service
can sometimes be "slow."

PALACE, THE ⊠

| 27 | 25 | 25 | $63 |

Cincinnatian Hotel, 601 Vine St. (6th St.), 513-381-6006;
www.palacecincinnati.com

"Attention to detail" is the hallmark of this "first-rate" longtimer
in Downtown's Cincinnatian Hotel, where "extraordinary", "artfully presented" Continental–New American cuisine is complemented by a cellar that boasts some "truly wonderful gems";
meanwhile, even commoners feel like "royalty" here thanks to
"exquisite service", live music and a stately dining room that's an
"oasis of civility", "elegance and style"; N.B. a post-*Survey* chef
change may outdate the above Food score.

PALOMINO

| 22 | 23 | 20 | $36 |

Fountain Pl., 505 Vine St. (5th St.), 513-381-1300; www.palomino.com

Its "primo location" ensures quick access to the Convention
Center and the Aronoff Center for the Arts plus "excellent views"
of "Fountain Square skaters" at holiday time, but "beautiful people" also head to this "slick" Downtown chain link – a "piece of
Seattle in Cincy" – for the "extraordinarily consistent" New
American–Med fare served by a "courteous and professional
staff"; the "lively", "loud" atmosphere is generally a plus, though
the "din" occasionally makes it hard to "enjoy your dinner."

Pho Paris

— | — | — | **M**

3235A Madison Rd. (bet. Brazee St. & Ridge Ave.), 513-871-1234;
www.phoparis.com
Star chef-restaurateur Jean-Robert de Cavel (Jean-Robert at
Pigall's) has scored another hit with this French-Vietnamese in
Oakley that offers up such fusion fare as five-spices salmon with
shallot compote; although the exterior is more strip mall than
sleek, the dining room appeals to couples with its silver-leafed
walls and collection of Eiffel Towers, while the black stone-topped
bar proves itself a great cocktail hour perch for hipsters.

PRECINCT, THE

26 | **21** | **24** | **$52**

311 Delta Ave. (Columbia Pkwy.), 513-321-5454; www.jeffruby.com
Carnivores (including "local celebs" and "professional ballplayers") crave the "mammoth portions" of "aged-to-perfection" steak
dispatched at Jeff Ruby's "white-tablecloth" Columbia-Tusculum
beefhouse, once a district police station; there are also raw bar
selections, a "fabulous cellar" and "outstanding service", all fit
for a "boys' night out" or to "impress a date"; however, a uniform
complaint is that "tables are too close together" ("busy nights
can be ear-shattering").

South Beach Grill at the Waterfront

☒ **25** | **22** | **24** | **$49**

14 Pete Rose Pier, Covington, 859-581-1414; www.jeffruby.com
It "feels like you are walking into a cruise ship" when you board
this floating surf 'n' turf palace – once again helmed by Jimmy
Gibson – moored in Covington; surveyors state it's "great for a special occasion" and "worth" the "steep" prices, thanks to "excellent" steaks, the "freshest seafood outside of the ocean" (including
sushi and a raw bar) and "sharp" service; the "view of Downtown
is hard to beat" and makes up for somewhat "tired" decor.

Sturkey's

26 | **19** | **23** | **$41**

400 Wyoming Ave. (Oak St.), Wyoming, 513-821-9200; www.sturkeys.com
"Personable" proprietors "Pam and Paul" please patrons of their
eponymous Eclectic, located in the suburban, "historic" village of
Wyoming, with "innovative", "fabulous food" that's "beautifully
presented" ("even the house salad is magnificent" and "desserts
are works of art in their own right"); a "friendly" staff fosters a "very
pleasant" atmosphere, while the decor is colorful and uncluttered –
even if a few aesthetes assess it as a little too "South Florida."

Cleveland

TOP FOOD RANKING

Restaurant	Cuisine
28 Johnny's Bar	Continental/N. Italian
27 Chez François	French
Phnom Penh	Cambodian
Lolita	Med./New American
Blue Point Grille	Seafood
Giovanni's Ristorante	Northern Italian
Flying Fig	American/Eclectic
26 Battuto	Italian
Classics	French
Sans Souci	French/Med.

OTHER NOTEWORTHY PLACES

Baricelli Inn	Continental
Fahrenheit	New American
fire	New American
Hyde Park Prime	Steakhouse
One Walnut	New American
Parallax	Seafood
Red the Steakhouse	Steakhouse
Sergio's Saravá	Brazilian
Three Birds	New American
Vivo	Northern Italian

	F	D	S	C

BARICELLI INN Ⓢ   26 | 25 | 25 | $57

Baricelli Inn, 2203 Cornell Rd. (Murray Hill Rd.), 216-791-6500; www.baricelli.com

Fromage fanatics smile and "say cheese" when focusing on the "exceptional" artisanal wedges paired with pours from a "great" 400-label wine list at this "elegant" East Side Continental where Paul Minnillo's cuisine is "creative and ever-changing" yet "consistently excellent"; diners also deem the "comfortable, quiet" setting in a "gracious" mansion-turned-B&B "conducive to talking, meeting or celebrating occasions" with the help of "impeccably" "attentive" staffers; and while some regard the rates as "reasonable", others shudder at "the size of the check."

Battuto Restaurant Ⓢ Ⓜ   26 | 20 | 23 | $43

12405 Mayfield Rd. (125th St.), 216-707-1055

At this East Side "oasis on a street of ketchup and egg noodles", chef-owners Mark and Giovanna Daverio conjure up "incredible", "inventive" variations on Italian classics (game, seafood, "excellent fresh" pasta) that servers present with "style and panache"; another "nice change" from nearby eateries is a "cozy" interior tinged with "modern-Euro coolness", leading patrons to pick this "relaxing place" when they aim to "linger over dinner with friends."

BLUE POINT GRILLE
27 ｜ 25 ｜ 24 ｜ $47

700 W. Saint Clair Ave. (6th St.), 216-875-7827;
www.hrcleveland.com
Fin fans have a merry time at this maritimer in the Warehouse District, voted Cleveland's Most Popular, where such "terrific fresh seafood" ("so many oysters, my wife found me attractive") in such a landlocked locale is a "rare treat"; meanwhile, the lofty, nautical-themed room with floor-to-ceiling windows is "stunning" for "special celebrations" and the "attentive" service falls "just short of palm-frond fans and hand-fed grapes" – so surveyors simply tune out "noise" from an often-"boisterous" business-class crowd.

CHEZ FRANÇOIS Ⓜ
27 ｜ 26 ｜ 28 ｜ $63

555 Main St. (Liberty Ave.), Vermilion, 440-967-0630;
www.chezfrancois.com
"Exemplary" attention from an "experienced staff" makes this "high-end special-occasion eatery" "worth the hike", as does "the best French food within 100 miles" ("foie gras to die for"); the converted sailmakers' loft on the Vermilion River (40 minutes west of Downtown) boasts a "charming", exposed-brick interior and a patio for "great alfresco dining", and also provides docking – but even the yachtsmen who weigh anchor admit the meals here are "kinda pricey"; N.B. jacket required in the dining room.

Classics Ⓔ Ⓜ
26 ｜ 28 ｜ 26 ｜ $67

InterContinental Hotel & Conference Ctr., 9801 Carnegie Ave. (E. 100th St.),
216-707-4100; www.classicsrestaurant.com
Revived in early 2003, this "incarnation" of a "special-occasion" classic resides in the InterContinental Hotel east of Downtown; it provides "first-class", "fairy-tale evenings" that are "worth the splurge", given an "opulent" atmosphere that's "polished in every way", "fanciful" yet "exacting" French preparations and "impeccable service" ("so many servers, you wonder who gets the tip"); yet to some it "borders on the pretentious"; N.B. gentlemen, please don a jacket – and leave children under 10 at home.

Fahrenheit Ⓔ
25 ｜ 22 ｜ 21 ｜ $44

2417 Professor Ave. (Jefferson Ave.), 216-781-8858;
www.fahrenheittremont.com
Simultaneously hot and "cool", Tremont's "ebullient urban bistro" draws a "boisterous" yet "mostly classy crowd" for chef-owner Rocco Whalen's "eclectic" New American fare "with flair" ("fantastic gourmet pizzas", Vietnamese chicken spring rolls); patrons praise the crew for "unobtrusive service with a smile" and call the art deco interior with open kitchen "trendy" and "chic"; however, many get overheated about "extreme noise" that makes it "difficult to carry on a conversation."

fire
25 ｜ 21 ｜ 22 ｜ $42

13220 Shaker Sq. (N. Moreland Blvd.), 216-921-3473;
www.firefoodanddrink.com
Shaker Square's flickering fortunes notwithstanding, "talented chef" Doug Katz's "lively" New American is still hot, offering "simply prepared" but "imaginative" seasonal cuisine cooked in brick ovens and tandoors ("phenomenal pork chops") as well as servers who are "usually" "downright charming"; meanwhile, the exposed-brick, open-kitchen environs spark heated debate – some term them "upscale" and "chic", others "noisy" and

"cramped" (with chairs so "uncomfortable" they "should be burned"); N.B. there's also patio dining in summer.

Flying Fig Ⓜ   27 | 21 | 24 | $40
2523 Market Ave. (W. 25th St.), 216-241-4243; www.theflyingfig.com
Foodies give far more than a flying fig for this "undiscovered gem" in trendy Ohio City; in fact, they lick their chops over chef-owner Karen Small's "brilliant", "unconventional" and "thoroughly satisfying" American-Eclectic concoctions, presented by servers "as entertaining as the menu"; though it's set on "one of the coziest streets in Cleveland", the dining room's sleek, minimalist decor "captures the feel of a Lower Manhattan eatery" – complete with "reverberating acoustics", so some may want to sup "on the streetside patio."

Giovanni's Ristorante Ⓢ   27 | 24 | 27 | $62
25550 Chagrin Blvd. (Richmond Rd.), Beachwood, 216-831-8625; www.giovanniscleveland.com
"Don't be fooled by the location" in a "suburban office building" – this "expensive" Beachwood "grande dame" is one of "Cleveland's classiest places", where "traditional" Tuscan dishes are "prepared to perfection" and paired with any of 700 wines; within the "lush" paneled main room, a "skilled" "black-tie" staff provides "superb" "old-school service"; cutting-edgers call the place a "throwback" that's "formal to the point of distraction", but well-wishers willing to "wear a jacket" (it's preferred) deem it "divine."

HYDE PARK PRIME STEAKHOUSE   25 | 22 | 24 | $49
123 W. Prospect Ave. (W. 2nd St.), 216-344-2444
26300 Chagrin Blvd. (Park East Dr.), Beachwood, 216-464-0688
Crocker Park Shopping Ctr., 21 Main St. (Crocker Rd.), Westlake, 440-892-4933
www.hydeparkrestaurants.com
The "business crowd" takes a seat at these outposts of the statewide chophouse chain, where a menu of "delectable", "mouthwatering" steaks (some "named after Cleveland sports figures") accords with the "masculine" feel of handsome, "wood-accented" rooms populated by "old guys with their trophy dates"; "superb service" from "personable" staffers makes patrons feel they "really count", but some bean-counters have a beef with the "expense-account" prices; N.B. the West Prospect branch is closed for renovations through fall 2006.

JOHNNY'S BAR Ⓢ   28 | 22 | 25 | $51
3164 Fulton Rd. (Trent Ave.), 216-281-0055
No Johnny-come-lately, this "outstanding" octogenarian just south of Downtown has once again been voted Cleveland's No. 1 for Food, so "dress up" and eat with the "'in' crowd"; the "sophisticated" Northern Italian–Continental cuisine has so many "twists and surprises", "you'll never tire" of it, let alone of the "high-end" 1,000-label wine list; meanwhile, paneled interiors with "faux-leopard carpets" give off a vintage vibe (there's also a patio) and "knowledgeable" staffers treat you "like a regular even if it's your first visit"; N.B. lunch Thursdays and Fridays only.

LOLITA   27 | 23 | 24 | $46
900 Literary Rd. (Professor Ave.), 216-771-5652; www.lolabistro.com
"I would eat shoe leather if Michael Symon cooked it for me" vow votaries of the chef/co-owner's "fantastic", "inventive" Med–New

American victuals (a "revelation" in this "pierogi and kielbasa town", and now offered in small-plate portions), plus 500 "well-valued" wines; the "cool-cat" Tremont 50-seater "pleases more than just your palate", since the "hip, chic" main room, all mocha walls and velvet furnishings, has "lots of energy" (read: "can get loud") and the "professional service" is usually "excellent."

One Walnut ☒ | 24 | 21 | 23 | $49 |
Ohio Savings Bldg., 1 Walnut Ave. (bet. 9th & 12th Sts.), 216-575-1111; www.onewalnut.com
Chef-owner Marlin Kaplan's "upscale" New American in Downtown's Ohio Savings Building is an "excellent business lunch destination" where "friendly", "professional" staffers serve up "mouthwatering" meals made "with flair and style" (including "just-right" degustation dinners), plus an all-domestic selection of wines; nonetheless, naysayers aren't nuts about "stuffy" environs that "resemble a bank lobby" or prices that are "sky-high by Cleveland's standards."

Parallax Restaurant & Lounge ☒ | – | – | – | E |
2179 W. 11th St. (Fairfield Ave.), 216-583-9999; www.parallaxtremont.com
Zack Bruell and David Schneider, the chef-manager team behind Z Contemporary Cuisine (one of Cleveland's Tops in the mid-'90s), reunite with this seafood-centric Tremont trendster turning out grilled fish and meats, along with a sushi selection; the contemporary setting is clean-lined, with earth tones and bamboo accents contributing a vaguely Asian feel.

PHNOM PENH ⬚ | 27 | 8 | 19 | $16 |
13124 Lorain Ave. (131st St.), 216-251-0210
1929 W. 25th St. (Carroll Ave.), 216-357-2951
www.ohiorestaurant.com
Ok, the "atmosphere is not luxurious", but this "quiet" West Side BYO delivers "tremendous value", turning out "exquisite" Cambodian rice and noodle dishes whose "brilliant flavors" put your "taste buds on sensory overload"; the "owners make you feel like family" and staffers "help you order", so chances are "once you dine here, you'll join the cult" of fervent fans; N.B. a West 25th Street branch opened post-*Survey* with the same menu and a more sophisticated decor.

Red the Steakhouse | – | – | – | E |
3355 Richmond Rd. (bet. Chagrin Blvd. & Woodland Rd.), Beachwood, 216-831-2252; www.redthesteakhouse.com
Trendy to look at, be in and pay for, this big, airy Beachwood steakhouse may be set in a strip-mall storefront, but it sports a very modern, monochromatic interior; meanwhile, the service proves professional as it doles out meaty, Med-tinged dishes that are accompanied by a rich list of California reds and lush libations like pomegranate martinis.

Sans Souci | 26 | 26 | 25 | $47 |
Renaissance Cleveland Hotel, 24 Public Sq. (bet. Superior Ave. & 3rd St.), 216-902-4095; www.sanssouicleveland.com
A culinary "Old Faithful" just off the lobby of Downtown's Renaissance Cleveland Hotel, this "classy", "romantic" special-occasion spot evokes a Provençal farmhouse via an enormous stone fireplace, beamed wooden ceiling and "murals depicting

countryside themes"; "marvelous" French-Med fare demonstrates the "kitchen's attention to detail", a "strong cellar" boasts
400 wines and "kind" staffers help create a "warm ambiance"
where diners can "converse without shouting"; still, since "this is
a place where people go to celebrate", you may encounter
"some noisy folks."

Sergio's Saravá — | — | — | M |

13225 Shaker Sq. (bet. N. Moreland & Shaker Blvds.), 216-295-1200;
www.sergioscleveland.com

Chef-restaurateur Sergio Abramof strikes again with this Shaker
Square hot spot where Brazilian-style entrees, raw-bar offerings
and a tapaslike menu of 'street plates' are accompanied by tropical cocktails and an international wine list; warm service and
South American rhythms attract locals and out-of-towners alike,
while a fireplace adds sizzle in winter and people-watching from
the patio proves a cool diversion from the summer's heat.

Three Birds ⑤ 25 | 24 | 22 | $47 |

18515 Detroit Ave. (Riverside Dr.), Lakewood, 216-221-3500;
www.3birdsrestaurant.com

"Even East Siders will cross the Cuyahoga" to visit this Lakewood
locale which has feathered friends chirping about the "whimsical",
"well-executed" New American entrees and perhaps "Cleveland's
prettiest garden patio" (with "fresh herbs grown" nearby); inside,
big windows and bright colors add "energy to a room" where eagle-
eyed eaters enjoy "people-watching" and "friendly", casually
attired staffers flit about; N.B. dinner only.

Vivo ⑤ 22 | 23 | 21 | $41 |

The Old Arcade, 347 Euclid Ave. (E. 4th St.), 216-621-4678;
www.vivo-cleveland.com

Located in Downtown's historic Old Arcade, this "high-gloss,
high-energy" Northern Italian brings "a Chicago feel to Euclid
Avenue"; its exposed-brick, lofty-ceilinged interiors are "classy",
the "inventive" cuisine is "delicious" and servers are "attentive
without overdoing it"; fans feel it's "great before or after the
theater" or on weekends when a DJ rocks the V Lounge downstairs, but foes feel the place is too "noisy" and the "food doesn't
warrant the expense."

Connecticut

TOP FOOD RANKING

	Restaurant	Cuisine
28	Thomas Henkelmann	New French
	Le Petit Cafe	French Bistro
27	Ibiza	Spanish
	Jeffrey's	Continental/New Amer.
	Jean-Louis	French
	Union League	French Bistro
	Métro Bis	New American
	La Colline Verte	New French
	Rest. du Village	French
	Cavey's	New French/N. Italian
	Max Downtown	New Amer./Steakhouse
	Carole Peck's	New American
	Da Pietro's	French/N. Italian
	Frank Pepe	Pizza
26	Frank Pepe's Spot	Pizza
	Sally's Apizza	Pizza
	Coromandel	Indian
	Meigas	Spanish/Tapas
	Cafe Routier	French Bistro
	Bernard's	French

OTHER NOTEWORTHY PLACES

Restaurant	Cuisine
Ann Howard	New American
Barcelona	Spanish/Tapas
Bentara	Malaysian
Bonda	New American
Bravo Bravo	Italian
Bricco	New American
Ching's Table	Pan-Asian
City Limits	Diner
Isla Montecristi	Pan-Latin
L'Escale	French
Mako of Japan	Japanese
Max's Oyster Bar	Seafood
Mayflower Inn	New American
Ocean 211	Seafood
Ondine	French
Peppercorn's Grill	Italian
Piccolo Arancio	Italian
Rebeccas	New American
Roomba	Nuevo Latino
Valbella	Northern Italian

Ann Howard Apricots　　　23 | 22 | 21 | $43 |
1593 Farmington Ave. (bet. Brickyard & Highwood Rds.), Farmington, 860-673-5405

"It doesn't get more charming than this" "enduring" New American overlooking the "scenic Farmington River" that offers "heavenly" outdoor dining, a "special-occasion white-tablecloth restaurant upstairs" with "elegant food" and a "comfy downstairs pub" that's less pricey; add in "outstanding service" and "excellent desserts", and you've got a perennial pleaser.

BARCELONA　　　　22 | 20 | 18 | $39 |
RESTAURANT & WINE BAR
4180 Black Rock Tpke. (Rte. 15, exit 44), Fairfield, 203-255-0800
18 W. Putnam Ave. (Greenwich Ave.), Greenwich, 203-983-6400
63 N. Main St. (bet. Ann & Marshall Sts.), Norwalk, 203-899-0088
971 Farmington Ave. (Main St.), West Hartford, 860-218-2100
www.barcelonawinebar.com

"You'll be grazing your way from tapas to paella" at this quartet of "lively hangouts"; the "unusual fare with Spanish flair", "superb wine list" and bar scene pack 'em in, but they may be "too popular for their own good" since "the noise level can exceed Barcelona's airport"; N.B. plans are afoot to open a branch in New Haven.

Bentara　　　　24 | 23 | 20 | $35 |
76 Orange St. (Center St.), New Haven, 203-562-2511; www.bentara.com

"Find a dish to warm your soul" at this "top-notch" Malaysian in New Haven's "developing Ninth Square neighborhood"; "spicy", "authentic roti appetizers, aromatic soups, lots of vegetarian options" and a straightforward signature filet of beef are complemented by an "award-winning wine list" and a "stylish" atmosphere fitted out with "ethnic" artifacts.

Bernard's Ⓜ　　　　26 | 23 | 25 | $60 |
20 West Ln./Rte. 35 (Rte. 33), Ridgefield, 203-438-8282;
www.bernardsridgefield.com

Chef-owner Bernard Bouissou "is a culinary genius and his wife, Sarah, must be his muse" at the "Frenchiest French restaurant" in Ridgefield, offering "exceptional" cuisine, a "splendid prix fixe Sunday brunch" ($35), "refined service" and a "comfortable" setting; while detractors are disappointed with the "dated, drab decor", most maintain this is an "inviting" "destination."

Bonda Restaurant & Wine Bar Ⓢ Ⓜ　　─ | ─ | ─ | E |
30 Charles St. (Franklin St.), Westport, 203-454-0840;
www.bondarestaurant.com

This savvy New American in Westport goes from gourmet, upscale deli by day to eclectic wine bar and bistro by night, offering a monthly changing, globally inspired menu that's driven by the well-traveled palates of brothers-in-law/co-owners Alex Sicre and James Cooper; the mix of abundant flavors, an unusual wine list and European ambiance is already attracting a crowd of well-heeled locals; N.B. open Wednesday–Saturday for dinner only.

Bravo Bravo Ⓜ　　　　26 | 20 | 23 | $40 |
Whaler's Inn, 20 E. Main St./Rte. 1 (Holmes St.), Mystic, 860-536-3228;
www.whalersinnmystic.com

Boosters say "bravo to this pearl of a waterside dining spot" in Mystic; "robust and surprisingly elegant tastes" along with "excellent service" make this Italian a "favorite", and it's gotten even better now that renovations have improved comfort and noise levels; though "cram-packed on weekends", this is a "restaurant that could make it in NYC."

Bricco
24 | 20 | 20 | $37

78 LaSalle Rd. (Farmington Ave.), West Hartford, 860-233-0220; www.restaurantbricco.com

"Expect to flash your bling" at the bar of this West Hartford New American – but "for once, it's not just the trendy atmosphere you're paying for", as chef-owner Billy Grant dishes up "consistently delicious" cuisine; "the open kitchen is entertainment in itself", and there's "a great patio for people-watching in the summer"; sure, it can be "loud and crowded", but that doesn't keep loyalists from "wishing they took reservations" for parties of less than six.

Cafe Routier
26 | 22 | 24 | $43

1353 Boston Post Rd. (I-95, exit 65), Westbrook, 860-399-8700; www.caferoutier.com

"Definitely not for truckers, despite what the name says", this "awesome" spot gives Westbrook denizens "bragging rights" for having "the best restaurant on the shoreline"; chef Jeff Renkl's cooking is a "combination of French bistro classics with Yankee sensibility and NYC panache", and the "good-hearted service" and "unstuffy atmosphere" also "make this a regular hang for fine diners of all stripes."

Carole Peck's Good News Cafe
27 | 20 | 23 | $45

694 Main St. S./Rte. 6 (Rte. 64), Woodbury, 203-266-4663; www.good-news-cafe.com

"Always on the short list" for "discerning foodies" is this "adventuresome" New American whose namesake chef-owner is dubbed "the Alice Waters of the East" for her "creative but not coy" cuisine "prepared with local and organic ingredients"; the fact that this casual, "jeans-and-loafers" "modern landmark" is located in "the antique haven" of Woodbury makes dining here even better news.

Cavey's ⬛Ⓜ
27 | 24 | 26 | $51

45 E. Center St. (Main St.), Manchester, 860-643-2751

What "a pleasant surprise to find such a high-quality", two-in-one restaurant "off the beaten path in historic Manchester", offering "always phenomenal Northern Italian upstairs" and what some call even "more phenomenal New French downstairs"; throw in "impeccable service" and "a wine list that even makes guests from Napa and Florence drool", and it's no wonder surveyors concur this is "the place to celebrate a momentous occasion."

Ching's Table
26 | 17 | 18 | $35

64 Main St. (Locust Ave.), New Canaan, 203-972-8550; www.chingsrestaurant.com

"Buffy-and-Brooks-Brothers" types "with pastel cardigans draped around their necks" pack into this "exceptional" Pan-Asian in New Canaan that "wakes up your taste buds" with "outstanding" dishes like "great duck" and "crispy snapper"; despite a "deafening noise level", it's "very popular", and "given how hard it is to get a reservation, Ching should add a few more seats at his table."

CITY LIMITS DINER
| 19 | 15 | 16 | $24 |

135 Harvard Ave. (I-95, exit 6), Stamford, 203-348-7000;
www.citylimitsdiner.com

This "high-energy", "always-crowded" Stamford eatery remains a "favorite" for its "diverse menu" of "comfort food done with flair"; if a few are fed up with "all the hype" (it's "better than a typical diner, but still a diner"), for most it remains a "tried-and-true option."

Coromandel
| 26 | 16 | 21 | $31 |

Goodwives Shopping Ctr., 25-11 Old Kings Hwy. N. (Sedgewick Ave.),
Darien, 203-662-1213; www.coromandelcuisine.com

"Long live India!" declare devotees of this "superb" subcontinental in Darien known for "innovative" cuisine that gives patrons the chance to "discover taste buds they never knew they had"; with "service that could not be friendlier or faster" and a "bargain lunch buffet", you "feel like you could be in London, New Delhi or Midtown."

Da Pietro's ⊠
| 27 | 18 | 25 | $62 |

36 Riverside Ave. (Boston Post Rd.), Westport, 203-454-1213

"Pietro Scotti is the Michael Jordan of chefs, so you may need an NBA salary to pay the bill" after a "truly great culinary experience" at his French–Northern Italian; "this is what happens when you do it because you love it" attest admirers who give A's to the "first-rate food and service" at "one of Westport's finest"; just note with "quarters this cramped, it's not the place to plot a bank heist."

Frank Pepe Pizzeria
| 27 | 11 | 14 | $18 |

236 Commerce Dr. (bet. Berwick Ct. & Brentwood Ave.), Fairfield,
203-333-7373
157 Wooster St. (Brown St.), New Haven, 203-865-5762 ⊅
www.pepespizzeria.com

"Pizza that will change your life" is the answer admirers offer for why it's "worth standing in a blizzard for an hour" for the "perfect", "crispy, thin-crust" Neapolitan-style pies at this 81-year-old "New Haven institution" where "the poor service is part of the legendary charm"; surveyors swear "the clam pies are the eighth wonder of the world" and the chief reason why this "local treasure" "has a special place in the hearts and arteries of many"; N.B. admirers applaud the fact that there is now a branch in Fairfield.

Frank Pepe's The Spot Ⓜ⊅
| 26 | 9 | 15 | $18 |

163 Wooster St. (Brown St.), New Haven, 203-865-7602

If you're "craving superior pizza and don't want to wait in big brother Pepe's longer lines, this spot fits the bill" with "great" pies; it's smaller and has a more "low-key vibe" than the original, but "it's like eating in the waiting room of a New Haven bus station" once you make it in.

IBIZA
| 27 | 23 | 26 | $49 |

39 High St. (bet. Chapel & Crown Sts.), New Haven, 203-865-1933;
www.ibizanewhaven.com

Executive chef Luis Bollo (also of Norwalk's Meigas) is at the "top of his game" at this "chic and unique" New Haven "showcase" for his "stunning", "cutting-edge" Spanish cuisine; "superior service", "eye-popping decor" and an "excellent wine list" add to the "fantastic", albeit "expensive", "world-class" experience.

Isla Montecristi ⓜ   – | – | – | M
57 Unquowa Rd. (off Post Rd.), Fairfield, 203-292-3058;
www.islamontecristi.com
Just a stone's throw from Fairfield's Community Theatre and the
train station, this Pan-Latin fusion hot spot is the place to stop before either destination for an authentic mojito or caipirinha and
some properly prepared ceviche; the vibrantly seasoned cuisine
will leave your taste buds humming the macarena, while the tropical decor and outdoor patio help to keep things lively.

JEAN-LOUIS   27 | 22 | 26 | $71
61 Lewis St. (bet. Greenwich Ave. & Mason St.), Greenwich,
203-622-8450; www.restaurantjeanlouis.com
"Food that Eiffel-towers over other French restaurants in the
area" is what supporters say about chef-owner Jean-Louis
Gerin's "rarefied" cuisine; meanwhile, a "top-notch" staff presides
over this "beautiful little island of grace and understated elegance in what is an increasingly flashy Greenwich scene"; although a few fume about the "claustrophobic" setting, more
maintain it's "a great place to spend your year-end bonus – all of it";
N.B. a post-*Survey* renovation may outdate the above Decor score.

JEFFREY'S   27 | 23 | 24 | $46
501 New Haven Ave. (Old Gate Ln.), Milford, 203-878-1910;
www.jeffreysofmilford.com
It's "small but it rocks" sums up Jeffrey Johnson's "classy" New
American–Continental overlooking the salt marshes in Milford,
where "superb cuisine", "impeccable service" and a "lovely"
candlelit setting make for an "excellent all-around" experience;
N.B. a post-*Survey* redo and a change to a more casual concep-
tual focus may outdate the above scores.

La Colline Verte ⓜ   27 | 24 | 27 | $57
Greenfield Hill Shopping Ctr., 75 Hillside Rd. (Bronson Rd.), Fairfield,
203-256-9242
"You'll feel pampered and happy, but never part of a snobby crowd"
at this "refined" Fairfield New French with the finesse to "make any
meal a celebration"; "you'll also pay credit-card-melting prices",
but the "heavenly cuisine", "beautiful" setting and "top-notch
service" are "worth it"; N.B. jackets for gents are recommended.

LE PETIT CAFE ⓜ   28 | 20 | 25 | $45
225 Montowese St. (Main St.), Branford, 203-483-9791;
www.lepetitcafe.net
Indeed, "nice things do come in small packages", as this "impeccable" Branford French bistro proves with its "deftly delivered",
$39.50 four-course prix fixe menu served Wednesday–Sunday;
chef-owner "Roy Ip is a magician who never disappoints",
service is "meticulous" and the setting is "warm" and "cozy"; it
all adds up to "one of the best bargains on the shore."

L'Escale   23 | 24 | 20 | $59
Delamar Hotel, 500 Steamboat Rd. (I-95, exit 3), Greenwich,
203-661-4600; www.lescalerestaurant.com
"During the summer, watch the hedge-fund managers pull up in
their yachts" at this "posh" Greenwich Provençal attached to the
Delamar Hotel, where "celebrity faces abound", the "seafood is
fresh and well prepared" and dining at a "terrace table" over-

looking the water is a "treat"; detractors declare it's "pricey", "noisy", service is "inept" and "divorcée seems to be the most popular entree" at the "sexy bar", but it's nevertheless made a big splash with the "big-spender" set; N.B. a post-*Survey* chef change may outdate the above Food score.

Mako of Japan Ⓜ 25 | 13 | 22 | $30
222 Post Rd. (Rte. 130), Fairfield, 203-259-5950
A "sushi bar where everybody knows your name" is how devotees describe this family-run Fairfield favorite for its "extremely friendly atmosphere" and "fabulous fresh food"; it's "small" and "not much to look at", but finatics simply aren't fazed; N.B. open for dinner only Wednesday–Sunday.

Max Downtown 27 | 25 | 24 | $48
City Place, 185 Asylum St. (bet. Ann & Trumbull Sts.), Hartford, 860-522-2530; www.maxrestaurantgroup.com
If you want to be at "the epicenter of the Hartford power scene" for "expense-accounters" or "really impress a date", head to the Max dining dynasty's "first-class" New American chophouse, where a "professional staff" serves "awesome steaks" and "serious martinis"; the bar action is "pretty good too" – "think polished, yet lively" with "many beautiful young things" to ogle; the only "ouch" is when the "wallet-wounding" bill arrives.

Max's Oyster Bar 26 | 24 | 23 | $43
964 Farmington Ave. (S. Main St.), West Hartford, 860-236-6299; www.maxrestaurantgroup.com
This "seafood standout in the school of Max's restaurants" is the hub of the "social universe in West Hartford", a "noisy" but "festive" spot that reels reviewers in with "amazingly fresh" ocean fare and "awesome tiered raw appetizers"; the comfy burgundy booths encourage lingering, but movers prefer to hit the "happening" bar "jammed with the moneyed, the single, the divorced and the thirsty."

Mayflower Inn & Spa, The 23 | 27 | 25 | $60
The Mayflower Inn & Spa, 118 Woodbury Rd./Rte. 47 (Rte. 109), Washington, 860-868-9466; www.mayflowerinn.com
Housed in a Relais & Châteaux Washington inn, this New American offers "great food that's flawlessly presented and served" against a backdrop of three "gorgeous rooms and gardens" that "ooze country charm with a soupçon of formality"; while detractors decry an "overpriced" and "overrated" "place that's a little too pleased with itself", most agree if you "dine on the terrace in summer with the one you love, the check won't hurt so much"; N.B. the spa boasts its own calorie-conscious dining room.

Meigas Ⓜ 26 | 21 | 25 | $53
10 Wall St. (bet. High & Knight Sts.), Norwalk, 203-866-8800; www.meigasrestaurant.com
"Aptly named (*meigas* means sorcerer)", this "worthy successor to Meson Galicia" "consistently performs magic" as it serves "sublime Spanish" spreads to its "sophisticated clients"; "toque-of-the-town" Luis Bollo's (also of New Haven's Ibiza) "creations are truly a source of joy", and they're complemented by "owner Ignacio Blanco's attentive, indulgent" staffers; this is "an occasion place, to be sure" (read: "pricey"), but "still, one of the tops in Norwalk."

Métro Bis Ⓢ
27 | 19 | 24 | $46

Simsburytown Shops, 928 Hopmeadow St./Rte. 10 (Rte. 44), Simsbury, 860-651-1908; www.metrobis.com

At this New American "culinary powerhouse" located in a Simsbury shopping plaza, the "creative" "food tastes like chef/co-owner Chris Prosperi enjoys his craft", and every member of the "professional" "staff can handle any question you can throw" at them about the "delectable meals"; the "small" space gets "noisy", but few mind, given the reasonable prices; *sans doute,* "Julia Child is smiling down upon this gem" – and you will too.

Ocean 211 Ⓢ
24 | 20 | 21 | $46

211 Summer St. (bet. Broad & Main Sts.), Stamford, 203-973-0494; www.ocean211.com

Though it's "near the movie theater", you'll want to "make an evening out of your meal" at this ocean of "serenity in Downtown Stamford", featuring "super-luxe seafood" ("the chef never met a fish he didn't love to cook") and "a nice selection of oysters" (about 20 varieties); you can expect "fine service", a "sophisti-cated NYC-type" vibe – and, some say, "Manhattan prices."

Ondine Ⓜ
26 | 24 | 25 | VE

69 Pembroke Rd./Rte. 37 (Wheeler Dr.), Danbury, 203-746-4900

"Use the smallest excuse to celebrate" at this "top-drawer" Danbury French favorite where chef-owner Dieter Thiel's cuisine, from the signature ebony-roasted duckling to the "marvelous soufflés", is "elegant", the room is "romantic" and the service is "*très français,* but without the Parisian attitude"; P.S. the $55 five-course prix fixe menu is a model of "value gourmet dining."

Peppercorn's Grill Ⓢ
26 | 20 | 23 | $42

357 Main St. (bet. Buckingham St. & Capital Ave.), Hartford, 860-547-1714; www.piccoloarancio.com

"You can't go wrong" at this "consistent standout" whose "wonder-ful Italian fare" "makes going out in Hartford worthwhile again" "for anyone who appreciates a complete food-and-wine experi-ence"; it's also "popular" with the "pre-theater crowd" because of its proximity to the Bushnell Center for the Performing Arts, and though certain servers "could be friendlier", the "competent staff" "can be counted on to get you out in time" for the show.

Piccolo Arancio Ⓢ
25 | 20 | 22 | $41

819 Farmington Ave./Rte. 4 (Rte. 10), Farmington, 860-674-1224; www.piccoloarancio.com

"Try the signature ravioli *all'arancia*" "with orange sauce", and "you'll want to go back" to this "unassuming" but "excellent" Farmington Italian that's the "sister of Hartford's Peppercorn's Grill"; for culinary "imagination and exceptional ingredients, this is an easy choice as one of the area's better" places; now, if they could just "get rid of the noise, you'd have perfection."

REBECCAS ⓈⓂ
26 | 20 | 23 | $65

265 Glenville Rd. (Riversville Rd.), Greenwich, 203-532-9270; www.rkateliers.com

It's "no Sunnybrook Farm" (in fact, the "contemporary interior" is somewhat "spartan"), but this Greenwich grandee is a "gourmet mecca" for "pilgrims who park their limos out front" and then en-joy chef/co-owner Reza Khorshidi's "sublime" New American dishes; critics may call it "pompous" and "seriously overpriced", but it remains "the place to be seen" (and to eat).

Restaurant du Village Ⓜ | 27 | 23 | 26 | $57 |

59 Main St. (Maple St.), Chester, 860-526-5301;
www.restaurantduvillage.com

You're actually in "charming little" Chester, but "the owners make you feel like you're in Alsace", "offering some of the most exquisite French cuisine" at this "central CT classic"; the "expert preparations" are matched by "expert service", and you won't find a prettier spot "in the middle of nowhere"; in short, it's "still the best" and further "comments are not needed – though reservations are."

Roomba | 25 | 23 | 21 | $43 |

1044 Chapel St. (bet. College & High Sts.), New Haven, 203-562-7666

"Hip, loud and vibrant", this "slice of Havana" "under the streets of Downtown New Haven" is "abuzz" with diners downing "strong mojitos" and "exciting" Nuevo Latino eats from chef/co-owner Arturo Franco-Camacho, a "specialist in tall food"; it'd be "perfect for a celebration", except that the staff is "full of attitude."

Sally's Apizza Ⓜ⊅ | 26 | 8 | 11 | $17 |

237 Wooster St. (Olive St.), New Haven, 203-624-5271

If there were a "password" to get into this "slice of heaven in New Haven's Little Italy" it would be "more coveted than the Hope diamond", for "the waits are excruciating"; "but when you sit down, you're rewarded" with a "paper-thin crispy pizza crust" and "sauce so good even cheese is an unworthy topping"; few seem to mind the "spare" digs, but many warn of "BYO service if you're not a regular."

THOMAS HENKELMANN Ⓢ | 28 | 27 | 27 | $74 |

Homestead Inn, 420 Field Point Rd. (Horseneck Ln.), Greenwich,
203-869-7500; www.thomashenkelmann.com

Voted Most Popular and No. 1 for Food in CT, this "transporting", "top-tier" New French set in a "charming" Greenwich inn is overseen by "chef extraordinaire Thomas Henkelmann" and his wife, Theresa; sure, "the size of the bill will stun you", but the "superb" cuisine, "enormously attentive service" and "lovely setting" with a view of "gorgeous gardens" all set "the gold standard for fine dining in Fairfield County"; N.B. jacket required.

UNION LEAGUE CAFE Ⓢ | 27 | 26 | 26 | $51 |

1032 Chapel St. (bet. College & High Sts.), New Haven, 203-562-4299;
www.unionleaguecafe.com

It's a "genteel crowd of visiting parents, their Yalie offspring, tweedy professors and urbane foodies" at this "constantly improving veteran" New Haven French bistro; chef-owner Jean-Pierre Vuillermet's "always exquisite" cuisine "respects and enhances the quality of seasonal ingredients", "the service is knowledgeable and – like the decor – is dignified without being stuffy."

Valbella Ⓢ | 25 | 24 | 24 | $62 |

1309 E. Putnam Ave./Rte. 1 (Sound Beach Ave.), Riverside, 203-637-1155;
www.valbellact.com

Oenophiles aim for "dining in the fabulous wine cellar" (which underwent a renovation and holds 20,000 bottles) at this Riverside Northern Italian "place to see and be seen", where "fantastic seafood and pasta" is served by a "superb staff" in "romantic" digs; it's "popular for local royalty" who shrug off the "high prices."

Dallas/Ft. Worth

TOP FOOD RANKING

Restaurant	Cuisine
29 French Room	American/French
28 York Street	New American
Abacus	Eclectic
Aurora	New American
Lola	New American
Saint-Emilion	French
27 Tei Tei Robata Bar	Japanese
Lonesome Dove	Southwestern
Pappas Bros.	Steakhouse
Café Pacific	Seafood
Teppo	Japanese
Del Frisco's	Steakhouse
Iris	New American
Nana	New American
Bonnell's	Southwestern
Local	New American
26 Al Biernat's	Steakhouse
Mercury Grill	New American
Goodhues Wood Fired	New American
Standard	New American

OTHER NOTEWORTHY PLACES

Angelo's	Barbecue
Bice	Italian
Cafe Aspen	New American
Capital Grille	Steakhouse
Chow Thai	Thai
Craft	New American
Grape, The	New American
Hibiscus	New American
Joe T. Garcia's	Tex-Mex
La Duni	Pan-Latin
Lavendou	French
Mansion on Turtle Creek	Southwestern
Mi Cocina	Tex-Mex
Modo Mio Cucina	Northern Italian
Nobu Dallas	Japanese/Peruvian
Oceanaire	Seafood
Reata	Southwestern
62 Main Restaurant	New American
Steel	Japanese/Vietnamese
Texas de Brazil	Brazilian/Steakhouse

ABACUS ☑

| 28 | 27 | 27 | $60 |

4511 McKinney Ave. (Armstrong Ave.), Dallas, 214-559-3111;
www.abacus-restaurant.com

A "crown jewel of high-end, new-style dining", this "chic" Knox-Henderson "favorite" from "genius" chef Kent Rathbun is a "proven winner" that's ranked Most Popular among Dallas/Ft. Worth restaurants thanks to "inventive", "fabulous" Eclectic fare, "divine service" and a "modern" and "elegant" (if somewhat "loud") interior; a few outsiders opine that the "excellent staff" is "a tad snooty" "if you're not a regular", but a vocal majority maintains that it's "always a treat."

Al Biernat's

| 26 | 24 | 25 | $55 |

4217 Oak Lawn Ave. (Herschel Ave.), Dallas, 214-219-2201;
www.albiernats.com

"Who doesn't love Al" Biernat, the "gracious host" and owner who "never forgets a name" at this Oak Lawn "steak haven", "a local favorite of the business set", "power brokers and beautiful people alike", where "succulent" cuts and "imaginative salads" are served in "huge portions" that are "easily shared"; the "personable service", "dark, clubby atmosphere" and "exceptional wine list" are other pluses, but those troubled by the "high prices" say it's "best to do this one on someone else's nickel – or $100 bill."

Angelo's Barbecue ☑ ⇆

| 24 | 15 | 16 | $14 |

2533 White Settlement Rd. (University Dr.), Ft. Worth, 817-332-0357;
www.angelosbbq.com

This "classic" Near West Ft. Worth spot is "a longtime institution" and a "shrine to smoked meat", dishing up "beef at its very finest" along with "schooners of cold draft beer"; with its "authentic Texana surroundings", including a weathered wood interior and an infamous "bear in the foyer" that "kids love", it "may look like a hole-in-the-wall, but isn't that where one finds the best BBQ?"

AURORA ☑

| 28 | 27 | 28 | $87 |

4216 Oak Lawn Ave. (Wycliff Ave.), Dallas, 214-528-9400;
www.auroradallas.com

Chef Avner Samuel, the "superbly talented enfant terrible of Dallas' culinary scene", "has outdone himself" at this "little jewel" in Oak Lawn, an "exotic and luxurious" "masterpiece" that's "over the top in every aspect" – from its "brilliant, creative" New American fare and "excellent service" to its "striking prices"; furthermore, gourmets "love" that "the focal point" of the "notable" interior is the "glass-enclosed kitchen", allowing you to "see the cooking theater", so "if your Gulfstream is in the shop and you can't go to Paris", "this is the place."

Bice

| – | – | – | E |

Crescent Court Complex, 100 Crescent Ct. (bet. Cedar Springs Rd. & Maple Ave.), Dallas, 214-922-9055; www.bicedallas.com

It's *amore* at first sight for the patrons of this haute Italian at Uptown's Crescent Court, where seafood and pastas take the spotlight; an offshoot of an original 1926 Milan flagship, it sports serene cream-and-mahogany interiors and plush banquettes that cater to couples and privacy-seeking luminaries; the white-jacketed servers waltz on multicolored wood floors, deftly avoiding handbag trees (an accessory at every table) that seem destined to display the blue-blood clientele's designer totes.

Bonnell's 🅂🅼   27 | 23 | 26 | $42
4259 Bryant Irvin Rd. (Southwest Blvd.), Ft. Worth, 817-738-5489;
www.bonnellsrestaurant.com

Chef-owner Jon "Bonnell must be the nicest chef in the city", so gracious are his hosting skills: he "makes sure his patrons have a wonderful time and a wonderful meal" at his discriminating Southwestern bistro in Southwest Ft. Worth; the combination of "inventive", "outstandingly presented" "Texas ranch cuisine" (featuring "interesting game" dishes), the room's "intimate ambiance" and his "friendly staff's" "great wine recommendations" help to ameliorate the "off-the-beaten-path" location.

Cafe Aspen 🅂   22 | 20 | 20 | $33
6103 Camp Bowie Blvd. (Bryant Irvin Rd.), Ft. Worth, 817-738-0838;
www.cafeaspen.com

How nice for West Ft. Worth to have this "popular spot" with "consistently" "excellent" New American fare, a "knowledgeable staff" and a "wonderful community feeling, where people know one another and the owner knows everyone" – be it the "blue-haired ladies at lunch" or those seeking "a great place for a business or pleasure" meal; some say the "setting leaves a bit to be desired", but more find the "nice, soothing decor" "charming."

CAFÉ PACIFIC 🅂   27 | 25 | 26 | $49
Highland Park Village, 24 Highland Park Village (bet. Mockingbird Ln. & Preston Rd.), Dallas, 214-526-1170

The "accommodating kitchen" at this "classy, longtime favorite" in Highland Park Village "consistently turns out excellent dishes", especially "first-class seafood", that are "superbly served" within an "upscale environment"; it's known as an "old-school meeting place" for a "slightly older crowd" of "old-money" "Dallas blue bloods", nouveau "billionaires", "celebrities" and assorted sundry "beautiful people", making for "great people-watching."

Capital Grille, The   25 | 25 | 24 | $55
Crescent Shops & Galleries, 500 Crescent Ct. (bet. Cedar Springs Rd. & Maple Ave.), Dallas, 214-303-0500; www.thecapitalgrille.com

Carnivores call this national chain link in Dallas the embodiment of the "classic Texas steakhouse", with "fabulous" meat, "huge" sides, an "excellent" wine selection and "devoted", "timely but unobtrusive" service; the "plush", "clubby" ambiance and "expensive" fare befit business dinners – "don't forget your platinum card" – though a cadre of critics calls the Uptown meatery "overrated" and "pretentious."

Chow Thai Addison   23 | 19 | 20 | $23
5290 Belt Line Rd. (Montfort Dr.), Addison, 972-960-2999;
www.chowthai.com

Chow Thai Pacific Rim
3309 Dallas Pkwy. (Parker Rd.), Plano, 972-608-1883;
www.ctpacificrim.com

"Go once and you'll be hooked" on these "upscale" spots owned by West Coast transplants Vinnie and Sam Virasin, a husband-and-wife duo who delivers "consistent" "wonderful" food that's a "fresh, California-style Thai (i.e. don't expect authentic)"; "despite the strip-mall location" at both the Addison and Plano branches, each is a "quiet place, perfect for lunch or dinner", with "lightning-fast service" and "fun decor."

Craft Dallas
– | – | – | VE |

W Dallas – Victory, 2440 Victory Park Ln. (N. Houston St.), Dallas, 214-397-4111; www.craftdallas.com

Bi-coastal chef-owner Tom Colicchio (of the NYC and LA outposts of the same name) transports his flavor-packed New American cuisine to this ultrachic space in the W hotel at Uptown's Victory Park; plush interiors set the tone for indulgent à la carte items that can be coupled with a selection from the two-story glass wine tower; the sum effect takes the city's dinner tab to new heights, and does the same with the lengthy valet parking lines; N.B. reservations are required on weekends.

DEL FRISCO'S DOUBLE EAGLE STEAK HOUSE
27 | 24 | 25 | $59 |

5251 Spring Valley Rd. (N. Dallas Tollway), Dallas, 972-490-9000
812 Main St. (8th St.), Ft. Worth, 817-877-3999
www.delfriscos.com

"A top contender" for "best steakhouse" ("which means a lot" in these parts), these North Dallas and Downtown Ft. Worth "gut-and wallet-busting à la carte" outposts not only have "excellent steaks" but also "spectacularly executed appetizers, sides and desserts", all served with "individual attention"; "don't be in a hurry", though, as you might have "a long wait", "even with reservations", and "be prepared for the bill", as the "wine list is off-the-chart expensive."

FRENCH ROOM ⑤ Ⓜ
29 | 29 | 29 | $80 |

Hotel Adolphus, 1321 Commerce St. (Field St.), Dallas, 214-742-8200; www.hoteladolphus.com

"There aren't enough superlatives to describe" this "gorgeous" "grande dame" in Downtown's Hotel Adolphus that's ranked No. 1 for Food among Dallas/Ft. Worth restaurants; "if you're looking for a romantic, old-world" venue in which "to celebrate an event, this is the place", with "spectacular", "expensive" French-American cuisine, an "impeccable but unpretentious" staff and "beautiful surroundings" ("including hand-painted ceilings" that remind swooning surveyors of "eating in a cathedral"), which adds up to a "wonderful experience" "to be savored"; N.B. jacket required.

Goodhues Wood Fired Grill ⑤
26 | 22 | 22 | $31 |

204 W. Virginia St. (Wood St.), McKinney, 972-562-7570; www.goodhuesgrill.com

It's "always a lovely evening" at this beloved boîte, "a true spot of light" in "quaint", "historic Downtown McKinney", whose "great menu" "changes subtly from visit to visit" but always offers "imaginative selections" of "high-end" New American "home cooking", including "fancy pastas"; "most important, it's quiet", guaranteeing that it's right on as a "special-occasion" spot.

Grape, The
25 | 21 | 23 | $36 |

2808 Greenville Ave. (Vickery Blvd.), Dallas, 214-828-1981; www.thegraperestaurant.com

"One of the darkest and oldest wine bars in Dallas", this "intimate" Greenville Avenue "neighborhood bistro" is a "foodie favorite", boasting "terrific" New American fare that's "consistently good, even with different chefs over the years"; "comparatively low markups" on its vino and an "educated, attentive staff" are other selling points, and the "romantic atmosphere" with its "cozy, close quarters" makes it a "perfect place to get engaged."

Hibiscus ⊠　　　　　25 | 24 | 25 | $53
2927 N. Henderson Ave. (off Rte. 75), Dallas, 214-827-2927;
www.hibiscusdallas.com
"Another home run for restaurateur Tristan Simon" and "genius chef" Nick Badovinus, this "swanky" Knox-Henderson New American offers up "gargantuan portions" of "delicious" "comfort food" in an interior that's "not what you expect from the name": "chic", "rustic and manly"; a few feel it "doesn't live up to expectations given all the accolades", but more maintain it's deservedly "busy" ("expect a wait").

Iris ⊠　　　　　27 | 22 | 25 | $52
5405 W. Lovers Ln. (Inwood Rd.), Dallas, 214-352-2727;
www.irisdallas.net
"Warm, welcoming owner" Suzie Priore "maintains a close watch over diners to make sure they're well cared for" at this "elegant bistro" on West Lovers Lane; its "quality menu" of "consistently excellent" New American fare renders "modern cooking with a great mix of flavors", which is "served by a very professional staff", and the walls of its "romantic room" are "adorned with local artists' work."

Joe T. Garcia's ⊘　　　　20 | 22 | 21 | $19
2201 N. Commerce St. (22nd St.), Ft. Worth, 817-626-4356;
www.joets.com
Sprawling across "several homes joined by a courtyard", this "cash-only" North Side "Ft. Worth landmark" is definitely "for the indecisive, because there's not much to select from" on its "simple menu" of "quintessential Tex-Mex" that fans describe as "*muy bueno*"; still, those who lament the "long waits" (no reservations for parties of less than 20) and "touristy" vibe insist it's "not about the food – it's about" "their famous margaritas"; P.S. the "fantastic grounds" provide "great outdoor dining", "especially near the pool."

La Duni Latin Cafe Ⓜ　　　25 | 22 | 20 | $29
4620 McKinney Ave. (Knox St.), Dallas, 214-520-7300
La Duni Latin Kitchen & Baking Studio
4264 Oak Lawn Ave. (Herschel Ave.), Dallas, 214-520-6888
www.laduni.com
A "great take on Latin, Caribbean and South American food" can be found at this "happening" Oak Lawn and Knox-Henderson Pan-Latin pair from "warm and friendly" chef-owner-partners Espartaco and Dunia Borga, who whip up "top-notch" fare, especially their "sinful", "luscious desserts" and "scrumptious, puffy popover sandwiches" ("a fantastic bargain" considering they're "still charging half of what they could/should ask"); in fact, "the only downside", supporters say, is "slow service."

Lavendou ⊠　　　　　24 | 22 | 23 | $40
19009 Preston Rd. (bet. Frankford Rd. & President George Bush Tpke.),
Dallas, 972-248-1911; www.lavendou.com
For "a touch of France", visit this far North Dallas bistro, a "lovely, serene place" offering "the feel and taste of Provence", with a "nice country interior" and "plants on the patio that screen the traffic noise and view of the parking lot well enough that you

can forget you are in a strip shopping center"; some say the staff "occasionally exhibits a little bit of attitude", but the service is generally "caring."

Local ⊠ Ⓜ | 27 | 24 | 25 | $46 |

2936 Elm St. (Hall St.), Dallas, 214-752-7500
An "exquisitely minimalist-chic" space "is the perfect setting for" a "savory" New American menu "combining upscale and down-home" at this "trendy", "intimate" spot in Deep Ellum's historic Boyd Hotel building ("book several weeks in advance"); the clientele is "gorgeous", and the "excellent food" "is fresh, organic and wonderful", though some give thumbs-down to the "fairly small portions", saying these examples of "minuscule nouvelle cuisine of days past" are "expensive for what's received."

LOLA ⊠ Ⓜ | 28 | 24 | 26 | $59 |

2917 Fairmount St. (Cedar Springs Rd.), Dallas, 214-855-0700;
www.lola4dinner.com
Foodies are "hard-pressed to think of a better meal" than the prix fixe menus (2-4 "courses of heaven", each a "sensational treat") offered at this Uptown New American, "one of this city's top" spots, whose "romantic dinners" are backed by an "extensive", "impeccable wine list", "personalized service" from a "knowledgeable" and "amazingly friendly" staff and an "old-house setting with great charm"; P.S. the on-site Tasting Room offers 10- and 14-course sampling menus that "change based on what's in season."

Lonesome Dove Western Bistro ⊠ Ⓜ | 27 | 24 | 24 | $50 |

2406 N. Main St. (24th St.), Ft. Worth, 817-740-8810;
www.lonesomedovebistro.com
"Highly recommended", the "always-satisfying" "gourmet Texan fare" at this "artfully winning" outpost "in a rustic, restored building" in Ft. Worth's Stockyards District comes from "celebrity chef" Tim Love, whose Southwestern cuisine (heavy on "wild game") is "cowboy fusion cooking that actually tastes as good as the menu descriptions"; the "helpful" servers are "ready and willing to explain anything on the menu", while the "cozy" yet "chic" decor includes a prominent bar "set for fine dining."

MANSION ON TURTLE CREEK, THE | 26 | 27 | 27 | $73 |

The Mansion on Turtle Creek, 2821 Turtle Creek Blvd. (Gillespie St.), Dallas, 214-559-2100; www.mansiononturtlecreek.com
"Still just about the best around town for a truly memorable outing", this Southwestern "classic" in the Uptown hotel of the same name is a "Dallas institution"; savvy surveyors insist it "deserves all the raves it gets" thanks to a "beautiful setting" (jacket required) blessed with "exquisite decor" in which "gracious staffers" "aim to please" – and, of course, "marvelous food" – all of which ensures its status as the "perfect place for any fancy night out"; N.B. the Food rating may not reflect the post-*Survey* departure of chef Dean Fearing.

Mercury Grill | 26 | 22 | 24 | $46 |

11909 Preston Rd. (Forest Ln.), Dallas, 972-960-7774;
www.mcrowd.com
For a "little NYC in Dallas", swan into this "sophisticated" Preston Forest spot, where there's "always something innovative" on "creative" and "nationally known chef" Chris Ward's" menu of

"high-priced", "stylishly presented" New American fare; adding to its "deserved reputation" is the "consistently superb service", which also "far exceeds expectations of a restaurant located in a strip mall at a busy North Dallas intersection."

MI COCINA
21 | 20 | 20 | $22

77 Highland Park Village (bet. Mockingbird Ln. & Preston Rd.), Dallas, 214-521-6426
11661 Preston Rd. (Forest Ln.), Dallas, 214-265-7704
7201 Skillman St. (Kingsley Rd.), Dallas, 214-503-6426
West Village, 3699 McKinney Ave. (Lemmon Ave.), Dallas, 469-533-5663
509 Main St. (bet. 4th & 5th Sts.), Ft. Worth, 817-877-3600
7750 N. MacArthur Blvd. (LBJ Frwy.), Irving, 469-621-0452
5760 Legacy Dr. (Parkwood Blvd.), Plano, 972-473-8777
4001 Preston Rd. (Lorimar Dr.), Plano, 469-467-8655
1370 W. Campbell Rd. (Coit Rd.), Richardson, 972-671-6426
www.mcrowd.com

Extremely "popular", this "locally owned chain" dominates the Tex-Mex scene via "consistent", "very-good-all-around" fare and decor that sports an "upscale" edge that's "welcoming to both singles and families"; sure, it's a "little noisy", but that's because many patrons "go here as much for the scene and the drinks", which, with the "multiple-hour wait", can mean you'll get "more than just dinner – this place can be your entire night's entertainment."

Modo Mio Cucina Rustica
23 | 18 | 20 | $32

Frankford Crossing, 18352 Dallas Pkwy. (Frankford Rd.), Dallas, 972-713-9559; www.modomio.net

A "consistent" menu of "well-prepared", "authentic offerings from Tuscany" can be found at this North Dallas Northern Italian storefront restaurant, a "neighborhood find" boasting a "wonderful house Chianti" that's quite quaffable; some find its location in "a nondescript strip mall" right off the Tollway a bit "weird", but most maintain it achieves a "cozy setting" with a "warm, intimate atmosphere."

Nana
27 | 28 | 26 | $65

Hilton Anatole Hotel, 2201 Stemmons Frwy., 27th fl. (Market Center Blvd.), Dallas, 214-761-7470; www.nanarestaurant.com

The "spectacular setting" with its "panoramic view of the Dallas skyline" instantly "elevates" this New American foodie temple on the 27th floor of the Market Center's Hilton Anatole Hotel to the realm of "very special special-occasion place", but fans insist it'd be "worthy even on the ground floor" thanks to a "top-drawer" staff and "amazingly creative chef" Anthony Bombaci's "exceptional food"; a few feel he's "a bit stingy" with the "expensive", "small portions", but a "dazzled" majority declares that "everything is outstanding."

Nobu Dallas
25 | 24 | 21 | $72

Hotel Crescent Ct., 400 Crescent Ct. (bet. Cedar Springs Rd. & Maple Ave.), Dallas, 214-252-7000; www.noburestaurants.com

Dallas foodies feel "lucky to have this" "world-class" restaurant in Uptown's Crescent Court complex, an outpost of Nobu Matsuhisa's "famous" Peruvian-influenced Japanese chain and a "true dining experience" thanks to "fabulous food" (including "awesome" "melt-in-your-mouth sushi") and "way-cool decor"; be warned, though, that the "noise" from the "trendy" clientele can make it "hard to converse", while the "outrageous" "expense-account pricing" has some insisting that "better value can be found elsewhere."

Oceanaire Seafood Room   26 | 24 | 24 | $49

Westin Galleria Hotel, 13340 Dallas Pkwy. (LBJ & Dallas N. Tollway), Dallas, 972-759-2277; www.theoceanaire.com

"Am I on a coast?" wonder wags wowed by the "beautifully presented" and "wonderfully fresh" seafood that "never fails to satisfy" at this "amazing" national-chain outpost in North Dallas' Westin Galleria Hotel; it's "a little pricey", but the "service is impeccable" too, as is the "classy, old-time luxury" of the "big and noisy room", whose "nautically themed" "art deco" "1930s liner decor is appropriate."

Pappas Bros. Steakhouse Ⓢ   27 | 24 | 25 | $57

10477 Lombardy Ln. (bet. I-35 & Northwest Hwy.), Dallas, 214-366-2000; www.pappasbros.com

"There is a lot of competition", but cognoscenti confide that this handsome Dallas steakhouse stands out from the herd thanks to "perfectly cooked" "slabs o' cow", "tasty sides", a "comprehensive wine cellar", "sommeliers who truly know what they're talking about" and "attentive, respectful" servers who "treat everyone like a VIP"; a vocal few, however, brand this "overpriced", "inconsistent" spot a bum steer.

Reata   23 | 25 | 23 | $40

Sundance Sq., 310 Houston St. (3rd St.), Ft. Worth, 817-336-1009; www.reata.net

You'll find there's "always a crowd" at this "fun cowboy-style" "Ft. Worth favorite" – "a true taste of Cowtown" and "a must for any visitor" to the area – that "looks as though it's straight off the *Giant* movie set"; its Southwestern menu has "inventive entrees and salads, as well as wonderful margaritas", and the staff is "accommodating", but the talk inevitably returns to the "amusing", "retro decor" and "rooftop dining" space "that's one of the prettiest places Downtown."

Saint-Emilion Ⓢ Ⓜ   28 | 25 | 27 | $48

3617 W. Seventh St. (Montgomery St.), Ft. Worth, 817-737-2781

"For a special evening" of "romance (especially if your significant other is a foodie)", this "wonderful French" "classic" in Ft. Worth's Cultural District is a "fabulous" option offering "elegantly executed preparations" of "incredible food" and a "unique wine list" crafted by a "perfectionist, with the namesake Bordeaux well represented", all in a "charming little house" with a "quaint", "intimate" vibe; P.S. surveyors say "stick to the blackboard specials."

62 Main Restaurant Ⓢ Ⓜ   23 | 21 | 23 | $49

62 Main St. (bet. Hwy. 26 & Main St.), Colleyville, 817-605-0858; www.62mainrestaurant.com

"Master" chef David McMillan, "formerly of Nana, is amazing everyone" at this "gourmet dining" venue, a "small, chic" restaurant "surprisingly located in suburban Colleyville"; its "creative, [daily] changing menu" of "blue-ribbon" New American cuisine features "fresh, quality ingredients" and is ferried to table by an "enthusiastic staff", sealing its status as "a lovely place for a grown-up evening out."

Standard Ⓜ

| 26 | 22 | 25 | $50 |

2816 Fairmount St. (Cedar Springs Rd.), Dallas, 214-720-9292; www.standarddallas.com

"Grand in a subtle way", this "modern" Uptown venue earns high praise for "excellent young chef" and co-owner Tim Byres' "inventive" and seasonally "changing menu" of "superlative" New American fare; an informed staff makes it "a good place to be a regular", assuming you can handle the "high prices" and "minimalist decor", with "stuffed pigeons perched high on a shelf", a decorative element that some find "bizarre."

Steel

| 24 | 25 | 20 | $48 |

Centrum Bldg., 3102 Oak Lawn Ave. (Cedar Springs Rd.), Dallas, 214-219-9908; www.steeldallas.com

Yes, this "trendy" Oak Lawn "place to be seen" is filled with "sports figures" and "young", "beautiful people", but supporters insist its "sexy", "urban-chic decor", "fantastic wine list" and "amazing" Japanese-Vietnamese cuisine (including "creatively presented sushi") "back up the flash"; a few find it "pretentious" and "noisy", but more maintain it's "a favorite place to take out-of-towners, who are surprised to find something other than steak in Dallas."

Tei Tei Robata Bar Ⓜ

| 27 | 24 | 23 | $44 |

2906 N. Henderson Ave. (Willis Ave.), Dallas, 214-828-2400; www.teiteirobata.com

A Knox-Henderson "hot spot", this "authentic robata grill" ("Teppo's more expensive brother") is "popular" for its "excellent Japanese cuisine" – including "rare options" of "outstanding" "high-end sushi", plus "hot rock–cooked Kobe beef" you "sear yourself"; the room is "chic" and the service "excellent", but those not content to "hobnob" at the "trendy bar" "rarely visit due to the no-reservations policy" during peak hours and the predictably "unbearable waits."

Teppo Yakitori and Sushi Bar Ⓜ

| 27 | 22 | 22 | $38 |

2014 Greenville Ave. (Prospect Ave.), Dallas, 214-826-8989; www.teppo.com

Bringing "consistently great" "West Coast–style sushi to Dallas", this Greenville Avenue sibling of Tei Tei (with a slightly younger but no less devout following) features a "big selection" of "excellent, super-fresh" raw-fish fare – "with the added bonus" of "amazing yakitori"; many also "love the cavelike atmosphere", but keep in mind that the "place doesn't take reservations" during prime time, so "expect a wait."

Texas de Brazil

| 24 | 21 | 24 | $48 |

15101 Addison Rd. (Belt Line Rd.), Addison, 972-385-1000
2727 Cedar Springs Rd. (bet. Carlisle & Woodrow Sts.), Dallas, 214-720-1414
101 N. Houston St. (Weatherford St.), Ft. Worth, 817-882-9500
www.texasdebrazil.com

It's "carnivore heaven" at these all-you-can-eat Brazilian steakhouses: "strolling waiters" proffer an endless, "one-price-fits-all" supply of "juicy" "meats on swords" abetted by a "huge, well-appointed salad bar" ("everything you ever wanted under a sneeze guard"); "upscale" and "classy", these "noisy" meateries are "impressive" for "out-of-town guests" but "not good date places": "after eating, you just want to go home and nap."

YORK STREET RESTAURANT ⊠ 🅼   28 | 22 | 27 | $56
6047 Lewis St. (Skillman St.), Dallas, 214-826-0968
A "showcase of fine dining", this "sublime" New American is "the place for foodies who want to experiment", as "only the finest and freshest ingredients make it onto the exquisite revolving menu" conceived by chef-owner Sharon Hage; "tucked on a side street in a converted house", it sits in a "strange location" next to a Lakewood gas station and seats fewer than four dozen – making reservations "essential."

Denver Area & Mountain Resorts

TOP FOOD RANKING

	Restaurant	Cuisine
28	Mizuna	New American
27	Highland's Garden Cafe	New American
	Del Frisco's	Steakhouse
	L'Atelier	French
	Sweet Basil	New American
	Cafe Brazil	Brazilian/Colombian
	Sushi Den	Japanese
	Flagstaff House	Eclectic/New Amer.
26	Six89 Kitchen/Wine	New American
	Matsuhisa	Japanese
	Keystone Ranch	New American
	John's	New American
	240 Union	New Amer./Seafood
	Montagna	New American
	Kevin Taylor	New American
	Alpenglow Stube	American/Bavarian
	Opus*	New American
	Capital Grille	Steakhouse
	Zengo	Asian/Nuevo Latino
	Grouse Mountain Grill	Regional American

OTHER NOTEWORTHY PLACES

Restaurant	Cuisine
Barolo Grill	Northern Italian
Frasca Food & Wine	Northern Italian
Full Moon Grill	Northern Italian
India's	Indian
Kitchen, The	Eclectic
La Tour	New French
Left Bank	French
Luca d'Italia	Italian
Mel's Restaurant	New American
Morton's	Steakhouse
New Saigon	Vietnamese
Piñons	Regional American
Potager	New American
Q's	New American
rioja	Mediterranean
Solera	New American
Steuben's	Regional American
Sushi Sasa	Japanese
Syzygy	New American
Z Cuisine Bistrot	French Bistro

---

* Indicates a tie with restaurant above

Alpenglow Stube Ⓜ   26 | 28 | 27 | $73

Keystone Resort, 21996 Hwy. 6 (atop North Peak Mtn.), Keystone,
970-496-4386; www.keystone.snow.com

"Both the altitude and the food take your breath away" at this
lodge atop the North Peak of Keystone (elevation: 11,444 ft.)
reachable only by gondola; the "romantic", old-world aerie
boasts "exquisite panoramas", roaring fireplaces and "outstanding" staffers who provide "nice sheepskin slippers" and "wonderful, creative" Bavarian-American cuisine; for this "peak
experience", "bring a fat wallet" and note that reservations are
required; N.B. limited hours in summer.

Barolo Grill Ⓢ Ⓜ   25 | 23 | 24 | $48

3030 E. Sixth Ave. (bet. Milwaukee & St. Paul Sts.), 303-393-1040;
www.barologrilldenver.com

"Warm and intimate" yet always "bustling", this dinner-only
"class act" in Cherry Creek "could hold its own anywhere"
thanks to "consistently excellent", "belt-expanding" Northern
Italian favorites, an "extensive", "expensive" list of nearly 1,000
regional wines and an "attentive" staff that regularly travels to
The Boot for educational tastings; some surveyors find the
"upsell" approach too "pushy", yet happily take a "seat by the
fireplace" to "watch the sparks . . . literally."

Cafe Brazil Ⓢ Ⓜ   27 | 16 | 22 | $32

4408 Lowell Blvd. (44th Ave.), 303-480-1877;
www.cafebrazildenver.com

Chef/co-owner Tony Zarlenga's "exciting", "exotic" Brazilian-
Colombian fare "astonishes the taste buds" at this "bright",
"unpretentious" 70-seater nestled in a "slightly folksy", "good-
looking location" in "not-quite-gentrified" Berkeley Park; "warm,
friendly" and "super laid-back" servers also add to the place's
"personality"; regulars advise reservations, but report "it's well
worth the wait" for such a "magical experience"; N.B. a mid-
Survey move may not be reflected in the Decor score.

Capital Grille, The   26 | 26 | 26 | $50

1450 Larimer St. (15th St.), 303-539-2500; www.thecapitalgrille.com

A formidable battleground in "Denver's steakhouse wars", this
"carnivore's-dream" chain link in Larimer Square brings beef
eaters "marvelous" chops, "very good seafood" and more than
400 wines via the ministrations of an "inspired" staff that "makes
everyone feel like a VIP"; the "clubby" quarters are "chic, sleek
and sophisticated" "without the stuffiness" of some competitors,
while the "see-and-be-seen" "bar excels"; and though "your
wallet will get a workout, who cares when you're treated like
royalty?"; N.B. free valet parking.

DEL FRISCO'S DOUBLE EAGLE   27 | 25 | 26 | $58
STEAK HOUSE

Denver Tech Ctr., 8100 E. Orchard Rd. (I-25), Greenwood Village,
303-796-0100; www.delfriscos.com

"Denver's elite" – including "pro ballplayers" (e.g. "the Broncos'
defensive unit") and other "celebs" – are among the "testosterone-
charged" "faithful" at this Greenwood Village chain chophouse;
they consider it "well worth the coronary risk" to chow down on
"succulent" "slabs of steer" and sides at this "clubby" "Western
parlor" where an "impeccable" staff is "out to please"; bellyachers

beef about a "loud crowd that likes to show off their money", apparently preferring fellow diners to be seen and not herd.

FLAGSTAFF HOUSE 27 26 27 $64
1138 Flagstaff Rd. (on Flagstaff Mtn.), Boulder, 303-442-4640;
www.flagstaffhouse.com
"Breathtaking views overlooking Boulder" from Flagstaff Mountain are by themselves "worth the high price of admission" to this "classic" hillside haven – but wait, there's more: loyalists laud the "imaginative, delicious" "French- and Asian-accented" New American–Eclectic fare as well as an "elegant", "romantic" dining room, a "spectacular" 20,000-bottle wine cellar and "white-glove" service; still, a minority finds the "whole experience" "hoity-toity" and "stuffy to the point of claustrophobia."

Frasca Food and Wine ☒ – – – E
1738 Pearl St. (bet. 17th & 18th Sts.), Boulder, 303-442-6966;
www.frascafoodandwine.com
Giddy gastronomes are arriving en masse to this Northeastern Italian noshery helmed by alums from California's famed French Laundry, including chef-owner Lachlan Mackinnon-Patterson and master sommelier Bobby Stuckey; their efforts pack the understated dining room with bona fide foodophiles and oenophiles who appreciate fare from the Friuli region complemented by 200 varieties of vino from small producers; N.B. Monday night's three-course tasting menu is one of Boulder's best deals.

Full Moon Grill 25 19 23 $38
Village Shopping Ctr., 2525 Arapahoe Ave. (bet. Folsom & 28th Sts.),
Boulder, 303-938-8800; www.fullmoongrill.com
For a "guaranteed happy experience", Boulderites head to this "cozy" shopping-center "gem" where the "consistently excellent" seasonal Northern Italian cuisine ("try the pear-and-polenta appetizer" and the "wonderful desserts") pleases both neighbors and visiting "urbanites" alike; picky eaters appreciate "knowledgeable" servers who "cheerfully honor requests", while tipplers toast "spectacular monthly wine dinners"; nonetheless, a few sigh the "tables are uncomfortably close" and take solace in patio seating.

Grouse Mountain Grill 26 25 25 $59
Beaver Creek Resort, 141 Scott Hill Rd. (Village Rd.), Beaver Creek,
970-949-0600; www.beavercreek.snow.com
When they want an "absolutely first-rate" "fine-dining" experience, the cognoscenti "come back" to this Beaver Creek Resort stalwart for "monstrous portions" of "creative", "outrageously delicious" Regional American fare ("fantastic without being too fancy") and 450 vintages, all "wonderfully presented" by an "attentive and professional" staff; the "elegant" yet "kid-friendly" setting offers a fireplace, "gorgeous views" and the "most comfortable chairs in the universe"; P.S. "ask for a table in the bar" near the jazz pianist.

HIGHLAND'S GARDEN CAFE ☒ Ⓜ 27 27 25 $43
3927 W. 32nd Ave. (bet. Osceola & Perry Sts.), 303-458-5920;
www.highlandsgardencafe.com
The "quintessential place for ladies of a certain age" ("take your mom"), this "impeccable" North Denver destination is a "treat for all the senses"; chef-owner Patricia Perry proffers a "shockingly

huge" New American menu featuring "creative", "challenging flavor combos" complemented by 300 wines and a "delightful staff"; and "luscious flora" blooming in "charming" "courtyard gardens" around the 1890 "Victorian manor" make for a "lovely summer meal on the patio."

India's
25 | 17 | 19 | $23

Tamarac Sq., 3333 S. Tamarac Dr. (Hampden Ave.), 303-755-4284
Still "the best Indian in town", this South Denver curry house has "regulars" raving about its "titillating", "flavorful and aromatic" food, including "impressive lamb vindaloo" ("every pore on your body will sweat"), "great vegetarian dishes" and a "value-priced" ($6.95) lunch buffet; yes, the "somber" staff has "a lot of rules" (e.g. "no shorts!") and the "colorful" room looks like "something out of a bad Bollywood movie", but spice cadets stay loyal "no matter how many" competitors "come and go."

John's 🗭 M
26 | 19 | 25 | $46

2328 Pearl St. (bet. 23rd & 24th Sts.), Boulder, 303-444-5232;
www.johnsrestaurantboulder.com
For an "intimate respite" from Boulder's "hectic Pearl Street Mall", epicures opt for this New American "classic charmer" set in a "delightfully quiet" cottage; "longtime faves" ("incredible Stilton filet mignon") are combined with "inventive" and "eclectic" "new offerings", and everything is served "gracefully" and with "professional" aplomb; though the decor seems "dated" to some, the spot remains a "standby."

Kevin Taylor 🗭
26 | 25 | 25 | $60

Hotel Teatro, 1106 14th St. (Arapahoe St.), 303-820-2600;
www.hotelteatro.com
Downtown Denver's Hotel Teatro is the stage for this "posh" Parisian-style haute house, an "elegant" and "rather formal" "special-occasion place"; foodies effervesce over the eponymous chef-owner's "delicately balanced" and "innovatively presented" New American cuisine ("perfection on a plate"), a "great" 900-label list and "truly dedicated" staffers who "cater to your every need"; but a few naysayers nitpick that prices are "ridiculous" and the scene "pretentious."

Keystone Ranch
26 | 25 | 25 | $70

Keystone Ranch Golf Course, 1437 Summit County Rd. 150 (Rd. D),
Keystone, 970-496-4386; www.keystone.snow.com
Keystone cognoscenti crow about this "consistently exceptional" 1930s ranch house with an "elegant" "Western ambiance" ("your own cabin in the hills, if your name happens to be Trump"); its "first-class" Colorado-style New American fare (bison, rack of lamb, wild game) is complemented by some 700 "interesting wines", while afterwards, the "tremendous" crew serves "wonderful desserts" and coffee in a "sitting room" complete with "roaring fireplace"; sure, it's "expensive", but "bring a fat wallet" and enjoy the "true mountain experience."

Kitchen, The
– | – | – | E

1039 Pearl St. (bet. 10th & 11th Sts.), Boulder, 303-544-5973;
www.thekitchencafe.com
Proving that the most convivial room in the house is, indeed, the kitchen, this chic Boulder Eclectic – a magnet for chowhounds and wine geeks – is known for its 12-ft. community table (made

from century-old Douglas fir), commitment to organic, local ingredients and eco-conscious sensibilities (the restaurant is
completely wind-powered); it all translates into a jubilant experience that's staffed by servers who are knowledgeable about the
daily-changing menu and 600-label wine list.

L'ATELIER | 27 | 23 | 23 | $44 |
1739 Pearl St. (18th St.), Boulder, 303-442-7233;
www.latelierboulder.com
Chef-owner Radek Cerny is once again a culinary "artiste-in-
residence", "cooking up French-inspired eats" for "NY-wannabes"
at his "charming" Boulder cafe; well-wishers wallow in the "dazzling", "imaginative" and "exquisitely presented" fare ("colorful
essences and reductions") served on "beautiful art-glass
dishes" in "good-size portions" that make for an "outstanding
value"; but claustrophobes cluck this 50-seater has "tables too
close together", resulting in "too many people in too small a space."

La Tour | – | – | – | E |
122 E. Meadow Dr. (I-70), Vail, 970-476-4403; www.latour-vail.com
At this Vail Contemporary French, chef-owner Paul Ferzacca
turns out a slew of seafood-centric Gallic goodies (sole meunière,
escargots), while half a dozen sommeliers are on hand to help
with the 350-label list of French and American wines (including 50
under $50); sleek, colorful and warm surroundings plus a conve-
nient village location also help turn diners into Tour-ists.

Left Bank | 25 | 21 | 24 | $62 |
Sitzmark Lodge, 183 Gore Creek Dr. (Bridge St.), Vail, 970-476-3696;
www.leftbankvail.com
Gallic "classics" ("fantastic bouillabaisse", "sauces that make
you want to lick your plate") without the "phony nouveau frills"
make this "sophisticated" stop at Vail's Sitzmark Lodge a must for
Francophiles (*"sans les enfants", s'il vous plait*) who also ooh-la-
la over the "outstanding wine list" and "relaxed" but "meticulous" service; sure, the "old-fashioned" decor might be a mite
"dated", but "it's all worth it"; N.B. closed Wednesdays.

Luca d'Italia ⩰ Ⓜ | 25 | 20 | 25 | $42 |
711 Grant St. (bet. 7th & 8th Aves.), 303-832-6600;
www.lucadenver.com
"Hey Dorothy, we're in Italy now", swear surveyors who swoon
over this "high-on-the-buzz-chart" Capitol Hill spot from chef-
owner Frank Bonanno (Mizuna); foodies feast on "fabulous" five-
course tasting menus as well as crab gnocchi "to make your Italian
grandmother smile", while an "outstanding" staff that's "caring
but not stuffy" traverses the "upscale", "minimalist", modern dining
room; though a few fret that the menu's "quirky" and "confusing",
most maintain the experience is "hip, happening and heavenly."

Matsuhisa | 26 | 21 | 21 | $64 |
303 E. Main St. (Monarch St.), Aspen, 970-544-6628;
www.nobumatsuhisa.com
"Omakase ... oh my goshe" gasp gourmets who gather at this
Aspen outpost of the "Nobu empire", where "refined Japanese
chow" and "world-class sushi" constitute a "culinary experience
not to be missed"; the decor is "down-home" vis à vis the coastal
siblings, comprising a "tastefully decorated" basement dining
room and a "swanky" upstairs lounge for sipping "tasty saketinis";

though there's grumbling about "indifferent service", most agree a dinner here is well "worth the wound" on your "bleeding wallet."

Mel's Restaurant & Bar
| 24 | 20 | 23 | $40 |

235 Fillmore St. (bet. 2nd & 3rd Aves.), 303-333-3979;
www.melsbarandgrill.com
The "mature 'in' crowd" "hangs out" at this "hardy perennial" in Cherry Creek, where a "pleasant atmosphere" is complemented by an "innovative", "eclectic" and "ever-changing" roster of "delicious and satisfying" New American fare; meanwhile, staffers who "take their jobs seriously" pour selections from a "stellar" cellar, and live piano music at the "terrific bar" "brings in both young city slickers and old-timers"; N.B. renovations completed after a 2004 fire outdate the Decor score.

MIZUNA ⊠ Ⓜ
| 28 | 22 | 27 | $49 |

225 E. Seventh Ave. (bet. Grant & Sherman Sts.), 303-832-4778;
www.mizunadenver.com
"Let's be frank": Frank Bonanno's "exceptional" Capitol Hill New American, rated No. 1 for Food in Colorado, is "best in breed, class and show"; gourmets are "dizzy with glee" over the "globe-trotting" goodies ("exquisite lobster mac 'n' cheese", "salads too pretty to eat") and "stunning wine list" from Denver's "most polished kitchen", while they say the "superb" service is "not just responsive but anticipatory"; and a recent expansion of the "lovely and intimate setting" to include a bar and private dining nook "means even more happy diners."

Montagna
| 26 | 26 | 27 | $66 |

The Little Nell Hotel, 675 E. Durant Ave. (Spring St.), Aspen, 970-920-6330;
www.thelittlenell.com
"Upscale, classy" and a touch "formal" (you'll find "few snow-boarders here"), this "brightly shining star" at Aspen's Little Nell Hotel is known for its "legendary service", "elegant outdoor dining" and "unbelievably creative", "indescribably delicious" New American cuisine ("spectacular desserts"), all bolstered by a 15,000-bottle list from "treasured master sommelier" Richard Betts; sure, "it's expensive, but worth it"; N.B. a post-*Survey* chef change may outdate the above Food score.

Morton's, The Steakhouse
| 25 | 22 | 25 | $60 |

1710 Wynkoop St. (17th St.), 303-825-3353
Denver Crescent Town Ctr., 8480 E. Belleview Ave. (DTC Blvd.),
Greenwood Village, 303-409-1177
www.mortons.com
"Chockablock" with "devoted carnivores" and "local celebrities" who store "their personal wine collections" here, these "clubby" cow palace chainsters in the Historic District and Greenwood Village bring in beef eaters for "dinner and a show": an "impecca-ble" "tag-team" staff presents a "food tour" of "plump and juicy" slabs later "seared to perfection" and served with "diabolically rich sides"; of course, as the "sizzling" meat "melts in your mouth", "funds in the wallet melt at a similar pace."

New Saigon
| 26 | 11 | 17 | $21 |

630 S. Federal Blvd. (bet. Center & Exposition Aves.), 303-936-4954;
www.newsaigon.com
With a menu the "size of a Tolstoy novel" (with "an entire section devoted to frogs' legs"), this "awesome", "authentic" "old-timer"

in a small South Denver strip mall remains an "inexpensive" way to "take your tongue on a trip to Vietnam"; "attentive" if sometimes "surly" servers "guide you" to a "truly wonderful" meal (the "best spring rolls", "fantastic smoothies"), and though "fancy folk" fret about the "nothing-special" interiors, the "food makes up for it."

Opus   26 | 23 | 25 | $44 |

2575 W. Main St. (Curtice St.), Littleton, 303-703-6787; www.opusdine.com
"Yes, Virginia, there really is great" food in the "land of the bland chain restaurants" announce "pleasantly surprised" diners who've found this "quaint" "storefront in downtown Littleton"; they talk up its "adventuresome", "exciting" and "wonderful" New American entrees presented with "panache" by "professional" servers in an "urban-chic" setting (some say "stark"); still, a vocal minority maintains the place "still feels like a work in progress", although they admit it's "trying hard."

Piñons   25 | 24 | 25 | $62 |

105 S. Mill St. (E. Main St.), Aspen, 970-920-2021; www.pinons.net
"No Aspen trip is complete" without dining at this "always excellent" Regional American "classic" from owner Rob Mobilian; in a "comfortable" room that feels like a "Southwestern art gallery" (or on a new patio), "cordial" staffers extend a "wonderful welcome" before "knowledgeably" discoursing on "Colorado cuisine" for the "gourmet Western palate" and "superb wines"; gripers groan about "off-the-chart" tabs, but converts counter that "even if the total bill comes to $5 per bite, it's worth every penny."

Potager ⓈⓂ   24 | 20 | 22 | $40 |

1109 Ogden St. (bet. 11th & 12th Aves.), 303-832-5788
Clearly a "Chez Panisse devotee", chef Terry Rippeto fashions her "eclectic, seasonal" New American fare from "sublime", "freshest-of-the-fresh" ingredients at this "funky" Capitol Hill "charmer"; add in a "breezy", "bohemian", "Euro-distressed" dining room, a "delightful garden" conducive to "romantic interludes" and a "friendly", "wine-savvy staff" that's up on the "thoughtful" "boutique" list, and you get a "Berkeley"-style "bistro that could – and does"; still, some sticklers' "high expectations" are "disappointed" by "loud acoustics" and staff "indifference"; N.B. no reservations.

Q's   25 | 23 | 23 | $42 |

Hotel Boulderado, 2115 13th St. (Spruce St.), Boulder, 303-442-4880; www.qsboulder.com
An "oasis within the People's Republic of Boulder" that's "far from the tree-hugging crowd", this "classy", "historic" New American in the Hotel Boulderado is a "great place to take your parents or have a business dinner"; servers "really care" and "outstanding" chef John Platt's "inspiring" seasonal menu is "heavenly" (though acrophobes assert his "artistic presentations" are "a little heavy on the towers"); "breakfast is awesome" too, especially if you sit on the "nice porch" overlooking the Pearl Street pedestrian mall.

rioja   – | – | – | E |

1431 Larimer St. (bet. 14th & 15th Sts.), 303-820-2282; www.riojadenver.com
The name refers not only to the provenance of the winsome wines dotting the eclectic, moderately priced list at this stylish hot spot on trendy Larimer Square, but also to the province inspir-

ing chef/co-owner Jennifer Jasinski's Med menu; a mix of locals and tourists dig into dishes like artichoke mousse–filled tortelloni, while swank singles belly up to a lively, copper-topped bar for sangria and small plates.

Six89 Kitchen/Wine Bar Ⓜ   26 22 24 $45
689 Main St. (7th St.), Carbondale, 970-963-6890; www.six89.com
Those in-the-know "hate to share the secret" of iconoclastic chef-owner Mark Fischer's Carbondale New American, but admit they "owe it" to him to spill the beans about his "passionate" "culinary artistry" ("each dish is more delicious than the last"); foodies are willing to journey "from Denver and then home the same night" for this "uplifting", "down-valley" experience that's enhanced by "genius sommelier" Bill Bentley's "stellar cellar" and "hospitable", "well-trained" servers who make everything "look effortless."

Solera Restaurant & Wine Bar Ⓜ   25 22 23 $45
5410 E. Colfax Ave. (Grape St.), 303-388-8429; www.solerarestaurant.com
"Rising star" Goose Sorensen elevated a "tough location" on a "seedy strip" in East Denver to a "superb neighborhood eatery" with his "innovative, playful!" and "fantastic" New American fare bolstered by an "incredible selection" of "reasonably priced wines"; thanks to "snappy service", a "quiet, calming" atmosphere and a "beautifully appointed patio" perfect for "starlit summer nights", it's "a delicious experience" for those "interested in food, not scenes"; P.S. "Wednesday wine tastings are a treat."

Steuben's   – – – M
523 E. 17th Ave. (bet. Pearl & Pennsylvania Sts.), 303-830-1001;
www.steubens.com
Citified cool cats have discovered this groovy Uptown temple of Regional American cuisine, where chef Matt Selby's nostalgic roster of comfort foods runs the gamut from deviled eggs to pan-roasted chicken; the retro setting (think Formica-topped tables and linoleum floors) is a funky throwback, while a hip cocktail menu offers raspberry-lime rickeys and the like; N.B. a separate take-out operation provides curbside service.

Sushi Den   27 23 20 $39
1487 S. Pearl St. (E. Florida Ave.), 303-777-0826; www.sushiden.net
"Beverly Hills meets the Rockies" at this "sleek", "modern" sushi specialist in Washington Park, where "beautiful people galore" gather for "artful and inventive" "ultra-fresh" fare ("creative rolls", "must-eat" sashimi) made from fish that's "flown in from Japan daily", along with "amazing banana cream pie"; some snipe that "service is pretentious" but admit the "food is worth the 'tude – barely" ("I wish it weren't so good, so I could stop going"); P.S. reservations for parties of five or more only, so "be prepared" for "long waits."

Sushi Sasa   – – – E
2401 15th St. (Platte St.), 303-433-7272
At chef-owner Wayne Conwell's fashionably minimalist Japanese in Platte River Valley, raw afishionados are falling hook, line and sinker for the usual smorgasbord of sushi, sashimi and rolls, plus a large selection of sake and an eight-course, $60 omakase menu; the blond-wood dining den is SoHo sleek, but serious voyagers set sail for the bar, where theatrical chefs ply patrons with the day's freshest offerings.

SWEET BASIL   27 | 22 | 24 | $51

193 E. Gore Creek Dr. (Bridge St.), Vail, 970-476-0125;
www.sweetbasil-vail.com

After 29 years, this "dynamic" Vail Village "landmark" "satisfies and stimulates" declare devotees of Colorado's Most Popular restaurant where patrons "never tire" of Bruce Yim's "clever, innovative" New American cuisine "with Asian touches", or of the "caring" staff, "great après-ski scene" and "beautiful views" of Gore Creek; sure, service can be "spotty", the reservation list fills "months in advance", and you might have to "sell your seat at the bar" to "help defray the cost", but the place's "energy and verve" endures; N.B. recent renovations may outdate the above Decor score.

Syzygy   25 | 23 | 23 | $58

520 E. Hyman Ave. (bet. Galena & Hunter Sts.), Aspen, 970-925-3700

"Syzygy – a word constructed from sizzle and energy?" wonder wordsmiths who agree this "great Aspen secret" "has both"; "wild-game master" Martin Oswald conjures up "terrific" New American dishes that aren't "drenched in sauces" for pairing with 600-plus bottles from a "superb wine list"; the setting also "has it all", with an "elegant", "tastefully simple" dining room and a lively bar offering "jumping jazz" Thursday–Saturday; it may be "expensive", but the "happening place" is "worth every dollar."

240 UNION   26 | 20 | 24 | $36

240 Union Blvd. (bet. 6th Avenue Frwy. & W. Alameda Pkwy.),
Lakewood, 303-989-3562; www.240union.com

This "beacon of exciting food in the culinary desert" of the Western suburbs is "alive, exciting and always busy" boast boosters who believe it's "a bargain for the quality of food you get"; the "modern" dining room is overseen by "superb" servers and chef Matt Franklin "a genius with seafood" in the open kitchen, creating "bright, innovative" and "consistently excellent" New American fin fare and "seasonal menus" whose "flavors sing on the plate" – perhaps that's one reason some snipe it's "too darn loud."

Z Cuisine Bistrot & Crêperie 🖼️Ⓜ️   – | – | – | E

2239 W. 30th Ave. (bet. Vallejo & Wyandot Sts.), 303-477-1111;
www.zcuisineonline.com

Sophisticates sit elbow-to-elbow at this evening bag–sized Parisian bistro proffering an ever-changing, seasonally driven French menu, along with a variety of dessert crêpes; chef/co-owner Patrick DuPays spends his spare time scouring Denver's farmer's markets for fresh ingredients and his excursions translate into dishes like cassoulet that are paired with a small but focused Gallic wine list; N.B. open Wednesday–Saturday for dinner only.

Zengo   26 | 27 | 24 | $44

1610 Little Raven St. (15th St.), 720-904-0965; www.modernmexican.com

What some call "the coolest-looking eatery in the West" is "unlike any other restaurant in Denver" rave respondents who revel in Richard Sandoval's "sassy", "bodaciously" "sexy", "urban hot spot" in River Park; so "snatch a seat at the chef's counter" to watch the busy kitchen concoct "exotic", "bizarre" and "deliciously unique" Asian–Nuevo Latino concoctions, complemented by "sublime drinks" and "smooth service"; still, a few grumblers growl that "deafening noise" derail "dinner conversation."

Detroit

TOP FOOD RANKING

	Restaurant	Cuisine
28	Rugby Grille	American/Continental
	Lark, The	Continental
27	Zingerman's	Deli
	Tribute	French
	Bacco	Italian
	Common Grill	Seafood
26	Five Lakes Grill	New American
	West End Grill	New American
	Il Posto Ristorante	Italian
	Rochester Chop House	Steakhouse

OTHER NOTEWORTHY PLACES

Beverly Hills Grill	New American
Cafe Bon Homme	New French
Coach Insignia	Seafood/Steakhouse
No. VI Chop House	Seafood/Steakhouse
Opus One	American/Continental
Oslo Sushi Bar	Japanese
Ristorante Café Cortina	Italian
Seldom Blues	New American
Sweet Georgia Brown	American
Traffic Jam & Snug	Eclectic

	F	D	S	C

BACCO ⌷   27 | 25 | 25 | $52
29410 Northwestern Hwy. (W. 12 Mile Rd.), Southfield, 248-356-6600; www.baccoristorante.com
The "pure-Italian" kitchen pays "attention to detail" as it dishes out "delectable food" with "wonderful flavors" at this "rather elegant", "pricey", "upscale" Southfield spot that regulars rank among the "best in Detroit"; there's also "top-notch service" from a "knowledgeable and friendly staff", as well as "great people-watching" at the bar and a "gorgeous", "contemporary" interior, all of which makes it "a place to be seen with the 'in' crowd."

Beverly Hills Grill   26 | 19 | 23 | $33
31471 Southfield Rd. (W. 13 Mile Rd.), Beverly Hills, 248-642 2355
"Always reliable", this "lively" Beverly Hills New American "favorite" "never disappoints" with its "amazing breakfasts", but it also gets "raves" for its "creative brunches", "delicious lunches" and "outstanding dinners" thanks to a "consistently stellar" kitchen and an "expertly trained staff"; true, the "casual" space is "crowded, small and noisy", but most maintain the "quality" "makes up for" the "drawbacks" – now "if only they would take reservations."

Cafe Bon Homme ⌧   26 | 20 | 23 | $55 |
844 Penniman Ave. (bet. Harvey & Main Sts.), Plymouth,
734-453-6260
"A lovely, welcoming experience" awaits at this "charming" New French "in the great little town of Plymouth", where "superb food" (including "sensational desserts") is paired with a "great wine list" and served by an "outstanding" staff in a "cozy", "quiet" setting; a few feel the "outdated decor" "is tired", but more maintain that the "quaint", "intimate atmosphere" helps "make every dinner there a special occasion."

Coach Insignia ⌧   – | – | – | VE |
Renaissance Ctr., 100 Renaissance Ctr., 71st fl. (Jefferson Ave.),
313-567-2622; www.mattprenticerg.com
Located on the 71st floor of the Renaissance Center, this latest venture from powerhouse restaurateur Matt Prentice pairs a land and sea menu with a 30-mile, 360-degree view of the skyline and river that draws both visiting executives and locals looking to pop the question; the menu ranges from aged Angus beef and wild salmon to an over-the-top 'Ultimate Surf & Turf' signature selection (a petite tenderloin with lobster tail and foie gras) that's bested only by the cellar's 600-label collection.

COMMON GRILL, THE Ⓜ   27 | 20 | 24 | $34 |
112 S. Main St. (bet. Middle & South Sts.), Chelsea, 734-475-0470;
www.commongrill.com
It's "worth the trip" to this "off-the-beaten-path" storefront spot "in the wonderful town of Chelsea" (an "hour's drive" from Detroit), thanks to "great chef" and owner Craig Common's "excellent seafood" menu, which offers "variety, freshness" and fish "as good as at an East Coast restaurant"; a "fun, bistro-like bustle" pervades the "always-crowded" dining room ("expect to wait to be seated"), but should it get too "high decibel", you can always opt for carryout at the adjacent Back Door market.

Five Lakes Grill ⌧   26 | 20 | 23 | $42 |
424 N. Main St. (Commerce Rd.), Milford, 248-684-7455;
www.fivelakesgrill.com
Fans feel like they've "died and gone to heaven" after a visit to this "fairly priced" New American where "excellent chef"-owner Brian Polcyn's "innovative" menu emphasizes "fresh, fresh, fresh" Michigan ingredients and includes "delightful twists on old favorites"; it's the type of "food you'll find nowhere else" and the storefront space offers a surprisingly "urbane atmosphere" given its location "in the quaint old town" of Milford, 40 minutes north of Detroit.

Il Posto Ristorante ⌧   26 | 24 | 24 | $51 |
29110 Franklin Rd. (Northwestern Hwy.), Southfield, 248-827-8070;
www.il-posto.com
"When you want to splurge", "dress up" and head to this "expensive, elegant Italian" in Southfield, where "classic" cuisine that "never disappoints" is "prepared flawlessly" from "the noblest of ingredients", then accompanied by a "great wine list" and "formally" served by "bona fide waiters from [The Boot]" in a "fabulous room"; some purport it's "pretentious", saying certain staffers are "supercilious", but more maintain it's a must for "memorable meals" of the "highest quality."

LARK, THE ⑤Ⓜ   28 | 26 | 28 | $81

6430 Farmington Rd. (W. Maple Rd.), West Bloomfield, 248-661-4466;
www.thelark.com

"Romance abounds" at this "still-superb" West Bloomfield "leg-end" "modeled after a Portuguese country inn" and ranked No. 1 for Popularity in the Detroit area; it offers an "outstanding menu" of "divine" Continental cuisine and the presence of "consummate hosts" and owners Jim and Mary Lark and their "educated, professional staff" contribute to the "fabulous dining experience"; N.B. the post-*Survey* departure of chef Kyle Ketchum may outdate the above Food score.

No. VI Chop House & Lobster Bar   26 | 24 | 25 | $56

Hotel Baronette, 27790 Novi Rd. (12 Mile Rd.), Novi, 248-305-5210;
www.mattprenticerg.com

"Fantastic food" is featured at this "first-class" surf 'n' turfer in the Hotel Baronette that has fans "salivating" over "some of the best steaks going", "divine morel bisque" and "wonderful" "sautéed lobster tails with whipped potatoes", plus "top-notch service to match"; some find the "dark wood" environs too "dimly lit" and the "manly prices" "sinful", but most agree this "favorite" is "worth the drive" to its "far-out" Novi location; P.S. the "catchy name is actually" a play on the town's moniker.

OPUS ONE ⑤   26 | 25 | 25 | $53

565 E. Larned St. (Beaubien St.), 313-961-7766;
www.opus-one.com

"Still a favorite" with "business- and theater-crowd" "movers and shakers", this "Downtown institution" "delivers on all levels" thanks to chef-partner Tim Giznsky's "interesting, varied menu" that offers "a mix of Traditional American" and Continental dishes, "owner Jim Kokas' superb wine list", a "professional staff" that "makes every guest feel special" and decor that has "a refreshing, modern look"; a few feel "there are better values", but more insist it's "fine dining the way it was meant to be."

Oslo Sushi Bar & Lounge ⑤   – | – | – | I

1456 Woodward Ave. (John R St.), 313-963-0300

Located at the intersection of sushi and American sensibility, this stylish, skinny Downtown venue creates a buzz with its modern interior, laid-back ambiance and super-fresh, scandalously low-priced morsels from Tokyo-born chef Kaku Usui; the upstairs is frequented by a mix of foreign auto execs and locals, while a younger crowd packs the downstairs lounge, savoring 12 different kinds of sake and a menu that, like the tides, changes twice a day.

Ristorante Café Cortina ⑤   26 | 24 | 24 | $53

30715 W. 10 Mile Rd. (Orchard Lake Rd.), Farmington Hills,
248-474-3033; www.cafecortina.com

"When you crave" "true Italian flavor", find your way to this "fabulous" Farmington Hills "favorite", a "beautiful cafe" where the "classic" cuisine (including "superb pastas") is "wonderfully prepared" using vegetables and "herbs grown in an [on-site] garden", and the "attentive", "smartly dressed" staff "makes you feel like family"; some fault the "high prices" and feel "the food and service can be a bit uneven at times", but a majority is won over by the "insanely romantic" ambiance.

Rochester Chop House

26 | **21** | **24** | **$39**

306 S. Main St. (3rd St.), Rochester, 248-651-2266;
www.kruseandmuerrestaurants.com

Though "beef rules" at this Rochester "Kruse & Muer operation" with "a private-club" feel and a "gracious" staff, it's "not your typical chophouse", as it's actually two restaurants in one: there's the "lively" Kabin Kruser's Oyster Bar up front and a "warm, friendly, intimate" dining room with live piano music (most nights) in the rear; it's known for "tempting" meats and "great lobster", but devotees insist that "everything is wonderful" – including the "great martinis"; N.B. a post-*Survey* redo may outdate the above Decor score.

RUGBY GRILLE ◑

28 | **26** | **28** | **$60**

Townsend Hotel, 100 Townsend St. (Pierre St.), Birmingham,
248-642-5999; www.townsendhotel.com

"You may have to mortgage your house, but it's worth it" for the "old-fashioned dining experience" at this "classy", "clubby" Continental-American that's rated No. 1 for Food in the Detroit area; "housed in the Townsend Hotel" ("where out-of-town celebs" "and musicians stay"), it's "reminiscent of the best intimate European restaurants", and its "exceptional" fare and "elegant service" appeal to "everyone who's anyone in Birmingham"; P.S. "you'll want to be seated inside" in the "tiny" Grille room rather than in the light-filled Gallery space.

Seldom Blues

– | **–** | **–** | **VE**

Renaissance Ctr., 400 Renaissance Ctr. (Jefferson Ave.), 313-567-7301;
www.seldomblues.com

At this sophisticated Renaissance Center supper club, diners listen nightly to jazz greats as they feast on a meat- and shellfish-focused New American menu from chef/co-owner Jerry Nottage; the upscale setting has a trendy, energetic ambiance, and its views of the river – from the dining room and the patio – are as apt to turn heads as the presence of celebrity co-owners Frank Taylor, former Detroit Lion Robert Porcher III and jazz flutist Alexander Zonjic.

Sweet Georgia Brown

– | **–** | **–** | **VE**

1045 Brush St. (Monroe St.), 313-965-1245; www.sweetgb.com

Local movers and shakers, policy makers and visiting celebrities enjoy this Greektowner's way with Southern-style American comfort foods taken to their deluxe utmost, in dishes like fried lobster, crabmeat-topped rib eye and desserts that look southward (bourbon pecan torte, berries with mint julep cream); the richly textured setting swings in the evenings with local and national jazz musicians (Wednesday–Saturday).

Traffic Jam & Snug

– | **–** | **–** | **M**

511 W. Canfield St. (2nd Ave.), 313-831-9470; www.traffic-jam.com

This Cultural Center institution – Detroit's first brewpub – makes cheeses and European-style beers in the same giant vats, all the better to anchor an Eclectic menu which ranges from inventive sandwiches made using bread from the on-site bakery to spinach lasagna (plus over-the-top desserts that feature the house's own dense ice cream); the culinary mélange is just right for a mixed clientele augmented by pre- and post-theater-goers, all of whom enjoy eccentric decor that features farm implements hanging from the ceiling.

TRIBUTE ⑤Ⓜ   27 | 27 | 25 | $76

31425 W. 12 Mile Rd. (Orchard Lake Rd.), Farmington Hills, 248-848-9393;
www.tributerestaurant.com

Acolytes "cannot say enough about" the "one-of-a-kind", "remarkable experience" at this "shining star" in Farmington Hills that "deserves all of its acclaim" for an "innovative menu" of "delicious", "decadent Classic French" fare with global accents, a "wonderfully attentive staff" and a "breathtakingly" "beautiful" space with "phenomenal ambiance"; nonetheless, "small portions", "over-the-top" prices and certain "haughty staffers" have some cautious types saving this "culinary masterpiece" for "a special-occasion" "splurge."

West End Grill ⑤Ⓜ   26 | 23 | 26 | $47

120 W. Liberty St. (Ashley St.), Ann Arbor, 734-747-6260;
www.westendgrillA2.com

"Make reservations well in advance" for a spot within the "quiet, candlelit setting" of this "romantic, intimate", "white-tablecloth" 65-seater located in the "heart of the action" in Downtown Ann Arbor; reviewers call it "a jewel" for "exquisitely prepared" New American cuisine that's "impeccably served" by a "solidly trained", "knowledgeable staff" and accompanied by a "fantastic wine list"; true, it's "always crowded" and "occasionally noisy", but you'll be "treated as if you're the only ones dining at the restaurant."

ZINGERMAN'S DELICATESSEN   27 | 16 | 21 | $17

422 Detroit St. (Kingsley St.), Ann Arbor, 734-663-3354;
www.zingermans.com

"Long lines" "out the door" mark this "legendary" Ann Arbor "institution", "a national treasure" that locals laud as the "best deli in America"; don't be dismayed by the "dizzying array of sandwiches", as the "knowledgeable", "personable staff" will "guide you through the huge selection" (though you may also need "help" handling the "humongous portions" and "high prices"), or by "the dreary sit-down area" "where your meal is brought to you", as you can always "carry out."

Ft. Lauderdale

TOP FOOD RANKING

	Restaurant	Cuisine
28	Sunfish Grill	New Amer./Seafood
27	La Brochette	Mediterranean
	Cafe Maxx	Eclectic/New Amer.
26	Canyon	Southwestern
	Cafe Martorano	Italian
	Casa D'Angelo	Northern Italian
	Eduardo de San Angel	Eclectic/Mexican
	Mark's Las Olas	Floribbean
	Galanga	Japanese/Thai
	Silver Pond	Chinese

OTHER NOTEWORTHY PLACES

Restaurant	Cuisine
Anthony's	Pizza
Blue Moon Fish Co.	Seafood
Cafe Vico	Italian
Cheesecake Factory	American
Chima	Brazilian/Steakhouse
Houston's	American
Johnny V's	Floribbean
Josef's	Northern Italian
Ruth's Chris	Steakhouse
3030 Ocean	New Amer./Seafood

F	D	S	C

Anthony's Coal-Fired Pizza | 25 | 14 | 20 | $20 |

2203 S. Federal Hwy. (SE 22nd St.), 954-462-5555
Weston Commons, 4527 Weston Rd. (Griffin Rd.), Weston, 954-358-2625
www.anthonyscoalfiredpizza.com
Even those demanding "NY pizza perfection" beat a path to this small Ft. Lauderdale storefront for "fantastic" pies like the "one-of-a-kind" eggplant Marino (named for the football Hall of Famer), a meatball version that's a "must" and other goodies including "excellent chicken wings"; waist-watchers weigh in and say this "gem" provides "the best excuse to cheat on a diet"; N.B. a Weston location opened post-*Survey*, with two more offshoots in the works.

Blue Moon Fish Co. | 25 | 24 | 22 | $44 |

4405 W. Tradewinds Ave. (E. Commercial Blvd.), 954-267-9888
10317 Royal Palm Blvd. (Coral Springs Dr.), Coral Springs, 954-755-0002
www.bluemoonfishco.com
Sit under the stars or take in the "beautiful" big blue at this Lauderdale Intracoastal eatery where the "splendid" view is matched by "superb" seafood, a "must-try" Sunday brunch and "gracious" service; dining at this "romantic" spot may be "pricey", but locals and "out-of-towners" alike aver it's "worth it"; N.B. the newer Coral Springs site is unrated.

CAFE MARTORANO ⑤　　26 | 18 | 20 | $61
3343 E. Oakland Park Blvd. (N. Ocean Blvd.), 954-561-2554;
www.cafemartorano.com
"Fast for a week" before going to this "small" no-menu, no-reserve
Ft. Lauderdale Italian serving "huge portions" of "fantastic" fare to
crowds who endure "painful waits", "attitude" from the staff and
enough "ear-cleaning noise" to make "Q-Tips unnecessary";
though it's "like dining in the middle of a dance floor" "after the
disco ball descends", regulars say this "crazy scene" "is worth it."

CAFE MAXX　　27 | 20 | 25 | $56
2601 E. Atlantic Blvd. (NE 26th Ave.), Pompano Beach, 954-782-0606;
www.cafemaxx.com
Darrel Broek and Oliver Saucy's Pompano Beach "stalwart" still
"amazes" after 21 years; the "dining adventure" features "incredible" New American–Eclectic fare including "outstanding
seafood" accompanied by "excellent" wines (with a "large selection by the glass"); while some scoff it's "a bit pricey", regulars
rave it's a "special-occasion place that should be your any-
occasion place" – especially given the recently redecorated digs.

Cafe Vico　　23 | 20 | 23 | $38
IHOP Plaza, 1125 N. Federal Hwy. (NE 11th Ave.), 954-565-9681;
www.cafevicorestaurant.com
Admirers appreciate the "winning" formula of "wonderful"
Italian food, "reasonable prices", a "friendly staff" and Marcos
Vico Rodrigues' "charm" (he "greets everyone like family") at this
"pretty" Lauderdale "favorite" in a shopping center; indeed, the
majority "counts on it" since it "never disappoints"; N.B. now
serves lunch Monday–Friday.

CANYON　　26 | 23 | 23 | $44
1818 E. Sunrise Blvd. (N. Federal Hwy.), 954-765-1950; www.canyonfl.com
While it may be hard to resist "the best prickly pear margaritas on
the planet", the "sensational" Southwestern fare also stands tall in
the opinion of many at this "hip", "high-energy" Ft. Lauderdale
"treasure"; the "worth-every-calorie desserts" are the crowning
touch and the service is "top-notch", but be aware that the
"small" digs and no-reserve policy mean you're headed for "too-
long" waits; P.S. grab a "quiet booth" "away from the racket."

CASA D'ANGELO　　26 | 20 | 24 | $49
Sunrise Square Plaza, 1201 N. Federal Hwy. (bet. E. Sunrise Blvd. &
NE 13th St.), 954-564-1234; www.casa-d-angelo.com
"As good as it gets", "celebrity chef" Angelo Elia's Tuscan treat
in Lauderdale offers up "beautiful" Italian fare with a "superb
wine list" in tow; it's "jam-packed with folks ready to spend the
cash", so it helps that the "attentive" staff's at the ready to calm
those unnerved by the "long waits."

CHEESECAKE FACTORY ◐　　20 | 18 | 19 | $26
600 E. Las Olas Blvd. (S. Federal Hwy.), 954-463-1999
Sawgrass Mills Oasis, 2612 Sawgrass Mills Circle (Flamingo Rd.),
Sunrise, 954-835-0966
www.thecheesecakefactory.com
It's the "best chain – ever" aver acolytes of this American duo voted
Most Popular in the Ft. Lauderdale area; they offer "encyclopedic"
menus featuring "giant-size portions" of everything, plus the leg-

endary "ultrarich" namesake desserts, all served by a "cheerful" staff; sure, "the line goes all the way to I-95" and it's so loud you may want to "bring your megaphone", but the reasonably priced fare and "kid-friendly" credo make it a "winner."

Chima Brazilian Steakhouse 25 | 25 | 24 | $52

2400 E. Las Olas Blvd. (SE 25th Ave.), 954-712-0580; www.chima.cc
Round up your "hungry" pals for this "festive", all-you-can-eat Ft. Lauderdale rodizio, a "carnivore's dream" where waiters dressed in full gaucho regalia roam the "beautiful", Brazilian-themed dining room and bring "skewer after skewer" bearing all kinds of "first-rate" meats; it adds up to a "big tab", but it's "worth the money."

Eduardo de San Angel ⊠ 26 | 22 | 25 | $50

2822 E. Commercial Blvd. (bet. Bayview Dr. & 28th Ave.), 954-772-4731; www.eduardodesanangel.com
Venturing beyond "chips and salsa" is this "exemplary" Eclectic-Mexican in Lauderdale, whose "magician" in the kitchen, chef-owner Eduardo Pria, cooks food "so good you'll want to order everything"; the "warm", "unobtrusive" service and "romantic" setting cap "memorable" meals that warrant "return visits."

Galanga 26 | 24 | 22 | $35

2389 Wilton Dr. (NE 8th Ave.), Wilton Manors, 954-202-0000; www.galangarestaurant.com
Winning over seasoned surveyors is this "stylish" Wilton Manors Asian offering "knockout" cuisine that fuses Thai and Japanese elements to "superb" effect, plus "helpful service" and a "gorgeous" "Zen-like" atmosphere; that it's "great" for "world-class people-watching" is another reason it's a "treat for the senses."

HOUSTON'S 21 | 20 | 21 | $32

2821 E. Atlantic Blvd. (Federal Hwy.), Pompano Beach, 954-783-9499; www.houstons.com
Floridians fare well at this Pompano Beach link in a national chain known for "rock-solid" American food, especially "great burgers" and the legendary, "fabulous" spinach dip; the "comfortable", "clubby" setting, "good service" and "active bar scene" is a testament to their "popularity" and reason for many to endure "long waits"; P.S. be sure to snag a "prized seat by the water."

Johnny V's 25 | 22 | 23 | $50

625 E. Las Olas Blvd. (Federal Hwy.), 954-761-7920; www.johnnyvlasolas.com
"It's the best thing to happen to Las Olas" say surveyors smitten with this "top-tier" Lauderdale venture from chef Johnny Vinczencz, whose "sumptuous" Spanish-Med influenced Floribbean cuisine draws "die-hard foodies", while grazers go for the "creative" tapas bar menu and oenophiles revel in "excellent" wines; the "sleek" setting seems to go hand in hand with the "beautiful" crowd."

Josef's ⊠ Ⓜ 25 | 22 | 25 | $43

Central Park Pl., 9763 W. Broward Blvd. (Nob Hill Rd.), Plantation, 954-473-0000
A "gourmet oasis" in the 'burbs, this "worthwhile" Plantation enterprise "delights" with a "delicious", "interesting" slate of Northern Italian fare from chef/co-owner Josef Schibanetz that's backed by a compact yet "interesting wine selection"; providing "hospitality" is his wife, Beth, who manages an "attentive" staff.

LA BROCHETTE BISTRO Ⓜ | 27 | 18 | 25 | $42 |

Embassy Lakes Plaza, 2635 N. Hiatus Rd. (Sheridan St.), Cooper City, 954-435-9090

This "winner" in Cooper City "exceeds expectations" with "beautifully presented", "first-rate" Med fare featuring "great seafood", signature rack of lamb and "excellent" grilled meats (there's wild game in season) brought to the table by a "sharp" staff; though "tucked away" in a strip mall, it manages to be "romantic", and an experience "you won't regret."

MARK'S LAS OLAS | 26 | 23 | 23 | $56 |

1032 E. Las Olas Blvd. (SE 11th Ave.), 954-463-1000; www.chefmark.com

When "you want to impress or be impressed", this Ft. Lauderdale "triumph" from Mark Militello fits the bill with "glorious" Floribbean fare, including lots of local seafood, that "tastes as good as it looks", a "professional staff" and a "modern" (albeit, "loud") setting; the few critics who claim it's "lost its edge" are outnumbered by those who still consider it at the "acme of South Florida's dining scene."

RUTH'S CHRIS STEAK HOUSE | 25 | 21 | 23 | $56 |

2525 N. Federal Hwy. (bet. Oakland Park & Sunrise Blvds.), 954-565-2338; www.ruthschris.com

Carnivores chris-ten this national chain's Ft. Lauderdale outpost a "consistent" performer considering its "tender", "tasty", "butter"-bedecked beef ("the best way to eat a steak") accompanied by "attentive service"; many stake their claim that the "clubby" confines are perfect for "impressing a client", even if the same surmise that the "high prices" are "out of line."

Silver Pond ◑ | 26 | 11 | 17 | $24 |

4285 N. State Rd. 7 (south of Commercial Blvd.), Lauderdale Lakes, 954-486-8885

Sinophiles swear by this "bustling" strip-mall eatery in Lauderdale Lakes, whose "unremarkable decor and service" are beside the point to "adventurous" diners who say the spot serves "real Chinese food" that includes "fresh fish" "plucked out of the tank"; its "favorite" status is confirmed by "lines during season."

SUNFISH GRILL Ⓢ Ⓜ | 28 | – | 23 | $51 |

2761 E. Oakland Park Blvd. (bet. Bayview Dr. & NE 27th Ave.), 954-564-6464; www.sunfishgrill.com

You'll be in seafood "heaven" when you dine at this "outstanding" New American ranked No. 1 for Food in Ft. Lauderdale thanks to chef-owner Anthony Sindaco's "out-of-this-world" (if "pricey") creations abetted by wife Erika's "delicious desserts" and a "crisp" staff; it may no longer be a "diamond in the rough" given a recent move to roomier quarters, but it remains "too good to miss", so surveyors are advised to "reserve way ahead."

3030 Ocean | 25 | 23 | 23 | $50 |

Marriott Harbor Beach Resort & Spa, 3030 Holiday Dr. (Seabreeze Blvd.), 954-765-3030; www.3030ocean.com

Patrons "almost forget they're in a hotel" when dining at this "sophisticated" New American seafooder in the Marriott, where Dean Max's kitchen offers "delectable", "beautifully plated" food served by a "superb" staff; a "lively" setting featuring a "great" bar helps make it one of Lauderdale's "best-kept secrets."

TOP FOOD RANKING

	Restaurant	Cuisine
28	Alan Wong's	Hawaii Regional
27	La Mer	New French
26	Hoku's	Pacific Rim
	Roy's	Hawaii Regional
	Chef Mavro	Hawaii Reg./New French
	Roy's Ko Olina	Hawaii Regional
	Orchids	American
	3660 on the Rise	Pacific Rim
	Hy's Steak House	Steakhouse
25	Ruth's Chris	Steakhouse

OTHER NOTEWORTHY PLACES

Restaurant	Cuisine
Bali by the Sea	Pacific Rim
d.k Steak House	Steakhouse
Duke's Canoe Club	Seafood
Indigo	Asian Fusion
L'Uraku	Pacific Rim
Michel's	French
Olive Tree Café	Greek/Mediterranean
Pineapple Room	Hawaii Regional
Sansei Seafood	Japanese/Pacific Rim
town	Italian

F	D	S	C

ALAN WONG'S
28	20	26	$58

McCully Ct., 1857 S. King St. (bet. Hauoli & Pumehana Sts.), 808-949-2526; www.alanwongs.com

Voted Most Popular and No.1 for Food in Honolulu, this restaurant located "away from the tourist fray" in Ala Moana "never ceases to amaze" fans of chef Alan Wong's "creative brilliance"; with Hawaii Regional dishes like the "heavenly ginger-crusted onaga", "amazing" tasting menus and "stealthlike", "unobtrusive service", it's "Pacific meets perfection", despite its "nondescript" second-floor space and "limited street parking"; P.S. make reservations "well in advance."

Bali by the Sea ⊠
24	26	24	$55

Hilton Hawaiian Village, 2005 Kalia Rd. (Ala Moana Blvd.), 808-941-2254; www.hiltonhawaiianvillage.com

"Expertly prepared seafood" that's "so fresh" "you swear it was just caught" and an "arty" chocolate replica of Diamond Head (it "smokes" via dry ice) delight diners at this Hilton Hawaiian Village Pacific Rim restaurant boasting an "idyllic" location that's "really by the sea"; you may have to book a few days in advance for the most "dramatic views", but with such a "warm and welcoming" atmosphere, you'll "dream about coming back."

CHEF MAVRO ⓜ   26 | 23 | 26 | $72
1969 S. King St. (McCully St.), 808-944-4714;
www.chefmavro.com
"From the moment you enter until the end of your meal", dinner
here is an "experience for all the senses" say fans of the "inspired" New French–meets–Hawaii Regional cuisine of chef
George Mavrothalassitis, who "often greets guests himself";
service is very "knowledgeable", the "wine pairings are outstanding" and the interior is "beautiful", so even if its Ala Moana
location "leaves a bit to be desired" and "portions are tiny", most
take one bite of the "homemade malasadas" dessert and declare
it all "fabulomavrous!"

d.k Steak House   – | – | – | E
Waikiki Beach Marriott Resort & Spa, 2552 Kalakaua Ave., 3rd fl.
(Kapahulu Ave.), 808-931-6280; www.dkrestaurants.com
Local celebrity chef D.K. Kodama (Sansei Seafood) has entered
the steakhouse fray with his newest venture in the Waikiki Beach
Marriott Resort & Spa, where prime beef that's dry-aged on-site
is complemented by a lengthy wine list from master sommelier
Chuck Furuya; whether you opt to sit in one of the intimate booths
in the modern, dimly lit dining room or out on the deck with its sunset
ocean views, keep in mind that reservations are required.

DUKE'S CANOE CLUB   17 | 22 | 17 | $31
Outrigger Waikiki on the Beach, 2335 Kalakaua Ave. (bet. Dukes Ln. &
Kaiulani Ave.), 808-922-2268; www.dukeswaikiki.com
"Wild, wacky" and "tons of fun", this "always packed", open-air,
oceanfront seafooder in the Outrigger Waikiki on the Beach is a
"tourist mecca" with a "great" breakfast buffet, "classic mahi
sandwiches", "kitschy Hawaiian cocktails" and a "famous hula
pie", all delivered with "a smile"; there's lots of "memorabilia"
honoring the "great surfing legend" Duke Kahanamoku, and
when the "hotties" show up for live music after sunset, it becomes
"*the* happening place."

HOKU'S   26 | 26 | 26 | $60
Kahala Hotel & Resort, 5000 Kahala Ave. (Kealaolu Ave.), 808-739-8780;
www.kahalaresort.com
For "sublime dining" with a "beautiful view of the ocean", this
Kahala Hotel & Resort restaurant is a "stunning" choice; feast on
a recently revamped menu of "creative", "phenomenal" Pacific
Rim fare among the "movers and shakers", revel in the "gracious" service and soak up the "romantic" ambiance "at sunset"
with the one you love; sure, it may "break the bank", but it leaves
you "happy to pay"; N.B. no casual attire allowed in the evenings.

Hy's Steak House   26 | 23 | 25 | $56
Waikiki Park Heights Hotel, 2440 Kuhio Ave. (Uluniu Ave.), 808-922-5555;
www.hyshawaii.com
"Excellent" slabs of beef grilled "exactly how you ordered" right
"before your eyes" on a glass-enclosed, kiawe-wood fire make
this "wonderful anachronism" in the Waikiki Park Heights Hotel a
"superb", "consistent" steakhouse "throwback to the '60s or
'70s"; a dimly lit, "old-world" setting complete with "curved
booths for cuddling" and "impeccable" service add to its appeal,
and meat mavens maintain they'd "eat there nightly" if they
could; N.B. there's live guitar Wednesday–Saturday.

Indigo ⌧   23 | 23 | 21 | $38
1121 Nuuanu Ave. (Hotel St.), 808-521-2900; www.indigo-hawaii.com

"Wow your taste buds" with Asian fusion eats from chef Glenn Chu, who "blends unique flavors for a multicultural feast" at this "*Sex-and-the-City*-meets-*South-Pacific*" "hipster" in Chinatown; it's a "favorite for the Downtown lunch crowd" and "trendy twenty- and thirtysomethings" seeking a happy hour full of "eclectic pupus" and "fantastic martinis" can head to the attached Green Room lounge; it can get "noisy" here, but it's also one of the most "provocative" settings around; P.S. "valet parking is recommended."

LA MER   27 | 28 | 27 | $78
Halekulani Hotel, 2199 Kalia Rd. (Lewers St.), 808-923-2311; www.halekulani.com

Both the "breathtaking" location overlooking "seductive" ocean waves and the royal service at this "landmark" in Honolulu's Halekulani Hotel are "unforgettable", as is "each bite" of chef Yves Garnier's "delectable" New French cuisine "with an island touch"; in short, it's "a taste of heaven" – so even if you need to wear a jacket and the "cost rivals that of NY's" top eateries, it's the "ultimate special date" choice.

L'Uraku   24 | 23 | 23 | $42
Uraku Tower, 1341 Kapiolani Blvd. (Piikoi St.), 808-955-0552; www.luraku.com

Since the departure of original chef Hiroshi Fukui in 2004, the quality of his "eclectic menu", along with "his unique presentations" of Pacific Rim "fusion food that works", have remained "excellent" at this Ala Moana eatery; the "upside-down", "hand-painted" umbrellas hanging from the ceiling and "attentive service" continue to draw fans back, as does a $28 weekend brunch buffet.

Michel's   25 | 26 | 25 | $64
Colony Surf Hotel, 2895 Kalakaua Ave. (Poni Moi Rd.), 808-923-6552; www.michelshawaii.com

It's "the place to go if you're in love" sigh surveyors who relish the "fantastic sunsets" and the "music of the surf caressing the shore" at this Classic French in the Colony Surf Hotel at the foot of Diamond Head; it's "dressy by Waikiki standards" (jackets for men are "requested but not required") and some say it "costs a bundle" – it's "only worth it if you have the view" – but others would happily return to feast on "sumptuous" standards like "steak Diane done tableside" and served by an "impeccable" "tuxedoed staff."

Olive Tree Café ⊭   23 | 10 | 15 | $17
4614 Kilauea Ave. (Pahoa Ave.), 808-737-0303

For "fabulous" and "authentic" Greek-Mediterranean fare, including "phenomenal fish souvlaki", head to this "popular neighborhood hangout" in Kahala, where "the counter service" and BYO policy keep the "prices low"; "parking and seating can be hard" and there's little decor, but it's "definitely worth" waiting amid "madhouse crowds" to sample this "hidden treasure."

Orchids   26 | 27 | 26 | $57
Halekulani Hotel, 2199 Kalia Rd. (Lewers St.), 808-923-2311; www.halekulani.com

With "amazing breakfasts", a "fantastic Sunday brunch" and a "view over the water at sunset that couldn't be any better", this open-air, beachside American in the Halekulani Hotel (just down-stairs from La Mer) is a "relaxing" choice; so "sip the most fabulous mai tai", feast on "superb" fare served by an "impeccable" staff, listen to the "lapping waves" and be "transported."

Pineapple Room   24 | 18 | 21 | $35
*Macy's, Ala Moana Shopping Ctr., 1450 Ala Moana Blvd. (Atkinson Dr.),
808-945-6573; www.alanwongs.com*
"Mega-talented" chef Alan Wong's "little-known outpost" is "oddly located" in the Ala Moana Shopping Center Macy's ("a gift to the ladies who lunch"); the "master's touch" is discernible in the "excellent" Hawaii Regional fare, especially the "to-die-for Kahlua pig BLT", but the prices "will leave some padding in your wallet" compared to his eponymous King Street spot; still, sour sorts snap over "inconsistent service" and a "view of the rooftop mall parking" lot; P.S. "reservations are a must."

ROY'S   26 | 21 | 24 | $50
*6600 Kalanianaole Hwy. (Keahole St.), 808-396-7697;
www.roysrestaurant.com*
This "original" Hawaii Kai "flagship" (of a 30-plus location chain) "put Hawaii Regional cuisine on the culinary map" and continues to thrill with its "unpretentious, eye-appealing and always delicious" offerings and seemingly "choreographed" service; while some suggest dining in the "quieter" downstairs section, others say "come early", head upstairs and "watch the beautiful sunset."

Roy's Ko Olina   26 | 23 | 25 | $47
*Ko Olina Resort & Marina, 92-1220 Aliinui Dr. (Kamoana Pl.),
Kapolei, 808-676-7697; www.roysrestaurant.com*
"There's a reason Roy has become so ubiquitous" in the islands, the Mainland and abroad: "fabulous" Hawaii Regional fare with "twists" and "creativity" that differ from location to location; for some, this Kapolei outpost is even "better than the [Honolulu] original" due to its "beautiful setting overlooking the Ko Olina Golf Course", its aloha "hospitality" and its "fabulous" fare (especially the signature macadamia-encrusted mahi mahi); so even if it's far away, most find it "well worth the drive"; N.B. also open for lunch.

Ruth's Chris Steak House   25 | 21 | 23 | $55
*Restaurant Row, 500 Ala Moana Blvd. (bet. Punchbowl & South Sts.),
808-599-3860; www.ruthschris.com*
"If you want a good steak" served "exactly how you like it", this chainster is "the place to go"; with dishes "generous enough for the local army", a "comfortable", "clubby" atmosphere on Restaurant Row and a "courteous" staff, it attracts locals as well as expense-accounters for a "very urban" yet "genteel" dining experience; N.B. a second location is set to open in Waikiki's soon-to-be-completed Beach Walk development.

Sansei Seafood   24 | 18 | 21 | $41
Restaurant & Sushi Bar
*Waikiki Beach Marriott Resort & Spa, 2552 Kalakaua Ave.
(Kapahulu Ave.), 808-931-6286; www.sanseihawaii.com*
For "a bit of sushi heaven" in "the islands", head to this "innovative" Pacific Rim–Japanese in the Waikiki Beach Marriott Resort & Spa, where everything from crispy Asian seafood ravioli to "fresh, fresh, fresh" sashimi is prepared by chef-owner D.K. Kodama and "his mom", who started the chain on Maui; the "cool,

mod" joint gets crowded with "locals lining up for early-bird specials" and visitors digging into those "generous portions", and diners are advised to call ahead for information on happy-hour and late-night bargains.

3660 on the Rise Ⓜ   26 20 24 $50
3660 Waialae Ave. (Wilhelmina Rise), 808-737-1177;
www.3660.com
The "innovative" Pacific Rim cuisine of chef Russell Siu, a "master of food and wine", "amazes" diners at this Kaimuki "favorite" where the menu includes an "ahi katsu appetizer that will melt in your mouth", a "to-die-for bread pudding" and a "delicious" lychee martini brought to table by an "engaging", "informal" staff; there's "no view" and the interior "looks like a coffee shop" to some, but others counter "who cares?" – this one "rises" higher than most.

town Ⓢ   – – – M
3435 Waialae Ave. (9th St.), 808-735-5900; www.townkaimuki.com
Restaurant-filled Waialae's latest addition has a hi-tech ambiance (concrete floors, highly polished steel tables) that's drawing a hip crowd to sample chef-owner Ed Kenney's contemporary Italian fare made with fresh, organic ingredients; along with lunch and dinner, the newcomer also serves breakfast Monday–Saturday, so drop by at any time of the day for a seat in the orange-and-white dining room or outside on the lanai.

Houston

TOP FOOD RANKING

Restaurant	Cuisine
28 Mark's American	New American
27 Da Marco	Italian
Brennan's	Creole
Bistro Moderne	French Bistro
Pappas Bros.	Steakhouse
Chez Nous	French
26 Cafe Annie	Southwestern
Frenchie's	Italian
Indika	Indian
Vic & Anthony's	Steakhouse
Remington, The	New American
Tony's	Continental
Churrascos	South American
Fogo de Chão	Brazilian/Steakhouse
Bank by Jean-Georges	Asian/New French
25 Kiran's	Indian
Strip House	Steakhouse
Capital Grille	Steakhouse
Shade	Eclectic/New Amer.
Artista	New American

OTHER NOTEWORTHY PLACES

Américas	South American
Backstreet Café	New American
benjy's	New American
Cafe Red Onion	Central/S. American
Carrabba's	Italian
Charivari	Continental
Fleming's Prime	Steakhouse
Goode Co. Texas Seafood	Seafood
Gravitas	New American
Hugo's	Mexican
Ibiza	Med./Spanish
Julia's Bistro	Nuevo Latino
La Griglia	Italian
Mockingbird Bistro	New American
Otilia's	Mexican
Pesce	Seafood
Quattro	Italian
Rainbow Lodge	New Amer./Seafood
t'afia	New American
Tony Mandola's	Seafood

subscribe to zagat.com

Américas ⧉   25 | 26 | 22 | $41 |

The Pavilion, 1800 Post Oak Blvd. (bet. San Felipe St. &
Westheimer Rd.), 713-961-1492; www.cordua.com
With "over-the-top" decor so "whimsical" it sends fans on flights
of fancy ("Dr. Seuss goes Mayan", "Disney on Quaaludes"), the
Cordúa family's "high-end" Galleria-area standby is an undisputed showplace; fortunately the "unforgettable" South
American specialties ("melt-in-your-mouth" churrasco steaks,
"amazing tres leches cake") are equally "dazzling" and well presented by an "attentive" staff; just be ready for the "ambient din."

Artista Ⓜ   25 | 25 | 23 | $41 |

Hobby Center for the Performing Arts, 800 Bagby St. (Walker St.),
713-278-4782; www.cordua.com
"The theater has a tough act to follow" applaud admirers of the
Cordúa family's "minimalist" New American in Downtown's Hobby
Center, featuring an ensemble of "stunning urban views" and
"superb", "creative" fare that spotlights the "tastes of South
America"; though the eclectic menu "confuses" some and parking
can be "tough", it's "ideal" for a curtain-conscious clientele.

Backstreet Café   24 | 22 | 21 | $32 |

1103 S. Shepherd Dr. (W. Clay St.), 713-521-2239; www.backstreetcafe.net
"Good ol' Southern food with a creative flair" – paired with
"exquisite" wines and served up by a "knowledgeable" staff –
attracts aficionados to this River Oaks New American "gem"; its
"laid-back" yet "sophisticated" setting with a "fabulous" courtyard
provides the "perfect atmosphere" for "a quiet business lunch or
a romantic dinner"; N.B. the "Sunday jazz brunch is wonderful."

Bank by Jean-Georges   26 | 26 | 24 | $53 |

Hotel Icon, 220 Main St. (Franklin St.), 832-667-4470; www.hotelicon.com
Yes, *that* Jean-Georges – Vongerichten – is behind this "top-
notch" showplace ensconced in the lobby of the historic
Downtown bank building that became the Hotel Icon; respondents rave that the "sublime" Asian–New French fusion cuisine
("amazing taste sensations" designed for "sophisticated palates") is matched by the "lush, decadent" decor ("take people
you want to impress"); the downside, say diners, is the *haute*
pricing – the place is "aptly named" because "you'll need a
mortgage to pay for your meal."

benjy's   23 | 20 | 20 | $31 |

2424 Dunstan St. (Kelvin Dr.), 713-522-7602; www.benjys.com
A "stark"-looking space in Rice Village, this New American
retains its "devoted following" with a "classy" menu of "creative",
"tasty" multinational munchies (including a "terrific" weekend
brunch) and a "cool" upstairs lounge; still, some say the eats are
"overshadowed" by the "see-and-be-seen" scene ("the better
you look, the better time you'll have") and that the servers, though
"knowledgeable" and "cheerful", can be "detached."

BISTRO MODERNE   27 | 26 | 24 | $52 |

Hotel Derek, 2525 West Loop S. (Westheimer Rd.), 713-297-4383;
www.bistromoderne.com
In its latest incarnation ("third time's the charm"), this "refreshing"
Galleria-area bistro at the Hotel Derek is practically a "piece of
Paris right here in the Lone Star State" – its "innovative", "so-

phisticated" French cuisine is proffered by "first-rate" servers in a "chic" room populated with "beautiful people"; *amis* assert that this "winner" is even "worth the aggravation" of trying to navigate the "impossible intersection" outside.

BRENNAN'S OF HOUSTON 27 26 26 $48

3300 Smith St. (Stuart St.), 713-522-9711;
www.brennanshouston.com

For a "true taste of N'Awlins", this Midtown "tradition" is a "must" for its "extravagant", "refined" Texas-inflected Creole cuisine, its "unmatched" 500-label wine cellar and an "elegant", "aristocratic" atmosphere that, of course, includes "exquisite service"; though weekenders relish the "decadent jazz brunch", regulars who "go there to be pampered" report dinner at the private kitchen table is "a marvelous experience"; N.B. jackets preferred.

CAFE ANNIE ☒ 26 24 25 $59

1728 Post Oak Blvd. (San Felipe St.), 713-840-1111;
www.cafe-annie.com

"Still grand" swoon supporters of chef/co-owner Robert Del Grande's Galleria-area "classic" – now over a quarter-century old – where the chef-owner's "inventive", "beautifully presented" and "incredibly delicious" Southwestern cuisine is paired with a wine list "as wide and deep as the Gulf"; the "treasure map" of a menu is matched by "professional and discreet service" and "posh" surroundings that provide "first-rate people-watching"; yet after so many years of "superior quality", some sense a "downhill" drift and suggest this "pricey" place is "resting on its laurels."

Cafe Red Onion 24 18 20 $22

1111 Eldridge Pkwy. (Enclave Pkwy.), 281-293-7500
3910 Kirby Dr. (Southwest Frwy./Hwy. 59 S.), 713-807-1122
12440 Northwest Frwy. (43rd St.), 713-957-0957 ☒
www.caferedonion.com

With outposts in Cypress Fairbanks, Upper Kirby and West Houston, this "fun, funky" trio is a "must-try" for its "adventurous" South and Central American *comida* (e.g. "eye-opening" pineapple salsa, "great seafood enchiladas") "elegantly presented" by a "friendly staff"; unsurprisingly, these "lively" locales can get "noisy and crowded" on weekends.

Capital Grille, The 25 25 24 $55

5365 Westheimer Rd. (Yorktown St.), 713-623-4600;
www.thecapitalgrille.com

Carnivores call this national chain link in Houston the embodiment of the "classic Texas steakhouse", with "fabulous" meat, "huge" sides, an "excellent" wine selection and "devoted", "timely but unobtrusive" service; the "plush", "clubby" ambiance and "expensive" fare befit business dinners – "don't forget your platinum card" – though a cadre of critics calls the meatery "overrated" and "pretentious"; N.B. dinner only.

CARRABBA'S ITALIAN GRILL 23 20 21 $25

Champions Village, 5440 FM 1960 W. (Champion Forest Dr.),
281-397-8255
7540 Hwy. 6 N. (Longenbaugh Dr.), 281-859-9700
11339 Katy Frwy. (N. Wilcrest Dr.), 713-464-6595
3115 Kirby Dr. (Branard St.), 713-522-3131

(continued)

CARRABBA'S ITALIAN GRILL
1399 S. Voss Rd. (bet. San Felipe & Woodway Drs.), 713-468-0868
750 Kingwood Dr. (Chestnut Ridge Rd.), Kingwood, 281-358-5580
2335 Hwy. 6 S. (Southwest Frwy.), Sugar Land, 281-980-4433
25665 North Frwy. (Rayford Rd.), The Woodlands, 281-367-9423
502 W. Bay Area Blvd. (I-45), Webster, 281-338-0574
www.carrabbas.com
Loyalists insist that the two "still-family-owned" locations (Upper Kirby District and Galleria) in this group – now an Outback subsidiary – are "far superior" to their brethren, with "outstanding" "classic" Italian dishes and "personal" service in a "warm, friendly" if often "noisy" atmosphere; the other branches, equally loud, are labeled "consistent", with "unusually competent" service and "tasty" food that's a "decent value."

Charivari ⓩ   25 | 19 | 24 | $40
2521 Bagby St. (McGowen St.), 713-521-7231; www.charivarirest.com
"Serious foodies" seek out this "undiscovered gem" in Midtown for "refined" Continental cuisine – including "excellent" seasonal menus emphasizing "white asparagus, wild mushrooms, truffles and other goodies" – delivered by a "friendly, effective" staff; the "old-world charm" extends to the place's "cozy, quiet" ambiance, though a few nouveau noshers term it "a bit stuffy" ("one feels compelled to produce a Medicare card at the door").

Chez Nous ⓩ   27 | 23 | 26 | $50
217 S. Ave. G (Staitti St.), Humble, 281-446-6717;
www.cheznousfrenchrestaurant.com
For "magnificent" French cuisine "prepared to perfection" ("every plate a work of art"), even far-flung foodies will "drive two hours on a fairly regular basis" to this chef-owned Humble "favorite" whose "intimate" atmosphere is enhanced by staffers who "make you feel like they want you there"; the only caveat is that this "jewel" – set in a residential neighborhood – can be "difficult to find."

Churrascos   26 | 21 | 22 | $37
Shepherd Sq., 2055 Westheimer Rd. (S. Shepherd Dr.), 713-527-8300
9705 Westheimer Rd. (Gessner Rd.), 713-952-1988
www.cordua.com
It's a trip to "Buenos Aires minus the airfare" proclaim gourmet gauchos who gallop over to chef-owner Michael Cordúa's "still fabulous" South American duo in Upper Kirby and West Houston; the namesake "mouthwatering" steaks "you can cut with a fork" are a "carnivore's delight", the sides and appetizers are "delicious" ("nothing beats those plantain chips") and the regional wines are "excellent"; factor in "prompt", "professional service" in "upscale" surroundings, and you've got "a Houston tradition"; P.S. the $15 three-course lunch is a "bargain."

DA MARCO ⓩ Ⓜ   27 | 21 | 24 | $50
1520 Westheimer Rd. (Ridgewood St.), 713-807-8857;
www.damarcohouston.com
Thanks to "amazing, sophisticated" *cucina* ("wonderful fried artichokes", "first-class" pasta, "consistently fabulous" entrees), most maintain chef/co-owner Marco Wiles' "intimate" Montrose "villa" is "easily the best Italian in town"; they credit "flawless"

execution, a "short" but "great" wine list, an "unpretentious atmosphere" and "knowledgeable" servers, but note that "excellence" has its price: "traffic jams" in the "tiny" bar, "cramped" seating and a "migraine-inducing" din.

Fleming's Prime Steakhouse & Wine Bar
25 | 23 | 23 | $50

River Oaks Ctr., 2405 W. Alabama St. (Kirby Dr.), 713-520-5959
The Woodlands Mall, 1201 Lake Woodlands Dr. (I-45),
The Woodlands, 281-362-0103
www.flemingssteakhouse.com

Contented carnivores have no beef with these "upscale" yet "laid-back" steakhouses, claiming they "do everything well": the "high-quality" rib-eyes are "delicious" and the wine list "extensive", while "cheerful" staffers "make you feel like kings and queens"; though a few find these places "noisy" and "overpriced", most consider this chain a "can't-miss" choice.

Fogo de Chão
26 | 21 | 25 | $51

8250 Westheimer Rd. (Dunvale Rd.), 713-978-6500;
www.fogodechao.com

An "insane onslaught" of flesh fare is ferried on skewers by "super-attentive gauchos" and paired with an "amazing salad bar" that "will even get respect from carnivores" at this "temple of gluttony" in West Houston, a "Brazilian-import" chain link that remains "true to its original concept"; its "all-the-meat-you-can-eat gimmick attracts lots of businessmen (not so many businesswomen) on expense accounts", but remember that it's "not for vegetarians – or the fainthearted."

Frenchie's ⊠
26 | 13 | 23 | $24

1041 NASA Pkwy. (Egret Bay Blvd.), 281-486-7144

"Despite the name", Italian's the game at this "casual", family-owned and family-friendly Clear Lake "standard" where "NASA eats lunch" and astronaut pics adorn the walls; regulars "treasure" the "tasty" *cucina* that comes in "huge", "steaming-hot" portions, and though the "popular" place can be a "zoo", service is "fast."

Goode Co. Texas Seafood
23 | 18 | 19 | $24

10211 Katy Frwy./I-10 W. (Gessner Dr.), 713-464-7933
2621 Westpark Dr. (Kirby Dr.), 713-523-7154
www.goodecompany.com

Goode friends gloat this pair of pescatoria "proves that Texas food can be excellent even if it's not barbecue or Mexican"; the "fresh" and "perfectly seasoned" fish comes in many forms ("don't leave without trying" the signature campechana) along with other Gulf Coast specialties ("good-as-it-gets" gumbo) ferried by "quick" servers; also transporting is the vehicle-themed decor – West U's "neat old" converted train car and an "antique racing boat" at the "more upscale" Memorial location.

Gravitas
22 | 18 | 16 | $34

807 Taft St. (McKinney St.), 713-522-0995; www.gravitasrestaurant.com

Owner-slash-"food genius" Scott Tycer lends his air of gravitas to this "hot" Midtown bistro, a "hip", "stark" space spotlighting "inventive" New American fare and "interesting" wines; prices are "reasonable" and "prospects look bright", but for now many diagnose "growing pains", as evidenced by "uneven", "uninformed" service and "terrible acoustics."

Hugo's
23 | 22 | 20 | $34

1600 Westheimer Rd. (Mandell St.), 713-524-7744;
www.hugosrestaurant.net

It's "not Tex-Mex", it's "haute Mexican" at chef/co-owner Hugo
Ortega's "sophisticated", "upscale" Montrose establishment,
where the "brilliant, innovative spins" on regional cuisine are
complemented by "killer" wine and tequila lists and "terrific"
margaritas; thanks in part to "accommodating" servers, the
"urban-chic" restored building is imbued with a "wonderful,
festive air", especially at Sunday brunch when there's "great live
music from local mariachi bands."

Ibiza
24 | 22 | 22 | $36

2450 Louisiana St. (McGowen St.), 713-524-0004;
www.ibizafoodandwinebar.com

Intrigued oenophiles do "double takes" when they see the "practically give-away prices" on this Midtowner's 500-label wine list,
but the "buzzy", "happening" Iberian is also favored by the "young
and beautiful" for its "creative" and "savory" Spanish-Med fare
("innovative small plates") served by "knowledgeable", "friendly"
personnel; as a result, this "trendy" yet "comfortable" setting
remains "popular for business lunches" and pre-theater dining.

Indika ☒ Ⓜ
26 | 22 | 24 | $32

516 Westheimer Rd. (Whitney St.), 713-984-1725; www.indikausa.com

Recently relocated to Montrose digs, chef-owner Anita
Jaisinghani's Indian "jewel" continues to "challenge diners" with
"sophisticated, stylized cuisine" – so "imaginative" that at times
it's "more like fusion" – matched with a "surprisingly good" wine
list; "prompt", "helpful" servers "explain everything", so even
"neophytes [can] make delicious choices."

Julia's Bistro ☒
22 | 19 | 20 | $33

3722 Main St. (W. Alabama St.), 713-807-0090; www.juliasbistro.com

"For a sophisticated business lunch" or "distinctive" dinner with
"out-of-towners", amigos opt for this "imaginative" Midtown
Nuevo Latino where the "eclectic flavors" of the "delicious"
grilled meats and fish (plus the many "unique sides") spice up a
setting that's "clean and modern" if a touch "industrial"; service
can be "rough around the edges", but staffers do "try hard."

Kiran's
25 | 23 | 23 | $30

4100 Westheimer Rd. (Midlane St.), 713-960-8472;
www.kiranshouston.com

At this "attractive" colonial-style Galleria-area subcontinental,
chef-owner Kiran Verma "loves her work and it shows"; her
"first-class", "seasoned-to-perfection" "aromatic delights"
"take Indian cuisine to new heights" with the help of an "affordable, varied" 400-label wine list; service is usually "efficient and
friendly" to boot; P.S. the "five-course tasting menu may well be
[the Houston area's] best restaurant value."

La Griglia
23 | 22 | 21 | $34

River Oaks Ctr., 2002 W. Gray St. (bet. McDuffie St. & Shephard Dr.),
713-526-4700; www.lagrigliarestaurant.com

Paesani praise this "boisterous", mural-filled River Oaks Italian
for the "finest seafood" and "excellent" free pizza bread, ably
served to an "elite" clientele; the "fabulous" bar is a "hot scene"

as well, but din-sensitive diners should "bring earplugs"; P.S. since its sale to the Landry's empire, some find the place "about the same", yet many fret quality and service have "dropped like a lead balloon."

MARK'S AMERICAN CUISINE | 28 | 26 | 27 | $55 |

1658 Westheimer Rd. (bet. Dunlavy & Ralph Sts.), 713-523-3800; www.marks1658.com

Worshipers at this converted Montrose church – a "cathedral to food" anointed Houston's No. 1 for Food and Popularity – sing hosannas over chef/co-owner Mark Cox's "breathtaking", "divinely inspired" seasonal New American creations ("amazing presentations") and "outstanding" 275-label wine list; the "spectacular" setting and "impeccable" service are two more reasons rhapsodic respondents christen this a downright "religious experience, as it should be"; yes, it's "expensive" ("you'll need to pray for a raise at work") and often "noisy", but most wouldn't alter a thing.

Mockingbird Bistro | 24 | 20 | 23 | $39 |

1985 Welch St. (bet. Hazard & McDuffie Sts.), 713-533-0200; www.mockingbirdbistro.com

River Oaks' "excellent neighborhood hideaway" has surveyors warbling the praises of its "creative", "upscale" New American cuisine and a "superb" 500-label wine list that can be explicated by "knowledgeable" servers; the "quasi-monastery" decor, though, gets mixed reviews: some find it "quaint", "eclectic" and "charming", others "weird" and "unpleasant" ("it looks like a cross between a cathouse and a diner").

Otilia's Ⓜ | 25 | 12 | 19 | $14 |

7710 Long Point Rd. (Wirt Rd.), 713-681-7203; www.otilias.com

Folks will tell ya they love this "out-of-the-way" Spring Branch "family favorite" – a converted Whataburger that's recently been expanded – for its "excellent" regional Mexican fare ("awesome" chile en nogada, "real-deal" mole) that "cannot be duplicated at any chain"; plus, there are "great staffers" to serve it all up in a simple, colorful setting.

PAPPAS BROS. STEAKHOUSE Ⓢ | 27 | 24 | 25 | $57 |

5839 Westheimer Rd. (Fountain View Dr.), 713-780-7352; www.pappasbros.com

"There is a lot of competition", but cognoscenti confide that this handsome Houston steakhouse stands out from the herd thanks to "perfectly cooked" "slabs o' cow", "tasty sides", a "comprehensive wine cellar", "sommeliers who truly know what they're talking about" and "attentive, respectful" servers who "treat everyone like a VIP"; a vocal few, however, brand this "overpriced", "inconsistent" spot a bum steer.

Pesce Ⓢ | 23 | 24 | 21 | $47 |

Upper Kirby Shopping Ctr., 3029 Kirby Dr. (W. Alabama St.), 713-522-4858; www.pescehouston.com

Pescavores are hooked on the "wonderful" fin fare and "pristine" oysters at this "reliable" Upper Kirby District seafooder, which boasts an "elegant" environment with a marble bar, "starched linens" and a "beautiful aquarium"; service ranges from "wonderful" to "pretentious", though, and both noise and cost can be high.

Quattro   25 | 25 | 25 | $51 |

Four Seasons Hotel Houston, 1300 Lamar St. (Austin St.), 713-276-4700; www.fourseasons.com

A "must for gourmands", this Italian at Downtown's Four Seasons (hence the name) is as "excellent" as "you'd expect from" this posh hotel chain – to wit, "spectacular" cuisine, hundreds of wines, "first-class" service and an "exceptionally tasteful" atmosphere "perfect for business lunches" or an "exquisite" Sunday brunch; the bar's "popular" happy hour also attracts nearby office workers.

Rainbow Lodge Ⓜ   24 | 28 | 24 | $46 |

1 Birdsall St. (Memorial Dr.), 713-861-8666; www.rainbow-lodge.com

"They got game!" assert admirers of this "stunning" "forest lodge" in River Oaks sporting "rustic-chic" interiors (wood, antiques, hunting and fishing gear and "mounted animal heads"), "picturesque" bayou views and "lush grounds"; "knockout wild game" "abounds" on the New American menu too (duck, elk, venison, boar) along with "highly recommended" seafood; service can be spot-on or "spotty", however, and you may need a pot of gold at the end of this rainbow – the tabs can be "expensive."

Remington, The   26 | 25 | 27 | $51 |

St. Regis Hotel, 1919 Briar Oaks Ln. (San Felipe Rd.), 713-403-2631; www.theremingtonrestaurant.com

This comparatively "unsung" New American in Houston's St. Regis Hotel triggers a 21-gun salute in honor of its "impeccable" staff's "unobtrusive" ministrations; the "meticulous" chef's "melt-in-your-mouth" cookery and the recently "updated" lipstick-red dining room are more reasons why this "oasis" is deemed "great" for a "romantic rendezvous" (or "people-watching" in the dark, wood-paneled bar), even if its elevated prices elevate some eyebrows.

Shade   25 | 21 | 21 | $32 |

250 W. 19th St. (Rutland St.), 713-863-7500; www.shadeheights.com

Fans feel they have it made in the shade at this "hip" "minimalist" Eclectic–New American "destination" in the Heights – "a breath of fresh air" "without a trace of stuffiness" thanks to "adventurous" yet "unpretentious" cuisine, a "laid-back" bar and a "narrow urban patio", plus "friendly, knowledgeable" service that includes the input of a "top-notch" sommelier; though a few take a dim view of the "long waits", most think it's all cool.

Strip House   25 | 25 | 23 | $52 |

The Shops at Houston Ctr., 1200 McKinney St. (San Jacinto St.), 713-659-6000; www.theglaziergroup.com

Patrons lick their chops at this "pricey" Downtowner where "strip means more than steak"; "flavorful" cuts of meat and "great" wines are served by a "sharp" crew in a "bordello" setting tricked out with "extremely sexy" "naked-lady" artifacts (e.g. photos of vintage burlesque queens, as at the NYC original); the theme – "risqué" and "edgy" to some, "hackneyed" "'50s-style porn" to others – has all agreeing it's "probably not a place to bring the family."

t'afia Ⓢ Ⓜ   24 | 17 | 22 | $40 |

3701 Travis St. (bet. W. Alabama & Winbern Sts.), 713-524-6922; www.tafia.com

Devotees are daffy about "culinary alchemist" chef/co-owner Monica Pope's Midtown "gem" where she conjures up "cutting-edge", "foodies'-delight" New American cuisine out of "wonderfully fresh" local ingredients and pairs it with a "terrific" Texas-accented wine list; most appreciate the efforts of "welcoming" staffers in the "hip", "minimalist", "loftlike" room, though a minority shrugs the whole scene's too "austere", "noisy" and "avant-garde"; N.B. there's a farmer's market here on Saturday mornings.

Tony Mandola's Gulf Coast Kitchen   24 | 18 | 22 | $33 |
River Oaks Ctr., 1962 W. Gray St. (McDuffie St.), 713-528-3474; www.tonymandolas.com
"You can't go wrong" with this "dependable" River Oaks seafooder's "delectable variety" of Gulf Coast-style shellfish, its "perfectly seasoned" slaw or gumbo that'll "make you weep"; chef-owner "Tony runs a tight ship" in this "lively", "friendly" "hangout", so though a few find the fare "overpriced", "no one seems to care."

Tony's ⊠   26 | 26 | 26 | $64 |
3755 Richmond Ave. (Timmons Ln.), 713-622-6778; www.tonyshouston.com
Recently relocated to a "sumptuous", "modern" space "with great art and a water wall", this tony Greenway Plaza–area "standard" is still the "best place to see and be seen" say the socially conscious; "exceptional" Continental cuisine is complemented by a "first-class wine list", and "the welcome is always gracious" even if the "excellent" service is occasionally "intrusive"; mere mortals find the vibe "snobby" and prices "very high" unless they're "celebrating special occasions."

Vic & Anthony's   26 | 26 | 24 | $53 |
1510 Texas Ave. (La Branch St.), 713-228-1111; www.vicandanthonys.com
A "guys' kinda place", this Downtown steakhouse near the "MLB and NBA venues" bases its appeal on "outstanding" steaks, a "variety of non-beef alternatives", "rich, decadent sides" and "excellent wines", all served up by an "obliging staff"; the "luxurious", "clubby" atmosphere also features a "terrific" bar that "makes you feel like Sinatra in 1962", so despite "close-together" tables, a "high" noise level and "astronomical" prices, a meal here is an "enjoyable" experience; N.B. lunch on Fridays only.

Kansas City

TOP FOOD RANKING

	Restaurant	Cuisine
27	Bluestem	New American
26	Stroud's	American
	Oklahoma Joe's	Barbecue
	Le Fou Frog	French Bistro
	American Rest.	New American
	Fiorella's Jack Stack	Barbecue
	Tatsu's	French
	Starker's Reserve	New American
	Danny Edwards'	Barbecue
25	Plaza III	Steakhouse

OTHER NOTEWORTHY PLACES

Restaurant	Cuisine
Café Maison	French Bistro
Café Sebastienne	New American
Circe	New American
40 Sardines	New American
Grand St. Cafe	Eclectic
Lidia's	Northern Italian
McCormick & Schmick's	Seafood
1924 Main	New American
Room 39	American
zin	New American

	F	D	S	C

AMERICAN RESTAURANT ☒   26 | 25 | 27 | $52
Crown Ctr., 200 E. 25th St. (Grand Ave.), 816-545-8000;
www.theamericanrestaurantkc.com
"Superb service" helps to make this "showpiece" at Hallmark's
Crown Center an "institution" and a "favorite of professionals and
gourmets alike" – especially now that "imaginative" toque Celina
Tio has "invigorated" the New American menu to go with the "excellent" 1,500-label wine list; "you feel grand gliding down the
staircase" into the "cathedral-like" dining room with its "magnificent" city views, although some snipe the "'80s decor" needs a
"face-lift"; P.S. at $24, the "three-course prix fixe lunch is a steal."

BLUESTEM   27 | 23 | 23 | $41
900 Westport Rd. (Roanoke Rd.), 816-561-1101; www.bluestemkc.com
Named after a variety of prairie grass, this "sophisticated" New
American set in the "simple, clean", "urban comfort" of an "intimate" Westport space has been voted KC's No. 1 for Food courtesy of "eclectic, adventurous" dishes that "balance the flavors"
of "local seasonal items" to "sublime" effect; for those who feel
the meals are a bit "expensive", there's now a chic but comfortable wine lounge serving signature cocktails and plenty of
appetizers priced under $10.

Café Maison　　　　　　　– | – | – | E
408 E. 63rd St. (Oak St.), 816-523-3400; www.cafemaisonkc.com
Brookside denizens have already discovered this bistro addition from chef-owner Ryan Kelly and his fiancée-partner Desiree Stone, where a Gallic lunch and dinner menu featuring dishes like seared foie gras served with toasted cinnamon brioche make way on Sunday afternoons for a set-price buffet brunch; there's also colorful, country-esque decor and a wine list that's understandably rich with French selections.

Café Sebastienne Ⓜ　　　　25 | 25 | 23 | $31
Kemper Museum of Contemporary Art, 4420 Warwick Blvd. (45th St.), 816-561-7740; www.kemperart.org
At this "striking" yet "serene" "urban escape", an "airy", mural-bedecked venue at the Kemper Museum of Contemporary Art near the Country Club Plaza, "outstanding" chef Jennifer Maloney pleases palates with "creative" New American cuisine (the "food they probably serve in heaven") brought around by a "relaxed" staff; prodigious partiers should note, however, that their "nighttime hours are limited" (Friday–Saturday only, until 9:30 PM).

Circe Ⓜ　　　　　　　　– | – | – | M
1715 W. 39th St. (Bell St.), 816-931-0596; www.circekc.com
After stints in other cities (including at NYC's Bouley Bakery), chef-owner Nathan Feldmiller has returned to KC to open this New American on 39th Street's Restaurant Row; the yearling is enchanting diners with straightforward but luxurious dishes – think duck club sandwiches – served in a minimalist space; roast suckling pig dinners on Friday nights add an exotic touch, while a wine list focused on small vintners keeps it simple.

Danny Edwards' Famous　　　26 | 9 | 17 | $14
Kansas City Barbecue Ⓢ
1227 Grand Blvd. (E. 13th St.), 816-283-0880
"Don't dress up" for lunch at second-generation pitmeister Danny Edwards' "git-down" "dump of a place" Downtown, but do expect to eat some of the "best 'cue in the rib capital of the world"; factor in a "friendly staff" and "price-is-right" tabs, and it's obvious why BBQ buffs "wish it were open more"; N.B. it closes at 2:30 PM.

FIORELLA'S JACK STACK　　　26 | 22 | 22 | $22
13441 Holmes Rd. (135th St.), 816-942-9141
101 W. 22nd St. (Wyandotte St.), 816-472-7427
9520 Metcalf Ave. (95th St.), Overland Park, 913-385-7427
www.jackstackbbq.com
"Who says authentic BBQ has to come from a greasy joint with Formica tables?" ask aficionados of this "high-toned" trio where the "posh" interiors perplex purists ("'cue with white linen napkins?") even as the "fork-tender brisket" and the city's "best sides" prove "addictive"; everyone agrees "it's worth the wait" – and given a no-reservations policy, "wait you will"; N.B. a Plaza location is set to open soon in the former K.C. Masterpiece space.

40 Sardines　　　　　　　24 | 21 | 22 | $40
11942 Roe Ave. (W. 119th St.), Overland Park, 913-451-1040;
www.40sardines.com
"Enterprising" chef-owners Michael Smith and Debbie Gold "wow" "epicurean adventurers" at their "refreshing" New

American in Overland Park, whipping up "imaginative and flavorful meals" and offering a "budget-friendly list of $20 wines" as well as a Thursday BYOB with no corkage fee; there's also an "engaging and thoughtful" staff, and though the "industrial but not hip" room can be "abominably noisy when crowded", reviewers report that changes "have improved the acoustics dramatically."

GRAND ST. CAFE   24 | 22 | 24 | $32
4740 Grand St. (47th St.), 816-561-8000; www.eatpbj.com
"Everything from burgers to steak and seafood" is served by a "friendly", "efficient" staff at this "upscale", "upbeat" Eclectic eatery near the Plaza that remains a "lively" "lunch venue for business or pleasure" and a "classic standby" for dinner; "try to sit outside" on the "best patio in town" suggest surveyors who blame "hard surfaces" for indoor "noise", while others ask "is the decor getting tired – or does it just seem that way because we go there so often?"

LE FOU FROG Ⓜ   26 | 19 | 22 | $38
400 E. Fifth St. (Oak St.), 816-474-6060; www.lefoufrog.com
Francophiles are *fou* for this "little bit of Paris" in the River Market area, a "charming", "funky" bistro where chef-owner Mano Rafael whips up "Midwestern portions" of daily-changing Gallic "*gastronomie*" (steak au poivre), plus "unusual" entrees like elk, and a "skillful" staff helps the con*fou*sed peruse "one of KC's finest wine lists"; so though foes fret about the "gritty" neighborhood, "tough-to-find" location and "elbow-to-elbow seating", most maintain the "wonderful meal" is "well worth it."

LIDIA'S   24 | 27 | 23 | $33
101 W. 22nd St. (Baltimore Ave.), 816-221-3722; www.lidiasitaly.com
TV chef and NYC culinary matriarch Lidia Bastianich is the force behind this "spectacular" showplace set in a "rehabbed" "brick station house" (note the "breathtaking" Dale Chihuly chandeliers) in the "revitalizing" Crossroads arts district; *amici* assert the "delicious" Northern Italian eats "sometimes achieve the sublime", while "value-priced" *vinos* are a boon for the "wine-challenged"; but the "disappointed" declare the place "has lost some of its spark", citing "uneven service" and "hit-or-miss" food.

MCCORMICK & SCHMICK'S   25 | 25 | 23 | $36
448 W. 47th St. (Pennsylvania Ave.), 816-531-6800;
www.mccormickandschmicks.com
"Seafood lovers" stranded "1,000 miles from an ocean" are "delighted" by the "staggering array" of "exceptional" fin fare at this Country Club Plaza chainster, voted the Most Popular restaurant in KC; a "happening place" for "movers and shakers" at lunch and "lively fun" after work ("top-notch" $1.95 "happy-hour eats"), this "yuppie" magnet provides "prompt service" and a "pleasant ambiance", plus a "beautiful stained-glass rotunda" and "patio overlooking the Plaza"; even if curmudgeons carp it can be "noisy", "packed" and "pricey", hooked habitués harrumph it's "worth every dollar."

1924 Main   – | – | – | M
1924 Main St. (19th St.), 816-472-1924; www.1924main.com
This New American housed in the lovingly renovated Rieger Building (the original tiled floors remain) brings the prix fixe concept to the Crossroads: for a set $38 ($15 at lunch), diners can

compile their own three-course meal, choosing from several selections at each stage; chef-owner Rob Dalzell's weekly changing menu offers optional wine pairings, while hard-liquor sippers can savor a serious selection of single-malt scotch.

OKLAHOMA JOE'S BARBECUE & CATERING

26 | 9 | 16 | $12

Shamrock Gas Station, 3002 W. 47th Ave. (Mission Rd.), 913-722-3366
11950 South Strang Line Rd. (119th St.), Olathe, 913-782-6858 🅱
www.oklahomajoesbbq.com

"Winners of umpteen contests", the "smoked-arts" practitioners at this Roeland Park favorite (and its Olathe sibling) turn out "moist", "tender, lean" KC-style meats and "fabulous" signature Carolina-style pulled pork; given its "down and dirty" gas station location, customers should keep in mind that there's "limited seating" for the "unlimited line" of 'cue connoisseurs.

PLAZA III THE STEAKHOUSE

25 | 21 | 25 | $43

4749 Pennsylvania Ave. (Ward Pkwy.), 816-753-0000;
www.plazaiiisteakhouse.com

"Great beef and this establishment both prove that some things do get better with aging" laud loyalists of this "old-line" "main-stay" on the Country Club Plaza; it's an "earthy", "dark-wood" den where "any CEO would feel comfortable" thanks to "perfect" porterhouses, a "fabulous" 350-label cellar and an "elegant, charming staff"; meanwhile, recent renovations to the dining room (including the addition of five private rooms) may outdate the above Decor score; P.S. the bar downstairs has the same full menu and "outstanding" jazz.

Room 39 🅱

– | – | – | I

1719 W. 39th St. (Bell St.), 816-753-3939; www.rm39.com

Every day is a daily special at this small West 39th Street American where chef-owners Ted Habiger and Andrew Sloan put a stylized spin on standards (e.g. bacon, egg and cheese panini, crispy root-vegetable fries) for breakfast, lunch and now week-night dinners (Monday–Thursday); if the custom-blended coffee and chai don't wake you up, the colorful walls surely will; N.B. a second location is expected to open in southern Johnson County.

Starker's Reserve 🅱 Ⓜ

26 | 24 | 25 | $45

201 W. 47th St. (Wyandotte St.), 816-753-3565;
www.starkersreserve.com

"Often overlooked" and "underpatronized", this second-story, "top-notch" New American on the Country Club Plaza is an "exquisite" "treasure" say surveyors who savor the "feeling of exclusivity" inside the "romantic", "casual French" room that "looks out on the activity" below; with "outstanding food", an "in-comparable" cellar of more than 1,500 wines and a "wonderful staff" that's "unobtrusive but available", this stalwart helps to make "special occasions" "elegant, intimate" and "memorable."

STROUD'S

26 | 14 | 22 | $19

5410 NE Oak Ridge Dr. (Vivion Rd.), 816-454-9600;
www.stroudsrestaurants.com

"Legendary fried chicken that deserves the rep", served with "otherworldly cream gravy", "extraordinary cinnamon rolls" and other Traditional American favorites "worth traveling long dis-tances for", is the draw at this "living memorial" to "Grandma's

farm cookin'" north of the river (the South KC original has closed);
the large 19th-century homestead offers "country atmosphere",
antique furniture and a live pianist, while "very friendly" staffers
help to keep patrons' spirits up during the "horrific waits";
N.B. no reservations.

Tatsu's   26 19 24 $37
4603 W. 90th St. (Roe Ave.), Prairie Village, 913-383-9801;
www.tatsus.com
"Consistency, thy name is Tatsu", declare visitors to this Prairie
Village "perennial" where the menu "changes very slowly – thank
God"; chef-owner Tatsu Arai continues to create "old-style"
"haute" "French cuisine of the first order" ("poached fish done
perfectly") in his "civilized" restaurant, assisted by an "exemplary"
staff; cutting-edge types crack, however, that the "place and its
clientele have aged together" and claim the "outdated" decor is
in "dire need of a face-lift"; N.B. Arai has opened a smaller, more
casual spinoff in Westport called Tatsu's Café & Bar.

zin Ⓜ   25 22 24 $40
1900 Main St. (19th St.), 816-527-0120; www.zinkc.com
Located in the "blossoming" Crossroads arts district, this "sexy",
"stunning", stripped-down New American with a "cool, urban
feel" "attracts a cultured crowd", especially on "First Fridays
when the galleries are open late"; hipsters dig into "innovative"
and "delicious" seasonal specialties (including a "worth-it" $60
tasting menu) and appreciate the "charming", "attentive" staffers'
"impeccable advice" about the "excellent wine list"; a few critics
cluck, however, that it's all too "trendy with a capital T."

Las Vegas

TOP FOOD RANKING

	Restaurant	Cuisine
28	Rosemary's	New American
	Lotus of Siam	Northern Thai
27	Nobu	Japanese/Peruvian
	Picasso	New French
	Michael Mina	Seafood
	André's	French
	Prime	Steakhouse
26	Steak House	Steakhouse
	Delmonico	Steakhouse
	Sterling Brunch	New American
	SW	Steakhouse
	Fleur de Lys	New French
	Alex	French/Med.
	Medici Café	New American
	Le Cirque	New French
	NOBHILL	Californian
	Bradley Ogden	New American
	Okada	Japanese
	Pamplemousse	French
	Todd's Unique Dining	Eclectic

OTHER NOTEWORTHY PLACES

Restaurant	Cuisine
Alizé	New French
Aureole	New American
Bouchon	French Bistro
Buffet at Bellagio	Eclectic
Capital Grille	Steakhouse
Commander's Palace	Creole
Craftsteak	Seafood/Steakhouse
Daniel Boulud	New French
Eiffel Tower	French
Emeril's New Orleans	Cajun-Creole/Seafood
Firefly	Spanish/Tapas
Gaetano's	Northern Italian
Guy Savoy	New French
Joël Robuchon	New French
L'Atelier Joël Robuchon	New French
Mesa Grill	Southwestern
MIX	French/New Amer.
Osteria del Circo	Northern Italian
Seablue	Seafood
Valentino	Italian

subscribe to zagat.com

Alex Ⓜ | 26 | 27 | 26 | $114 |

*Wynn Las Vegas, 3131 Las Vegas Blvd. S. (Desert Inn Rd.), 702-770-9966;
www.wynnlasvegas.com*

One of Sin City's "very best" chefs, Alex Stratta, has earned the
first-name clout to head up this "Wynn top draw" where diners
"descend a grand staircase" "Dolly Levi"–style to a "lavish",
European-style room to savor "extraordinarily conceived"
French-Med meals served on "gorgeous china"; the staff "goes
out of its way to ensure a wonderful evening", and "perfect
touches" like "the seat-side purse ottoman" for a clientele "who
actually remembers to dress" guarantee a reprieve from "the
shorts-and–flip-flops" "Vegas culture"; N.B. no children under five.

Alizé | 26 | 26 | 25 | VE |

*Palms Casino Hotel, 4321 W. Flamingo Rd. (Arville St.), 702-942-7777;
www.alizelv.com*

"Against all the out-of-town invaders", local institution André
Rochat "holds his own" at his "magical" New French "splurge"
"atop the Palms Hotel" where, "if you can tear your eyes away
from the chef's stunning plates", you're treated to "an awesome,
infinite view of the lights and sights"; in fact, "it's hard to decide
which is more fabulous: the food, the vista", the "impeccable
service" or "a wine list that would make Bacchus cry" – each
is "off the charts"; N.B. they prefer if you don't bring your
children under 10.

André's | 27 | 25 | 26 | $69 |

*Monte Carlo Resort, 3770 Las Vegas Blvd. S. (bet. Harmon &
Tropicana Aves.), 702-798-7151*
401 S. Sixth St. (bet. Bonneville St. & Bridger Ave.), 702-385-5016 Ⓢ
www.andrelv.com

"Go to the original for homey and the hotel for classy", but enjoy
the same "fantastic" French fare at André Rochat's eponymous
eateries in a "rustic, charming" "cottage" Downtown and tucked
behind "sound-proof doors" in a "Louis XIV–style" room in the
Monte Carlo; "everything is rich, rich, rich", but diners "basking
in the full glory of butter, cream and foie gras" "done to perfection" and presented by a "gracious" staff find it all "*magnifique!*"

AUREOLE | 25 | 27 | 24 | $76 |

*Mandalay Bay Resort, 3950 Las Vegas Blvd. S. (Mandalay Bay Rd.),
702-632-7401; www.charliepalmer.com*

"Book your bachelor party" in the "vaulted" front of Charlie
Palmer's Mandalay Bay outpost for a "high-tech, super-sexy"
"dining fantasy" complete with "acrobatic" "angels" "on bun-
gees" "who fetch the good stuff" from the "extravagant wine
tower", or let the "attentive" staff usher you and your date to the
back for a "romantic dinner" "while the swans glide by" outside;
either way, "bring your bank book, as the bill" for the "sublime"
New American offerings and a bottle from the "computerized
wine list" "can rise as high as those lovely" ladies soaring
for your vino.

Bouchon | 24 | 24 | 23 | $57 |

*Venetian Hotel, 3355 Las Vegas Blvd. S. (bet. Flamingo &
Spring Mountain Rds.), 702-414-6200; www.bouchonbistro.com*

"Genius" Thomas Keller "graces Vegas" with this French bistro,
an outpost of the Yountville "classic" in the Venetian Hotel's

Venezia tower "far away" from the "razzmatazz"; "casual gourmands" flock here for "power breakfasts" featuring "light-as-a-feather sourdough waffles" or dinner's "luscious rotisserie chicken", nesting in the "Parisian" interior or on the "lovely" patio; service might be "so-so", but the kitchen "earns" its "buzz" by "proving you don't have to be expensive to be excellent."

Bradley Ogden
26 | 24 | 25 | $80

Caesars Palace, 3570 Las Vegas Blvd. S. (Flamingo Rd.), 702-731-7731; www.caesars.com

"What a treat" to dine at this "wonderful" Caesars casino destination where the "celebrity" namesake "is actually in", "working his wonders" with an "always changing menu" of "deliciously innovative" New American dishes; the "portions are small" but the "flavors are big", and the "impeccable" staff is "without pretension" – it might even give you "a tour of the kitchen" for a "charming" topper to an "elegant but comfortable" evening that's "well worth your hard-earned dollars."

BUFFET AT BELLAGIO, THE
24 | 19 | 19 | $31

Bellagio Hotel, 3600 Las Vegas Blvd. S. (Flamingo Rd.), 702-693-8255; www.bellagio.com

"Loosen your belt good" because "all anyone could want" to eat is "deftly prepared" and "well presented" at the Bellagio's "high-end" Eclectic paean to "pigging out"; the "feast" (from "unlimited cracked crab" and Kobe beef to "Asian specialties like congee" and "exotic choices such as venison") is so "fresh, flavorful and inventive", it "elevates the genre", so despite "hungry" "hordes" and a "banquet-hall" atmosphere, gourmands ask "can I live here?"

Capital Grille, The
25 | 23 | 24 | $58

Fashion Show Mall, 3200 Las Vegas Blvd. S., 3rd fl. (Spring Mountain Rd.), 702-932-6631; www.thecapitalgrille.com

"They take their meat seriously" – and with a wine "list as long as your arm", they treat their vinos the same – at this "white-tablecloth" chophouse chainster upstairs in the Fashion Show Mall; "thick, flavorful" steaks prepared using "classic techniques and sauces" combine with "super" service and a "typically clubby", "dark-wood" room to make for a "power-lunch" destination, with a "phenomenal" city view to boot.

Commander's Palace
25 | 23 | 25 | $57

Desert Passage at Aladdin, 3663 Las Vegas Blvd. S. (Harmon Ave.), 702-892-8272; www.commanderspalace.com

It's "not quite as good as New Orleans", but you can still score "lick-the-plate-good" Creole cuisine in the desert at the Aladdin's "excellent re-creation" of the Louisiana "classic"; the dishes are "sinfully" "delicious", but there's lots more to "put on your happy face" for: lunchtime's "hefty" martinis are a 25-cent "bargain" (as is the $18.80 prix fixe menu), and a band serves "mellow jazz with your turtle soup" during the "excellent" weekend brunch; even better, the "service is so genteel", "it's straight out of the Big Easy."

Craftsteak
25 | 24 | 24 | $70

MGM Grand Hotel, 3799 Las Vegas Blvd. S. (Tropicana Ave.), 702-891-7318; www.mgmgrand.com

"As expected", Tom Colicchio's MGM Grand chop-and-seafood house delivers "superior quality", "flawless execution" and dining empowerment: "choose what your cow ate before" it hit the plate, then "build your own meal with a bountiful selection" of sides to go with your "sublime" beef (or lamb, pork, fowl or fish); the wine list is "tremendous", the "groovy staff" is "helpful" and the "un-Vegas-like setting" ("not old boy, but metrosexual") is as "delightfully unadorned" as the meat; if you can afford the "high prices", you'll "enjoy it immensely."

Daniel Boulud Brasserie | 25 | 25 | 24 | $74 |

Wynn Las Vegas, 3131 Las Vegas Blvd. S. (Desert Inn Rd.), 702-770-9966; www.wynnlasvegas.com
"No matter where Daniel opens restaurants, you can be assured" of an "exceptional" experience, as evidenced by this "magical" New French namesake with a patio overlooking the Wynn's water wall, "lake, trees" and surreal, near-submerged statues; while a few note "the service is not perfected", the restaurant more than makes up for it via "impressive dishes" (including the "famous" "burger stuffed with short ribs") that "have the innovative yet traditional touches you would expect from a Boulud eatery", plus a "chic, relaxing" setting that's "consistent with the db" mode; N.B. no children under five.

DELMONICO STEAKHOUSE | 26 | 23 | 25 | $67 |

Venetian Hotel, 3355 Las Vegas Blvd. S. (bet. Flamingo & Spring Mountain Rds.), 702-414-3737; www.emerils.com
"Everything Emeril touches turns to gold", including this "hunk-of-meat heaven" in the Venetian; the beef is "impeccably aged" and "seasoned to perfection", the wine list is to "drool over" and the sides are so "orgasmic", "even the potato chips are divine"; what's more, the synchronized servers "know how to put on a great show", but the "dark, simple" room could be less "noisy" and "more interesting to match the quality of the fare" – book the pricey chef's table instead "for a feast to be remembered."

Eiffel Tower | 22 | 26 | 22 | $70 |

Paris Las Vegas, 3655 Las Vegas Blvd. S. (bet. Flamingo Rd. & Harmon Ave.), 702-948-6937; www.eiffeltowerrestaurant.com
Want to "fall in love again"? – ride the glass elevator to this "romantic" "special-occasion" destination atop the namesake monument at the Paris and "get a window seat facing the Strip", because "watching the Bellagio water show is dreamy" from above, particularly combined with a "classic" French meal; you may even make "a trip to The Little White Wedding Chapel" afterward, if your mood isn't dampened by "prices as high as the view", "disappointing" dishes and "lookie-loos who interfere with timely service."

Emeril's New Orleans Fish House | 23 | 19 | 22 | $55 |

MGM Grand Hotel, 3799 Las Vegas Blvd. S. (Tropicana Ave.), 702-891-7374; www.emerils.com
"Kick your dinner plans up a notch" at this MGM spot for "oh-my-God"-good, "spicy, down-home Louisiana" seafood, a "bam! bam!" "sign of the times that you can get fantastic food of all sorts in Vegas"; dishes "bursting" with "flavors, colors and textures" match a "trendy" "remodel" (which may outdate the Decor score), while the staff manages to lend "a smaller feel to the huge" space; still, those who find the "TV chef's" empire "spread thin" and "overhyped" say "the trouble with Emeril's is there's no Emeril here."

Firefly ◐ | 23 | 17 | 21 | $29 |
3900 Paradise Rd. (bet. Flamingo Rd. & Twain Ave.), 702-369-3971;
www.fireflylv.com
"Tasty little plates" of "easy-to-share" tapas "keep on comin'" to
your table thanks to "helpful" servers at this East Side Spaniard
that's "nowhere near as stuffy or expensive" as its Strip counter-
parts, and does without those "ringing slot machines", too;
decorwise it may be a bit "blasé inside", so "sit on the patio"
instead, where pitchers of "dangerous" sangria go down easier.

Fleur de Lys | 26 | 26 | 25 | $90 |
Mandalay Bay Resort, 3950 Las Vegas Blvd. S. (Mandalay Bay Rd.),
702-632-9400; www.fleurdelyssf.com
Chef-owner Hubert Keller "nourishes all the senses" at the "Vegas
branch of his SF legend", this "dreamy" "jewel box" in Mandalay
Bay where the "sexy" decor features "3000+ unforgettable pink
roses on the wall", the "out-of-this-world" New French fare is
"artistically impressive" and the "spectacular service" helps
ensure a "peaceful" experience; choose a three-, four- or five-
course "exquisite" prix fixe (or "a vegetarian menu" or an almost-
"daunting" cheese sampling) and pair it with a flight from the
"amazing wine list" to "impress anyone from a date to a client."

Gaetano's | 23 | 22 | 23 | $38 |
Siena Promenade, 10271 S. Eastern Ave. (Siena Heights Dr.),
Henderson, 702-361-1661; www.gaetanoslasvegas.com
"Real class act" 'Tano' Palmeri "makes you feel at home" in his
"wonderfully friendly" yet "elegant" "family-operated" namesake in Henderson where "the customer is first" on the list for
"personal care"; "it's not the cheapest Italian in town", but it's
"worth the price" for "excellent", "authentic Northern" standards and "innovative specials" – even snobs call it "not bad for
a neighborhood place."

Guy Savoy, Restaurant Ⓜ | – | – | – | VE |
Caesars Palace, 3570 Las Vegas Blvd. S. (Flamingo Rd.), 877-346-4642;
www.caesarspalace.com
The renowned Parisian chef introduces his haute New French
cuisine to the U.S. with this branch of his eponymous establishment housed in Caesars Palace; the sleek yet intimate space,
designed by Jean-Michel Wilmotte, includes three private dining
rooms, a chef's table, champagne and wine bar, and glass-
enclosed patio overlooking the Roman Plaza and the Strip; the bill
of Savoy fare features a 10-course tasting 'menu prestige' at
$290, while the wine list boasts some 1,500 labels, primarily from
France; N.B. closed Mondays and Tuesdays.

Joël Robuchon | – | – | – | VE |
MGM Grand Hotel, 3799 Las Vegas Blvd S. (Tropicana Ave.),
702-891-7925; www.mgmgrand.com
Foodies headed to this first stateside restaurant from the ac-
claimed Joël Robuchon aren't likely to be disappointed with the
$350, 16-course tasting menu at his New French fete in the MGM;
à la carte signatures include scallops cooked in their shells with
lemon-and-seaweed butter, Brittany lobster beneath a melting
saffron wafer and confit of lamb with semolina couscous, all supported by a 750-bottle wine list and served in an interior lavishly
reminiscent of a 1930s Parisian mansion; in other words, ooh-la-la.

L'Atelier de Joël Robuchon — | — | — | E |

*MGM Grand Hotel, 3799 Las Vegas Blvd. S. (Tropicana Ave.),
702-891-7358; www.mgmgrand.com*

The more casual of the namesake master chef's two New French
ventures in the MGM, this restaurant offers a small number of tables
plus service around a U-shaped counter for the ultimate open-
kitchen experience; the menu changes seasonally, and specialties include the legendary truffled mashed potatoes, roasted rack
of lamb with thyme, free-range quail stuffed with foie gras and
desserts such as a chartreuse soufflé with pistachio ice cream,
all served amid lively decor accented with red and black.

Le Cirque | 26 | 26 | 25 | $88 |

*Bellagio Hotel, 3600 Las Vegas Blvd. S. (Flamingo Rd.), 702-693-8100;
www.bellagio.com*

"Turn your frown upside down" when you step from the Bellagio
casino into this "elegant" "temple of gastronomy", where ring-
master Sirio Maccioni's "synchronized servers" deliver "superb"
New French cuisine and "delectable desserts", albeit at "steep
prices"; "lusciously colored", overstuffed chairs and banquettes
make the "intimate" room feel like "sitting inside a jewel box",
and a window table ensures a "great view of the fountains" for an
"elegant" evening; P.S. children under 12 are not allowed, so hire
a babysitter and savor a "memorable experience."

LOTUS OF SIAM | 28 | 12 | 21 | $23 |

*Commercial Ctr., 953 E. Sahara Ave. (bet. Maryland Pkwy. &
Paradise Rd.), 702-735-3033; www.lotusofsiamlv.com*

"Take a trip off the beaten path" to this "hole-in-the-wall" "hidden
treasure" east of the Strip and "don't let the location fool you": it
may be in a shopping center, but whatever is "lacking in decor"
is made up for with "transcendental" Northern Thai cuisine, like
beef that will make you "weep with delight", "staggeringly good
tom yum soup" and "ethereal sour sausage"; each "outstanding", "authentic" and yet "inexpensive" dish pairs perfectly with
one of the many German wines ("amazing Rieslings") on offer.

Medici Café | 26 | 26 | 26 | $51 |

*Ritz-Carlton, Lake Las Vegas, 1610 Lake Las Vegas Pkwy.
(Grand Mediterra Blvd.), Henderson, 702-567-4700; www.ritz-carlton.com*

"Far in the boondocks" of Henderson is an "out-of-the-way gem"
where "sublime" New American cuisine is served amid "elegant", silk-and-brocade environs with a "wonderful view" of the
Ritz-Carlton's Florentine gardens; "brunch is delicious", lunch is
"fantastic" and dinner is "a special evening every time", while
the "romantic" setting "provides a serenity that's often hard to
get in Las Vegas."

Mesa Grill | 24 | 22 | 22 | $54 |

*Caesars Palace, 3570 Las Vegas Blvd. S. (Flamingo Rd.), 702-731-7731;
www.caesarspalace.com*

Sure, "it would be nice if [Bobby Flay] were present" (he stops in
once a month or so), but even if he's in NYC, this "impressive"
Caesars "offshoot" of the TV toque's "ultra-creative"
Southwestern flagship is "his place from the time you enter to
leaving"; the seasonal menu's "beautiful presentations" and
"distinctive flavors" "restore your faith in celebrity chefs", and
they're backed up by "personable service" in a "stylish" yet "re-

laxing" space; "if you like a little spice in your meal", this "could become a regular haunt" because it's "flay-bulous!"

MICHAEL MINA
27 | 24 | 26 | $82

Bellagio Hotel, 3600 Las Vegas Blvd. S. (Flamingo Rd.), 702-693-8255; www.michaelmina.net

San Francisco "master chef" Michael Mina feeds fish to the whales (aka "high rollers") at this seafooder, an "inspired" spot for "exquisite" eating *à* "*la mer*" in the Bellagio conservatory; "try the signature" "huge and delicious lobster pot pie" accompanied by a bottle from the "excellent wine list" and "treat yourself with their caviar service"; the dishes are so "outstanding", the service so "congenial" and the space (with open kitchen) so "chic, simple and cosseting" (if "noisy") that the "sky-high prices" are "worth it."

MIX
23 | 27 | 22 | $82

Mandalay Bay Resort, 64th fl., 3950 Las Vegas Blvd. S. (Mandalay Bay Rd.), 702-632-9500; www.chinagrillmgt.com

"Dine in an egg-shaped pod" "in a room straight out of a Kubrick film" with "hundreds of glass spheres hanging from the ceiling", a new lounge and "the best view this side of a Vegas showgirl" from atop Mandalay Bay; the "outrageously chic and decadent" experience extends to the French–New American fare, courtesy of über-chef/co-owner Alain Ducasse and chef de cuisine Bruno Davaillon, who "keep your *bouche* amused" throughout; all this and "mind-blowing service" make for a "top-of-the-world" "winner" – at "equally high prices."

NOBHILL
26 | 25 | 25 | $80

MGM Grand Hotel, 3799 Las Vegas Blvd. S. (Tropicana Ave.), 702-891-7337; www.michaelmina.net

"You'd think you're in the city" by the Bay at Michael Mina's "San Francisco treat" in the MGM Grand serving the "talented" toque's "creative" "contemporary Californian cuisine"; carb lovers say "the most delicious things ever tasted" are the complimentary "mashed-potato sampler" and the "steaming-hot bread fresh from the oven" with three kinds of butter, but Atkins dieters also "spend their winnings" on the "exceptional" fare, "incredible wine list", "attentive" staff and all-around "swankiness."

NOBU ●
27 | 22 | 23 | $71

Hard Rock Hotel, 4455 Paradise Rd. (bet. Flamingo Rd. & Harmon Ave.), 702-693-5090; www.nobumatsuhisa.com

"Be adventuresome and trust your waiter – they won't steer you wrong" – at this east-of-Strip outpost in Nobu Matsuhisa's "unique" empire of Peruvian-accented Japanese eateries, which is "notorious" for "cutting-edge sushi like you've never had before", "don't-miss miso cod" and other "fabulous fusion" fare; the "tranquil" "garden" setting is "wonderful" for a "first date", if you "come with your checkbook" and avoid it on "hotter-than-a-royal-flush" weekends when "noisy crowds" fueled by "sake in bamboo stalks" "turn it into a sort of nightclub."

Okada
26 | 27 | 24 | $72

Wynn Las Vegas, 3131 Las Vegas Blvd. S. (Desert Inn Rd.), 702-770-9966; www.wynnlasvegas.com

"Another Wynn winner", this Japanese specializes in "excellent teppanyaki" and "must-try robata" cooking, not to mention "fantastic sushi", served in a "visually stunning" "Zen garden" featuring a "floating pagoda table" and "floor-to-ceiling windows that showcase" the hotel's "famous mountain", lake and "lit waterfall"; "first-rate service" goes with the "gorgeous food and decor"; N.B. a post-*Survey* chef change may outdate the above Food score.

Osteria del Circo
25 | 25 | 23 | $61

Bellagio Hotel, 3600 Las Vegas Blvd. S. (Flamingo Rd.), 702-693-8150; www.bellagio.com

The Maccionis' "'discount'" eatery in the Bellagio delivers "all the pomp and circumstance you expect from a high-caliber" restaurant "without the fuss" and with "less expense than its big brother", Le Cirque; the "inventive, savory" Tuscan cuisine is to be "toothed with a maximum joy", but the real "show" is in the "buoyant atmosphere", thanks to the "colorful, circus"-like decor and a fountain view from "coveted tables ringside to the floor-to-ceiling windows"; now someone should tell the staff in this "fantasy menagerie" to lose their "New York attitude."

Pamplemousse Ⓜ
26 | 23 | 25 | $52

400 E. Sahara Ave. (bet. Joe W. Brown Dr. & Paradise Rd.), 702-733-2066; www.pamplemousserestaurant.com

"Named by Bobby Darin", this "traditional French" "gem" that was favored by the "Rat Pack" is an "oldie but still goodie" thanks to chef-owner George LaForge's "excellent, classic", "quirky menu (they recite it to you)" and the "romantic shanty" setting east of the Strip; the "fabulous waiters" "pamper you" with "remarkable crudités", followed by an "outstanding" meal.

PICASSO
27 | 28 | 27 | $102

Bellagio Hotel, 3600 Las Vegas Blvd. S. (Flamingo Rd.), 702-693-8255; www.bellagio.com

Las Vegas' Most Popular restaurant is this "intoxicating" "MoMA-meets-Bacchus" "splurge" in the Bellagio, where chef Julian Serrano's "exquisite" Spanish-inflected New French dishes are "meticulously honed" "masterpieces", just like the "beautiful" namesake original paintings on the walls; other enticements include "perfect wines", "gorgeous flowers", "a view of the dancing fountains" and a "gracious" staff that "treats you as an honored guest"; of course, it's "expensive", but "it still costs less than 15 minutes at blackjack"; N.B. closed Tuesdays.

PRIME STEAKHOUSE
27 | 27 | 26 | $83

Bellagio Hotel, 3600 Las Vegas Blvd. S. (Flamingo Rd.), 702-693-8255; www.bellagio.com

"Sink into the lavish seats" and "begin an evening of delight" at this steakhouse from Jean-Georges Vongerichten, where a "pampering" staff serves "heaven on a plate (and in a glass)"; "if the Rat Pack were still around, they'd congregate here" for "marvelous" meat, "martini-centric drinks", "theatrical decor" and "fantastic" fountain views, "all of which scream 'ring-a-ding Vegas'"; just "know that you'll be spending a ton" and you'll "want to dress up" to dine among the "famous people"; N.B. cigars are permitted on the patio only.

ROSEMARY'S
28 | 21 | 26 | $52

W. Sahara Promenade, 8125 W. Sahara Ave. (bet. Buffalo Dr. & Cimarron Rd.), 702-869-2251; www.rosemarysrestaurant.com

Tucked "way off the Strip" on the West Side, this "not-to-be-missed" New American from chef-owners Michael and Wendy

Jordan is Las Vegas' "ultimate epicurean event", a "hidden treasure" that's toppled Nobu to become No. 1 for Food in Las Vegas; "fabulous tastes and flavors" are served in a "pretty" space that "belies its strip-mall location", while "excellent prix fixes" and "exceptional" service that "goes above and beyond expectations" make it "worth every penny of the cab ride."

Seablue | 24 | 22 | 23 | $63 |

MGM Grand Hotel, 3799 Las Vegas Blvd. S. (Tropicana Ave.), 702-891-3486; www.michaelmina.net

The "knowledgeable servers are eager to describe and recommend the ultrafresh seafood preparations" on Michael Mina's "fabulous, innovative" (but "not overly elaborate") menu at this "global" oceanic "experience" in the MGM, where other list "twists" include "great 'build-your-own' salad" and "melt-in-your-mouth Kobe rib-eye"; given prices that are "high but not off the charts" and "hip" decor featuring a "cool fish tank", "you won't feel blue" here.

Steak House | 26 | 21 | 24 | $47 |

Circus Circus Hotel, 2880 Las Vegas Blvd. S. (Circus Circus Dr.), 702-794-3767; www.circuscircus.com

"Fred and Barney" could order up a couple of "dead-bang perfect" brontosaurus-sized steaks and "kick it old-school" style at this "dark woods–and–leather" meat mansion in Circus Circus, where the "huge", "excellent" cuts come with "soup or salad and sides included" (and offset by a limited wine list), at "amazingly" prehistoric prices; all this and "the best Sunday brunch out there" lure "real-deal" hunters to venture "past the kiddies and clowns" in the "bizarre hotel" to get in.

Sterling Brunch Ⓜ | 26 | 19 | 23 | $60 |

Bally's Las Vegas Hotel, 3645 Las Vegas Blvd. S. (Flamingo Rd.), 702-739-4111; www.ballyslasvegas.com

Yes, it's only open on Sundays (9:30 AM–2:30 PM), but for a "delightful experience" fueled by "free-flowing Perrier Jouët", this Bally's New American brunch venue is "absolutely grand"; "feel free to pile your plate five deep with grilled lobster and top them off with good-quality American sturgeon caviar", finishing your meal with "unusual and decadent desserts"; just "bring a credit card with a large limit" and be prepared to deal with "crowds"; N.B. reservations are recommended.

SW Steakhouse | 26 | 26 | 25 | $74 |

Wynn Las Vegas, 3131 Las Vegas Blvd. S. (Desert Inn Rd.), 702-770-9966; www.wynnlasvegas.com

Surveyors savor "steak you can cut with a fork" at this "fabulous" chophouse in the Wynn, where the room is as "breathtaking" as the fare, with "chic" decor and a patio overlooking the "lake and forest with a water show at night"; "sensational service" and an "amazing and reasonable wine list" help make this an "excellent" part of the high-rolling scene; N.B. the post-*Survey* departure of chef Eric Klein may outdate the above Food score.

Todd's Unique Dining Ⓩ | 26 | 18 | 26 | $39 |

4350 E. Sunset Rd. (bet. Green Valley Pkwy. & W. Sunset Rd.), Henderson, 702-259-8633; www.toddsunique.com

"Finally, fabulous food that doesn't cost an arm and a leg and involve a smoke-filled room or a trip past dinging machines" sigh

Henderson's hungry who hail this "winner" in a "quiet mall"; chef-owner Todd Clore brings the Eclectic sensibilities he honed at the Sterling Brunch to a daily changing menu including "innovations" like goat-cheese won tons with raspberry-basil sauce; "also high on the list" of its "charms" are the "reasonably priced wines" and "personal service", while "the only true negative" is the "lousy decor."

Valentino Las Vegas 24 | 22 | 23 | $72

Venetian Hotel, 3355 Las Vegas Blvd. S. (bet. Flamingo & Spring Mountain Rds.), 702-414-3000; www.welovewine.com
This is "food to live for" laud loyalists of Piero Selvaggio's "sleek" Italian in the Venetian where a "mind-boggling" "wine list the size of a phone book" and chef Luciano Pellegrini's "fantastic" "twists on the expected" add up to a much-appreciated sibling of the Santa Monica flagship; but a portion are put off by the "pretentious" service and "noisy grill" section (head to the more formal dining room instead), insisting there are "better places in town for this kind of cash."

Long Island

TOP FOOD RANKING

Restaurant	Cuisine
28 Kotobuki	Japanese
Polo	New American
27 Kitchen à Bistro	French Bistro
Peter Luger	Steakhouse
Mill River Inn	Eclectic/New Amer.
La Plage	Eclectic
Chachama Grill	New American
Maroni Cuisine	Eclectic/Italian
Le Soir	French
26 Mirabelle	French
Dario's	Northern Italian
Orient, The	Chinese
Panama Hatties	New American
On 3	New American
Siam Lotus	Thai
La Piccola Liguria	Northern Italian
Il Mulino	Northern Italian
Barney's	French/New Amer.
Piccolo	Italian/New Amer.
Da Ugo	Northern Italian

OTHER NOTEWORTHY PLACES

American Hotel	American/French
Bryant & Cooper	Steakhouse
Cheesecake Factory	American
Coolfish	New Amer./Seafood
Della Femina	New American
Frisky Oyster	Eclectic
Harvest on Fort Pond	Med./Northern Italian
Jimmy Hays	Steakhouse
Louis XVI	New French
Mio	Northern Italian
Mirko's	Eclectic
Nick & Toni's	Mediterranean
Palm	Seafood/Steakhouse
Plaza Cafe	New American
Rialto	Northern Italian
Robert's	Italian
Starr Boggs	New Amer./Seafood
Stone Creek Inn	French/Med.
Tellers Chophouse	Seafood/Steakhouse
Trattoria Diane	Northern Italian

American Hotel, The
| 25 | 23 | 23 | $59 |

The American Hotel, 49 Main St. (bet. Bay & Washington Sts.),
Sag Harbor, 631-725-3535; www.theamericanhotel.com

A combo of "19th-century charm and Hamptons chic", this "classic" Sag Harbor hotel garners garlands for "top-flight" French-American cuisine and a "fabulous" 2,500-label wine list that's "thicker than a phone book"; "attentive but not fawning" servers "meet every need" in the antiques-filled dining rooms or on the "perfect" porch, so though a few grumble it's "stuffy", "snooty" and "pricey", admirers assert they "never regret paying the bill"; N.B. a post-*Survey* chef change may outdate the above Food score.

Barney's Ⓜ
| 26 | 23 | 24 | $59 |

315 Buckram Rd. (Bayville Rd.), Locust Valley, 516-671-6300;
www.barneyslv.com

"Don't wait for a special occasion" to "search out" this "hidden gem" in Locust Valley urge surveyors who swoon over its "sensational", "inventive and mouthwatering" French–New American cuisine and "excellent" 250-label wine list; the "charming" space feels "like a country inn" and "impeccably" "professional" staffers make visitors "feel like royalty" – so though it's indubitably "expensive", all agree that the experience is "worth every penny."

BRYANT & COOPER STEAKHOUSE
| 25 | 19 | 21 | $58 |

2 Middle Neck Rd. (Northern Blvd.), Roslyn, 516-627-7270;
www.bryantandcooper.com

"Pack your appetite and your wallet" and go to this "meat lovers' paradise" in Roslyn for "colossal" steaks ("melt-in-your-mouth filets"), "wonderful" seafood and "great sides" in a decidedly "masculine" setting; the tables are so close together some feel "packed in like cattle" and you can expect waits even if you've booked a table, but the service is "friendly and accommodating."

Chachama Grill
| 27 | 14 | 23 | $43 |

Swan Nursery Commons, 655-8 Montauk Hwy. (S. Country Rd.),
East Patchogue, 631-758-7640; www.chachamagrill.com

"The secret's out": at this "quiet", "family-run" spot set in a "dreary" East Patchogue storefront, "every bite is a taste sensation"; an "unexpected" "gem", it serves "excellent" New American specialties "beautifully prepared" and "uniquely presented", and delighted diners declare they "don't know what's better, the staff or the food"; P.S. the three-course early-bird is "a steal."

CHEESECAKE FACTORY, THE ◐
| 21 | 18 | 17 | $28 |

Mall at the Source, 1504 Old Country Rd. (Merchants Concourse),
Westbury, 516-222-5500; www.thecheesecakefactory.com

"They have a winning formula" "based on price/value ratio" alone calculate consumers of this Westbury chain link; "humongous portions" of "delicious" Traditional American eats plus "incredible" cheesecake and a "cavernous" yet "comfortable" space equal "everyone's favorite"; servers are "friendly" but "not always on the ball" and you can "grow old waiting" amid the "noisy" conditions.

COOLFISH
| 24 | 22 | 21 | $47 |

North Shore Atrium, 6800 Jericho Tpke. (Michael Dr.), Syosset,
516-921-3250; www.tomschaudel.com

"Off the beaten path" in a Syosset office park ("who knew?"), this "hard-to-find" New American seafooder is worth the search considering its, yes, "cool fish" and equally "cool vibe"; the flagship in chef-owner Tom Schaudel's fleet, it's known for "creative", "classy" dishes served by an "accommodating" crew in quarters that have "verve", and though it's "a little pricey", the early-bird special (Sunday–Friday) is "a terrific deal."

Dario's ⊠　　　26 | 18 | 24 | $52
13 N. Village Ave. (bet. Merrick Rd. & Sunrise Hwy.), Rockville Centre, 516-255-0535
This "simply wonderful" family-owned Rockville Centre special-occasioner, one of "the best on Long Island", provides a culinary experience "of the highest degree": "excellent", "sophisticated" Northern Italian cuisine that's "worth the splurge" brought to table by a "friendly" and "utterly professional" staff that "knows how to take care of people"; the room may be "small" and "non-descript", but overall delighted diners declare Dario "da bomb."

Da Ugo ⊠　　　26 | 18 | 23 | $48
509 Merrick Rd. (Long Beach Rd.), Rockville Centre, 516-764-1900
"For that special occasion", reviewers recommend this Rockville Centre "hideaway" serving "top-notch" Northern Italian in a "charming", "romantic setting" where kids are scarce ("don't go without an AARP card"); the food is "worth sitting on your neighbor's lap for" – a good thing since "quarters are tight" – but service can be an issue ("regulars get the royal treatment" but "infrequent visitors are often disappointed"); nevertheless, this "class act" remains a "tough reservation."

Della Femina　　　24 | 22 | 21 | $58
99 N. Main St. (Cedar St.), East Hampton, 631-329-6666; www.dellafemina.com
You can have a "true Hamptons experience" at this East Hampton New American, a "perennial favorite" for "delicious" meals in a "lively" (read: "crowded and noisy") "see-and-be-seen" atmosphere that provides "neck-craners" with choice "celeb-spotting" opportunities; pleasingly "professional" service and "classy" yet "casual" decor are further reasons that for most it "matches the hype" and is "well worth" prices "as high as the quality."

Frisky Oyster　　　25 | 21 | 20 | $51
27 Front St. (bet. 1st & Main Sts.), Greenport, 631-477-4265; www.thefriskyoyster.com
"NYC hits the North Fork" at this "fantastic" "SoHo"-esque "hot spot" in Greenport, where "imaginative" Eclectic dishes "emphasizing local ingredients" present a "superb blend of flavors"; given that the "owner is super-accommodating", the "service professional" and the atmosphere "sophisticated", no wonder it's "easier to get a reservation at the White House on a Saturday night."

Harvest on Fort Pond　　　26 | 22 | 22 | $46
11 S. Emery St. (S. Euclid Ave.), Montauk, 631-668-5574; www.harvest2000.com
The "bountiful portions" of "rustic" Mediterranean–Northern Italian cuisine are "meant to be shared" at this Montauk "jewel", which has rapt reviewers raving that the "food is incredible", the "helpful" staffers are "professional" and the "serene setting" with its "amazing sunset views" across Fort Pond is ever so "romantic" – but "go with a group" if you hope to finish the

"humongous" servings; "reservations are a must", and if possible, insiders advise "snagging a seat in the Tuscan-style garden."

Il Mulino New York
26 | 22 | 22 | $80

*1042 Northern Blvd. (bet. Old Northern Blvd. & Searingtown Rd.),
Roslyn Estates, 516-621-1870; www.ilmulinonewyork.com*

"Primo" Northern Italian cuisine in "copious quantities" "comes to Roslyn" crow those cognoscenti who cheer for the "outstanding" food that's served in a "beautiful room" at this "hot spot"; despite service that can be "inconsistent" (even "pretentious"), and "outrageous" prices that warrant "bringing your banker along", a reservation here is still "just as hard to get" as at its "Manhattan cousin."

Jimmy Hays
25 | 21 | 22 | $51

4310 Austin Blvd. (Kingston Blvd.), Island Park, 516-432-5155

Reviewers rave "the beef is tops" at this Island Park meatery that "deserves its popularity" for serving some of "the best steak on the South Shore"; not only is the filet mignon "outstanding", the "fish is excellent" as well, and an "efficient" staff keeps things moving; the decor comes close to matching the first-rate food, so most maintain it's "a good experience all around" – just beware the "heart-attack prices."

KITCHEN À BISTRO ⊉
27 | 9 | 21 | $35

532 N. Country Rd. (Lake Ave.), St. James, 631-862-0151

"For people who care more for food than ambiance", this "superb" St. James French bistro delivers "fabulous value" in the form of "spectacular", "cutting-edge", "five-star" cuisine ("outstanding seafood", desserts "straight from heaven") at "rock-bottom prices", plus a "satisfying" BYO policy; "young, energetic" staffers "love what they do", and although the "lilliputian" 30-seat room is "cramped" and "lacks atmosphere", nobody seems to mind – almost all avow it's "worth the one-month wait" for reservations (accepted Friday–Sunday only); N.B. cash only.

KOTOBUKI Ⓜ
28 | 16 | 21 | $33

86 Deer Park Ave. (Main St.), Babylon, 631-321-8387
377 Nesconset Hwy. (Rtes. 111 & 347), Hauppauge, 631-360-3969

"Plain and simple" sushi "so fresh it's still swimming" explains why this Babylon and Hauppauge Japanese duo has been voted No. 1 for Food in LI; "the wait is insufferable at peak times" ("reservations would be nice"), "the tables are too close for comfort" and there's "no ambiance" to speak of, but finatics agree "it's all worth it" because the food is "heaven to the taste buds" and the "kind" staffers are "helpful to first-timers"; N.B. the Babylon branch completed a renovation post-*Survey*.

La Piccola Liguria Ⓜ
26 | 19 | 25 | $52

*47 Shore Rd. (bet. Mill Pond & Old Shore Rds.), Port Washington,
516-767-6490*

Don't bother "looking at the menu" – at this "stellar" Northern Italian in Port Washington, the servers memorize an "array of specials" so "extensive" it "almost takes your breath away"; once you choose from the "diverse", "authentic" selections, the result is a "meal to remember", with the "owner and his fine staff" "treating you like a king"; seating is "cozy" (some might say "tight") and getting a reservation is "tough", but it's worth whatever it takes for one of the Island's "best" dinners.

La Plage   27 | 20 | 23 | $52

131 Creek Rd. (Sound Rd.), Wading River, 631-744-9200
Serving "spectacularly creative" fare that "you'd expect at a NYC
place *du jour*", this "hideaway" in Wading River is an "absolute
gem"; the "top-notch", "artistically plated" Eclectic fare "sparkles",
and the "wonderful staff" maintains a "laid-back atmosphere";
some say the "beach-house setting" is a bit too "rustic", but supporters who savor the "black-tie food in a khaki-pants ambiance"
sigh "thank God it's hard to find" – otherwise, "we'd never get in."

Le Soir   27 | 20 | 23 | $45

825 Montauk Hwy. (west of Nicolls Rd.), Bayport, 631-472-9090
Chef-owner Michael Kaziewicz "gets better every year" rave
"regulars" of this "special" Bayport French; they *soir* by his "consistently excellent", "complex" cuisine and appreciate the "lovely",
"attentive" service and "unpretentious" country feel – all of which
has surveyors sighing "if only there were one of these in every
town"; since there isn't, the weekday all-inclusive dinner special,
"one of the best values on the Island", is definitely "worth the trip."

Louis XVI Ⓜ   26 | 27 | 25 | $72

600 S. Ocean Ave. (Masket Dock), Patchogue, 631-654-8970;
www.louisxvi.org
A "magnificent dining experience" awaits at this "opulent"
waterfront château in Patchogue, where the "gorgeous", "elab-
orately decorated" environs are "enhanced" by "drop-dead
ocean views"; "spectacular" New French cuisine comes in a
"top-notch" tasting menu or a prix fixe that "offers great variety",
and service is "impeccable"; it's a "must-see at least once in a
lifetime" – just be sure to "bring your best plastic."

Maroni Cuisine ⊠⍪   27 | 14 | 22 | $43

18 Woodbine Ave. (bet. Main St. & Scudder Ave.), Northport,
631-757-4500; www.maronicuisine.com
Michael Maroni is a "fabulous chef-owner" "worthy of NYC" rave
reviewers about this "lilliputian" 24-seat hideaway in Northport;
order his tasting menu and you'll savor "a hundred bits of
heaven" (well, 12 or 13 courses anyway); the food is Eclectic with
an Italian bent, and while it can be "pricey", it's all "of delectable
quality"; so whether you dine in this "itty-bitty space" or "take
out", prepare for a truly "unique" and "amazing" experience.

MILL RIVER INN   27 | 22 | 26 | $68

160 Mill River Rd. (bet. Lexington Ave. & Oyster Bay-Glen Cove Rd.),
Oyster Bay, 516-922-7768; www.millriverinn.com
Year after year one of Long Island's top-rated restaurants, this
tiny Oyster Bay New American–Eclectic "hideaway" continues to
turn out "sterling" cuisine that, matched with an "excellent wine
list", "impeccable service" and a "warm", "romantic" setting,
makes for a perfect "special-occasion" meal; "first-class" cre-
dentials notwithstanding, the experience feels more like "going
to a friend's house for dinner" – albeit a "wealthy friend."

Mio   26 | 20 | 22 | $53

1363 Old Northern Blvd. (bet. Bryant Ave. & Roslyn Rd.), Roslyn,
516-625-4223; www.mio-restaurant.com
"You won't be singing solo" at this Roslyn Northern Italian now
that it has been "discovered" and is drawing diners in droves

with its "innovative" and "superbly prepared" fresh pastas and other classic dishes, personal attention from chef-owner Dino Vlacich and "hip" setting "reminiscent of" The Boot; there are a few grumbles about "noisy" acoustics and "pricey" tabs, but most don't notice much once they've taken a bite of the "melt-in-your-mouth" edibles.

Mirabelle ⓜ　　　　　　26 | 22 | 25 | $66
404 N. Country Rd. (Edgewood Ave.), St. James, 631-584-5999;
www.restaurantmirabelle.com
"*C'est magnifique*" enthuse epicures about this St. James "treasure" where "masterful" chef-owner Guy Reuge "never fails to surprise and thrill" with "amazing" French fare that "sings", the wine list is "exquisite" and service is "always gracious" and "civilized"; some find the "subtle" space a bit "plain" for such an "extravagant experience", but others appreciate the "cozy" ambiance; P.S. the $25 prix fixe lunch is the "best deal in town", and there's a special Friday night bistro menu.

Mirko's ⓜ　　　　　　25 | 21 | 23 | $63
Water Mill Sq., 670 Montauk Hwy. (Old Mill Rd.), Water Mill, 631-726-4444
One of "the best in the Hamptons", this "wonderful" Water Mill legend dwells in a "strange location" that's worth seeking out for "tip-top" Eclectic cuisine enjoyed in "pretty and romantic" (if "cramped") quarters; it's "hard to get a reservation in season" and the greetings here range from "the warmest" and "most gracious" to "snobby" depending on whom you ask (insiders advise "only go if you are known to them"), but "once inside" the "swell crowd" and "culinary magic" are truly "memorable."

Nick & Toni's　　　　　　24 | 20 | 21 | $60
136 N. Main St. (bet. Cedar St. & Miller Terrace), East Hampton,
631-324-3550; www.nickandtonis.com
"Still great after all these years", this "rustic" East Hampton Med retains an army of admirers thanks to "sophisticated" seasonal menus that emphasize "outstanding" organic ingredients and an "excellent" staff that helps sustain a "warm and friendly" atmosphere; by now, however, everyone knows it's "a hit with all the celebs", so in season it's almost "impossible to get in" without offering "your first-born" or having "the Spielbergs in your party."

On 3 ⓩ　　　　　　26 | 21 | 24 | $56
32 Railroad Ave. (off Glen Head Rd.), Glen Head, 516-656-3266
Reviewers rhapsodize that "all the elements work" at this chef-owned "first-rate" Glen Head spot; the "innovative" New American cuisine is "excellent" "down to the smallest detail" and matched by "impeccable" service from a "very professional" crew; though the "tiny" room is sometimes loud, its "upscale", "upbeat" decor lends it a "movie-set feel", and "outdoor seating in the bungalow" can even "make you forget you're on Long Island"; N.B. bringing kids is not encouraged.

Orient, The　　　　　　26 | 11 | 19 | $21
623 Hicksville Rd. (Central Ave.), Bethpage, 516-822-1010
"You'll think you're in Chinatown" at this "excellent" Bethpage Chinese offering a "tremendous selection" of "authentic", "unusual dishes and old favorites" (Cantonese, Hunan and Szechuan) plus a "super" weekend dim sum that "rivals favorites in Flushing"; owner Tommy Tan is a "gracious host" who's "al-

ways willing to recommend the best dishes" and "make anything you ask for, any way you like it."

Palm | 25 | 18 | 23 | $61 |

The Huntting Inn, 94 Main St. (bet. Davids & Hunting Lns.), East Hampton, 631-324-0411; www.thepalm.com
Contented carnivores call East Hampton's link in the "top-drawer" surf 'n' turf chain "the best in the Palm" family; the standard "enormous portions" of "perfectly prepared" steaks and lobster are served in the "historic" Huntting Inn (circa 1699) by a staff that works "like a well-oiled machine", plus celeb sightings ("Sarah Jessica Parker, Brad Pitt") are de rigueur – so "who cares that the bill is monstrous?"

Panama Hatties | 26 | 23 | 25 | $69 |

Post Plaza, 872 E. Jericho Tpke. (2 mi. east of Rte. 110), Huntington Station, 631-351-1727; www.panamahatties.com
At this Huntington Station "gourmet's delight" owned by exec chef Matthew Hisiger, connnoisseurs are "continually amazed" by the "excitingly creative" and "artistically presented" New American cuisine, and find the personnel even "friendlier since Hisiger bought the place"; the "bundles-of-bucks" prices and "sophisticated atmosphere" seem to some a "surreal" contrast with the "strip-mall setting", but most figure that's the flip side of having "upper-echelon NYC quality in your own neighborhood."

PETER LUGER ⊜ | 27 | 16 | 21 | $60 |

255 Northern Blvd. (bet. Lakeville Rd. & Little Neck Pkwy.), Great Neck, 516-487-8800; www.peterluger.com
"Incredibly" "succulent" steaks that are "the best of the best" have made this Great Neck "classic" Long Island's No. 1 for Popularity for the 12th straight year; yes, the decor could use "a peppy marinade" and the "curt" "old-time waiters" can exhibit "attitude", but it's "worth every penny (and you'll need quite a few)"; P.S. "no vegetarians and no Visa" (cash, check, debit or Peter Luger cards only).

Piccolo | 26 | 21 | 24 | $53 |

Southdown Shopping Ctr., 215 Wall St. (bet. Mill Ln. & Southdown Rd.), Huntington, 631-424-5592; www.piccolorestaurant.net
Admirers "can't say enough" about the "amazing" New American–Italian fare, particularly the extensive list of "innovative specials", at this "fabulous" Huntington haunt; the "knowledgeable waiters" "treat you as an honored guest", and the "enchanting" ambiance with "delightful piano players" helps make it a "perfect place to celebrate romance"; add a 400-bottle wine list, and "no wonder the crowds keep coming" – it's "first-class all the way."

Plaza Cafe | 25 | 21 | 24 | $51 |

61 Hill St. (bet. First Neck & Windmill Lns.), Southampton, 631-283-9323; www.plazacafe.us
"Brilliant" chef Doug Gulija creates "incredible" New American cuisine (he has seafood "down to a science"), and when you combine it with "one of the most interesting wine lists on Long Island", "dining doesn't get much better than this"; add a "top-notch staff" (without "that frenetic Hamptons attitude") and a "romantic" room with a big stone fireplace, and this Southampton "gem" delivers a "true NYC-quality eating experience."

POLO RESTAURANT
| 28 | 27 | 26 | $64 |

Garden City Hotel, 45 Seventh St. (bet. Cathedral & Hilton Aves.), Garden City, 516-877-9353; www.gchotel.com

This "class act" in the Garden City Hotel once again earns "high marks" all around from pleased patrons who praise the "outstanding", "knowledgeable" staff, the recently refurbished "formal" decor and the "spectacular" New American cuisine "of the highest quality"; everything combines to create an "indulgent" dining experience "right out of *The Great Gatsby*" – "it breaks the bank", but it's "almost perfect."

Rialto Ⓜ
| 26 | 18 | 23 | $49 |

588 Westbury Ave. (bet. Glen Cove Rd. & Post Ave.), Carle Place, 516-997-5283

The "top-notch" Northern Italian fare is "among the finest Long Island has to offer" avow *amici* of this "quiet" "old-world" Carle Place "gem" where the "tuxedoed waiters" "fawn on you" and the welcoming owner "makes you feel like you're a special guest in his home"; sure, it's "expensive" (the penny-wise protest that "the price of the fish might drown you"), but it's a "lovely place."

Robert's
| 25 | 21 | 21 | $56 |

755 Montauk Hwy. (Water Mill traffic light), Water Mill, 631-726-7171

With "unbelievable" Italian cuisine and "accommodating" service in an "intimate" "country-house" setting, this Water Mill destination has its clientele cheering; the kitchen creates "fabulous blends of taste and texture", and the "grown-up atmosphere" feels "more like New England than the Hamptons"; sure, pettifoggers pout about staffers who can be "arrogant" and "pushy", and it's "pricey" too, but enthusiasts insist it's "worth every penny."

Siam Lotus Thai Ⓜ
| 26 | 16 | 23 | $31 |

1664 Union Blvd. (bet. 4th & Park Aves.), Bay Shore, 631-968-8196; www.siamlotus.info

Flower power is evident at this "affordable" Bay Shore Thai, decorated in pink and green to evoke the eponymous blossom, and considered one of "LI's best" Siamese; the "sublime" food is "so full of flavor" ("ask for the heat and you'll get it") that a meal is "great from start to finish"; add in "personalized" service from owner Danny Poom and his "gracious" staff, and the combo is "worth the trip from anywhere" laud loyalists.

Starr Boggs
| 25 | 24 | 20 | $56 |

6 Parlato Dr. (Library Ave.), Westhampton Beach, 631-288-3500

We "call him Four-Star Boggs" and we "thank heavens he's back" swoon Starr-gazers smitten with this "legendary" East End chef; "he's done it again" at his outpost in Westhampton Beach, where everything on the seafood-centric New American menu is "imaginative" and you dine in "gorgeous rooms" decorated with Warhol prints or in the "breathtaking back garden"; "the only thing prettier and richer than the food is the crowd", so it's too bad the "young" servers can sometimes be so "unprofessional."

Stone Creek Inn
| 26 | 24 | 24 | $57 |

405 Montauk Hwy. (bet. Carter Ln. & Wedgewood Harbor), East Quogue, 631-653-6770; www.stonecreekinn.com

"Chef-owner Christian Mir continues to impress year after year", and his talent is "showcased" in his "imaginative" and "perfectly prepared" French-Mediterranean "haute cuisine", well matched with the "varied wine list" and "professionally" served in this "elegant" "historic house"; it's "everything a great night out should be" and "well worth a trip" to East Quogue from anywhere; P.S. "the prix fixe menu" available on some days "is a steal" at this dinner-only spot.

Tellers American Chophouse   25 | 26 | 22 | $61

605 Main St. (Rte. 111), Islip, 631-277-7070; www.tellerschophouse.com
"Soaring ceilings and huge windows" distinguish this Islip surf 'n' turfer named for its "spectacular" setting in a 1927 bank building; the "brontosaurus-size" rib-eyes and the "extra dividends" of "tasty sides" captivate carnivores, as do servers who remain "gracious" "no matter how busy"; some happily exchange the "noisy" main dining room for the "intimate" upstairs Gallery, while others warn "you'll be ignored" up there "like a counterfeit $20 bill"; still, most maintain this meatery is "worth every cent."

Trattoria Diane Ⓜ   25 | 21 | 22 | $52

21 Bryant Ave. (bet. Roosevelt Ave. & Skillman St.), Roslyn, 516-621-2591
"Inspired food" in an "intimate" setting makes for an "elegant evening" enthuse epicures who've dined at this "sophisticated" yet "charming" Northern Italian trattoria in Roslyn; the "imaginative Tuscan menu" "changes with the seasons" and the quality is always "outstanding" ("you can't resist" the "wonderful breads" made in-house and the "even better desserts"); the staff is "accommodating" as well, and the $29.95 Sunday prix fixe may be "the deal of the decade."

Los Angeles

TOP FOOD RANKING

	Restaurant	Cuisine
28	Matsuhisa	Japanese
27	Mélisse	French/New Amer.
	Sushi Nozawa	Japanese
	Leila's	Californian
	Saddle Peak	New Amer./Steakhouse
	Shiro	French/Japanese
	Nobu Malibu	Japanese
	Piccolo	Italian
	Angelini Osteria	Italian
	Katsu-ya	Japanese
	Spago	Californian
	Frenchy's Bistro	French Bistro
	La Cachette	New French
	Josie	New American
	Water Grill	Seafood
	Derek's	Californian/French
	Providence	New American
	Yujean Kang's	Chinese
	Hump, The	Japanese
	Chinois on Main	Asian

OTHER NOTEWORTHY PLACES

A.O.C.	Californian/French
Belvedere, The	New American
BLD	New American
Brent's Deli	Deli
Café Bizou	Californian/French
Campanile	Californian/Med.
Capo	Italian
Chaya Brasserie	Asian/Eclectic
Cheesecake Factory	American
Christine	Med./Pacific Rim
Cut	Steakhouse
Depot, The	Eclectic
Grace	New American
Grill on the Alley	American
Hamasaku	Japanese
Hotel Bel-Air Restaurant	Californian/French
JiRaffe	Californian
Mimosa	French Bistro
Mori Sushi	Japanese
Valentino	Italian

Angelini Osteria Ⓜ   27 17 22 $46
7313 Beverly Blvd. (Poinsettia Pl.), 323-297-0070;
www.angeliniosteria.com
"Gino [Angelini] is a genius!" rhapsodize regulars of this Beverly
Boulevard Italian famed for the "best branzino imaginable" and
other "excellent, authentic" dishes complemented by an
"awesome wine list" and served by a "wonderful" staff; it's
"loud", "crowded" and though tables "can't be squeezed any
closer", at least you can "sit hip-to-hip with the hippest" (yes,
"those boorish louts next to you are celebrities") while experiencing an "outstanding" meal.

A.O.C.   26 23 24 $51
8022 W. Third St. (Crescent Heights Blvd.), 323-653-6359;
www.aocwinebar.com
Gourmets love to "graze" on Suzanne Goin's "innovative", "inventive" and straight-up "incredible" Cal-French small plates –
matched by a "jawdropping selection" of wines by the glass – at
this modern, "minimalist" and "convivial" LA "foodie heaven"
staffed by a "knowledgeable", "gracious" crew; reservations
remain "hard to get" (perhaps because aficionados urge "come
with an adventurous group" for wider sampling) but walk-ins can
perch at the bar or the cheese station and charcuterie; of course,
it'll cost you ("$1 per molecule").

Belvedere, The   24 26 26 $68
The Peninsula Hotel of Beverly Hills, 9882 Little Santa Monica Blvd.
(Wilshire Blvd.), Beverly Hills, 310-788-2306; www.peninsula.com
Even after the departure of longtime chef Bill Bracken, fans insist
this "fine-dining establishment" in the Peninsula Beverly Hills is
"still a powerhouse", offering "wonderful", "not overly solicitous" service and current toque Sean Hardy's "delectable" New
American fare, including mac 'n' cheese "to die for" and a "spectacular" Sunday brunch, amid "exquisite" surroundings; a few
feel it's "not what it once was" (although still "expensive"), but to
most it remains a "perfect spot for that special occasion."

BLD   – – – M
7450 Beverly Blvd. (N. Vista St.), 323-930-9744;
www.bldrestaurant.com
Grace's Neal Fraser expands his territory with this casual New
American (its name is an acronym for 'breakfast, lunch and
dinner') in the Fairfax space that's been, variously, Red, Opaline
and Cafe Capo; in this case, Fraser and his partners have created
a light-filled room with floor-to-ceiling windows, tables inside and
out and a moderately priced menu that's built around the coziest
of comfort foods.

Brent's Deli   26 12 21 $19
19565 Parthenia St. (bet. Corbin & Shirley Aves.), Northridge,
818-886-5679; www.brentsdeli.com
Fans feel like they "died and went to pastrami heaven" at this
Northridge deli, a "local treasure" dishing out "immense" help-
ings of "corned beef like my mother never made" and other "old-
school" "Jewish soul food" choices that are "well worth the
drive and the wait for a table"; the "nice folks" serving you are
"very accommodating", another reason the "decor is so unim-
portant here"; N.B. a Westlake Village branch is in the works.

CAFÉ BIZOU
23 | 19 | 21 | $31

91 N. Raymond Ave. (Holly St.), Pasadena, 626-792-9923
14016 Ventura Blvd. (bet. Costello & Murietta Aves.), Sherman Oaks,
818-788-3536
www.cafebizou.com

Chef-owner Neil Rogers and partner Philippe Gris get kisses from "regulars" of this "popular" Pasadena and Sherman Oaks pair of "crowded" Cal-French bistros where the "consistently delicious food" delivers "incredible bang for the buck" and the "nominal [$2] corkage fee" is "a wine collector's delight"; but while some like "knowing what to expect" from the "never-changing" bill of fare, many more "bemoan" that the "tired menu" offers "no surprises", saying it's "time to" "freshen it up a bit" with "something new."

CAMPANILE
26 | 24 | 24 | $53

624 S. La Brea Ave. (bet. W. 6th St. & Wilshire Blvd.), 323-938-1447;
www.campanilerestaurant.com

Chef-owner Mark Peel's Cal-Med has been a "winner for a long time" and his "urban-rustic cuisine" continues to "excite and delight" at this "world-class" La Brea "destination restaurant"; with its "beautiful, historic setting" (built by Charlie Chaplin), "sophisticated" social and "power scene", "exceptional" wines and "top-notch" service, the place "keeps packing them in" – especially for "can't beat" "Thursday night grilled cheese" and the "awesome Saturday and Sunday brunch."

Capo ☒ Ⓜ
24 | 22 | 22 | $76

1810 Ocean Ave. (Pico Blvd.), Santa Monica, 310-394-5550

Bruce Marder's "extremely expensive" Santa Monica Italian is "one of the most exclusive rooms in town", "catering to industry royalty and their courts" with "incredible wood-grilled steaks" and a "great wine list"; the "beautiful, cozy" dining room with its open fireplace provides a "great" backdrop according to most, though a few naysayers mutter the emphasis is on eyeing "collagen and carpaccio" in a "minuscule" setting that "lacks creature comforts."

Chaya Brasserie
23 | 22 | 21 | $51

8741 Alden Dr. (bet. George Burns Rd. & Robertson Blvd.),
West Hollywood, 310-859-8833; www.thechaya.com

With a "creative" Asian-Eclectic menu, an "awesome happy hour" with "the tastiest raspberry martinis in the city" and central WeHo location, this still "hip after all these years" spot is "the unofficial New Line [Cinemas] commissary", and comes equipped with an "attentive" staff that knows all about "catering to big egos"; the skylit setting can be "noisy" and "the scene a little overwhelming" at times, but most maintain it's "tried-and-true."

CHEESECAKE FACTORY
20 | 18 | 18 | $25

11647 San Vicente Blvd. (bet. Barrington Ave. & Wilshire Blvd.),
310-826-7111
364 N. Beverly Dr. (Brighton Way), Beverly Hills, 310-278-7270
4142 Via Marina St. (Admiralty Way), Marina del Rey,
310-306-3344
2 W. Colorado Blvd. (Fair Oaks Ave.), Pasadena, 626-584-6000
605 N. Harbor Dr. (190th St.), Redondo Beach, 310-376-0466
Sherman Oaks Galleria, 15301 Ventura Blvd. (Sepulveda Blvd.),
Sherman Oaks, 818-906-0700

(continued)

(continued)
CHEESECAKE FACTORY
Thousand Oaks Mall, 442 W. Hillcrest Dr. (Lynn Rd.), Thousand Oaks,
805-371-9705
Warner Center Trillium, 6324 Canoga Ave. (Victory Blvd.),
Woodland Hills, 818-883-9900
www.thecheesecakefactory.com
"Come hungry, leave deaf" and wear your "fat jeans" quip cronies
of this "cacophonous", "convivial" American chain (voted LA
and Orange County's Most Popular) offering "something for
everyone" from its "encyclopedic" menu, including "every imaginable flavor of cheesecake"; there's "always a long wait" for a
table in the "cavernous" rooms, but "you can't beat the value" of
the "King Kong–sized portions" and "reasonable tabs."

Chinois on Main   27   20   22 $58
2709 Main St. (Hill St.), Santa Monica, 310-392-9025;
www.wolfgangpuck.com
"Wolfgang Puck's version of Asian cuisine" is French-influenced,
"innovative" and "way too expensive, but worth every single
penny"; whole sizzling catfish, curried oysters, Chinese chicken
salad and other "tantalizing" signature dishes are paired with
"exciting wines" and served "family-style" by an "attentive"
staff; the room is "unapologetically noisy" ("take guests if you're
not on speaking terms"), "über-crowded" and "cramped", but
this "miracle of longevity" in Santa Monica is "still spectacular.

Christine   27   19   24 $40
Hillside Vlg., 24530 Hawthorne Blvd. (Via Valmonte), Torrance,
310-373-1952; www.restaurantchristine.com
"Christine [Brown] is a genius" exult acolytes of her long-
standing, "always-enjoyable" eponymous restaurant where
"innovative" Med–Pacific Rim cuisine is served by a "personable
and knowledgeable" staff; just note that "one of the treasures of
Torrance" can be "cramped" and "crowded", so "sit on the
second floor if you want a quiet conversation."

Cut ⊠   –   –   –   VE
Four Seasons Regent Beverly Wilshire, 9500 Wilshire Blvd.
(El Camino Dr.), Beverly Hills, 310-275-5200; www.fourseasons.com
After spending several years in Las Vegas, Wolfgang Puck returns
home to open a talk-of-the-town steakhouse in the Beverly Hills
Four Seasons; designed by Richard Meier (of the Getty fame), the
ultraminimalist room features white-on-white decor, a multipartite
open kitchen and polished wood tables with place mats rather
than tablecloths; the menu is similarly au courant, with steaks
that come with pedigrees, along with mix-and-match sauces and
sides; N.B. there's an adjoining lounge called Sidebar.

Depot, The ⊠   24   21   22 $39
1250 Cabrillo Ave. (Torrance Blvd.), Torrance, 310-787-7501;
www.depotrestaurant.com
Chef-owner Michael Shafer prepares Eclectic cuisine that's
"inventive", "delicious" and "full of character", inspiring fans to
call his upscale cookery inside a "historic" Torrance train station
"one of the finest restaurants in the South Bay"; "auto execs" in
particular park it here at lunch – one of the peak times when you
can "expect to be very cozy with your neighbor."

Derek's ⬛Ⓜ   27 | 23 | 25 | $56

181 E. Glenarm St. (Marengo Ave.), Pasadena, 626-799-5252;
www.dereks.com

Derek Dickenson "continues to please" with his "upscale", "elegant" Pasadena Cal-French "hidden" in a strip mall, a "foodies' hangout" thanks to "masterful" cuisine, "impeccable" service and a "quiet, well-appointed" interior; an "extensive but not overwhelming" wine list also makes it a "favorite for wine dinners", and fans agree it's a "wonderful place for a celebration" or "romantic evening", albeit in an "odd location"; N.B. jackets suggested.

Frenchy's Bistro Ⓜ   27 | 17 | 23 | $48

4137 E. Anaheim St. (bet. Termino & Ximeno Aves.), Long Beach,
562-494-8787; www.frenchysbistro.com

"Absolutely terrific French cuisine" earns rave reviews for this Long Beach strip-mall "sleeper", "a little jewel" in an "industrial area"; the "charming hosts" serve "classic" and "nouvelle" dishes such as "second-to-none" lamb shank and lobster bisque that "can make you whimper" in delight; while the setting is "cramped" and some say "I wish they'd up the quality of the room a bit", most maintain "it's everything a neighborhood bistro should be."

Grace Ⓜ   25 | 24 | 24 | $58

7360 Beverly Blvd. (Fuller Ave.), 323-934-4400; www.gracerestaurant.com

"Inspired chef" Neal Fraser delivers a "unique" "gastronomic experience" at this "true winner" on Beverly Boulevard via an "inventive" New American menu ranging from an "outstanding selection of meats" to "incredible vegan and vegetarian selections", all prepared with "fresh" ingredients and paired with "beautiful wines that aren't overly expensive"; a "sophisticated" and "elegant" yet "unstuffy" room and "knowledgeable", "never-intrusive" staff are other reasons it's considered to be "one of the top restaurants" around.

Grill on the Alley, The   23 | 20 | 23 | $54

9560 Dayton Way (Wilshire Blvd.), Beverly Hills, 310-276-0615;
www.thegrill.com

A "who's who of producers and execs" can be seen power-lunching in the "coveted booths along the wall" at this "brass-rail", "old-school" Beverly Hills American, where "comfort food at its best", "professional", "no-attitude" service and a "serious approach to bartending" are par for the course, and the tabs are "not for the faint of wallet"; still, "people-watching is the real allure" here, even if some grouse the "high-profile clientele" makes it "difficult to reserve at lunch."

Hamasaku ⬛   25 | 17 | 20 | $56

11043 Santa Monica Blvd. (Sepulveda Blvd.), West LA, 310-479-7636;
www.hamasakula.com

"Innovation and thoughtfulness" are hallmarks of the "truly great sushi" fashioned from "fresh ingredients" at this "wonderful Japanese" "tucked away" in a West LA "mini-mall", where customers enjoy "name dropping when ordering" from the "expansive menu" of specialty rolls with "celebrity" monikers; the "warm owner" helps create a "home-away-from-home" vibe, and the environment's great for "stargazing while grazing", but be warned that its "trendy" reputation means "the wait can be agonizing"; N.B. a branch on Melrose is in the works.

Hotel Bel-Air Restaurant
26 | 29 | 27 | $69

Hotel Bel-Air, 701 Stone Canyon Rd. (Sunset Blvd.), Bel-Air, 310-472-1211; www.hotelbelair.com

"It's like stepping into paradise" at this "luxurious", "incredibly romantic" Bel Air venue ranked No. 1 for Decor and Service in LA; "walk in the gardens" before dining in the "elegant" interior or on the "heavenly" terrace upon "exquisitely prepared", "very evolved" Cal-French fare ("with an endless blue-chip wine list") served by staffers who "practically read your mind"; it's a "wonderful experience" that's "worth" the "high price" – even if a few find the "excellent food" "not quite up to" the "fabulous" celeb-centric ambiance.

Hump, The
27 | 23 | 22 | $57

Santa Monica Airport, 3221 Donald Douglas Loop S. (Airport Ave.), Santa Monica, 310-313-0977

Self-described "sushi purists" swoon over the "sublime", "swimmingly fresh" fish served at this "hidden" Japanese literally "on the tarmac" at the Santa Monica Airport, where the "luxe" setting and "dramatic" view through the wall-to-wall windows "impress" almost as much as the chef's "breathtaking" performance; true foodies say "try the omakase", though be warned that dinner may "still be moving when it arrives at your table" – and the price "will shock the senses."

JiRaffe
26 | 21 | 23 | $51

502 Santa Monica Blvd. (5th St.), Santa Monica, 310-917-6671

"Foodies" "can't wait to go back" to this "pillar" of the Santa Monica dining scene, an "A-list" "treat" thanks to "consistently excellent", "upscale" Californian cuisine and "impeccable" service in a "cozy", yet "noisy", setting (insiders advise "try upstairs to escape the noise"); though some complain the "menu hasn't changed much", the "mainstays" are "lovely and delicious" and the Monday 'Bistro Night' prix fixe is a "steal."

Josie
27 | 23 | 25 | $58

2424 Pico Blvd. (25th St.), Santa Monica, 310-581-9888; www.josierestaurant.com

A "wonderfully imaginative" menu of "inspiring" French- and Italian-accented New American cuisine prepared with "fresh, honest", "Farmers Market" ingredients and "great cuts of wild game" draws a "grown-up" crowd to Josie La Balch's "sophisticated" "oasis" located "off the beaten track" in Santa Monica; the service is "top-notch" and the surroundings "comfortable", if sometimes "noisy", and though it's "certainly not cheap", most declare the overall experience a "grand slam."

Katsu-ya
27 | 14 | 18 | $38

11777 San Vicente Blvd. (Montana Ave.), 310-207-8744
16542 Ventura Blvd. (Hayvenhurst Ave.), Encino, 818-788-2396
11680 Ventura Blvd. (Colfax Ave.), Studio City, 818-985-6976

"Be adventuresome" advise cool Kats who crave the "phenomenal", "inventive sushi concoctions" and "interesting, progressive" cooked items at these Japanese siblings along Ventura Boulevard's sushi row (with a Philippe Starck–designed Brentwood baby brother that opened post-Survey); some "traditional" raw-fish "purists" pout that they did "not get the experience [they] were looking for", while others insist the "unpredictable service" "leaves something to be desired", but they're still "always crowded" ("make a reservation").

La Cachette | 27 | 25 | 25 | $61 |

10506 Little Santa Monica Blvd. (Thayer Ave.), Century City, 310-470-4992; www.lacachetterestaurant.com

As the name suggests, this "intimate restaurant" in Century City is rather "hidden away", but "satisfied" surveyors sigh "it's well worth looking for" thanks to "innovative" "top chef" and owner Jean Francois Meteigner, whose "exquisite", "light" New French food is ferried by a "smooth" staff; the "lovely", "romantic" rooms feature "great acoustics", making for "quiet and refined" meals, but the "celebrity sightings", "bejeweled" "mature" clientele and "elegant decor" all add "sparkle" to the "wonderful dining experience."

LEILA'S Ⓜ | 27 | 19 | 24 | $43 |

RE/MAX Plaza, 706 Lindero Canyon Rd. (Kanan Rd.), Oak Park, 818-707-6939; www.leilasrestaurant.com

The "sophisticated, demanding clientele" of this "relaxed, elegant" Californian "hidden in a shopping center" in Oak Park "can't believe such a gourmet restaurant" exists all the way "out in the hinterlands"; chef Richie DeMane's "unique", weekly changing menu features "exciting, often spicy" creations that are "unfailingly well-done", and the "caring staff" provides "excellent service" – though some suggest the "decor could use some upscaling" to match.

MATSUHISA | 28 | 17 | 23 | $71 |

129 N. La Cienega Blvd. (bet. Clifton Way & Wilshire Blvd.), Beverly Hills, 310-659-9639; www.nobumatsuhisa.com

Acolytes give "a deep bow to the master", Nobu Matsuhisa, whose "original temple" in La Cienega is ranked LA's No. 1 for Food for its "outstanding" Peruvian-accented Japanese cuisine, including the "freshest, best sushi in town" and a "divine" omakase served in a private room that "still surprises"; service is "solid" but the "small" dining room can feel "like a sardine can" when it's "packed"; N.B. the restaurant is scheduled to close in early 2007, to be replaced by Nobu Matsuhisa, which will occupy the space of the former L'Orangerie down the road.

MÉLISSE Ⓢ Ⓜ | 27 | 25 | 26 | $84 |

1104 Wilshire Blvd. (11th St.), Santa Monica, 310-395-0881; www.melisse.com

"Allow several hours to enjoy" the "otherworldly" experience at Josiah Citrin's Santa Monica destination, showcasing the "breathtaking artistry" of his French–New American cuisine, with "gorgeous" wine pairings recommended by sommelier Brian Kalliel and a cheese cart that'll "make one say *sacré chèvre*"; the service is "impeccable without being pretentious" and the ambiance is "flawless" – "you'll be pampered, stuffed and much poorer", but most agree it's "worth every penny."

Mimosa Ⓢ | 22 | 18 | 21 | $42 |

8009 Beverly Blvd. (bet. N. Edinburgh & N. Laurel Aves.), 323-655-8895; www.mimosarestaurant.com

Francophiles laud the "truly French experience" at this "dependable" Beverly Boulevard bistro where a "limited" but "wonderful" menu of Gallic "country food", including "very good" daily specials, is served "without attitude" in the mirrored dining room or on the "pleasant" patio; for many, though, the "warm, intimate" ambiance is the "main ticket."

Mori Sushi ⊠   26 | 19 | 22 | $66

11500 W. Pico Blvd. (Gateway Blvd.), West LA, 310-479-3939
"Minimalist presentation provides maximum sensual pleasure" at Morihiro Onodera's "sophisticated" West LA Japanese where the "most authentic offerings" of "phenomenally fresh" sushi and other "classic" dishes are presented with "no gimmicks" on "his handmade pottery" in a "spartan, yet warm", room; for acolytes it's a veritable "religious experience" – as long as you "don't think about the cost."

Nobu Malibu   27 | 20 | 23 | $65

3835 Cross Creek Rd. (PCH), Malibu, 310-317-9140;
www.nobumatsuhisa.com
Malibu residents say "*domo arigato*" to Nobu Matsuhisa for this "sublime" sushi spot that serves "mouthwatering" sushi and "inventive" "fusion" dishes to "beautiful people" and "celebrities" in a "laid-back" setting; the servers are "knowledgeable", though at times they seem to have "their minds on their next auditions", and while the "strip-mall location" "may not be TriBeCa", most agree the experience is "worth the drive" – and, "hopefully, you can pay off your credit card over a few months."

Piccolo   27 | 17 | 25 | $44

5 Dudley Ave. (Speedway), Venice, 310-314-3222;
www.piccolovenice.com
"People line up around the block" to get into this "no-reservations" "tiny closet of a place" off the beach in Venice" serving "gorgeous, authentic" Italian cuisine, including "exceptional homemade pastas" and "stellar ragouts", with the "funky" "street scene at your toes"; the service is "friendly and professional" and the prices "reasonable", but cognoscenti caution "tell only the people you like best, because you'll probably end up sitting in each other's laps."

Providence   27 | 24 | 27 | $84

5955 Melrose Ave. (Cole Ave.), 323-460-4170;
www.providencela.com
An "experience extraordinaire" is how fans describe dining at Michael Cimarusti's "A-list" New American on Melrose, where "creative combinations of fresh ingredients" go into "flawless" seafood specialties and "magnificent" terra firma offerings, and the tasting menus "paired with recommended wines" are "superb"; the front-of-house staff is "delightful" and the service "impeccable" in the "beautiful", "elegant" space, and even if there may be an "unduly restrictive" corkage policy and "huge" prices, satisfied groupies are calling it one of "LA's most exciting" destinations.

SADDLE PEAK LODGE Ⓜ   27 | 27 | 26 | $59

419 Cold Canyon Rd. (Piuma Rd.), Calabasas, 818-222-3888;
www.saddlepeaklodge.com
"Away from it all" but "worth the drive" to Calabasas for diners game for a "culinary adventure", this New American steakhouse housed in a "rustic" mountain cabin specializes in "impressive", "exotic game meats", served by a "well-trained, friendly" staff;

while some find the "mounted trophies" on the walls "disconcerting" ("is that my dinner staring down at me?"), the "amazing" interior makes others "feel like you're in a very exclusive hunting lodge – without Dick Cheney shooting you in the face."

Shiro Ⓜ | 27 | 18 | 24 | $46 |

1505 Mission St. (Fair Oaks Ave.), South Pasadena, 626-799-4774; www.restaurantshiro.com

Chef-owner Hideo Yamashiro is a "master with fish" gush groupies of his "tiny", "serene" Franco-Japanese in South Pasadena, where "every dish is wonderful", especially the "ethereal whole catfish on a ponzu sauce lake"; the staff makes you "feel like one of the family", and though some complain the decor "isn't consistent with the food or service", most agree the experience is "worth the trip – and the price tag."

SPAGO | 27 | 25 | 24 | $70 |

176 N. Cañon Dr. (Wilshire Blvd.), Beverly Hills, 310-385-0880; www.wolfgangpuck.com

Wolfgang Puck is "still the gracious showman who visits your table" at his "expensive, flashy" "institution" in Beverly Hills, a "heavenly" "culinary experience you will not forget", with Lee Hefter's "amazing", "innovative" Californian cuisine and "stellar" desserts by Sherry Yard served by a "skillful" staff in an "inspiring" room full of "glamorous" people, including "A-list celebrities"; still, some demur at the "hefty price tag" and "too much glitz."

SUSHI NOZAWA Ⓢ | 27 | 6 | 14 | $56 |

11288 Ventura Blvd. (bet. Arch & Tropical Drs.), Studio City, 818-508-7017

"Don't expect to be coddled" at this sushi "purist's heaven" in Studio City, where "master" Kazunori Nozawa's "passion for perfection" and "dictatorial" mien are "not everyone's cup of sake", but whose "vibrant tasting" fare is "second to none" in the minds of many; while the mini-mall space is "lacking in decor", the "stars do tend to light up the room", where they, like the rest, must learn to "sit down, shut up, and eat" – some of the "best damn sushi anywhere."

Valentino Ⓢ | 25 | 22 | 25 | $71 |

3115 Pico Blvd. (bet. 31st & 32nd Sts.), Santa Monica, 310-829-4313; www.welovewine.com

Although "fantastic, refined" Italian cuisine is one part of the winning equation at this Santa Monica "expense-account" classic that gets "better with each passing year", an "amazing" wine list longer than a "phone book" (i.e. 3,000 labels), a "consummate" host in owner Piero Selvaggio and "courteous" service all play a role; if the "plush" decor seems somewhat "dated", most don't seem to mind, for this restaurant is still "the king" in this corner of the world.

Water Grill | 27 | 24 | 25 | $61 |

544 S. Grand Ave. (bet. 5th & 6th Sts.), 213-891-0900; www.watergrill.com

In simple words, "the best seafood in town" is in store for patrons at this Downtown "special-occasion" "classic" whose "deserved acclaim" rests on its "superb" food (in this case the work of chef David LeFevre) complemented by "consistently excellent" service, "sophisticated" ocean liner-esque decor and "interesting" wines; P.S. "bring your executive platinum credit card to fund the evening."

Yujean Kang's 27 | 16 | 22 | $37

67 N. Raymond Ave. (bet. Holly & Union Sts.), Pasadena, 626-585-0855
"Everything is unusual, appealing and brightly flavored" at this Pasadena "winner" where the eponymous chef-owner creates "gourmet" "Chinese food like you've never had it" (followers have been known to "quack for the tea-smoked duck"); it's an "extremely good value for the money" (and especially a "bargain for lunch") and an "attentive" staff provides "polite service", though some say the "decor needs updating" and quip "dim sum of the lights."

TOP FOOD RANKING

	Restaurant	Cuisine
28	Francesco	Peruvian
27	Romeo's Cafe	Northern Italian
	Nobu Miami Beach	Japanese/Peruvian
	Chef Allen's	New World
	Matsuri	Japanese
26	Ortanique on the Mile	New World
	Prime One Twelve	Seafood/Steakhouse
	Azul	Asian/Med.
	Mark's South Beach	New American
	Norman's	New World
	Joe's Stone Crab	Seafood
	Osteria del Teatro	Northern Italian
	Shoji	Japanese
	Pascal's on Ponce	New French
	Talula	New American
	AltaMar	Seafood
	Toni's Sushi	Japanese
25	Capital Grille	Steakhouse
	La Dorada	Seafood/Spanish
	Palme d'Or	New French

OTHER NOTEWORTHY PLACES

Cacao	Nuevo Latino
Casa Tua	Northern Italian
Cheesecake Factory	American
Escopazzo	Italian
Houston's	American
Jaguar Restaurant	Pan-Latin
Lan	Pan-Asian
Michy's	Mediterranean
Nemo	New American
North One Ten	New American
Off the Grille	Caribbean
Pacific Time	Pan-Asian
River Oyster Bar	Seafood
SushiSamba dromo	Japanese/S. American
Tamarind	Thai
TapTap	Haitian
Timo	Italian/Mediterranean
Versailles	Cuban
Vix	Eclectic
Wish	New American

AltaMar Ⓜ　　　　　　　　26 | 15 | 21 | $41
1223 Lincoln Rd. (Alton Rd.), Miami Beach, 305-532-3061
You may "have passed it a hundred times" and never noticed this "low-key" "neighborhood gem"; finatics swear it is one of the "best on SoBe" for Claudio Giordano's "exquisite" Med-inspired seafood and for daily specials that are "the stars of the show"; it's a "rare find" that comes with "modest prices" and, blessedly, "no attitude."

Azul　　　　　　　　　　　26 | 27 | 25 | $66
Mandarin Oriental Hotel, 500 Brickell Key Dr. (8th St.), 305-913-8358;
www.mandarinoriental.com
"Cool" and "sublime", this Med-Asian in the Mandarin Oriental soars with "the best" combination in the city – "spectacular", swoonworthy food, a "gorgeous" room, "breathtaking views" of Downtown and "polished" service; though it may be "pricey", and many "miss" chef Michelle Bernstein, in the minds of the majority, this "class act" continues to thrive "at the top."

Cacao Ⓢ　　　　　　　　　25 | 24 | 23 | $51
141 Giralda Ave. (bet. Galiano St. & Ponce de Leon Blvd.),
Coral Gables, 305-445-1001; www.cacaorestaurant.com
Enthusiasts admire this "amazing" Coral Gables Nuevo Latino, where you can indulge in "exotic", "extraordinary" fare from the "incredible" Edgar Leal in a "pretty", "jewel-box" setting enhanced by "lighting that makes everyone gorgeous", an "excellent staff" and a "knowledgeable" sommelier; it's "expensive", but the "spectacular desserts" help make it "worth every penny."

Capital Grille, The　　　　　25 | 24 | 25 | $57
444 Brickell Ave. (SE 5th St.), 305-374-4500; www.thecapitalgrille.com
Downtown lobbyists laud this "high-class" DC-based steakhouse as "the best of the big-name [steakhouse] chains"; the "beautiful", "clubby" room features "dark wood" appointments, cigar storage rooms and "extensive" wine list, while the "exceptional staff" serves "flawless" fare featuring "awesome" steaks and seafood, and "great sides"; P.S. "raise capital" before you go.

Casa Tua ❶　　　　　　　　24 | 27 | 22 | $79
Casa Tua, 1700 James Ave. (17th St.), Miami Beach, 305-673-1010;
www.casatualifestyle.com
The "rich and famous" find "glorious" goings-on at this "gorgeous" Northern Italian SoBe "hideaway" in a "beautiful" converted home that makes you feel "like you're at a Tuscan villa"; though the garden is "wonderful" and the fare "top-notch", it may be wise to "reserve early", bring a "corporate credit card" to cover the "outrageous" tabs and expect to detect "pretentious" airs in the air.

CHEESECAKE FACTORY　　　20 | 18 | 19 | $26
Aventura Mall, 19501 Biscayne Blvd. (NE 195th St.), Aventura,
305-792-9696
CocoWalk, 3015 Grand Ave. (Virginia St.), Coconut Grove,
305-447-9898 ❶
Dadeland Mall, 7497 N. Kendall Dr. (88th St.), Kendall, 305-665-5400
www.thecheesecakefactory.com
It's the "best chain – ever" aver acolytes of these South Florida Traditional Americans whose "encyclopedic" menus feature "giant-size portions" of everything – from "burgers to Thai" – and

the legendary, "unbelievable", "ultrarich" namesake desserts, all served by a "cheerful", "efficient" staff; sure, "the line goes all the way to I-95" and it's so loud you may want to "bring your megaphone", but the "consistently good", reasonably priced fare and "kid-friendly" credo make it a "winner."

CHEF ALLEN'S | 27 | 22 | 25 | $65 |

19088 NE 29th Ave. (bet. 28th Ave. & NE 191st St.), Aventura, 305-935-2900; www.chefallens.com

The "genius" evident in "inimitable" chef-owner Allen Susser's "top-notch" New World fare has helped him earn his "well-deserved reputation" and puts his "high-end" Aventura venue into the "classic" category in the hearts of admirers; "every bite" of food is a "sheer delight", and though a few fuss that the decor "could use an upgrade", the "polished staff" will make you "feel like royalty."

Escopazzo ❶ | 25 | 19 | 23 | $57 |

1311 Washington Ave. (bet. 13th & 14th Sts.), Miami Beach, 305-674-9450; www.escopazzo.com

Those who've discovered SoBe's "great" family-run "jewel" go *pazzo* over the "stunning", "sophisticated" Italian fare accompanied by "exceptional" wines and "fantastic" service in "romantic" quarters; it "more than surpasses its reputation", and that it caters to a well-heeled crowd is little surprise when you consider the "pricey" tabs.

FRANCESCO ⊠ | 28 | 17 | 24 | $43 |

325 Alcazar Ave. (bet. Le Jeune Rd. & Salzedo St.), Coral Gables, 305-446-1600; www.francescorestaurant.com

Nabbing the No. 1 ranking for Food in Miami is this *pequeña* Peruvian on Coral Gable's Restaurant Row with "tiraditos that melt in your mouth", "out-of-this-world squid ink pasta" and "amazing ceviche", as well as a "value wine" list that's "ripe for the picking"; savvy surveyors see eye to eye that even if the decor is "unspectacular", the "efficient" staff and "terrific" cooking make for an experience "as close as it gets to being in Lima."

HOUSTON'S | 21 | 20 | 21 | $32 |

201 Miracle Mile (Ponce de Leon Blvd.), Coral Gables, 305-529-0141
17355 Biscayne Blvd. (NE 172nd St.), North Miami Beach, 305-947-2000
www.houstons.com

Floridians fare well at these links of a national chain known for "rock-solid" American food, especially "great burgers" and the now legendary, "fabulous" spinach dip; the "comfortable", "clubby" setting, "consistently good service" and "active bar scene" is a testament to their "popularity" and reason for many to endure "long waits."

Jaguar Restaurant ❶ | 23 | 24 | 25 | $29 |

3067 Grand Ave. (Virginia St.), Coconut Grove, 305-444-0216; www.jaguarspot.com

"Beautiful people" pounce on this "impressive" kitten exciting Coconut Grove epicures with "wonderful", "reasonably" priced Pan-Latin cuisine and standout seviche; factor in "gorgeous", tropical decor, a "great" bar scene and "smart" service, and few will dispute that it's likely to be around awhile.

JOE'S STONE CRAB ⓜ

| 26 | 19 | 22 | $58 |

11 Washington Ave. (1st St.), Miami Beach, 305-673-0365;
www.joesstonecrab.com

A "treasured institution" and Miami's Most Popular spot for the fifth straight year, this 1913 South Beacher "lives up to the hype" with "the best stone crabs on earth" accompanied by "great" hash browns and an obligatory "killer Key lime pie" served by legions of "wholly professional" veterans in a setting akin to a "glorified diner"; whether you "claw your way in" or endure the "hellish" wait, be ready to "shell out" a lot of cash; N.B. closed from August till mid-October.

La Dorada ⓓ

| 25 | 19 | 23 | $60 |

177 Giralda Ave. (Ponce de Leon Blvd.), Coral Gables,
305-446-2002

This "elegant" Spanish "sleeper" in Coral Gables proffers "exceptional" seafood (with fresh catch flown in daily) that's brought to table by "flawless servers"; for many, it's a "memorable" experience, even if some aver that given the "shocking prices", the fish "should be made out of 18 carats"; N.B. closed Sundays in summer.

Lan ⓜ

| 23 | 11 | 20 | $23 |

Dadeland Station, 8332 S. Dixie Hwy. (84th St.), Kendall, 305-661-8141;
www.lanpanasian.com

Overlook the "odd" shopping-mall locale and "simple decor" at suburbia's "best-kept secret", a Pan-Asian "jewel" in Kendall capturing kudos for its "tasty" fare including "fresh sushi", "yummy noodles" and an "amazing lunch special"; the "friendly" staff and "reasonable prices" keep it "popular."

Mark's South Beach

| 26 | 22 | 24 | $63 |

Hotel Nash, 1120 Collins Ave. (bet. 11th & 12th Sts.), Miami Beach,
305-604-9050; www.chefmark.com

"Break out the Gucci" and "head to the hull" of the Hotel Nash where "celebrity chef"-owner Mark Militello "elevates" palates by turning out "trendy, yet tremendous" New American preparations that continue to "break new ground" "without being weird"; the "welcoming" staff makes its mark, too; P.S. even though the "gorgeous" decor may evoke "the '30s", the prices are strictly "21st century."

MATSURI ⓜ

| 27 | 14 | 21 | $28 |

5759 Bird Rd. (Red Rd.), South Miami, 305-663-1615

The "best sushi in town", an "extensive", "authentic" menu and "fair prices" account for the acclaim of this "unassuming" South Miami strip-maller that "mustn't be overlooked"; it's the standby for many (especially for "lots of Japanese patrons"), so don't be surprised if the staff's stymied "when it gets busy."

Michy's ⓜ

| – | – | – | E |

6927 Biscayne Blvd. (bet. NE 69th & 70th Sts.), 305-759-2001

Finally in a room of her own, Michelle Bernstein (ex Azul at the Mandarin Oriental), one of Miami's most cherished culinary figures, has helped create this Upper East Side Mediterranean; '70-ish orange and royal-blue decor provides a lively backdrop for the toque's whimsical and bold menu of small plates, which can total up to a big tab.

Nemo ☻ 25 | 22 | 22 | $54
100 Collins Ave. (1st St.), Miami Beach, 305-532-4550;
www.nemorestaurant.com
Superlatives stream in for this "low-key" New American that
charms with "fabulous" fare, "stellar fish" dishes, a "great raw
bar" and a Sunday brunch that ranks among "the greatest
around"; the "light-hearted, terrific staff" helps make for an
"unbeatable", though "pricey", time; P.S. snare a seat in the
"beautiful" courtyard or patio for a uniquely "SoBe experience."

NOBU MIAMI BEACH ☻ 27 | 23 | 23 | $71
The Shore Club, 1901 Collins Ave. (20th St.), Miami Beach, 305-695-3232;
www.noburestaurants.com
Nobu Matsuhisa's "chichi" South Beach branch of his NYC flagship "shines as brightly as the trendy, flashy crowd" ready for
"mind-blowing" Japanese-Peruvian cuisine (the black cod miso
is "an undisputed classic"), "remarkably un-SoBe service"and
the inevitable "killer waits" in an "ultramod" blue-tiled setting; do
yourself a favor, though, and "bring your Amex Black card" and
"make sure your date's worth it"; N.B. only takes reservations for
parties of six or more.

NORMAN'S Ⓢ Ⓜ 26 | 23 | 25 | $66
21 Almeria Ave. (Douglas Rd.), Coral Gables, 305-446-6767;
www.normans.com
After more than a decade at the pinnacle of the Miami dining
scene, "master" chef-owner Norman Van Aken's "world-class",
eponymous eatery in Coral Gables remains the benchmark for
"original", "seductively delicious" New World fare served in a
"classy" setting by a staff that "makes you feel important";
though you'll "pay top dollar" for the privilege of dining here, it's
"worth whatever it costs."

North One 10 25 | 21 | 25 | $48
11052 Biscayne Blvd. (110th St.), Biscayne Shores, 305-893-4211;
www.northone10.com
"Prepare to be dazzled" at this "first-rate" blond-wood and glass-
accented "jewel" in Biscayne Shores; chef Dewey LoSasso's
"superb" New American cuisine transports you to a "gastronomic paradise", while wife Dale commands the dining room and
guarantees "efficient" service.

Off the Grille Bistro – | – | – | I
12578 SW 88th St. (bet. SW 125th & 127th Aves.), Kendall, 305-274-2300;
www.offthegrille.com
Hot off the grill is this fast Kendall Caribbean counter cafe that's
been currying favor with its mojo-marinated meats and chicken
plus other bargain dishes; though in a nondescript shopping
center, the restaurant, with its steel beams and metal tables,
looks more SoHo than strip mall.

Ortanique on the Mile 26 | 23 | 23 | $51
278 Miracle Mile (Le Jeune Rd.), Coral Gables, 305-446-7710;
www.cindyhutsoncuisine.com
It may be tough to "combine fine dining with Caribbean influences",
but chef-owner Cindy Hutson "pulls it off" with her "exciting"
New World fare that's "a party for the palate" at this "paradise"
on Miracle Mile in Coral Gables; though the space is "tight", the

staff does an "incredible job", and the "beautiful", tropical-themed setting puts this "gem" where it should be – "at the top of everyone's list."

Osteria del Teatro ☒   26 | 15 | 24 | $54

1443 Washington Ave. (Española Way), Miami Beach, 305-538-7850
"You can't go wrong" at this SoBe standby where the quarters are "tight" and the loyal audience applauds the "excellent" Northern Italian standards, "attentive service" and "window seating" that allows you to "watch the world go by"; if the hostile hiss the "high" tabs, others offer that it "would be a bargain at twice the price"; N.B. after 10 PM, night-owls can get the $18 'twilight special.'

Pacific Time   25 | 19 | 21 | $55

915 Lincoln Rd. (bet. Jefferson & Michigan Aves.), Miami Beach, 305-534-5979; www.pacifictimerestaurant.com
Officially a "classic", this fixture on the SoBe culinary firmament delights with chef-owner Jonathan Eismann's "stunningly good", "exotic" Pan-Asian cooking hitched to "informed" service, and scores with an "excellent" 300-label wine list that may "not offer many bargains", but is in keeping with the "posh" setting; P.S. insiders advise "dine early" – or outside – if you want to avoid the "din."

Palme d'Or ☒ Ⓜ   25 | 25 | 25 | $70

Biltmore Hotel, 1200 Anastasia Ave. (Granada Blvd.), Coral Gables, 305-445-1926; www.biltmorehotel.com
For a taste of "five-star hotel dining found only in Europe", this "elegant" New French in Coral Gables' historic Biltmore Hotel ranks among the "best in South Florida" thanks to the "astonishing" small-plates menu devised by chef Philippe Ruiz, "superb service" and "romantic" environs; it's there "when you want to splurge" for a trip to "gastronomic heaven"; N.B. closed Sundays and Mondays.

Pascal's on Ponce ☒   26 | 19 | 23 | $53

2611 Ponce de Leon Blvd. (bet. Almeria & Valencia Aves.), Coral Gables, 305-444-2024; www.pascalmiami.com
"Thank goodness" for this Coral Gables "gem" where the kitchen turns out "stand-out" New French food under the direction of chef Pascal Oudin, while wife Ann-Louise oversees a floor crew who "make everyone feel important"; the "charming", though "tight", quarters recently received a "face-lift", and a new liquor license may make it even more of a "must."

Prime One Twelve ◗   26 | 24 | 22 | $70

112 Ocean Dr. (1st St.), Miami Beach, 305-532-8112; www.prime112.com
It's always prime time at this "sceney" SoBe steakhouse/seafooder that "blows its competitors away" with "perfect" (and "pricey") oversized steaks, "delicious ceviche" and desserts that induce "outer body experiences"; you may have to wait "forever" – "even with a reservation" – but at least the "hot bar" area offers complimentary bacon and "celeb sightings."

River Oyster Bar, The ☒   24 | 22 | 22 | $40

650 S. Miami Ave. (SW 7th St.), 305-530-1915; www.therivermiami.com
There's more than just the "amazing oysters" at this "civilized" "winner", an "upscale", yet "comfortable" seafooder near the

Miami River that attracts fans with "the best ceviche in town", "heavenly calamari" and other "superb" items; the "trendy crowd" fishes for catch over drinks at the "inviting" mahogany bar.

ROMEO'S CAFE ⓈⓂ   27 | 19 | 27 | $69 |
2257 SW 22nd St./Coral Way (bet. 22nd & 23rd Aves.), 305-859-2228; www.romeoscafe.com
"Give yourself over to Romeo" Majano's "creativity" at his "small" Coral Gables Northern Italian, where the "exquisitely planned" (there's "no printed menu"), "magnificent" six-course meals are "prepared to your taste" and where the "charming" service (No. 1 in Miami) makes you feel "like you're the only one there"; "romantics" report that the "dimly lit" setting means "your date won't see your tears when the check arrives."

Shoji ⓿   26 | 20 | 21 | $49 |
100 Collins Ave. (bet. 1st & 2nd Sts.), Miami Beach, 305-532-4245; www.shojisushi.com
SoBe sushiphiles sign on to this "top-flight" Japanese using "impeccably fresh" fish in "fantastic" fare that goes "far beyond" the norm; "attentive service" and a "romantic garden" make it a neighborhood "favorite", and though tabs run high, it's still "cheaper" than others in its league; N.B. a new chef has replaced Shingo Inoue.

SushiSamba dromo ⓿   22 | 23 | 17 | $47 |
600 Lincoln Rd. (Pennsylvania Ave.), Miami Beach, 305-673-5337; www.sushisamba.com
This "trendy" SoBe version of an NYC-based hit brings "hotties" and hipsters a swinging menu of "delicious" Japanese, Peruvian and Brazilian fusion fare featuring "creative" sushi in presentations that would satisfy "artists"; the "sex" factor is abetted by concoctions of "killer" cocktails and a "gorgeous", "loungey" interior, and while the staff may be "haughty", few seem to care given the "great" atmosphere.

Talula Ⓜ   26 | 20 | 22 | $52 |
210 23rd St. (bet. Collins Ave. & Dade Blvd.), Miami Beach, 305-672-0778; www.talulaonline.com
Situated on an "unassuming corner" of South Beach is this "outstanding" New American bistro created by the "talented" and married Andrea Curto-Randazzo and Frank Randazzo; their "fine-dining oasis" provides a "serious gastronomic experience" where the food "sings" in a town where it's often "all about looks"; praise extends to the "comfortable", brick-walled setting and "friendly servers."

Tamarind Ⓜ   ▽ 24 | 16 | 22 | $26 |
946 Normandy Dr. (71st St.), Miami Beach, 305-861-6222
Chef-owner (and cookbook author) Vatcharin Bhumichitr's art-filled "sleeper" in Miami Beach's Normandy Isle proffers "beautiful presentations" of "excellent" Thai fare that combines classic dishes with street-food specialties; prices that are "a steal" and a "welcoming staff" turn it into an "unexpected treasure."

TapTap Haitian   21 | 21 | 17 | $28 |
819 Fifth St. (bet. Jefferson & Meridian Aves.), Miami Beach, 305-672-2898
For some "Haitian flavor with SoBe flair", consider this "funky" "off-the-beaten-path" standby, where you can wash down the

"delicious", "authentic" cooking with "awesome drinks"; though naysayers knockknock "slow service", "beautiful", "colorful" decor and "excellent music" (Thursdays–Saturdays) help atone for it.

Timo   23 | 20 | 21 | $45 |
17624 Collins Ave. (bet. 175th Terr. & 178th St.), Sunny Isles Beach, 305-936-1008; www.timorestaurant.com
Join the "good-looking crowd" at this Sunny Isles Italian-Med in a strip mall; it's a "terrific find", thanks to chef Tim Andriola's "sensuous" cuisine and "hip" atmo overseen by a "solid", "accommodating" front of the house; devotees declare it's now officially "on the North Miami radar."

Toni's Sushi Bar ●   26 | 17 | 22 | $41 |
1208 Washington Ave. (12th St.), Miami Beach, 305-673-9368; www.tonisushi.com
The fish's "always fresh" and the room's "always packed" at this SoBe "institution" whose "ultratasty" Japanese fare coupled with an "interesting sake list" has helped win over fans; one caveat: some say the seats are "tiny", so come early for a spot at the sushi bar where the "accommodating" staff makes you feel "relaxed."

Versailles ●   21 | 15 | 18 | $22 |
3555 SW Eighth St. (SW 35th Ave.), 305-444-0240
"Everyone from high-society types to drag queens" makes a pilgrimage to this "lively" late-night Little Havana "landmark" to "rub elbows with politicians", chow down "cheap" Cuban eats or simply "discover the wonders of café con leche" in a "huge", "kitschy" complex; even those who quip "it's a tourist trap" (with so much "gold and mirrors" "you really ought to be wearing sunglasses") agree that "everybody should eat here at least once."

Vix ● Ⓜ   ▽ 25 | 29 | 21 | $80 |
Hotel Victor, 1144 Ocean Dr. (bet. 11th & 12th Sts.), Miami Beach, 305-428-1234; www.hotelvictorsouthbeach.com
New and "ultrachic", this South Beach hot spot in the "posh" Hotel Victor entrances enthusiasts with its "incredible", Jacques Garcia–designed, "jellyfish"-themed decor and "spectacular" Eclectic food that makes you feel like you're taking a culinary trip "around the world"; though it's "pricey", it's still "phenomenal" and "worth all the hype."

Wish   24 | 25 | 22 | $61 |
The Hotel, 801 Collins Ave. (8th St.), Miami Beach, 305-674-9474; www.wishrestaurant.com
Romantics retreat to this "serene" South Beach "favorite" where the "superb", "playful" Asian-influenced New American creations coupled with a "fabulous" Todd Oldham–designed space, featuring an "enchanting", tropical garden, make believers out of many; while prices are "stiff", come once, many insist, and your "only compulsion will be to return."

Milwaukee

TOP FOOD RANKING

	Restaurant	Cuisine
29	Sanford	New American
26	Eddie Martini's	Steakhouse
	5 O'Clock Club	Steakhouse
	Immigrant Room	New American
	Bacchus	New American
25	River Lane Inn	Seafood
	Coquette Cafe	French
	Riversite, The	American
	Osteria del Mondo	Northern Italian
	Sake Tumi	Asian

OTHER NOTEWORTHY PLACES

Barossa	New American
Dancing Ganesha	Indian
Lake Park Bistro	French
Maggiano's	Italian
Mr. B's	Steakhouse
P.F. Chang's	Chinese
Potbelly Sandwich	Sandwich Shop
Roots	Asian/Californian
Saffron Indian Bistro	Indian
Singha	Thai

	F	D	S	C

BACCHUS | 26 | 26 | 26 | $56 |

Cudahy Towers, 925 E. Wells St. (Prospect Ave.), 414-765-1166;
www.bacchusmke.com

"Milwaukee arrives" courtesy of this "snazzy" Downtown "in-a-class-by-itself" "jewel" that's "definitely a place to indulge" your taste for New American cuisine (it "doesn't get much better" than this) served within a "posh" setting; even admirers, though, assert that the "over-attentive staff just needs to relax a bit"; N.B. lunch and cocktails can be had in the glass-enclosed conservatory space.

Barossa Ⓜ | 20 | 17 | 19 | $35 |

235 S. Second St. (Oregon St.), 414-272-8466;
www.barossawinebar.com

"Fresh", "inventive organic creations" that are pleasing to "vegetarians and carnivores alike" (e.g. chicken Eos, a popular item at the "excellent" Sunday brunch) help define this "lovely" New American restaurant in Walker's Point, a "hidden gem" that "everyone wants to like" – in part because its "calm, warming" atmosphere makes it "great for social and business dinners" alike; still, some warn that it "can get pricey depending on what one orders."

Coquette Cafe ⊠   25 | 21 | 23 | $36

316 N. Milwaukee St. (St. Paul Ave.), 414-291-2655;
www.coquettecafe.com

"Is this France?" local Europhiles ask about this "lively" "little bit of Paris" in the "newly hippified" Third Ward, "friendly and creative chef" Sanford 'Sandy' D'Amato's source for "hearty", "innovative" French cuisine "at affordable prices"; the "cozy", "casually elegant" atmosphere is "great for a pre-show meal" at one of the nearby theaters, and D'Amato's new adjacent Harlequin Bakery is "all it was promised to be."

Dancing Ganesha   22 | 18 | 20 | $33

1692-94 N. Van Buren St. (Brady St.), 414-220-0202;
www.dancingganesha.com

"Innovative" and "delicious" "Indian food in a classier atmosphere than most" defines this East Sider that's run by mother-daughter team Usha and Ami Bedi; menu vets know to order one of the inventive nightly specials (including fish and "veg options"), but novices needn't fear, as the "knowledgeable staff" will be happy "to explain it all"; N.B. there's also a casual bar menu.

EDDIE MARTINI'S   26 | 24 | 26 | $54

8612 Watertown Plank Rd. (86th St.), 414-771-6680;
www.eddiemartinis.com

"It's back to the '50s" at this "real gem" of a West Side steakhouse "institution", a classic for "incredible" steaks ("my mouth is watering just thinking about them") and "unbelievable" martinis that's "popular with doctors" from the nearby medical complex and other "Milwaukee bigwigs"; its "sophisticated" "old supper club–like" interior has some convinced that "Frank and Dean are still with us", but remember that the "big drinks" are matched by "big tabs", so "bring extra cash."

5 O'CLOCK CLUB STEAK HOUSE ⊠Ⓜ   26 | 12 | 22 | $46
(fka Coerper's 5 O'Clock Club)

2416 W. State St. (24th St.), 414-342-3553

Clock-watchers "can't stop eating once [they] start" tucking into the "enormous portions" of "to-die-for" steaks at this Central City standby; its "kitsch", "time-warp-into-the-'50s" decor "will bring back memories of the classic steakhouse experience of days gone by", and "the servers will make you feel like you're visiting an older relative's house" – though some "don't like" the "required stop at the bar", where you "order a drink and dinner before getting to your table."

IMMIGRANT ROOM & WINERY, THE ⊠   26 | 26 | 26 | $64

American Club, 419 Highland Dr. (School St.), Kohler, 920-457-8888;
www.destinationkohler.com

For "a fine-dining experience of the highest caliber", "gourmets" go to this "wonderful" "Wisconsin treasure" in Kohler's American Club resort, one of the "finest hotels in the Midwest", where the "elegant" New American fare comes with a "nice wine list" and "doting service" ("at these prices, it should be"); "now *this* is a place for romance and privacy" say fans of its six different dining rooms, which "take you back to the old days"; P.S. if the tab's too high, remember that "the prices on bottles and cheese in The Winery [next door] are extremely fair."

LAKE PARK BISTRO
25 | 27 | 25 | $50

(aka Bartolotta's Lake Park Bistro)
Lake Park Pavilion, 3133 E. Newberry Blvd. (Lake Park Rd.),
414-962-6300; www.lakeparkbistro.com
"It's wonderful to sit by the windows" and revel in the "exquisite" Lake Michigan view (especially "heavenly" at sunset) at this "treat" located in Frederick Law Olmsted–designed Lake Park, where "lots of new twists on old classics" make the "ooh-la-la fabulous French cuisine" "worth every decadent calorie"; factor in a "romantic atmosphere" and staffers who "pay attention to all the details" and it adds up to a "great place for a special occasion" or "the perfect date."

MAGGIANO'S LITTLE ITALY
20 | 19 | 20 | $31

Mayfair Mall, 2500 N. Mayfair Rd. (North Ave.), Wauwatosa,
414-978-1000; www.maggianos.com
Regulars "rely" on this "red-sauce" "Italiano" chain joint (Milwaukee's Most Popular) for its "can't-lose formula" of "affordable", "hearty" "standards" served "family-style" in a "boisterous" "retro" atmosphere where "everyone always seems to be having a great time" – but some dissenters who knock what they call a "faux" vibe and "obscenely large portions" of "blah", "cookie-cutter" cuisine believe it's better to "bring the kids [than] the Italian food lovers."

Mr. B's: A Bartolotta Steakhouse
23 | 20 | 24 | $49

17700 W. Capitol Dr. (Calhoun Rd.), Brookfield, 262-790-7005;
www.mrbssteakhouse.com
Bringing "a bit of the Bartolotta touch" and "consistency" to Brookfield, this cousin of Lake Park Bistro and Bacchus is the "steakhouse of record" for many "locals", "wow"-ing with "excellent", "personal service" from a "terrific staff" that transports "mouthwatering" cuts and "great drinks" in a "stylish yet casual" space; a word of warning from vets to first-timers, though – "remember that this kind of quality comes at a price."

Osteria del Mondo ⊠
25 | 22 | 22 | $48

1028 E. Juneau Ave. (Astor St.), 414-291-3770; www.osteria.com
"Remaining solidly [near] the top of the ladder in Milwaukee", this Downtown Northern Italian delivers "outstanding meals" courtesy of chef/co-owner Marc Bianchini, who "never ceases to amaze" with "elegant fare" that's "inventive" "without being strange"; combined with "wonderful service" and a "comfortable setting" (including "a great patio"), it amounts to a "fine-dining" experience that's "not to be missed"; N.B. a separate cigar lounge and valet parking are available.

P.F. CHANG'S CHINA BISTRO
20 | 20 | 19 | $28

Mayfair Mall, 2500 N. Mayfair Rd. (North Ave.), Wauwatosa,
414-607-1029; www.pfchangs.com
Flatterers of this "friendly" foursome favor its "non-traditional", "varied" Mandarin-style munchables made from "fresh", "identifiable ingredients", plus its "excellent cocktails" and Great Wall of Chocolate dessert ("as big as" the real thing) offered in "upscale-casual" confines with "tasteful decor"; but while adherents assert they "look for" outposts of the "consistent chain" "in every city", foes find the feel "formulaic" and fault the fare as "faux Chinese", saying it's "not for purists."

POTBELLY SANDWICH WORKS
20 | 15 | 18 | $9

135 W. Wisconsin Ave. (Plankinton Ave.), 414-226-0014
17800 W. Bluemound Rd. (bet. Brookfield & Calhoun Rds.),
Brookfield, 262-796-9845
www.potbelly.com

"There's a reason the lines are out the door" at this beloved "fast-food" duo "at the top of their game" with "tasty sandwiches" that "satisfy" "addicts"; though some "first-time"-ers complain of a "confusing ordering system", most insist the "unbelievably speedy" counter staff has it "down to a science", ensuring "you'll never waste a lot of time getting your food."

River Lane Inn ⊠
25 | 18 | 24 | $37

4313 W. River Ln. (Brown Deer Rd.), 414-354-1995

"From [Wednesday] lobster night to the always-changing fish specials on the chalkboard", this "longtime favorite" (sibling to Mequon's Riversite) set in a turn-of-the-century building in an "off-the-beaten-path" North Shore location "still delivers" "consistently great" seafood ferried by "friendly servers" in a "low-key" setting – no wonder it continues to "attract a crowd."

Riversite, The ⊠
25 | 23 | 26 | $46

11120 N. Cedarburg Rd. (Mequon Rd.), Mequon, 262-242-6050

"The always reliable, elegant sister to the River Lane Inn" on the North Shore, this "very popular" place in Mequon keeps dinner "creative" thanks to "artist"-chef Tom Peschong, whose Traditional American specialties are "superb"; "fabulous warm service" from a "stellar staff" that's "knowledgeable about" the "unbeatable wine list" and a "glorious setting" affording a "great view of the Milwaukee River" also make it "worth the drive."

Roots Restaurant & Cellar
25 | 23 | 21 | $37

1818 N. Hubbard St. (Vine St.), 414-374-8480; www.rootsmilwaukee.com

A "class act all the way", this "wonderful place" in Brewers Hill "puts together delicious creations" of Californian-Asian "comfort food" (using some "organically grown local produce" from co-owner Joe Schmidt's nine-acre Cedarburg farm) in "surprisingly inventive combinations that really work"; "perched above the city", its bi-level location also offers "drop-dead views" of Downtown Milwaukee, so "whether upstairs or down" expect an "always-enjoyable" experience; N.B. the Cellar offers a less-formal menu.

Saffron Indian Bistro Ⓜ
∇ 25 | 14 | 20 | $24

17395D-1 W. Blue Mound Rd. (bet. Brookfield & Calhoun Rds.),
Brookfield, 262-784-1332

"Your palate will thank you for the exotic trip" after a visit to this "unassuming and unpretentious" Brookfield strip-mall spot serving "lots of uncommon but delicious specialties from India" that offer an "innovative" respite from the "Americanized" offerings of some other subcontinental venues – indeed, the "food is much nicer than the appearance of the restaurant would suggest"; P.S. don't miss the "great buffet" offered daily at lunch.

Sake Tumi ⊠
25 | 24 | 23 | $34

714 N. Milwaukee St. (bet. Mason St. & Wisconsin Ave.), 414-224-7253;
www.sake-milwaukee.com

"Don't let the corny", *Laugh-In*–style name" "fool you into thinking this isn't a high-quality experience" advise addicts "hooked" on this "amazing" Asian, an "absolute must" Downtown whose "ambitious and well-executed menu has something for everyone" – from "trendy" fusion dishes to traditional Japanese and Korean BBQ fare; also, the "lively dining room" and "fun", "swanky" upstairs Buddha Lounge are "where the beautiful people go to eat sushi" and revel in a "cool vibe."

SANFORD ☒　　　　29 | 26 | 28 | $66
1547 N. Jackson St. (Pleasant St.), 414-276-9608;
www.sanfordrestaurant.com
"Words can't describe" the "world-class" experience at this "hits-on-all-cylinders" East Side New American "gem" that's definitely "in a league by itself" (as evidenced by the fact that it's ranked No. 1 for Food in Wisconsin); eponymous toque-owner Sandy D'Amato gets "all the details right" – from the "sophisticated" "gourmet" fare, to the "unbeatable" service provided by "friendly caring staffers" who can "feel your table's mood", to the "intimate", "ultramodern" dining room; P.S. "try the chef's 'Surprise'", an "especially fabulous seven-course" tasting menu.

Singha Thai　　　　24 | 13 | 18 | $19
2237 S. 108th St. (Lincoln Ave.), 414-541-1234
Singha Thai II
780 N. Jefferson St., 414-226-0288
www.singhathairestaurant.com
"Delicious food" at a "good value" makes for a "great Thai" experience at this West Side "favorite" "hidden in a strip mall"; to be sure, the "uninspired", "no-ambiance" decor keeps some diners away, but folks who flip for the "authentic" fare ("their pad Thai is a favorite") insist the "picturesque" cuisine more than compensates; P.S. the Downtown branch opened recently.

Minneapolis/St. Paul

TOP FOOD RANKING

Restaurant	Cuisine
28 Bayport Cookery	New American
La Belle Vie	Med./New French
27 D'Amico Cucina	Northern Italian
Vincent	French Bistro
Manny's	Steakhouse
Levain	New American
Alma	New American
26 Oceanaire	Seafood
Lucia's	New American
Ristorante Luci	Italian

OTHER NOTEWORTHY PLACES

Cosmos	Eclectic
Cue	New American
Dakota Jazz	Regional American
Five	New American
112 Eatery	Eclectic
Solera	Spanish/Tapas
St. Paul Grill	American
20.21	New American
Zander Cafe	New American
Zelo	Italian

	F	D	S	C

Alma ☒   27 | 21 | 24 | $39
528 University Ave. SE (6th Ave.), Minneapolis, 612-379-4909;
www.restaurantalma.com
"A treasure", this Dinkytown "destination" "near the University" of
Minneapolis is "always packed" thanks to a "constantly changing
menu" of "astonishingly good" New American cuisine courtesy
of chef Alex Roberts, who is "dedicated to fresh local ingredients"
and "sustainable" agriculture; the "spruced-up storefront" space
is "beautiful" yet "homey", and the "attentive" staff provides
"welcoming service", making it "a class act all the way" – though
some sigh "if [only] it were a little cheaper."

BAYPORT COOKERY Ⓜ   28 | 20 | 25 | $51
328 Fifth Ave. N. (Rte. 95), Bayport, 651-430-1066;
www.bayportcookery.com
"A pleasant 30-minute drive from Downtown" through the
"beauty of the St. Croix River area", this "small storefront" spot
"wows" with "amazing" New American food (voted No. 1 in the
area) offered via "excellent", "ever-changing and imaginative"
prix fixe or à la carte meals; it's a "lovely place for a romantic dinner", so "get reservations well in advance"; P.S. "the annual
springtime morel festival is not to be missed."

Cosmos   25 | 26 | 24 | $55 |
Graves 601 Hotel, 601 First Ave. N. (6th St.), Minneapolis,
612-677-1100; www.cosmosrestaurant.com
"Exquisite" Eclectic cuisine is "exceptionally served" by a "top-notch" staff within a "sophisticated setting" at this "sleek dining room" located in the Warehouse District's "über-hip" Graves 601 Hotel; "the food tastes as good as it looks", and the "beautiful-people" "clientele isn't far behind" in the appearance department, making for a "super-chic" environment that seems "far, far away from Minneapolis."

Cue Ⓜ   – | – | – | E |
Guthrie Theater, 806 Second St. S. (Chicago Ave.), Minneapolis,
612-225-6499; www.cueatguthrie.com
The arresting new Jean Nouvel–designed Guthrie Theater has tapped local top toque Lenny Russo (of Heartland in St. Paul) to oversee the kitchen of this New American; here, the chef offers his signature fare fine-tuned and served to posh palates within a glass contemporary setting alongside the Mississippi River.

Dakota Jazz Club & Restaurant   – | – | – | E |
1010 Nicollet Mall (10th St.), Minneapolis, 612-332-1010;
www.dakotacooks.com
Supporters trumpet the metro area's best supper/jazz club and its snazzy David Shea-designed venue smack in the middle of the high-traffic Nicollet Mall (all the better to lure out-of-towners); local foodies and hepcats alike also hail chef Jack Riebel's (ex La Belle Vie) robustly Regional American menu.

D'AMICO CUCINA Ⓩ   27 | 25 | 27 | $52 |
Butler Sq., 100 N. Sixth St. (2nd Ave.), Minneapolis, 612-338-2401;
www.damico.com
With "top-flight, creative Northern Italian cuisine" and a "superb wine list", this "fancy standby" in the Warehouse District is "a can't-miss choice" "for special nights out", and "still the one to beat for entertaining clients" ("try the unparalleled and inventive tasting menu"); the "Tuscan"-like "atmosphere is soothing", "the mood is formal but not uptight" and the "attentive staff" "spoils you rotten" – but be sure to "bring a well-stuffed wallet."

Five Ⓜ   – | – | – | E |
2917 Bryant Ave. S. (Lake St.), Minneapolis, 612-827-5555;
www.fiverestaurant.com
Chef Stewart Woodman (whose résumé includes positions at NYC's Alain Ducasse and Le Bernardin) named his new New American after Uptown's former Fifth Precinct police station, where he now books the city's glitterati who arrive for the modern, artful cuisine and for the setting that boasts a streetside bar, a Fred-and-Ginger staircase leading to the bistro area and a more sedate fine-dining room.

LA BELLE VIE   28 | – | 27 | VE |
510 Groveland Ave. (Hennepin Ave.), Minneapolis, 612-874-6440;
www.labellevie.us
"There's not a bad choice on" the "imaginative Med"–New French menu at this "chef-owned" venue, relocated to the big city from small-town Stillwater, where the "care and attention is evident in the ingredient selection and preparation"; similarly, the

"service is impeccable" and the "lovely wine list is well chosen and fairly priced", making the "experience worth every nickel."

Levain ⌀ Ⓜ   27 17 22 $50
4762 Chicago Ave. (48th St.), Minneapolis, 612-823-7111; www.restaurantlevain.com

Hidden in "out-of-the-way" South Minneapolis, this New American can be nearly "impossible to spot", so look for the "little red door" behind which awaits "fabulous chef Steven Brown's" "trendy NY restaurant–style food (with NY prices)" complemented by an "exemplary wine list"; some decry the "noisy, noisy, noisy" atmosphere and quip that the fare's "as amazing as the decor is sparse", but most suggest you "do not miss" this "rare find."

Lucia's Ⓜ   26 20 24 $35
1432 W. 31st St. (Hennepin Ave.), Minneapolis, 612-825-1572; www.lucias.com

A "pioneer of nouvelle Minnesota cooking", this "upscale neighborhood joint" "in the heart of Uptown" is "always a treat", offering a "small", "balanced" and "frequently changing menu" of New American food made from "fresh, locally produced" provender "cooked in creative ways" by chef-owner Lucia Watson; the "simple", "intimate environment" is further enhanced by a "friendly staff" that makes "excellent service" look "effortless"; P.S. check out her "good wine bar" and new bakery/flower shop next door, too.

MANNY'S STEAKHOUSE   27 20 25 $53
Hyatt Regency, 1300 Nicollet Mall (Grant St.), Minneapolis, 612-339-9900; www.mannyssteakhouse.com

"Still the benchmark" for local chophouses, this "meat eaters' nirvana" in Downtown's Hyatt Regency boasts an "accomplished staff" that serves "perfectly prepared, Flintstone-sized steaks" to a "fairly formal, business-oriented" crowd; some suggest the "old boys' club" decor is "a bit too male" ("women eat steak too!"), but most "satisfied carnivores" suggest you "save your pennies and appetite – you'll need both"; P.S. with its "photographs of past guests", "the bar is definitely the place to sit for ambiance."

OCEANAIRE SEAFOOD ROOM   26 23 25 $51
Hyatt Regency, 1300 Nicollet Mall (Grant St.), Minneapolis, 612-333-2277; www.theoceanaire.com

The "fish is flown in fresh and tastes like it" at this "special-occasion" "seafood palace" in Downtown's Hyatt Regency, a "loud, crowded" outpost of a locally owned national chain that's the Most Popular restaurant "in landlocked Minneapolis"; the kitchen "doesn't miss a beat" in orchestrating an "amazing fish adventure" ("the old standbys are better than you remember, but try their more creative fare – it's excellent"), and the "elegant and attentive" service befits the "swank", "'30s-style" room reminiscent of a "grand ocean liner."

112 Eatery ●   – – – M
112 N. Third St. (1st Ave. N.), Minneapolis, 612-343-7696; www.112eatery.com

The city's after-hours chefs vie for seats with local foodies at this slim, exposed-brick Warehouse District entry offering Isaac Becker's distinctly Eclectic roster (think fried egg and harissa sandwich on one end, and sweetbreads on the other); warmth here is supplied by both the crowds and the chef's wife, Nancy, who runs the front of the house.

Ristorante Luci ⊠ M | 26 | 17 | 24 | $34 |
470 Cleveland Ave. S. (Randolph Ave.), St. Paul, 651-699-8258; www.ristoranteluci.com

"Fine", "authentic Italian" fare "like your mamma would have cooked if she were a native" of The Boot is the forte of this "crowded but cozy" "neighborhood restaurant" in Highland Park, where "superb meals" that would be "a bargain at twice the price" are offered "in a pretension-free atmosphere"; P.S. it can be "hard to get a reservation", so regulars recommend you call "two weeks in advance – the food is worth" the extra effort.

Solera | 24 | 24 | 21 | $39 |
900 Hennepin Ave. (9th St.), Minneapolis, 612-338-0062; www.solera-restaurant.com

"Colorful Gaudí-inspired decor" that's "sensual without being overwrought" evokes "sunny Spain" at this "new favorite" Downtown ("from the folks who brought us La Belle Vie") that "tantalizes" with "an unending list of tasty tapas" "made for sharing" and ferried by a "friendly, helpful" staff; it's not every "epicurean's dream come true", though, with some wondering "what all the hype's about" and warning that those "teeny-tiny" dishes "quickly add up, pricewise"; nevertheless, "the rooftop terrace is all the rage."

ST. PAUL GRILL | 24 | 24 | 24 | $43 |
St. Paul Hotel, 350 Market St. (5th St.), St. Paul, 651-224-7455; www.stpaulgrill.com

"Grand dining in a grand room of a grand hotel" sums up the appeal of this "grande dame" in Downtown St. Paul that "continues to impress" with its "classy", "clubby atmosphere", "gorgeous mirrored bar" and "wonderful view of Rice Park"; it's where the "old-money" crowd meets for "true power lunches" and "excellent pre-theater" dinners of "well-done Traditional American" fare "graciously served" – no wonder well-wishers willingly "spend too much, eat too much and always adore it."

20.21 | – | – | – | E |
Walker Art Center, 1750 Hennepin Ave. (Vineland Pl.), Minneapolis, 612-253-3410; www.wolfgangpuck.com

The Walker Art Center has lured Wolfgang Puck to operate this finer-than-thou eatery; uniformly attired in determinedly upscale funk, the city's cognoscenti meet in the spare, classy digs to dine on the chef's signature Asian-influenced New American eats, peruse a wine list that incites sticker shock in moral Minnesotans, and beg for a window seat to drink in the Downtown skyline view.

VINCENT ⊠ | 27 | 23 | 24 | $48 |
1100 Nicollet Mall (11th St.), Minneapolis, 612-630-1189; www.vincentarestaurant.com

"A welcome oasis", this Downtown "chef-owned gem" is helmed by "imaginative", "charismatic" toque Vincent Francoual, who "sincerely cares what his clients think" and garners *beaucoup de "mercies"* from them for giving his "high-end French Bistro" fare a "Contemporary" American interpretation then pairing it with a "thoughtful wine list"; the "top-notch staff" and "elegant, minimal decor" with "hardwoods, high ceilings and loads of windows" for "people-watching on Nicollet Mall" "complete the package"; P.S. "try the chef's table" in the kitchen.

Zander Cafe   25 | 18 | 22 | $35

525 Selby Ave. (bet. Kent & Mackubin Sts.), St. Paul, 651-222-5224
"Thank goodness for a great neighborhood place we can afford" – so say Selby sorts smitten with this "warm and friendly" "jewel", the "signature restaurant" of chef-owner Alexander "Zander" Dixon ("the Zorro of gastronomy"), who concocts a "creative, inventive" New American menu; the "smart and casual staff", "a wine list to boggle the mind" and "live jazz some nights" are additional attributes that will "keep you coming back" to its "funky, hip" "storefront setting."

ZELO   23 | 25 | 22 | $39

831 Nicollet Mall (9th St.), Minneapolis, 612-333-7000; www.zelomn.com
"The best thing to happen to Minneapolis" next to "Jesse Ventura leaving the state" might be this "chic" Italian Downtown where "beautiful bankers" do that "single" "metrosexual thing"; "creative, modern cooking" (with some Asian thrown in) and decor to match, featuring "dark wood and contemporary decorations galore" in a space staffed by "attentive" servers, make it "a good place to impress a date", or a "pickup" scored in the "happening" bar "where (old) boy meets (young) girl", if he's lucky.

New Jersey

TOP FOOD RANKING

Restaurant	Cuisine
28 Nicholas	New American
Ryland Inn	New French
27 DeLorenzo's	Pizza
Cafe Panache	Eclectic
Cafe Matisse	Eclectic
Scalini Fedeli	Northern Italian
Serenade	New French
Saddle River Inn	French/New Amer.
Augustino's	Southern Italian
Origin	New French/Thai
Whispers	New American
Gables, The	Eclectic
Washington Inn	American
Dining Room	New American
La Isla	Cuban
26 Stage House	New French
Bernards Inn	New American
Chez Catherine	French
Latour	American/French
Rosemary and Sage	New American

OTHER NOTEWORTHY PLACES

Amanda's	New American
Anthony David's	Eclectic/N. Italian
Bistro Olé	Portuguese/Spanish
Blu	New American
Blue Point Grill	Seafood
Cucharamama	South American
CulinAriane	New American
David Burke Fromagerie	New American
Fascino	Italian
Frog and the Peach	New American
Giumarello's	Italian
Hamilton's	Mediterranean
Ixora	French/Japanese
Perryville Inn	American
Pluckemin Inn	New American
Rat's	New French
Sagami	Japanese
Siri's	French/Thai
Zafra	Pan-Latin
Zoe's by the Lake	French

AMANDA'S
| 26 | 25 | 24 | $43 |

908 Washington St. (bet. 9th & 10th Sts.), Hoboken, 201-798-0101;
www.amandasrestaurant.com

Still "wonderful", this "romantic" Hoboken "jewel" in a "beautiful" restored brownstone is renowned for its "fabulous", "creative" New American menu, "thoughtfully" selected wines, "impeccable" service and "lovely" decor – "and how can you beat their early-bird special?"; a "stupendous bargain" at $14 per person.

Anthony David's
| 26 | 20 | 21 | $37 |

953 Bloomfield St. (10th St.), Hoboken, 201-222-8399

Admirers "love, love, love" chef-owner Anthony Pino's "tiny", "first-class" Hoboken BYO, where the "superb", "evolving" Eclectic–Northern Italian fare is complemented by what many consider an "excellent cheese selection"; fans are also quite fond of the "wonderful" weekend brunch and "jazzy, casual" ambiance; here's a tip: "book a reservation in advance."

Augustino's ∅
| 27 | 19 | 24 | $37 |

1104 Washington St. (bet. 11th & 12th Sts.), Hoboken, 201-420-0104

Expect a "treat" if you're "lucky enough" to reserve at this "intimate" Hoboken Southern Italian, where the prize is "glorious" "homespun" cooking, a "tiny", "cozy" brick-walled dining room and "mouthy" but "ultrafriendly" waitresses who "act like you're a regular"; be sure to call ahead – "unless you know someone."

BERNARDS INN, THE
| 26 | 26 | 25 | VE |

27 Mine Brook Rd. (Quimby Ln.), Bernardsville, 908-766-0002;
www.bernardsinn.com

Chef Corey Heyer's tenure at the "grande dame" of "special-occasion" dining in Bernardsville has been "extraordinary", and the "magic" of this "classic" in the land of "blue bloods" remains on all fronts, from the "blue-ribbon" New American cuisine to "superb" service to an "incredible wines"; though the prices may seem "exorbitant", the experience here is likely to be "memorable."

Bistro Olé Ⓜ
| 26 | 19 | 23 | $36 |

230 Main St. (bet. Cookman & Mattison Aves.), Asbury Park,
732-897-0048; www.bistroole.com

Adding a second dining room has given more folks a chance to check out chef Wil Vivas' "lively", "exceptional" cooking, a "celeb"-worthy greeting from host-owner Rico Rivera and "enthusiastic" service at this "swanky" Spanish-Portuguese "pearl" in Asbury Park; P.S. "the waits to get in" can be "insane."

Blu Ⓜ
| – | – | – | E |

554 Bloomfield Ave. (bet. Park St. & Valley Rd.), Montclair, 973-509-2202;
www.restaurantblu.com

Chef-owner Zod Arifai (ex Charlie Trotter's in Chicago, and Bouley in NYC) gives Montclair this small storefront BYO that's joined the ranks of Jersey's more important openings; propelled by artful presentations of seafood-strong New American fare and a modern-retro setting, it's quickly become the darling of the local scene.

Blue Point Grill
| 26 | 15 | 21 | $34 |

258 Nassau St. (Pine St.), Princeton, 609-921-1211;
www.bluepointgrill.com

Scoring points for its "amazing" "variety" of "flawless", "super-fresh" seafood preparations "kept simple" is this "casual"

Princeton BYO that's usually "packed to the gills"; the "great" raw bar and "efficient" staff keep "hooking" 'em despite "long" lines and "noise."

CAFE MATISSE M
27 | 26 | 26 | $60

167 Park Ave. (bet. E. Park Pl. & Highland Cross), Rutherford, 201-935-2995; www.cafematisse.com

A "go-to place" for a "special-occasion" "splurge", this "romantic" Rutherford BYO in a "charmingly decorated" renovated firehouse wows with a "consistently amazing" Eclectic menu, a "pastry chef who works wonders" and a "knowledgeable" staff that "pays attention to details"; the "velvet chairs" and "jeweled chandeliers" add to "beautiful" decor even the maestro would have approved; P.S. there's a wine shop up front – "how perfect is that?"

CAFE PANACHE Z
27 | 21 | 25 | $52

130 E. Main St. (Rte. 17), Ramsey, 201-934-0030

It's no surprise that reservations are "hard to come by" at "one of Bergen's best", a Ramsey BYO via "magician" chef-owner Kevin Kohler that "delights" both "palate" and soul with an "ever-changing" menu of "terrific" Eclectic fare incorporating "fresh" ingredients "sourced from local farmers"; "impeccable" service and a recent decor "upgrade" adds to a "wonderful" experience.

Chez Catherine Z M
26 | 21 | 24 | $57

431 North Ave. (E. Broad St.), Westfield, 908-654-4011; www.chezcatherine.com

Edith and Didier Jouvenet are "doing a marvelous" job carrying on the tradition set by their predecessor; their "cozy" French "landmark" in Westfield treats its audience to "beautiful" preparations of sometimes "otherworldy" cuisine and service from a "first-class" staff, making it a "superb" choice for a "special day or date."

Cucharamama M
25 | 27 | 22 | $41

233 Clinton St. (bet. 2nd & 3rd Sts.), Hoboken, 201-420-1700; www.cucharamama.com

Maricel Presilla's "amazing" Hoboken South American a block away from her sister restaurant, Zafra, "will delight your senses" with "powerful flavors" and an "ingenious use of ingredients" revealed in the "phenomenal" fare that's backed by "sexy", "swanky" sub-equatorial decor; "small" and sometimes "tough to get into", those who don't mind "waiting" are glad they did.

CulinAriane Z M
— | — | — | E

33 Walnut St. (Pine St.), Montclair, 973-744-0533

Purveying both a globally inspired New American menu and a stylish setting is this fledgling, off-the-beaten-path Montclair newcomer that's run by husband-and-wife chef team Ariane and Michael Duarte (she's in charge of the savories, while he's responsible for pastries); the 30-seat BYO has quickly become a contender in this restaurant-savvy town – and a tough reservation to snag; N.B. there's sidewalk seating in the summer.

David Burke Fromagerie M
— | — | — | E

26 Ridge Rd. (Ave. of Two Rivers), Rumson, 732-842-8088; www.fromagerierestaurant.com

NJ fans of David Burke (of NYC's davidburke & donatella) needn't B&T-it for his fanciful New American fare: the celebrity chef has acquired Rumson's Classic French mainstay, Fromagerie (he ap-

prenticed here some 25 years ago), and renovated not only the interior (which now sports a more contemporary look), but also
tweaked the menu, which bears a few of the toque's signatures –
pastrami smoked salmon and cheesecake pops.

DELORENZO'S TOMATO PIES ⓂⒹ̷　　27 | 8 | 15 | $15
530 Hudson St. (bet. Mott & Swann Sts.), Trenton, 609-695-9534
If all the "universe" were filled with competitors, this Trenton
"institution" with "zero" decor and no bathroom might still "sur-
pass" all others for its "thin-crust", "perfectly crisp" pies; "join
the line" "around the corner" to gain admission to the No. 1 pizza
spot in our *Survey* – again – that offers up its "brilliant" creations
to legions of fawning followers.

Dining Room, The ⒮Ⓜ　　　　27 | 26 | 26 | $69
Hilton at Short Hills, 41 JFK Pkwy. (Rte. 24), Short Hills, 973-379-0100;
www.hiltonshorthills.com
Reserve this "elegant" and "formal" Hilton New American near
the Mall at Short Hills for those "momentous life events", or if
you're just in the mood to indulge in the "epitome of fine dining in
NJ"; it's "tops" in every way, from the "exquisitely prepared"
food, to the "romantic" ambiance to the "superb" service – but
remember to bring a "Brinks truck" to pay for it.

Fascino ⒮　　　　　　　26 | 20 | 24 | $47
331 Bloomfield Ave. (bet. Grove & Willow Sts.), Montclair, 973-233-0350;
www.fascinorestaurant.com
"Top-notch", this "bustling" Montclair BYO run by the "warm and
talented" DePersio family is "so hot" that "reservations" are
almost "impossible" to get since there have been "nothing but
raves" about its "outstanding" "nouveau" Italian cuisine (save
space for some "dreamy desserts"), "superb" service and
"cool", "sleek" decor; in simple words, it's "fantastic."

FROG AND THE PEACH, THE　　　26 | 23 | 24 | $57
29 Dennis St. (Hiram Sq.), New Brunswick, 732-846-3216;
www.frogandpeach.com
An example of "excellence on all fronts" is New Brunswick's
"favorite" son, a New American that "continues to amaze" repeat visitors with "innovative", "brilliantly executed" food, "top-
notch" service and a "superb" wine list; it's "still one of the finest"
and "most beautiful" restaurants in the state, but "oy! the prices"
are not for the faint of heart.

Gables, The　　　　　　　27 | 22 | 25 | VE
Green Gables Inn, 212 Center St. (bet. Bay & Beach Aves.),
Beach Haven, 609-492-3553; www.gableslbi.com
Though there are no written menus, acolytes who deem this
Victorian Beach Haven BYO "wonderful" don't seem to mind,
since the Eclectic food on the five-course prix fixe is "phenomenal"; it's true, "you never know what you're going to get", but you
can bet the farm there'll be "accommodating" service and a "romantic" setting during your "enchanted evening."

Giumarello's Ⓜ　　　　　25 | 23 | 23 | $48
329 Haddon Ave. (bet. Cuthbert Blvd. & Kings Hwy.), Westmont,
856-858-9400; www.giumarellos.com
"Be prepared to spend" – though it'll be "well worth it" – is the
dish on this "family"-operated Italian in Westmont associated

with "excellent" food and service; the "romantic", "peaceful" patio takes you "far away from the suburbs", but some say the experience is enhanced by sipping "great" martinis at the bar and watching "off-duty lawyers" playing "pickup."

Hamilton's Grill Room
| 25 | 20 | 22 | $47 |

8 Coryell St. (N. Union St.), Lambertville, 609-397-4343;
www.hamiltonsgrillroom.com

"Outstanding" grilled fare cooked before you, a "charming" courtyard location alongside the Delaware Canal and rustic decor distinguish this Med BYO, a "treasure" in Lambertville; "bring a date" and "eat outside" some advise, or to while away the time, "grab a drink at the nearby Boat House bar."

Ixora M
| 25 | 21 | 23 | $51 |

407 Hwy. 22 E. (Rte. 523), Whitehouse Station, 908-534-6676;
www.ixoranj.com

This Whitehouse Station "strip-mall" "sleeper" may not be one of New Jersey's "best-kept secrets" for long, not after an across-the-board jump in its ratings this year, a testimony to its "pristine sushi" and other "outstanding" items on the "innovative" Japanese-French fusion menu, as well as the "elegant, modern" decor and "helpful, unobtrusive" staff.

La Isla
| 27 | 10 | 19 | $19 |

104 Washington St. (bet. 1st & 2nd Sts.), Hoboken, 201-659-8197;
www.laislarestaurant.com

"Ridiculously small" but packing the energy of a supernova, this "festive", "diner-esque" Hoboken BYO cooks up "the best Cuban food you've ever had" that arrives via a "quick" and "busy, busy" floor crew; the "multitudes" willing to wait for a table is evidence of its "popularity"; N.B. no reservations taken.

Latour M
| 26 | 22 | 24 | $49 |

6 E. Ridgewood Ave. (Broad St.), Ridgewood, 201-445-5056

Chef-owner Michael Latour's "fabulous" French-American cuisine matched by "consistently top-notch" service and an "elegant", "lovely and low-key" setting have put this "quaint storefront" "by the train" in Ridgewood on many a "must" list; it is "popular", "small" and utterly "charming" – and "tough to get a reservation."

NICHOLAS M
| 28 | 24 | 28 | $79 |

160 Rte. 35 S. (bet. Navesink River Rd. & Pine St.), Middletown,
732-345-9977; www.restaurantnicholas.com

Though the setting is "sophisticated" and "calm", the "tasting menu delivers a roller-coaster" ride "for the taste buds" at Melissa and Nicholas Harary's "spectacular" Middletown New American (No. 1 for Food in New Jersey); you may have to "mortgage the Shore house" to experience its "culinary masterpieces", but it's a "place to celebrate" offering a "Mercedes meal" complete with an "impeccable", "unobtrusive" staff: just call it "perfect"; N.B. the new bar/lounge area seats up to 30.

Origin
| 27 | 20 | 20 | $34 |

10 South St. (Morris St.), Morristown, 973-971-9933
25 Division St. (Main St.), Somerville, 908-685-1344 M
www.originthai.com

You may ask yourself if "the flavors are from France, Thailand or heaven"? admit those awed by these paeans to fusion fare in

Morristown (the new sibling) and Somerville (the older, but recently expanded original); no matter, exult those who dub these BYOs "a delight for all five senses" and a "true adventure in eating", and even if the crowds often "overwhelm" the staff, diners are "transported by the first bite."

Perryville Inn Ⓜ 26 | 24 | 24 | $52
167 Perryville Rd. (I-78, exit 12), Union Township, 908-730-9500;
www.theperryvilleinn.com
"A country classic" in Hunterdon County is this "perfect getaway" in a "historic" 1813 Colonial building where "consistently" "well-executed" American fare courtesy of chef-owner Paul Ingenito "hits a homer"; it makes for an "exquisitely romantic" dinner, prompting partisans to brag it's a "find off Route 78."

Pluckemin Inn, The Ⓢ – | – | – | VE
359 Rte. 202/206 S. (Pluckemin Way), Bedminster, 908-658-9292;
www.pluckemininn.com
High class, high concept and high prices define this Bedminster New American, a rebuilt Colonial-style manse that's rapidly becoming the in place to be in Somerset Hills; the menu (now under the care of new executive chef David Felton) includes a pastry-wrapped 'brik' of halibut, hamachi tartare and avocado ice cream; it's supplemented by a 2,100-label wine list and 10,000 bottles stored in a three-story tower that dominates each of the four plush, posh dining rooms.

Rat's Ⓜ 24 | 27 | 23 | $64
Grounds for Sculpture, 16 Fairgrounds Rd. (Sculptors Way), Hamilton,
609-584-7800; www.ratsrestaurant.org
Look up "beautiful" in Webster's and find a picture of this "destination" Hamilton New French in the "whimsical" and "alluring" Grounds for Sculpture; stroll through the "otherworldly" sculpture gardens before or after settling in to the "gourmet" food complemented by a wine list that "justifies repeat visits"; and even if some find the staff a bit "snooty", the consensus is it's "worth going here at least once."

Rosemary and Sage Ⓜ 26 | 19 | 23 | $50
26 Hamburg Tpke. (I-287, exit 53), Riverdale, 973-616-0606;
www.rosemaryandsage.com
"All you seek is here" at this 60-seat Riverdale home for "foodies", where "new items are added regularly" to an "outstanding" New American menu and the "lovely owners" "pay attention to details"; with "interesting, affordable" wines and a value prix fixe, "you won't be disappointed"; N.B. Wednesday–Sunday, dinner only.

RYLAND INN, THE 28 | 27 | 26 | $87
Rte. 22 W. (Rte. 523), Whitehouse, 908-534-4011;
www.rylandinn.com
"The magic of culinary excellence" inspires acolytes to worship at the "granddaddy of NJ restaurants" (the state's Most Popular restaurant), a showcase for the "gastronomic wizardry" of "brilliant" chef Craig Shelton; since 1991, devout diners have been making pilgrimages to this country inn in Whitehouse to savor "magnificent" New French fare (bolstered by the on-site organic garden), service that "misses nothing" and "superbly" selected wines; all of the above begs the question "how can you improve perfection?"

Saddle River Inn ⊠Ⓜ
27 | 25 | 25 | $59

2 Barnstable Ct. (bet. E. Allendale Ave. & W. Saddle River Rd.),
Saddle River, 201-825-4016; www.saddleriverinn.com

"Once you open the doors, the enchanted journey begins" at this
Saddle River "gem" in a "quaint barn" that "oozes country elegance", a "veteran" creating "exceptional" French–New
American food "without novelties", "foams or fussiness"; with a
"chef-owner who really cares", and who "understands the
subtleties of good service", it's no surprise this BYO "continues to
perform at the top of its game."

Sagami Ⓜ
26 | 15 | 21 | $35

37 W. Crescent Blvd. (Haddon Ave.), Collingswood, 856-854-9773

Still "heaven in the raw for fans" is the sushi that's "as fresh as
you can get on this side of the world" at Collingswood's 32-year-
old Japanese BYO; for "flawless" fish, you'll have to settle for
"low-ceilinged" quarters, but it's a small concession, since this
mainstay continues to bring "joy" to its loyal fans; N.B. before
dinner, drop by Moore Brothers Wines.

SCALINI FEDELI ⊠
27 | 25 | 24 | $64

63 Main St. (Parrot Mill Rd.), Chatham, 973-701-9200;
www.scalinifedeli.com

"Culinary heaven on earth", this "beautiful", "world-class"
Chatham Northern Italian "pampers" patrons lucky enough to get
in – what can be a long wait for a reservation is forgotten after
tasting Michael Cetrulo's "magical" prix fixe "wonders" served
by a "staff that knows the right amount of schmooze"; the only issue, for many, is deciding which of the "divine" creations to order.

Serenade
27 | 26 | 26 | $66

6 Roosevelt Ave. (Main St.), Chatham, 973-701-0303;
www.restaurantserenade.com

Hitting all the high notes with surveyors, this "magnificent" New
French in Chatham (from the union of "husband-chef" James
Laird and "wife-in-front" Nancy Sheridan Laird) is "fabulous from
start to finish", with "breathtaking" food, an "incredible wine list"
shepherded by a "very user-friendly" sommelier, "understated
service" and a "magical setting"; all in all, this one will "impress"
"even people from NYC."

Siri's Thai French Cuisine
25 | 20 | 23 | $37

2117 Old Marlton Pike (Mimosa Dr.), Cherry Hill, 856-663-6781;
www.siris-nj.com

Don't be "fooled" by the strip-mall location, since there's "terrific" fare to spare at this "upscale" BYO Cherry Hill mainstay
whose "reasonably" priced food successfully fuses "the best of
Thai and French" cuisines; factor in "impeccable" service from
"knowledgeable" folks, and you can see why it's been a "special"
spot for years.

Stage House Restaurant & Wine Bar
26 | 24 | 24 | $62

366 Park Ave. (Front St.), Scotch Plains, 908-322-4224;
www.stagehouserestaurant.com

Even in the post–David Drake era, "it all still works" at this "romantic" "gem on the sleepy main drag" of Scotch Plains where
New French fare is served in a "charming" 1737 building; dig into
the seasonal "market menu" insiders advise, or relax "in front of

a roaring fire in the winter" over dishes that are "perfectly refined and ready" for what's on the "incredible wine list"; N.B. a more casual dining area opened post-*Survey*.

Washington Inn
| 27 | 25 | 26 | $54 |

801 Washington St. (Jefferson St.), Cape May, 609-884-5697; www.washingtoninn.com

"Unlike the weather, you can always count on it to be great" say diehards of this American that's "as good as it gets in Cape May", an "always on-the-money", "up-to-date" "favorite" with "fantastic" fare and an "outstanding" 900-bottle wine list; other restaurants "should send their staff here for training", since "no detail is forgotten", so even though it may be "tough on the pocketbook", the entire package is deemed "total class all the way."

Whispers
| 27 | 23 | 25 | $52 |

Hewitt Wellington Hotel, 200 Monmouth Ave. (2nd Ave.), Spring Lake, 732-974-9755; www.whispersrestaurant.com

If the "sublime" is what you seek, by all means try this chandeliered New American "wonder" in Spring Lake offering an "awesome, intimate dining experience" that's even more "memorable in the off-season"; its "heavenly" fare, BYO status and staff "on standby" to serve may soften the screams of those who say you'll need "a high credit limit" on that platinum.

Zafra
| 25 | 18 | 19 | $30 |

301 Willow Ave. (3rd St.), Hoboken, 201-610-9801

"Close your eyes and blindly point to anything on the menu" at this "superior" Hoboken Pan-Latino with "too many delicious dishes to highlight" and too little room to make folks feel anything other than "cramped"; still, chef-scholar Maricel Presilla makes it a "pleasure to dine" at her "colorful" BYO whose "high-quality" fare turns any meal into an "affordable" experience; in simple words, go and "wait on line" if you must.

Zoe's by the Lake Ⓜ
| 26 | 23 | 25 | $51 |

112 Tomahawk Trail (2 mi. east of Rte. 15), Sparta, 973-726-7226; www.zoesbythelake.com

Called "a miracle in the boondocks of northwestern New Jersey", this bi-level "find" has gushers grateful for its "seriously thoughtful" French menu that "grabs your attention" and for the "scrumptious food that keeps it"; with a staff that "charms", and "classy, understated elegance" pervading the setting overlooking Seneca Lake, this one would be "outstanding anywhere."

New Orleans

TOP FOOD RANKING

Restaurant	Cuisine
28 August	Continental/New French
Brigtsen's	Contemp. Louisiana
Bayona	New American
Stella!	New American
Alberta	French Bistro
Cuvée	Creole/Continental
27 La Provence	French
Mosca's	Italian
Vizard's on the Avenue*	Creole/Mediterranean
Jacques-Imo's Cafe	Creole
Clancy's	Creole
Dakota, The	Contemp. LA/New Amer.
Galatoire's	Creole/French
K-Paul's	Cajun
Herbsaint	New Amer./French
Dick & Jenny's	Creole/French
26 Upperline	Contemp. Louisiana
Dickie Brennan's	Steakhouse
Irene's Cuisine	Southern Italian
Lilette	French Bistro

OTHER NOTEWORTHY PLACES

Antoine's	Creole
Arnaud's	Creole
Brennan's	Creole/French
Broussard's	Creole/French
Café Adelaide	Creole
Café Degas	French Bistro
Cochon	Cajun
Emeril's	Contemp. Louisiana
Iris	New American
La Petite Grocery	Contemp. Louisiana
Lola's	Spanish
Muriel's	Creole
New Orleans Grill	New American
Nine Roses	Vietnamese
NOLA	Contemp. LA/Creole
Pelican Club	New American
Peristyle	Contemp. LA/French
Ralph's on the Park	Contemp. LA/Creole
Rib Room	Steakhouse
RioMar	Seafood/Spanish

---

* Indicates a tie with restaurant above

ALBERTA 🖼Ⓜ 28 | 21 | 24 | $54

5015 Magazine St. (Robert St.), 504-891-3015

Regulars whisper "don't tell" about this year-old, unmarked Uptowner where fans are "floored" by chef Melody Pate's "intricate", "avant-garde" French bistro food; though some say it's "pricey", most are "charmed" by the "kind, ebullient staff" and "hip", "jewel box" setting with "honey-colored" lighting that flatters "everyone" – so naturally "reservations are a must."

Antoine's 24 | 24 | 24 | $55

713 St. Louis St. (bet. Bourbon & Royal Sts.), 504-581-4422;
www.antoines.com

"You can feel the history" in this "beautiful", circa-1840 French Quarter "landmark", a Creole "grande dame" known for "classics" like oysters Rockefeller (which was invented here and "lives up to the hype"); it's long been a "special-occasion" destination for "New Orleans society" and a tourist "must-do", and admirers report "new energy" post-Katrina, finding service "more attentive" and the recently introduced Sunday jazz brunch "simply magical."

Arnaud's 26 | 25 | 26 | $50

813 Bienville St. (bet. Bourbon & Dauphine Sts.), 504-523-5433;
www.arnauds.com

"Old school . . . but wow" say those dazzled by this "jewel of the Quarter", a "fabulous reminder of times that were", serving "remarkable", "traditional" Creole cuisine in an "elegant" tile-paved dining room (with the house Mardi Gras museum located upstairs); from its Sunday brunch – when the "jazz is fine and the milk punch potent" – to its "gracious" service, it remains a "quintessential", if "expensive", Crescent City "original."

AUGUST 🖼Ⓜ 28 | 28 | 27 | $58

301 Tchoupitoulas St. (Gravier St.), 504-299-9777;
www.restaurantaugust.com

"Spectacular" dishes blending "European style" with "a touch of the bayou" enchant guests at this "elegant" CBD Continental–New French, ranked No. 1 in New Orleans for Food, where chef John Besh crafts a "daring" menu showcasing pristine local ingredients; the "drop-dead gorgeous" surroundings, a "warm", "knowledgeable" staff and presentation "so beautiful you hesitate to mess up the plate", it's "pricey", but you'll be "too blissed out to notice."

BAYONA 🖼Ⓜ 28 | 25 | 26 | $53

430 Dauphine St. (bet. Conti & St. Louis Sts.), 504-525-4455;
www.bayona.com

Fans of the "original", "peerless" New American cuisine with "global influences" created by "masterful" celeb chef-owner Susan Spicer say it "doesn't get any better" than this French Quarter "favorite", whose Creole-cottage setting has a "gracious", slightly "formal" interior and a "lovely patio"; the prix fixe options remain "a deal", and though Katrina ruined the wine cellar, an "amazing new wine list" is in place.

BRENNAN'S 25 | 24 | 24 | $51

417 Royal St. (bet. Conti & St. Louis Sts.), 504-525-9711;
www.brennansneworleans.com

"One of those places that defines old New Orleans", this Creole-French cornerstone of the Brennan "family dynasty" and birthplace of "addictive bananas Foster" invites a "tourist"-heavy French Quarter crowd to "linger" over its famous, "decadent" "three-hour breakfast", which costs big bucks "if you do it right"; "first-rate" dinners, "Southern hospitality", a "pleasant" if "dated" dining room and a "beautiful courtyard" are pluses, and if some say "overrated", more concur "you gotta go" "at least once."

BRIGTSEN'S 🗷 Ⓜ︎   28 22 27 $47

723 Dante St. (Maple St.), 504-861-7610; www.brigtsens.com
"Genius" chef Frank Brigtsen and his "exquisite", "imaginative interpretation" of "Louisiana home cooking" provide a "true NOLA experience" at this "charming Creole cottage" in Riverbend; the blue-ribbon wine list, lively people-watching and a staff that "treats you like family" while displaying "excellent attention to detail" round out a meal that's more than "worth the cab ride"; N.B. book early.

Broussard's   24 25 25 $51

819 Conti St. (Bourbon St.), 504-581-3866;
www.broussards.com
At this "top-notch" yet relatively "underrated" "Quarter landmark", longtime chef-owner Gunter Preuss prepares "fresh", "delicious" Creole-French fare with an "artistic" touch; the tastefully decorated dining room and "fantastic" courtyard, combined with "high-end service" that's "old fashioned (in a good sense)", make it a "favorite romantic spot."

Café Adelaide   24 24 24 $44

Loews New Orleans Hotel, 300 Poydras St. (S. Peters St.), 504-595-3305;
www.cafeadelaide.com
Owners Ti Martin and Lally Brennan, along with chef Danny Trace (Commander's Palace), preside over this "fine outpost of the Brennan empire" inside the CBD's Loews Hotel; the "Creole-inspired but not Creole-limited" menu offers "tasty", "clever reworkings of local seafood dishes", and service is generally "on its game", so even if some find the "modern" room overly "lobby"-like, the "New Orleans elite" is hooked.

Café Degas Ⓜ︎   24 22 21 $32

3127 Esplanade Ave. (Ponce de Leon St.), 504-945-5635;
www.cafedegas.com
Edgar himself would say *"très charmant"* to this "arty" "touch of France" on the Esplanade Ridge "down the street from NOMA"; it serves "affordable", "delectable" "classic bistro fare" on an enclosed deck reminiscent of a "tiny" "tree house" (indeed, a pecan tree grows right inside), making it a "cheery" destination whether for a "first date", Sunday brunch or "dinner with friends."

Clancy's 🗷   27 22 25 $45

6100 Annunciation St. (Webster St.), 504-895-1111
"Sublime smoked soft-shell crab" and "ooh-la-la" "oysters with Brie" among other "exquisite" dishes tantalize a "tony", "table-hopping" "who's who" of "old New Orleans" at this "country club"–style Creole that some call the "Galatoire's of Uptown"; it can be "noisy and crowded" but "stands out as the quintessential locals' favorite", since it's "tucked away from all things touristy" and the "tuxedoed servers" have an "excellent rapport" with regulars.

Cochon ☒ 25 | 22 | 23 | $35
930 Tchoupitoulas St. (bet. Andrew Higgins Dr. & S. Diamond St.),
504-588-2123; www.cochonrestaurant.com
Locals "pigging out" on "tapas-style plates" of "authentic", pork-centric Cajun cuisine say "cheers for Donald Link" (also of Herbsaint), the chef/co-owner who fires up "dynamite" Southern Louisiana cooking inside this new Warehouse District "temple of swine"; the "fab" staff, open kitchen with wood-burning oven and "upscale-casual picnicky decor" guar-ontee it's a "real fun spot" to "bring friends" and "sample a little of everything."

Cuvée ☒ 28 | 26 | 26 | $55
St. James Hotel, 322 Magazine St. (bet. Gravier & Poydras Sts.),
504-587-9001; www.restaurantcuvee.com
Even in "the darkest days" just after Katrina, this Creole-Continental "shining light" in the CBD maintained "exceptional" standards, starting with chef Bob Iacovone's "outstanding", "creative" local cuisine with rich touches (e.g. "last meal"–worthy duck confit); the "wonderful" "French-focused wine list", "polished service" and "warm, dark decor" of exposed brick and gas lamps also help secure its rep as a "special-occasion" "gem."

Dakota, The ☒ 27 | 23 | 25 | $49
629 N. Hwy. 190 (¼ mi. north of I-12), Covington, 985-892-3712;
www.thedakotarestaurant.com
This Cuvée sibling wins accolades as the "most accomplished restaurant on the Northshore" thanks to the likes of "excellent game", "fabulous crab and Brie soup" and other "decadent, delicious" New American–Contemporary Louisiana dishes; factor in "awesome wines", "exceptional service" and a setting enriched by deep colors and "great art on the walls" and most agree it's "worth the drive across the Causeway."

Dick & Jenny's ☒ Ⓜ 27 | 21 | 24 | $37
4501 Tchoupitoulas St. (Jena St.), 504-894-9880; www.dickandjennys.com
Following what many call a "seamless" change of owners post-Katrina, this clapboard-cottage bistro on a "working-class" Uptown block remains "beloved" by locals thanks to "sumptuous", "soulful" Creole-French "comfort food" that "reflects the seasons" and comes at "very reasonable prices"; with the same "friendly" servers and "laid-back", "folk-art" atmosphere, it continues to draw fans who roll with the no-reserving policy by "lazing" away the "long waits" sipping cocktails while "relaxing on the patio rockers."

Dickie Brennan's Steakhouse 26 | 25 | 25 | $53
716 Iberville St. (bet. Bourbon & Royal Sts.), 504-522-2467;
www.dickiebrennanssteakhouse.com
"Astounding steaks" "so tender they practically melt on the plate" wrangle French Quarter frequenters to this "beef eater's paradise" from the Brennan clan; the menu comes through with "all the extras" plus a "superior" wine selection, and the "clubby", "masculine" wood-paneled rooms, "well-trained" staff and hefty price tag are exactly what you'd expect "when you need that meat."

EMERIL'S 25 | 24 | 25 | $59
800 Tchoupitoulas St. (Julia St.), 504-528-9393; www.emerils.com
"Don't let the celebrity-chef status hold you back" say a bevy of "bam!" believers who laud this Lagasse flagship in the Warehouse

District for "robustly flavored", "earthy" eats that "capture the essence of New Orleans–style haute cuisine"; its "crisp" service, "sleek" looks and high "energy" ("the chef's bar is what I call 'dinner and a show'") please most, though dissenters knock it as a "tourist mecca" that needs to kick it "down a notch" in terms of "noise" and cost.

GALATOIRE'S M 27 | 26 | 27 | $51

209 Bourbon St. (Iberville St.), 504-525-2021; www.galatoires.com
"You could see Blanche DuBois sipping a Sazerac" at this "old-line", "almost cultish" French Quarter centenarian – the city's Most Popular restaurant – a "'dress up and live large' kinda place" where "bigwigs" and "ladies in hats" find "gastronomic heaven" in "classic" Creole-French fare; for best results, snag a table in the tiled downstairs room ("where the action is"), "get to know your waiter" ("let him choose for you") and don't be surprised if a leisurely lunch "turns into dinner", especially on Fridays; N.B. jackets required after 5 PM and on Sundays.

Herbsaint ☒ 27 | 22 | 25 | $45

701 St. Charles Ave. (Girod St.), 504-524-4114; www.herbsaint.com
In "top form" post-Katrina, the kitchen at this Warehouse District "winner" turns out "stellar" New American–French fare with a "Southern twist" and a touch of "whimsy", thanks to "truly talented" chef Donald Link; its "chic" dining room is both "casual" and "electric", energized by "enticing" cocktails, a "wonderful wine list" and "smart service" – in sum, "another home run" from co-owner Susan Spicer.

Irene's Cuisine ☒ 26 | 22 | 23 | $41

539 St. Philip St. (Chartres St.), 504-529-8811
"Locals love" this "dark", "romantic" trattoria that tourists seem to "find with their noses" as the scent of "delectable" Southern Italian food permeates its French Quarter block; inside, "cozy, quirky" dining rooms, a "delightful staff" and "great piano bar" keep spirits soaring – but since no reserving can mean "painful" waits, you'd best show up early, add your name to the list and "take the opportunity" to explore the area.

Iris ☒ 25 | 19 | 23 | $40

8115 Jeannette St. (S. Carrollton Ave.), 504-862-5848;
www.irisneworleans.com
Chef Ian Schnoebelen and co-owner Laurie Casebonne (both ex Lilette) make this new Carrollton "gem" "shine", serving "fresh", "imaginative" New American meals – not to mention "superb martinis"; early-comers add that the "small but charming" cottage setting and "knowledgeable staff" heighten the appeal of this "hot" spot that's "quickly become a local favorite."

Jacques-Imo's Cafe ☒ 27 | 21 | 22 | $33

8324 Oak St. (S. Carrollton Ave.), 504-861-0886;
www.jacquesimoscafe.com
Fans of Jack Leonardi's "big-flavored", "down-home" Creole soul cooking at this Carrollton "dive" assure you'll be "sighing in bliss and loosening your pants" before you can say "alligator cheesecake" (a "must-try"); sure, many bemoan the "insanely long" waits that can run over an hour, but even so most call this "funky", "boisterous" "Tulane" fave "a blast" that "could only exist in New Orleans."

K-Paul's Louisiana Kitchen ⏣

27 | 21 | 24 | $48

416 Chartres St. (bet. Conti & St. Louis Sts.), 504-596-2530;
www.kpauls.com

"Not the cliché you'd expect", the French Quarter birthplace of blackened redfish maintains high standards thanks to "flavor virtuoso" Paul Prudhomme and his "complex, sophisticated interpretation" of "robustly" spiced Cajun food; "long waits" are often a prelude to the "hot and pricey" fare, but "spirited" service and a "charming", "casual" atmosphere that encourages "talking to people you don't know" help ensure "a good time."

La Petite Grocery ⏣Ⓜ

26 | 24 | 24 | $45

4238 Magazine St. (General Pershing St.), 504-891-3377

Raves abound for chef Anton Schulte (ex Peristyle and Clancy's) and his "welcome addition to Uptown", serving "sophisticated", "inventive" Contemporary Louisiana–French cuisine amid "understated" surroundings in a renovated former corner grocery; despite the "din", fans find it a "perfect blend of special-occasion restaurant and neighborhood bistro", whose "simple" "Parisian style", "polished service" and "blissful" bites make you think "you're on the Left Bank."

La Provence Ⓜ

27 | 26 | 26 | $46

25020 Hwy. 190 (bet. Lacombe & Mandeville), Lacombe, 985-626-7662;
www.laprovencerestaurant.com

After 34 years, "treasured" toque Chris Kerageorgiou still turns out "superb" French "comfort food to die for" at this unexpected "bit of Provence" on a highway in rural Lacombe; "romantic" meals "you'll remember for a lifetime" are enhanced by "lovely hearth fires" and "welcoming" service, and the "excellent" three-course prix fixe offers real "value"; N.B. closed Mondays and Tuesdays.

Lilette ⏣Ⓜ

26 | 23 | 23 | $46

3637 Magazine St. (Antonine St.), 504-895-1636;
www.liletterestaurant.com

Whether for an "intimate dinner" or "sybaritic lunch", this "top-tier" French Uptowner impresses with "inventive combinations" of "fresh seasonal ingredients" by "brilliant" chef-owner John Harris; "chic" yet "relaxed", it draws "young professionals" and other locals who "love the booths" as well as the "cool bar" (complete with "sexy drinks"), all tended by a "friendly", "unrushed" staff.

Lola's ⊄

26 | 19 | 21 | $26

3312 Esplanade Ave. (bet. N. Broad & N. Carrollton Aves.), 504-488-6946

Iberia buffs "wish there were more" "warm", "lovely little" "date" spots like this inexpensive Mid-City BYO, which serves "authentic" Spanish dishes such as "top-notch pork loin" and "paella that rocks"; the no-reserving policy translates into patrons "waiting outside in lounge chairs" and "sipping the wine they've brought for dinner", gearing up for a glorious "garlic experience" – "vampires beware."

Mosca's ⏣Ⓜ⊄

27 | 12 | 20 | $38

4137 Hwy. 90 W. (bet. Butler Dr. & Live Oak Blvd.), Avondale, 504-436-9942

"I'd do dishes to eat here!" exclaim devotees of this hallowed "old roadhouse" in Avondale, which plates up a "garlic-powered" Italian menu of "authentic", "inspired" creations like chicken à la grande and oysters Mosca, served "family-style" to a crowd that always includes a few fascinating "characters"; insiders say "call first to get directions", "bring at least six people so you can get everything on the menu" and "take cash."

Muriel's Jackson Square 　　　23 | 26 | 22 | $42

Jackson Sq., 801 Chartres St. (St. Ann St.), 504-568-1885; www.muriels.com

"Imaginatively decorated" rooms "ranging from haunting to haunted" beguile guests (and "ghosts") at this "festive", "romantic" Creole "overlooking Jackson Square"; from its "rich and tasty creations" at a "fair price" to its "smiling service" and "historic charm" – particularly in the "decadent" Seance Lounge where you "feel like a sultan" – it's "what the French Quarter is all about"; N.B. the Food rating may not reflect a recent chef change.

New Orleans Grill 　　　24 | 28 | 25 | $63

Windsor Court Hotel, 300 Gravier St. (bet. S. Peters & Tchoupitoulas Sts.), 504-522-1992; www.windsorcourthotel.com

A "world-class" setting embellished with plush banquettes, floral arrangements and other "formal, elegant" touches is the hallmark of this "posh" Windsor Court Hotel destination; though a few find the atmosphere "stuffy" most recommend this CBD "classic" for "a special night out with all the trimmings" – so "dress up" and prepare to feel (and spend) "like royalty"; N.B. the new chef's internationally influenced New American menu may outdate the Food score.

Nine Roses 　　　25 | 15 | 17 | $20

1100 Stephens St. (Westbank Expy.), Gretna, 504-366-7665

Both "adventurous" newcomers and longtime pho fans savor the "brilliant Vietnamese" dishes served at this "authentic" West Bank "family" spot; since the menu is "phone book"–sized, the portions "generous" and the prices gentle, it's an "excellent place to get people together and use the lazy Susan."

NOLA 　　　26 | 23 | 24 | $51

534 St. Louis St. (bet. Chartres & Decatur Sts.), 504-522-6652; www.emerils.com

"Delicious Creole-inspired" Contemporary Louisiana cuisine "served with style" draws the masses to Emeril's "alternative" French Quarter outpost, which many find "hipper" and "more casual" than his namesake venue; most agree it's a "good value" for the price and "runs like a clock", though the "touristy" crowd ups the "noise" to "stratospheric levels."

Pelican Club Ⓢ Ⓜ 　　　26 | 24 | 23 | $48

312 Exchange Pl. (Bienville St.), 504-523-1504; www.pelicanclub.com

"Cozy, clubby" and "off the beaten path in the French Quarter", this "upscale" New American set in a 19th-century townhouse is "well worth seeking out" for "wonderful meals" with a seafood emphasis; regulars recommend "dressing up", bringing a "large group" and starting off with a cocktail at the "great bar with live piano" on weekend nights.

Peristyle Ⓢ Ⓜ 　　　26 | 24 | 24 | $55

1041 Dumaine St. (Burgundy St.), 504-593-9535

Most 'style mavens agree that chef-owner Tom Wolfe does this French Quarter mecca "proud" by serving "refreshing", "well-realized" French–Contemporary Louisiana fare that boasts an "innovative melding of flavors"; yes, some still "miss Anne Kearney", but as consolation, the "long-term staff" is "attentive" "without being pretentious", complementing the "historic" "charm" of this "teeny bistro with big food."

Ralph's on the Park Ⓜ   24 | 27 | 24 | $43 |
900 City Park Ave. (N. Alexander St.), 504-488-1000;
www.ralphsonthepark.com
Ralph Brennan's "beautiful" renovation of an 1860 building "over-looking City Park's magnificent oaks" wins the highest praise for its "sweeping vista", "stunning dining room" and "swinging bar"; most agree that the French-accented Contemporary Louisiana cuisine served by an "accommodating staff" "lives up to the Brennan tradition", and the location makes it "perfect" for ladies who lunch before visiting the nearby "sculpture garden at NOMA."

Rib Room   25 | 25 | 25 | $50 |
Omni Royal Orleans, 621 St. Louis St. (Chartres St.), 504-529-7046;
www.omnihotels.com
"A great place for beef in a seafood town", this "sophisticated" steakhouse is a "longtime favorite of French Quarter residents" thanks to its "famous prime rib" among other cuts; a "power-lunch" scene, warm "hospitality" and window seats for "watching people walk by" on Royal Street add to the allure, though opinions differ as to whether the polished new look is "reinvigorating" or has turned a "one-of-a-kind place" into a typical "nice hotel restaurant."

RioMar Ⓢ   25 | 19 | 21 | $37 |
800 S. Peters St. (Julia St.), 504-525-3474;
www.riomarseafood.com
"Ceviche rules the menu" at this Warehouse District fintasia serving "inventive", "fresh seafood" prepared with "Spanish and Latin American flair" by "serious chef" Adolfo Garcia; the "moderately priced wines", "boisterous" atmosphere and "thoughtful", "efficient" service also impress, and even fish-phobes can't complain since "everyone looks beautiful after a couple of sangrias."

STELLA!   28 | 25 | 26 | $56 |
Hôtel Provincial, 1032 Chartres St. (bet. St. Philip St. & Ursuline Ave.),
504-587-0091; www.restaurantstella.com
"Incredibly ambitious" chef Scott Boswell crafts an "innovative" New American menu starring "superlative" "experimental Creole fare" with "surprising flavor combinations", making this "intimate" hotel dining room and patio "tucked away in the Quarter" "worth the exclamation point"; if some cry "expensive", others are "shouting 'Stella!' all night" after their "memorable meal"; N.B. closed Tuesdays and Wednesdays.

Upperline Ⓜ   26 | 24 | 25 | $45 |
1413 Upperline St. (bet. Prytania St. & St. Charles Ave.), 504-891-9822;
www.upperline.com
"Wonderful chef" Ken Smith and "consummate hostess" JoAnn Clevenger ("a hoot") have "kept the torch lit" at this "quirky" Uptowner, serving "splendid", "inventive" Contemporary Louisiana cuisine with the option of an "excellent" seven-course 'Taste of New Orleans' menu; on par with the food is the setting inside a lofty 1877 house, whose four dining rooms are decorated

with paintings from Clevenger's collection and graced by "fine", "cordial service", creating a "first-rate" experience.

Vizard's on the Avenue 🅢 Ⓜ   27 | 24 | 25 | $48

Garden District Hotel, 2203 St. Charles Ave. (Jackson Ave.), 504-529-9912

Foodies, socialites, "movers and shakers" swarm to this "lively" post-Katrina newcomer inside the Garden District Hotel, eager to tuck into veteran chef Kevin Vizard's "spellbinding", "superb" Creole-Mediterranean fare; it's "chic" ambiance and "pleasant" staff also help make it "worth" the expense – particularly if you nab "a table looking out on the avenue"; N.B. reservations strongly suggested.

New York City

TOP FOOD RANKING

Restaurant	Cuisine
28 Le Bernardin	French
Daniel	New French
Sushi Yasuda	Japanese
per se	French/New Amer.
Peter Luger	Steakhouse
Gramercy Tavern	New American
Café Boulud	French
Bouley	New French
Jean Georges	New French
27 Annisa	New American
Chanterelle	French
Masa	Japanese
Gotham Bar & Grill	New American
Roberto's	Italian
Alain Ducasse	New French
Veritas	New American
Aureole	New American
Sushi Seki	Japanese
Sushi of Gari	Japanese
Nobu	Japanese
Tomoe Sushi	Japanese
Babbo	Italian
Grocery, The	New American
Saul	New American
La Grenouille	French

OTHER NOTEWORTHY PLACES

Balthazar	French Brasserie
Blue Hill	New American
Buddakan	Asian Fusion
Buddha Bar	Asian Fusion
Café des Artistes	French
Carnegie Deli	Deli
Danube	Austrian
Del Posto	Italian
dévi	Indian
Eleven Madison Park	New American
Four Seasons	Continental
Il Mulino	Italian
Milos	Greek/Seafood
Modern, The	French/New American
Morimoto	Japanese
Oriental Garden	Chinese/Seafood
Palm	Steakhouse
Picholine	French/Med.
River Café	New American
Shun Lee Palace	Chinese
Spice Market	Southeast Asian
Sripraphai	Thai
Tavern on the Green	American
Telepan	New American
21 Club	American
Union Square Cafe	New American

Alain Ducasse ⊠   27 | 27 | 28 | $215

Jumeirah Essex House, 155 W. 58th St. (bet. 6th & 7th Aves.), 212-265-7300; www.alain-ducasse.com

Everything's "extraordinary" at this "over-the-top" Central Park South "temple to modern French food", where "sublime", "sophisticated" flavors (via exec chef Tony Esnault), "cosseting" service and "old-style opulence" make for a "gastronome's paradise"; yes, it's "big bucks" for a "pageant" staged "for a select few", so bring your banker along for this "once-in-a-lifetime experience"; N.B. the restaurant is relocating to a new space in the St. Regis Hotel (2 E. 55th Street) by early spring 2007.

Annisa   27 | 22 | 26 | $70

13 Barrow St. (bet. 7th Ave. S. & W. 4th St.), 212-741-6699; www.annisarestaurant.com

An "oasis of civility in rambunctious Greenwich Village", Anita Lo's "other-worldly" New American "labor of love" serves "exquisite", "beautifully presented" food (including a "ticket-to-heaven" tasting menu) served by a "solicitous" staff in a "minimalist", "Zen-like" setting; it "doesn't come cheap", but "stellar experiences" seldom do.

Aureole ⊠   27 | 26 | 26 | $83

34 E. 61st St. (bet. Madison & Park Aves.), 212-319-1660; www.charliepalmer.com

"Wonderful from start to finish", Charlie Palmer's East Side New American "treasure" is "still aglow" thanks to chef Dante Boccuzzi's "impeccable" food "artfully presented" by a "classy" staff in an "opulent", flower-bedecked townhouse; for those without a "full wallet", the $35 prix fixe lunch is the ticket.

BABBO ◑   27 | 23 | 25 | $74

110 Waverly Pl. (bet. MacDougal St. & 6th Ave.), 212-777-0303; www.babbonyc.com

"Every bit as fabulous as you've heard", Mario Batali and Joe Bastianich's "masterful" Village Italian is *numero uno* for pairing "inspired" food with an "encyclopedic" wine list; those snaring an "impossible" reservation find the service "smart", the carriage house setting "surprisingly relaxed" and being "bombarded with a big bill" bearable for a dinner that's "last-meal-on-earth good"; by the way, "upstairs is better if you want to talk."

Balthazar ◑   23 | 23 | 19 | $52

80 Spring St. (bet. B'way & Crosby St.), 212-965-1414; www.balthazarny.com

The "never-ending bustle" is part of the "unflagging charm" of Keith McNally's "piping hot" SoHo brasserie where "delightful" French food is served by a "convivial" crew in a setting that accurately recalls "Paris in the 1920s"; it's hard to beat for "stargazing grazing" amid "fabulous" folk, "shoppers" and "tourists", and hard to believe it's now celebrating its 10th anniversary, without slowing down or missing a beat.

Blue Hill   26 | 22 | 25 | $68

75 Washington Pl. (bet. MacDougal St. & 6th Ave.), 212-539-1776; www.bluehillnyc.com

A "little bit of foodie heaven" off Washington Square, Dan Barber's "haute organic" New American employs "superb" local ingredients in its "quietly inventive" preparations, paired with "stellar" wines; "gracious" staffers and an "understated" yet "lovely" setting "increase the enjoyment" while road-trippers recommend their upstate outlet, Blue Hill at Stone Barns.

Bouley ● ⎸28⎸26⎸27⎸$91⎸
120 W. Broadway (Duane St.), 212-964-2525; www.davidbouley.com
"Food heaven from the first glance to the last dab of the napkin", David Bouley's "rarefied" TriBeCa New French is "quintessential Manhattan dining", pairing "sumptuous" cuisine with "memorably wonderful" wines; the "swank", vaulted-ceiling setting "oozes romance", the "mind-reading" staffers "serve with élan" and the offerings are "so exquisite, they don't seem so expensive."

Buddakan ● ⎸23⎸27⎸22⎸$63⎸
75 Ninth Ave. (16th St.), 212-989-6699; www.buddakannyc.com
Philadelphia restaurateur Stephen Starr's "huge", "happening" contender in Chelsea Market purveys a "delicious" Asian fusion menu served by a "precise, helpful" team; still, as good as it is, the food is outshone by the "incredible", "goes-on-forever" theatrical setting that's centered around a "jaw-dropping" main dining hall; it's already so crowded that a woman could get pregnant going to the bar.

Buddha Bar ● ⎸▽ 18⎸27⎸17⎸$61⎸
25 Little W. 12th St. (bet. 9th Ave. & Washington St.), 212-647-7314; www.buddhabarnyc.com
Spun-off from the Paris original, this "enormous" Meatpacking District newcomer features a "Vegas"-like interior incorporating a 17-ft. Buddha and private pagodas; but given the "awesome bar scene" incorporating lots of long legs and short skirts, dining isn't necessarily the top priority – what with the "standard", pricey Asian fusion items and staffers who "don't seem to care."

Café Boulud ⎸28⎸23⎸26⎸$77⎸
Surrey Hotel, 20 E. 76th St. (bet. 5th & Madison Aves.), 212-772-2600; www.danielnyc.com
Bertrand Chemel is behind the burners at this Upper East Side sibling of Daniel, and he's up to the challenge, creating "stunning" French cuisine "with finesse and depth" paired with one of NYC's "most thoughtful wine lists"; "sophisticated" service, "handsome yet unfussy" decor and a chic, designer-dressed crowd make the place feel like your typical "neighborhood bistro for billionaires."

Café des Artistes ● ⎸22⎸26⎸23⎸$66⎸
1 W. 67th St. (bet. Columbus Ave. & CPW), 212-877-3500; www.cafenyc.com
"*Très romantique*", festooned with a "riot of flowers" and Howard Chandler Christy's "magical" murals of gamboling nymphs, this "sumptuous" Lincoln Center–area "grande dame" via George and Jenifer Lang is one of NYC's "most beautiful" dining rooms; equally "lovely" is the French cuisine presented by a "thoughtful staff" – no wonder this 90-year-old remains a consistent "crowd-pleaser" – as well as a favorite place for proposing.

Carnegie Deli ●⌀≠ ⎸21⎸8⎸12⎸$26⎸
854 Seventh Ave. (55th St.), 212-757-2245; www.carnegiedeli.com
You can "feel your arteries swell" simply by reading the menu at this "fabled" Midtown deli where "jaw-dislocating sandwiches"

make for world-class "cholestofests"; "chaotic" quarters, a quintessential "NY tableau" crowd (hey, there's Woody) and "mouthy", "Ice Age"–era servers add up to a "must experience" that "never gets old."

Chanterelle ⊠ | 27 | 26 | 27 | $93 |

2 Harrison St. (Hudson St.), 212-966-6960; www.chanterellenyc.com

"Simplicity reigns supreme" at David and Karen Waltuck's 28-year-old TriBeCa "treasure", a "paragon" of "luxurious dining" with "knockout" French cooking, "graceful" service that "never skips a beat" and a "lovely", understated room with "pin-drop quiet" and "ample table spacing"; all this "joy" comes with a "premium price tag", leading bargain-hunters to tout the "unbeatable" $42 prix fixe lunch.

DANIEL ⊠ | 28 | 28 | 28 | $112 |

60 E. 65th St. (bet. Madison & Park Aves.), 212-288-0033; www.danielnyc.com

A "total experience for the senses", Daniel Boulud's East Side "tour de force" (voted No. 2 for Food) inspires "awe" with its "incomparable" New French menu, "exceptional wine list", "read-your-mind" service and "opulent" room; epicures who feel "like a million bucks" put their money where their mouth is, trading in their "retirement savings" for the "phenomenal tasting menu."

Danube ●⊠ | 26 | 27 | 25 | $86 |

30 Hudson St. (bet. Duane & Reade Sts.), Manhattan, 212-791-3771; www.davidbouley.com

To "dine like a Hapsburg", try David Bouley's "august" Austrian "fantasy" in TriBeCa, a "culinary marvel" for "sumptuous, smart" Viennese dining with a French twist topped off with "heavenly" desserts; the "gracious" service and "enchanting", Klimt-esque backdrop make the "fin de siècle" "come to life", so the "élan" is "worth the money", especially if you waltz in early for a warm-up in the "sexy" bar.

Del Posto | 23 | 26 | 23 | $90 |

85 10th Ave. (16th St.), 212-497-8090; www.delposto.com

The Batali-Bastianich juggernaut takes an ultra-"civilized" turn (think "Babbo meets Bouley") with the arrival of this "grand" new Way West Chelsea powerhouse, a "peaceful" marble-and-mahogany extravaganza with "nice spacing between tables" and "upscale" touches like valet parking and a piano player; the modern Italian menu is "haute", tabs are "stiff" and "head mama" Lidia Bastianich is on board, so there's a more "formal" approach; P.S. check out the primo private rooms.

dévi | 24 | 22 | 21 | $55 |

8 E. 18th St. (bet. B'way & 5th Ave.), 212-691-1300; www.devinyc.com

"Culinary wizards" Suvir Saran and Hemant Mathur are behind this "serious" Flatiron Indian serving "sumptuous" yet "refined" dishes that "match the best in London"; "lush", "pretty-as-a-picture" decor and "knowledgeable" service add to the "high-end", "high-priced" mood.

Eleven Madison Park | 26 | 26 | 25 | $66 |

11 Madison Ave. (24th St.), 212-889-0905; www.elevenmadisonpark.com

"Sublime" food, "impeccable" service and a "swank", high-ceilinged deco setting "all come together" at Danny Meyer's "touch-of-class" New American off Madison Square Park; it "hasn't skipped a beat" under new chef Daniel Humm, remaining "reliable" for a "special occasion" that's "expensive but worth it."

Four Seasons 🛇
26 | 27 | 26 | $86

99 E. 52nd St. (bet. Lexington & Park Aves.), 212-754-9494; www.fourseasonsrestaurant.com
"Whatever the season", there's "unparalleled" cuisine and "sophisticated" service under the aegis of Alex von Bidder and Julian Niccolini at this "superb" Midtown Continental, a "modernist beauty" that's the "epitome of luxurious decadence"; it's best in the Grill Room for the super "power-broker" lunch or the Pool Room for a simply "memorable occasion", but the overall "ambiance reminds you why you came to NYC – and why you brought all those "C-notes to burn."

Gotham Bar & Grill
27 | 25 | 26 | $70

12 E. 12th St. (bet. 5th Ave. & University Pl.), 212-620-4020; www.gothambarandgrill.com
"Superb", "soaring" dishes by chef Alfred Portale "continue to amaze" at this "chic yet approachable" New American "perennial" in the Village, also known for its "high ceilings" and "gracious", "on-point" service; all agree the overall "celebratory" mood will make "you feel like a million bucks" and even though the check may "break the bank", the $25 prix fixe lunch is a "flat-out steal."

GRAMERCY TAVERN
28 | 26 | 27 | $76

42 E. 20th St. (bet. B'way & Park Ave. S.), 212-477-0777; www.gramercytavern.com
Again voted No. 1 for Popularity, this Flatiron "standard bearer" via Danny Meyer "seems to get better every year", offering an "extraordinary" New American menu, "comfortably elegant" surroundings and "impeccable service"; in short, it's a "fabulous place to spend a bundle", though regulars report you'll find the "same quality" for less dough in the walk-in–friendly front room; N.B. Michael Anthony (ex Blue Hill at Stone Barns) is now overseeing the kitchen following the departure of founding chef Tom Colicchio.

Grocery, The 🛇
27 | 17 | 25 | $55

288 Smith St. (bet. Sackett & Union Sts.), Brooklyn, 718-596-3333
It's "all about the food" at this upmarket Carroll Gardens New American where "delightful" chef-owners Charles Kiely and Sharon Pachter purvey "artfully crafted" seasonal fare that shines with "fresh, pure flavors"; "flawless service" and a "delightful garden" in back add to its allure, but it's so "tiny" (and popular) that "reservations are hard to come by."

Il Mulino 🛇
27 | 18 | 23 | $83

86 W. Third St. (bet. Sullivan & Thompson Sts.), Manhattan, 212-673-3783; www.ilmulinonewyork.com
"You're showered with food from the moment you sit down" at this "classic" Village "experience" that's still the "gold standard" for "old-school Italian dining"; sure, "tables are tight" and it's "difficult" – verging on "impossible" – to get a table, but the 'in' crowd says "unbuckle your belt and take out a loan" (or "rob a bank") – it's "worth it"; N.B. lunch is more casual, less expensive and easier to book.

Jean Georges 🍽

28 | 26 | 27 | $98

Trump Int'l Hotel, 1 Central Park W. (bet. 60th & 61st Sts.),
212-299-3900; www.jean-georges.com
An "absolutely ethereal" experience, Jean-Georges
Vongerichten's New French flagship in Columbus Circle offers
always "inventive" food in a "chicly understated", Adam Tihany–
designed setting; it's "heavenly" dining, prices included, but the
"royal-treatment" service alone will make you "feel important
just being there", so "break the piggy bank and go for it" – or
go try the $24 prix fixe lunch in the "more casual" Nougatine Room.

La Grenouille 🍽 Ⓜ

27 | 27 | 27 | $94

3 E. 52nd St. (bet. 5th & Madison Aves.), 212-752-1495;
www.la-grenouille.com
Among the last of the city's "old guard", this justly renowned
Midtown French restaurant "serves up dreams" via "sublime"
classic "haute cuisine" and "perfectly pitched service" in a
"stunning", "serene" space abloom with "famously" "gorgeous
flowers"; *oui*, such "glamorous" repasts "come dear", but you'll
leave "feeling like a million bucks."

LE BERNARDIN 🍽

28 | 27 | 28 | $106

155 W. 51st St. (bet. 6th & 7th Aves.), 212-554-1515; www.le-bernardin.com
"All superlatives are warranted" when it comes to the "celestial
experiences" at Maguy LeCoze's French Midtown "temple to seafood"; the "stellar service" and "serene", "luxurious" quarters
alone place it in a "league of its own", but chef Eric Ripert
"approaches perfection" with his "stunningly well-executed"
and "beautifully presented" cuisine that "takes your breath
away" (and is once again voted No. 1 for Food in NYC); yes, it's
"very expensive", but if you can swing it "by all means, go";
P.S. the $51 prix fixe lunch is "a steal."

Masa 🍽

27 | 25 | 26 | $446

Time Warner Ctr., 10 Columbus Circle, 4th fl. (60th St. at B'way),
212-823-9800; www.masanyc.com
To fully savor the "once-in-a-lifetime" "evening of theater and
sensations" presented by legendary chef Masayoshi Takayama,
just "check your guilt at the door" of this Zen-like Japanese – a
"model of simple, tranquil excellence" – and don't even try to
"justify" the "insane" $350 kaiseki-style prix fixe that makes it
NYC's most costly eatery; just be warned that after sampling
these "perfect morsels" you may be "spoiled for any other sushi."

Milos, Estiatorio ❶

26 | 23 | 22 | $72

125 W. 55th St. (bet. 6th & 7th Aves.), 212-245-7400; www.milos.ca
At this Midtown "piscine Parthenon" plan on "impeccable" "Greek
cooking for the Aristotle Onassis crowd" – namely, fish "just pulled
from the sea" and "vegetables so crisp they echo when you bite
them"; a "knowledgeable" crew and "airy" quarters evocative of
a Mykonos "marketplace" help justify the "hefty bill", and those
less rich than Croesus opt for "bargain" prix fixe menus.

Modern, The 🍽

25 | 26 | 23 | $75

Museum of Modern Art, 9 W. 53rd St. (bet. 5th & 6th Aves.),
212-333-1220; www.themodernnyc.com
"Living up to" its "spectacular" setting overlooking MoMA's
sculpture garden, Danny Meyer's "divine" French–New American

makes a "sleek" showcase for Gabriel Kreuther's "phenomenal" prix fixe dinners that are "a rare treat" – at "rarefied prices", while the larger front bar area's "more casual" Alsatian bites are "equally delicious" and "half the cost"; either way, it's the "perfect finish" to a day at the museum – in fact, perfect any day!

Morimoto ● | 23 | 25 | 22 | $88 |
88 10th Ave. (16th St.), 212-989-8883; www.morimotonyc.com
"Destined to become a destination", this "over-the-top" West Chelsea Japanese is already a "scene" thanks to "genius" architect Tadao Ando's "sophisticated" setting and the "wonderful textures and flavors" of Iron Chef Masaharu Morimoto's "impressive" (and "eye-wateringly expensive") omakase dinners; still, the "friendly" servers "need training", and critics carp that the cuisine is "not always on the mark."

Nobu | 27 | 22 | 23 | $76 |
105 Hudson St. (Franklin St.), 212-219-0500;
www.myriadrestaurantgroup.com
Nobu Matsuhisa's "celebrity-gawker's paradise" in TriBeCa remains a "true classic" where the "transcendent" Japanese fusion fare with Peruvian touches will "set you back a month's rent" but is "well worth" the splurge – and the "monthlong wait for a reservation"; N.B. the "more accessible" Next Door adjunct offers "equally compelling" dining at slightly lower rates, and is "easier to get into" since it's first come, first served.

Oriental Garden | 24 | 11 | 16 | $29 |
14 Elizabeth St. (bet. Bayard & Canal Sts.), 212-619-0085
You can't do better for fresh fish "from the tanks" than at this taste of "Chinatown's high end", a surefire source of "superior" "Cantonese-style seafood" that also features "top-notch" dim sum; if the "brusque" service and "institutional" setting is "standard"-issue, high quality and modest prices mean most simply dive in.

Palm | 24 | 17 | 21 | $64 |
250 W. 50th St. (bet. B'way & 8th Ave.), 212-333-7256 ●
837 Second Ave. (bet. 44th & 45th Sts.), 212-687-2953 ⑤
840 Second Ave. (bet. 44th & 45th Sts.), 212-697-5198
www.thepalm.com
These "warhorse" chophouses are "the real deal" for "man-size" "slabs" of beef and "monster lobsters", along with "old-fashioned" "surly" service and plenty of "bustle"; they're "hard on the wallet" and seem "stodgy" to some, but "you can't knock" a "NY icon"; P.S. the founding site on the west side of Second Avenue with all the "entertaining celebrity caricatures" is "where you want to be."

PER SE | 28 | 27 | 28 | $287 |
Time Warner Ctr., 10 Columbus Circle, 4th fl. (60th St. at B'way),
212-823-9335; www.perseny.com
In a "life-altering" "league of its own", Thomas Keller's "apex of dining" "never fails to thrill" via the "ethereal" "finesse" of its French–New American tasting menus and "incomparable" service; the Time Warner Center setting affords "spectacular" Columbus Circle and Central Park views from Adam Tihany's discreetly "opulent" space and sets the scene for "culinary bliss" that justifies the "overblown prices", so per-se-vere with the "all-time-headache" reservations routine – "you're worth it."

PETER LUGER STEAK HOUSE ⌿   28 | 14 | 19 | $68

178 Broadway (Driggs Ave.), Brooklyn, 718-387-7400;
www.peterluger.com

"Devout" carnivores go on "pilgrimage" to this "venerable" Williamsburg cow "Valhalla" that's the No. 1 steakhouse in NYC for the 23rd year running; its "matchless" "marbled beef" is of such "juicy" "perfection" that fans freely forgive the "crusty" service and "macho" "Bavarian beer hall" setting; they also say "fuhgeddabout the menu" and stick with those porterhouses, and "bring lots of cash" to cover those plastic-less "prime" prices.

Picholine   26 | 24 | 25 | $83

35 W. 64th St. (bet. B'way & CPW), 212-724-8585;
www.artisanalcheese.com

"*J'adore*" coo enthusiasts as Terry Brennan's West Side "class act" "continues to soar" with an "exquisite" French-Med menu (featuring an "unsurpassed cheese-cart" encore), "standout" service and an atmosphere of bourgeoise "elegance" that validates the "big bucks" spent; a $38 Saturday prix fixe lunch eases the pinch; N.B. a post-*Survey* redo, which added a front wine-and-cheese bar, may outdate the above Decor score.

River Café   26 | 27 | 25 | VE

1 Water St. (bet. Furman & Old Fulton Sts.), Brooklyn, 718-522-5200;
www.rivercafe.com

"Bring the love of your life" and take in the "magnificent" skyline view at this "special-occasion" Dumbo destination "tucked under the Brooklyn Bridge"; its "exquisite" New American cuisine, "flower-filled" interior and "gracious" service work in "artful" harmony, but it's that "fantastic view of the harbor" (and the prix fixe tab) that will "take your breath away."

Roberto's ⌸   27 | 20 | 22 | $49

603 Crescent Ave. (Hughes Ave.), Bronx, 718-733-9503

"Believe the hype" report the legion fans of Roberto Paciullo's "superb" Salerno cuisine at this Arthur Avenue–area Italian; while the "no-reservations" policy may mean "outrageous waits", it's a "far-and-away" "favorite" where savvy diners "let the chef" do the ordering.

Saul   27 | 20 | 24 | $54

140 Smith St. (bet. Bergen & Dean Sts.), Brooklyn, 718-935-9844;
www.saulrestaurant.com

"You can taste chef-owner Saul Bolton's passion for food" on every plate at this Boerum Hill New American offering a "perfect combination" of "neighborhood friendliness and elegant cuisine", not to mention "solicitous, well-informed" service; even "Manhattanites don't mind" making the schlep, especially since the tabs offer "great bang for your buck."

Shun Lee Palace ●   23 | 20 | 22 | $53

155 E. 55th St. (bet. Lexington & 3rd Aves.), 212-371-8844;
www.shunleepalace.com

"Still going strong" after 35 years, Michael Tong's "formal" Midtown "landmark" provides "top-of-the-line" "gourmet" Chinese fare and "impeccable service" in "elegant" surroundings; repeating the phrase "holy amazing food" may help distract you when the "huge bill" arrives.

Spice Market ⬤
22 | 26 | 19 | $57

403 W. 13th St. (9th Ave.), 212-675-2322;
www.jean-georges.com
"Hanging lanterns and diaphanous curtains" play a role in the "spectacular", "exotic", "transporting" decor scheme at Jean-Georges Vongerichten's "spicy hot" SE Asian duplex in the Meatpacking District that serves "elevated" Thai-Malay-Vietnamese street food to a "pretty-people" clientele; portions may be as "skimpy" as the staff's "pajama"-like uniforms, but most agree that the prices, while "not cheap", represent a "relative bargain" for a fab "JGV" venture; N.B. the private rooms downstairs are spicy too.

Sripraphai ⊘
27 | 14 | 17 | $22

64-13 39th Ave. (bet. 64th & 65th Sts.), Queens, 718-899-9599
Voted NYC's No. 1 Thai, this Woodsider's "out-of-this-world", "real-deal" dishes "awaken taste buds" with "fiery hot" flavors that lead aficionados to jump "on the 7 train"; a "lovely garden", "smiling service" and super-"cheap" checks mitigate the "cafeterialike" setup and cash-only rule.

Sushi of Gari Ⓜ
27 | 11 | 19 | $70

402 E. 78th St. (bet. 1st & York Aves.), 212-517-5340
"Wow" – the "creativity is unsurpassable" at chef Gari Sugio's Upper East Side Japanese, where the staff "guides you through an amazing assortment" of "life-altering" sushi; the space is "bare-bones" with "tables on top of each other" and you'll need a "bank loan" before leaving, but "concentrate on the food" and all else will be forgotten.

Sushi Seki ⬤⊠
27 | 14 | 20 | $57

1143 First Ave. (bet. 62nd & 63rd Sts.), 212-371-0238
Sushi "masterpieces" as "delectable as they are beautiful" make this "late-night" (till 3 AM) East Side Japanese a "dangerous habit"; no, it "isn't cheap", and the setup's "rather plain", but nonetheless cognoscenti cheer "*kanpai!*" and join the "line out the door."

SUSHI YASUDA ⊠
28 | 22 | 24 | $75

204 E. 43rd St. (bet. 2nd & 3rd Aves.), 212-972-1001;
www.sushiyasuda.com
"Prepare to be wowed" at this "sublime" Grand Central–area "temple" that is once again voted the No. 1 Japanese in NYC thanks to chef Naomichi Yasuda's "amazingly fresh" "traditional" preparations that will "redefine your idea of sushi"; the "elegant", "serene" light-wood setting and "attentive but not overbearing" service create a "Zen-like ambiance" that helps you cope with the "breathtaking prices."

Tavern on the Green
14 | 24 | 16 | $61

Central Park W. (bet. 66th & 67th Sts.), 212-873-3200;
www.tavernonthegreen.com
It's "a tourist trap, but who cares" when you can revel in "the magic of Central Park" at this West Side "landmark"; "everyone should go once" to experience the "spectacular" setting and "gorgeous" decor that's "like being inside a Fabergé egg", but just "don't expect much" from the "uninspiring" Traditional American fare; P.S. it's "great for private parties."

Telepan
| 25 | 20 | 23 | $67 |

72 W. 69th St. (bet. Columbus Ave. & CPW), 212-580-4300;
www.telepan-ny.com
Upper Westsiders have a "new star" to cheer in ex–JUdson Grill chef Bill Telepan's "civilized" New American near Lincoln Center; expect an "innovative but unfussy" menu (including "mid courses along with starters and mains") served in a "minimal", "Prada-green" setting complete with a "charming bar area" – it's "expensive", but given the "quality", open seats are rare.

Tomoe Sushi ◪
| 27 | 8 | 17 | $39 |

172 Thompson St. (bet. Bleecker & Houston Sts.), 212-777-9346
Come "rain, snow or heat", there's "always a line of drooling patrons" in front of this no-reservations, no-decor Village Japanese famed for "stellar" "jumbo-size" sushi at "rock-bottom prices"; the fish is "tender and melty" enough to make some sniff "Nobu-schmobu", so "hire someone to wait on line for you."

21 Club ◪
| 22 | 24 | 24 | $69 |

21 W. 52nd St. (bet. 5th & 6th Aves.), 212-582-7200; www.21club.com
"You can feel the history" at this "essential" Midtown American, a "legendary" former speakeasy that still attracts "captains of industry" with its solid "traditional" menu, "gracious" service and "old-money", "country-club" airs; for maximum enjoyment, bring a "large wallet", "wear a jacket and tie" (it's required) and request a "tour of the hidden wine cellar downstairs"; P.S. there are also plenty of private party rooms.

UNION SQUARE CAFE
| 27 | 22 | 26 | $63 |

21 E. 16th St. (bet. 5th Ave. & Union Sq. W.), 212-243-4020;
www.unionsquarecafe.com
The "granddaddy of Danny Meyer–ville" is this Union Square "classic" that remains at the "top of every NYer's list" thanks to its "winning formula" of Michael Romano's "exemplary" New American cuisine, a "wonderful" wine list, "warm" decor and "welcoming" staffers who "make the experience unforgettable"; getting a reservation may be the only hard part in what's otherwise a "truly happy experience."

Veritas
| 27 | 22 | 25 | $85 |

43 E. 20th St. (bet. B'way & Park Ave. S.), 212-353-3700;
www.veritas-nyc.com
"Serious" oenophiles swoon for Scott Bryan's Flatiron New American that's "famous" for a wine list the "size of *War and Peace*" along with a "drool"-worthy $72 prix fixe–only menu; although it offers "nothing but winners", the "understated room" and "personal service" make it feel as if it's "still undiscovered."

Orange County, CA

TOP FOOD RANKING

Restaurant	Cuisine
27 Hobbit, The	Continental/French
Basilic	French/Swiss
Tabu Grill	Seafood/Steakhouse
Ramos House	New American
26 Pinot Provence	French
Napa Rose	Californian
Cafe Zoolu	Californian
Studio	Californian/New French
Mastro's	Steakhouse
Golden Truffle	Caribbean/French

OTHER NOTEWORTHY PLACES

Antonello	Italian
Blue Coral	Seafood
Bluefin	Japanese
Cheesecake Factory	American
Houston's	American
P.F. Chang's	Chinese
Roy's	Hawaii Regional
Ruth's Chris	Steakhouse
Stonehill Tavern	New American
Tradition by Pascal	French

F	D	S	C

Antonello ☒ | 23 | 23 | 23 | $51 |
3800 Plaza Dr. (Sunflower Ave.), Santa Ana, 714-751-7153; www.antonello.com
Blessed with a "stunningly beautiful" "fairy-tale" setting, this "upscale" South Coast Plaza Village "landmark" lures the "Lamborghini set" for "gracious" meals of "classic yet imaginative" Italian fare served by a "top-notch staff" and supported by a "great wine cellar"; a few outsiders say "expect to be ignored if you're a nobody", though, adding you "can get better elsewhere at a more appetizing price", but insiders insist it's "superb all the way."

BASILIC ☒ Ⓜ | 27 | 21 | 27 | $54 |
217 Marine Ave. (Park Ave.), Newport Beach, 949-673-0570; www.basilicrestaurant.com
Voters deem this "quaint and cozy" "touch of Europe" hidden on teensy Balboa Island "an absolute treasure" thanks to chef-owner Bernard Althaus' "consistently superb" menu of "unusual and outstanding" Swiss-French "classics" (including "authentic raclette") offered within "romantic", "unassuming" quarters whose "intimate ambiance" is heightened by a "friendly, witty" staff that makes diners "feel welcome"; no surprise then that fans insist "dining here is well worth the parking challenge."

Blue Coral
– – – VE

Fashion Island, 451 Newport Center Dr. (bet. San Miguel & San Nicolas Drs.), Newport Beach, 949-856-2583; www.bluecoralseafood.com

From the minds behind Fleming's (its next-door neighbor), this classy new Fashion Island seafooder is making a splash with the upmarket OC crowd thanks to pristine shell and fin fare served by an indulgent staff in an airy setting that evokes the sea via elliptical lines, azure hues and illuminated glass; look for the back-lit vodka wall that glitters with scores of brands, stirred tableside into martinis and seasonal specialty libations.

Bluefin
∇ 28 22 21 $50

Crystal Cove Promenade, 7952 E. PCH (Crystal Heights Dr.), Newport Coast, 949-715-7373; www.bluefinbyabe.com

"Sublime sushi" "is just the start" at this sleek new spot on the "luxurious Crystal Cove" Promenade; swooning supporters of "fabulous chef"-owner Takashi Abe (previously of Abe) insist "anything he makes is wonderful" owing to his "intricate presentations" of "fresh and clever" "French-accented" Japanese dishes that are simply "beyond delicious"; sure, "reservations are a must" and "you pay a premium to be by the beach", but it's "worth it" – and there's always the "lunch omakase that's still a steal."

Cafe Zoolu Ⓜ
26 16 24 $40

860 Glenneyre St. (bet. St. Anne's Dr. & Thalia St.), Laguna Beach, 949-494-6825

A mixed tribe of locals and visitors "loves" to "sit at the bar" and watch "magician chef-owner Michael [Leech] in his tiny kitchen" at this "quaint" Laguna "haunt" where the "funky" digs are "real small" but the portions of "outstanding" Californian eats are "gigantic" (you'll want to "split the enormous entrees", such as the "best swordfish anywhere"); insiders advise you to "make reservations" to assure your spot, saying "there's no one who do the foodu like they do."

CHEESECAKE FACTORY
20 18 18 $25

Brea Mall, 120 Brea Mall (Imperial Hwy.), Brea, 714-255-0115 ◐
Irvine Spectrum Ctr., 71 Fortune Dr. (Pacifica St.), Irvine, 949-788-9998
42 The Shops at Mission Viejo (I-5), Mission Viejo, 949-364-6200
Fashion Island, 1141 Newport Center Dr. (Santa Barbara Dr.), Newport Beach, 949-720-8333
www.thecheesecakefactory.com

"Come hungry, leave deaf" and wear your "fat jeans" quip cronies of this "cacophonous", "convivial" American chain (voted LA and Orange County's Most Popular) offering "something for everyone" from its "encyclopedic" menu, including "every imaginable flavor of cheesecake"; there's "always a long wait" for a table in the "cavernous" rooms, but "you can't beat the value" of the "King-Kong-sized portions" and "reasonable tabs."

Golden Truffle, The ⓈⓂ
26 13 20 $47

1767 Newport Blvd. (bet. 17th & 18th Sts.), Costa Mesa, 949-645-9858

"Creativity abounds" at "imaginative" chef-owner Alan Greeley's "quirky little gem" "squished" into a "downscale strip mall" on Costa Mesa's main drag, where the "absolutely amazing" French-Caribbean fare shines and the "wine list is sure to have something" "you haven't seen before"; grail-seekers "don't seem to mind" the "goofy decor" with "no atmosphere", considering this "un-chain" "anomaly" "an oasis" in "all too dry OC."

HOBBIT, THE Ⓜ   27 | 24 | 28 | $71

2932 E. Chapman Ave. (Malena St.), Orange, 714-997-1972; www.hobbitrestaurant.com

"Delectable" French-Continental fare and an "impeccable" staff that makes diners "feel like personal guests" of owners Debra and Mike Philippi have earned this "simply amazing" "special-occasion treat" in Orange our No. 1 ranking for Food in OC; the "dining adventure" ("four hours of epicurean bliss") "begins with champagne and hors d'oeuvres" in the "amazing wine cellar" and continues upstairs in the "charming old Spanish home" with "a truly unique seven-course, prix fixe menu" that's "more than dinner" – it's "a terrific one-of-a-kind experience"; N.B. reservations required.

HOUSTON'S   21 | 20 | 20 | $32

Park Pl., 2991 Michelson Dr. (Jamboree Rd.), Irvine, 949-833-0977; www.houstons.com

"Always a good bet for a business lunch or date", this national chain delivers a "short, simple" selection of American dishes – the "ribs and shoestring fries are especially good", and some locations have "added sushi" – in an "urban, hip" environment "with dim lighting, deep booths" and "prompt" service; some fans, though, feel that certain branches' "no-reservations policy is a turnoff."

MASTRO'S STEAKHOUSE   26 | 23 | 23 | $68

633 Anton Blvd. (Park Center Dr.), Costa Mesa, 714-546-7405; www.mastrossteakhouse.com

"Simply the best bling-bling fleshfest anywhere" gush groupies of this "popular", "dark" and "swanky" "expense-account" Costa Mesa steakhouse that caters to the "young-money", "Mercedes or Bentley" crowd with "huge", "succulent" steaks and "worthy" sides, "perfect" martinis and "seamless", albeit "snobby", service; N.B. there's "loud" live music to boot.

Napa Rose   26 | 25 | 26 | $61

Grand Californian Hotel, 1600 S. Disneyland Dr. (Katella Ave.), Anaheim, 714-300-7170

"Save a trip to Napa" by savoring "serious" "wine-country cuisine" in Anaheim at this "unexpected" "stunner" in the Grand Californian Hotel, where a "seasonal" menu of "creative" "complex dishes" is "prepared with excitement" and paired with an "amazing", "extensive" list of vinos ("including an unmatched by-the-glass" selection); factor in "impeccable" service from a "savvy" staff and a "lovely", "elegant" setting and you have a "shining star of OC dining" that brings "a touch of grandeur" to Disneyland's empire.

P.F. CHANG'S CHINA BISTRO   20 | 19 | 18 | $26

Irvine Spectrum Ctr., 61 Fortune Dr. (Irvine Center Dr.), Irvine, 949-453-1211
The Shops at Mission Viejo, 800 The Shops at Mission Viejo (Crown Valley Pkwy.), Mission Viejo, 949-364-6661
Fashion Island, 1145 Newport Center Dr. (Santa Barbara Dr.), Newport Beach, 949-759-9007
www.pfchangs.com

Fans of this "always bustling" Chinese chain "don't care if it's not authentic", for the "inventive", "updated take" on Middle Kingdom cuisine is "consistently good" and "affordably priced", which is why "there's always a wait to get in"; the "dark", "chic" quarters are "comfortable", if "noisy", and service is "quick", but foes liken the "faux" fare to "Pat Boone doing a cover of Chinese opera."

PINOT PROVENCE   26 | 25 | 25 | $55

The Westin South Coast Plaza Hotel, 686 Anton Blvd. (Bristol St.), Costa Mesa, 714-444-5900; www.patinagroup.com

"This is a restaurant in a hotel, not a hotel restaurant" explain allies of this *très, très bien* Costa Mesa "treasure" that's applauded for "sophisticated", "often sublime" feasts of "artistic" French fare from "amazing" chef Florent Marneau, gilded by "extensive" wine offerings; the "refined surroundings" are "plush" but "relaxed", and "almost-perfect" service from a "professional" staff helps to "set the gold standard" for "awesome" dining, "before the theater" or when "entertaining friends or clients."

RAMOS HOUSE CAFÉ M   27 | 21 | 23 | $28

31752 Los Rios St. (Ramos St.), San Juan Capistrano, 949-443-1342; www.ramoshouse.com

"All diets are off" swear disciples of "creative" chef-owner John Q. Humphreys, whose "pure genius" is evident in his "original", "sublimely good" takes on "made-from-scratch" New American dishes with a "touch of the South" ("the crab hash will change your life") at this "quaint" "alfresco" venue "secluded" within San Juan Capistrano's "historic district"; all told, it's a "most unusual" destination that's "well worth the long drive from LA", but surveyors "sad" about its "day-only" hours shout "with food this good, we need to demand dinner too!"

ROY'S   24 | 22 | 22 | $48

Fashion Island, 453 Newport Center Dr. (San Miguel Dr.), Newport Beach, 949-640-7697; www.roysrestaurant.com

Roy Yamaguchi is "king" of the "aloha experience" with his "model" chain delivering "imaginative" (and "expensive") Hawaiian/Regional cuisine, including "crazy good" fish and "kung pao calamari that'll knock your flip-flops off", as well as "awesome drinks"; service is "so good that you believe you're on vacation" in the "tasteful" surroundings, but some find the scene "too loud" and "crowded."

RUTH'S CHRIS STEAK HOUSE   26 | 21 | 23 | $57

2961 Michaelson Dr. (Jamboree Rd.), Irvine, 949-252-8848; www.ruthschris.com

Pros promise "you can't go wrong" at this national chain with its "sizzling" steaks "perfectly broiled and seasoned", "seafood specials that never let you down" and "awesome" sides, served by an "attentive but discreet" staff that "lets you relax and enjoy"; the "dark" "atmosphere isn't much" and it's "not for the budget minded", but "huge portions make the prices seem reasonable."

Stonehill Tavern M   ▽ 24 | 26 | 24 | $68

St. Regis Resort Monarch Beach, 1 Monarch Beach Resort (Niguel Rd.), Dana Point, 949-234-3318; www.michaelmina.net

The "gorgeous" St. Regis Resort Monarch Beach is the venue for "yet another excellent Michael Mina establishment", situated in the former Aqua space with an "awesome" new interior design by Tony Chi (NY's Asiate, MObar) that features marble floors and "elegant" floor-to-ceiling wine storage; the "genius" chef's kitchen turns out "perfect executions" of "sophisticated" New American creations, and despite occasionally "confused" service, early enthusiasts declare it a "great new hit for OC."

Studio
26 | 28 | 27 | $85

Montage Resort & Spa, 30801 S. PCH (Montage Dr.), Laguna Beach, 949-715-6420; www.studiolagunabeach.com

With its "amazing clifftop location", "majestic" "views of the Pacific Ocean" and "sumptuous" yet "understated" interior, this "simply divine" venue in Laguna's "luxurious" Montage Resort & Spa is ranked No. 1 for Decor in OC, but patrons also praise it for its "pampering" staff's "seamless service" and "wonderful chef" James Boyce's "stunning" Cal–New French creations, which "always challenge the taste buds"; of course, you'll pay "exorbitant prices" for such an "unforgettable" meal, but at least you'll "feel like a billionaire."

TABU GRILL
27 | 20 | 22 | $50

2892 S. PCH (Nyes Pl.), Laguna Beach, 949-494-7743; www.tabugrill.com

"Tiny and tasty" is the verdict on this "funky" PCH "jewel" "south" of Laguna Beach, where "inventive and delicious" Pac Rim-accented surf 'n' turf dinners are fashioned from "first-rate ingredients"; "parking is difficult" to "impossible", "as is getting in" – the space is so "cramped" that "the kitchen is [practically] in the dining room", making reservations "a must" – but admirers insist the "terribly crowded" conditions lend "real energy" to the evening.

Tradition by Pascal
26 | 21 | 24 | $55

(fka Pascal)

1000 N. Bristol St. (Jamboree Rd.), Newport Beach, 949-263-9400; www.pascalnewportbeach.com

"One of the very best in OC", this recently rechristened "special place" is known for "serious" feasts from a "splendid" "*très* French" menu sprinkled with some "unique dishes" that reveal chef-owner Pascal Olhat's "personal touch" – all "exquisitely" served in a "surprisingly elegant" "strip-mall" site that's "even more fabulous" after a "sophisticated" renovation; some critics call the vibe "a bit stuffy" and report an "unmemorable" experience, but more insist it's "a fantastic evening" ("why go to France when the food is better here?").

TOP FOOD RANKING

Restaurant	Cuisine
27 Le Coq au Vin	French
Victoria & Albert's	New American
Chatham's Place	Continental
Del Frisco's	Steakhouse
Taquitos Jalisco	Mexican
26 Primo	Italian/New Amer.
Norman's	New World
California Grill	Californian
Amura	Japanese
25 K Restaurant	Eclectic
Jiko	African
Ruth's Chris	Steakhouse
Seasons 52	New American
Thai House	Thai
Roy's Orlando	Hawaii Regional
Enzo's On The Lake	Italian
Antonio's La Fiamma	Italian
Vito's Chop House	Steakhouse
24 Boma	African
Palm	Steakhouse

OTHER NOTEWORTHY PLACES

Antonio's Cafe	Deli/Italian
Blue Bistro	Eclectic
Boheme, The	New American
Café de France	Contin./French Bistro
Chef Justin's	European/Floribbean
Chez Vincent	French Bistro
Christini's	Italian
Doc's Rest.	New American
Emeril's Orlando	Creole/Louisiana
Emeril's Tchoup Chop	Asian/Polynesian
Fleming's Prime	Steakhouse
Flying Fish Café	New Amer./Seafood
Hue	Asian Fusion/New Amer.
Kres Chophouse	Steakhouse
MoonFish	Seafood/Steakhouse
Shari Sushi	Japanese
Thai Thani	Thai
Todd English's bluezoo	Eclectic/Seafood
Venetian Room	Continental
Wolfgang Puck Cafe	Californian

Amura 26 20 19 $33
Plaza Venezia, 7786 W. Sand Lake Rd. (bet. Della Dr. & Dr. Phillips Blvd.), 407-370-0007
55 W. Church St. (bet. S. Garland & S. Orange Aves.), 407-316-8500
Colonial Town Ctr., 950 Market Promenade Ave. (Townpark Ave.), Lake Mary, 407-936-6001
"Sushi lovers will be delighted" by this "trendy" trio's "King Kong portions" of "super-fresh seafood" and "inventive rolls" "with an edge" selected from a "seemingly endless list of options"; a few frown on service that "could be quicker", but most find them "funky, vibrant" and "aglow with ambiance"; N.B. the locations in Dr. Phillips and Lake Mary also offer teppanyaki.

Antonio's Cafe & Deli 23 17 19 $24
611 S. Orlando Ave. (Maitland Ave.), Maitland, 407-645-1039; www.antoniosonline.com
"A slice of genuine in a sea of fake", this "bustling" "quintessential neighborhood Italian deli", cafe and wine store is "great for a quick meal" of "reasonably priced" sandwiches, pizzas and other "authentic" dishes; regulars say "you can count on seeing someone you know on every visit" to this "tried-and-true" Maitland standby and they also appreciate that you can "choose from its huge retail wine selection" for only a $5 corkage fee.

Antonio's La Fiamma Ristorante 25 22 23 $42
611 S. Orlando Ave. (Maitland Ave.), Maitland, 407-645-1035; www.antoniosonline.com
For what some claim is the "best Italian food outside of Italy", head to this "immensely popular" Maitland mainstay owned by local legend Greg Gentile, where "wonderful, authentic", "zesty dishes like mama made" are accompanied by a "can't-beat" wine list; "though sometimes noisy", it has a "lovely atmosphere" courtesy of servers who "treat you like a family member" and a dining room with "romantic lake views."

Blue Bistro & Grill 24 17 21 $43
815 N. Mills Ave. (E. Park Lake St.), 407-898-5660; www.bluebistroandgrill.com
"You simply cannot beat the value" at this "Asian-influenced" Eclectic "secret" that offers up "edgy", "NYC-quality food at Orlando prices" in the form of an "always delicious", ever-changing menu served with "personal attention" amid "technopop" decor; it's "small" and located "on an otherwise gritty stretch" of the ViMi District, but its supporters advise "go for the food – it's worth it."

Boheme, The 23 25 22 $53
Westin Grand Bohemian, 325 S. Orange Ave. (bet. Jackson & South Sts.), 407-581-4700; www.grandbohemianhotel.com
"It's like eating in an art gallery" observe ardent admirers of this "elegant" Downtown destination in the Westin Grand Bohemian, where "beautiful-looking" New American "creations" and "incredible service" are complemented by "cosmopolitan", "Klimt-meets-Dietrich" decor and nightly live piano in the lounge; it's "big-city food at big-city prices", but "worth it" "for a special occasion", "business lunch" or "quality-over-quantity" Sunday jazz brunch.

Boma
24 | 24 | 22 | $33

Disney's Animal Kingdom Lodge, 2901 Osceola Pkwy. (Sherbert Rd.), Lake Buena Vista, 407-938-4722; www.disneyworld.com

"Take a safari and never leave your table" at this "unique" buffet in Disney's Animal Kingdom Lodge, where "an excellent spread" mingles "exotic African preparations" for "adventurous palates" with "common but well-prepared American dishes" for kids and "picky eaters"; the "amazing variety of flavors" extends to "mouthwatering desserts" and a small but "fantastic South African wine list", all served in a themed setting that's "done remarkably well, without being campy."

Café de France ⊠ Ⓜ
24 | 19 | 22 | $40

526 S. Park Ave. (Fairbanks Ave.), Winter Park, 407-647-1869; www.lecafedefrance.com

"Feel like you're in Paris" at this "quaint" "neighborhood bistro" in Winter Park, an "old standby" for "always-fresh, well-prepared food" that combines "venerable, traditional French fare" with more "creative" Continental offerings; "unpretentious yet consummately gracious", it's "a longtime favorite" "for romantic occasions", with a "lovely" (if "small") setting that's enhanced by sidewalk seating on Park Avenue.

CALIFORNIA GRILL
26 | 25 | 24 | $50

Disney's Contemporary Resort, 4600 N. World Dr., 15th fl. (Contemporary Resort Access Rd.), Lake Buena Vista, 407-939-3463; www.disneyworld.com

Located on the 15th floor of Disney's Contemporary Resort, the Orlando area's Most Popular restaurant is an "unparalleled" "retreat", from its "inventive" if "expensive" Californian cuisine and "exemplary staff" to its "upscale" ambiance and a "wine list that's second to none"; "make your reservations ahead of time" and "request a window seat" to catch the "spectacular" view of the nightly "fireworks exploding over the Magic Kingdom"; N.B. the post-*Survey* departure of chef John State may outdate the above Food score.

CHATHAM'S PLACE
27 | 19 | 26 | $53

7575 Dr. Phillips Blvd. (Sand Lake Rd.), 407-345-2992; www.chathamsplace.com

At this "heavenly" "local favorite" in Dr. Phillips, "a serious kitchen" spins out "creative", "pricey but excellent" Florida-tinged Continental fare that's served by "attentive and gracious" "professionals"; it's located "out of the way" "in an office building", but its supporters say the "small but special" space has an "intimate", "old-world ambiance", plus nightly guitar music that sets a "very romantic" tone.

Chef Justin's Park Plaza Gardens
22 | 21 | 21 | $42

319 Park Ave. S. (New England Ave.), Winter Park, 407-645-2475; www.parkplazagardens.com

Chef Justin Plank's "innovative" European-Floribbean preparations and an "enthusiastic yet unobtrusive staff" have eaters enamored with this "staple in the Winter Park food scene"; but a "unique" dining room that's more like "an indoor garden with huge trees" is what really makes this a "festive" destination, as does sidewalk seating that's "great for a glass of wine while you watch the beautiful people walk by on Park Avenue."

Chez Vincent
23 | 17 | 24 | $42

533 W. New England Ave. (Pennsylvania Ave.), Winter Park, 407-599-2929; www.chezvincent.com

A "most hospitable chef-owner" and a "friendly", "highly trained" staff are just the beginning at this "small", "charming" French bistro in Winter Park "that's big on service" and even more focused on producing "wonderful" Gallic fare; still, a few fickle types find the cuisine to be "a noble attempt" that's "hit-or-miss", while others claim the "cramped" setting offers "little privacy" and "no ambiance."

Christini's Ristorante Italiano ●
24 | 21 | 24 | $59

The Marketplace, 7600 Dr. Phillips Blvd. (Sand Lake Rd.), 407-345-8770; www.christinis.com

At this "warm", "intimate", "old-world Italian" in Dr. Phillips, you'll get everything you expect from a "New York–style" restaurant – "epicurean delights", a "romantic" ambiance, "top-notch service" – "delivered in a charming and endearing way" ("a rose is given to the ladies" as they're seated); satisfied surveyors say this "standard-bearer" is "suited to special occasions", although they admit the prices may be designed for "expense-account" and "tourist budgets only."

DEL FRISCO'S PRIME STEAK & LOBSTER ⃞
27 | 18 | 25 | $58

729 Lee Rd. (I-4), Winter Park, 407-645-4443; www.delfriscosorlando.com

"Don't change a thing!" cry carnivores captivated by this Winter Park chophouse "for a man to love", where what some believe is "the best steak at any restaurant, in any city, at any price" plus "lobsters better than in Maine" are served in "huge portions" by an "excellent", "old-school" staff; a "very good wine list" and "typical", "dark-wood and leather" decor rounds out the "expense-account" experience.

Doc's Restaurant ⃞
23 | 21 | 20 | $38

1315 S. Orange Ave. (Copeland Dr.), 407-839-3627; www.docsrestaurant.com

"The 'doctor' is in" at this "great new restaurant" owned by a local physician and "hidden" near the Orlando Regional Medical Center, where "eager-to-please" chef Neil Connolly conjures up an "interesting menu" of "fresh, creative" New American fare; a stylishly "casual" "sleeper", it has "lots of ambition", but cautious types take a "time will tell" attitude, noting that the food can be either "brilliant or just average"; N.B. there's live music Thursday–Saturday.

EMERIL'S RESTAURANT ORLANDO
24 | 22 | 23 | $52

Universal Studios CityWalk, 6000 Universal Blvd. (Vineland Rd.), 407-224-2424; www.emerils.com

This culinary "island of adventure" in Universal Studios CityWalk provides a "sophisticated break from the theme parks" via Emeril Lagasse's "delicious", "memorable" Contemporary Louisiana–Creole cuisine – "close your eyes and you're in NOLA" – plus "friendly service" and "great wines"; however, it's "pricey" and can get "packed" with "tourists" "in tank tops and shorts", leading some to suggest "a novel idea: a dress code"; P.S. "make reservations in advance."

Emeril's Tchoup Chop   23 | 26 | 23 | $53

Royal Pacific Hotel & Resort, 6300 Hollywood Way (Universal Blvd.),
407-503-2467; www.emerils.com

Über-chef Emeril Lagasse "outdid himself" with this high-end,
"visually stunning" Asian-Polynesian restaurant in Universal's
Royal Pacific Hotel, a "jaw-dropping" David Rockwell–designed
"feast for the eyes" *and* the palate with its "interesting mix" of
"creative and delicious" dishes that wield "the wow factor in
spades"; "attentive but not intrusive" service adds to the "unbelievable experience", while regulars recommend sitting "at the
food bar to watch the kitchen" at work – it's "a must."

Enzo's On The Lake ⊠   25 | 22 | 22 | $51

1130 S. Hwy. 17-92 (Wildmere Ave.), Longwood, 407-834-9872;
www.enzos.com

"A big-city-quality restaurant in a small 'burb", this "Italian
delight" in Longwood "has been cranking out first-rate meals forever", from an "amazing antipasti table" to "authentic", "fresh,
flavorful, fabulous" classics that are "worth the splurge" – "you
can taste the love in the handmade pasta"; it's the "perfect blend
of true hospitality" and "lovely" lakeside setting, and its "bustling,
lively" energy has a "buzz" that "keeps 'em coming back."

Fleming's Prime Steakhouse & Wine Bar   23 | 23 | 22 | $53

933 N. Orlando Ave. (Rte. 423), Winter Park, 407-699-9463;
www.flemingssteakhouse.com

"Definitely a cut above the rest" rave reviewers about this Winter
Park link in a national chophouse chain that proves a "consistently excellent" choice for "large portions" of "fabulous steak
and perfect side dishes", enhanced by "attentive service",
"warm decor" and a "fantastic wine list" that includes over 100
selections by the glass; though foes find it "misses the mark for
the prices", more insist you're "in for a lovely evening."

Flying Fish Café   24 | 23 | 22 | $46

Disney's BoardWalk Resort, 2101 N. Epcot Resorts Blvd.
(Buena Vista Dr.), Lake Buena Vista, 407-939-3463;
www.disneyworld.com

"Fish must fly in straight from the ocean" to this "oasis" in
Disney's BoardWalk Resort that offers up "delicious" New
American seafood that "couldn't be fresher if you caught it earlier
that day"; patrons praise it as "a real restaurant in the land of
make-believe", with "excellent service", "delightful" decor and
"people-watching on the boardwalk after dinner", but they warn
that "it can sometimes get noisy"; P.S. sitting at the "counter to
see the chefs at work is a real treat!"

Hue – A Restaurant   24 | 23 | 21 | $44

629 E. Central Blvd. (Summerlin Ave.), 407-849-1800;
www.huerestaurant.com

"Wear all black and you'll be fine" as you dine at this "avant-
garde" Thornton Park bistro where a "splash of South Beach
style" plus New American–Asian "fusion cuisine" make it "the
coolest place to eat" according to "Downtown hipsters" and
"beautiful people"; a few fuss about "inconsistent service", but
all in all it's a "lively scene" with outdoor seating "for watching
the world go by" and an "awesome disco brunch" on the third
Sunday of every month.

Jiko – The Cooking Place

25 | 25 | 25 | $48

Disney's Animal Kingdom Lodge, 2901 Osceola Pkwy. (Hwy. 192), Lake Buena Vista, 407-939-3463; www.disneyworld.com

"Let your taste buds be adventurous" counsel safari-seekers who trek to this "sleek", "serene" spot in Disney's Animal Kingdom Lodge for chef Anette Grecchi Gray's "sumptuous", "African-inspired cuisine" featuring sub-Saharan spices on foods from an array of cultures at what most consider "fair prices"; the "exotic tastes" are complemented by a "tantalizing" "South African wine selection" and served by a "friendly, helpful" staff – in short: "wow! what an experience."

Kres Chophouse ●ⒹⓏ

22 | 24 | 22 | $49

17 W. Church St. (S. Orange Ave.), 407-447-7950

Sporting "ultraswanky", "classical-meets-Asian decor", this "elegant, urban" Downtown chophouse is "a certified hit" with "beautiful people" who champion the "awesome" but "expensive" menu and "great steaks" as well as a "see-and-be-seen bar" ideal "for after-work drinks"; nevertheless, a few chide the food and service as "not always consistent", hinting that this may be "a triumph of style over substance."

K Restaurant Wine Bar Ⓩ

25 | 20 | 22 | $46

2401 Edgewater Dr. (Vassar St.), 407-872-2332; www.krestaurantwinebar.com

This "bustling" "culinary prize" in Orlando's College Park "takes chances" via "talented" chef-owner Kevin Fonzo's "to-die-for" "food art", a "pricey", "ever-changing menu" chock full of "scrumdiddlyumptious" Eclectic eats that are served by a "charming, down-to-earth staff"; it also boasts a "solid wine list" and "yummy desserts", and the "pleasant", "casual", recently expanded setting is enhanced by local artwork, leading most reviewers to give this K an "A++."

LE COQ AU VIN Ⓜ

27 | 19 | 25 | $46

4800 S. Orange Ave. (Holden Ave.), 407-851-6980; www.lecoqauvinrestaurant.com

"Julia Child would be proud" of South Orlando's "longtime favorite", this "farm-style French" that "year after year" is the area's No. 1 for Food courtesy of chef-owner Louis Perrotte's "unpretentious yet spectacular" seasonally changing menu; "quaint", "country-style decor", "professional service" and "decent prices" make it "a pleasure to eat" at this "petite treasure" "hidden" away in an unlikely locale, leading patrons to plead: "shhh! don't tell anyone"; P.S. there are now half-portions, meaning you'll "have room for the spectacular soufflé."

MoonFish Restaurant

23 | 23 | 21 | $47

The Fountains, 7525 W. Sand Lake Rd. (International Dr.), 407-363-7262; www.fishfusion.com

Regulars rave about this "lively" Dr. Phillips surf 'n' turfer that turns out "excellent sushi" ("anything raw that's legal!"), plus "mammoth portions" of "awesome" seafood and steaks; it can get "loud", but respondents report that "entertaining", "inviting decor" – including "restrooms that defy description" – helps make it "a great place to bring out-of-towners"; nevertheless, a few find it "sometimes good, sometimes average" and take note of the "big prices."

Norman's

26 | 26 | 26 | $72

Ritz-Carlton Orlando, Grande Lakes, 4012 Central Florida Pkwy. (John Young Pkwy.), 407-393-4333; www.normans.com

"South Florida's best chef rocks Orlando!" declare devotees "in love with New World cuisine" thanks to the Ritz-Carlton's "superb" dinner-only offshoot of chef-owner Norman Van Aken's Coral Gables original; the tasting menu is "the way to go" and "worth the price" (five courses for $90), while a "gorgeous room" and "terrific service" make for "elegant dining on all levels"; in short, "on a scale of one to five, it's a 10!"

Palm

24 | 21 | 24 | $56

Hard Rock Hotel, 5800 Universal Blvd. (Vineland St.), 407-503-7256; www.thepalm.com

"An oasis of attentive service and superb dining", this chophouse in Universal's Hard Rock Hotel "is where you go for beef if you're on the attractions side of Orlando", offering "enormous portions" of "always consistent" steaks and lobster, plus desserts that you'll want to "save room for"; dissenters deem it "middle of the pack", but most find this "satisfying" chain link "as good as the ones in NYC without the attitude", i.e. "don't expect power brokers."

Primo

26 | 26 | 24 | $58

JW Marriott Orlando, Grande Lakes, 4040 Central Florida Pkwy. (John Young Pkwy.), 407-393-4444; www.marriott.com

At this "primo experience" in South Orlando's JW Marriott Grande Lakes, "foodies will not be disappointed" by the "glorious" New American–Italian "surprises" from "amazing" Maine-based maestro Melissa Kelly, whose menu includes organic touches and "emphasizes fresh, local produce (often from the chef's own garden)"; the same "exquisite care given" to the "intriguing pastas" and "highest-quality seafood" can also be seen in the "attentive service" and "casual but elegant setting."

Roy's Orlando

25 | 23 | 22 | $49

Plaza Venezia, 7760 W. Sand Lake Rd. (Dr. Phillips Blvd.), 407-352-4844; www.roysrestaurant.com

Roy Yamaguchi "is king of Hawaiian Regional cooking, even in Orlando" enthuse admirers of this Plaza Venezia chain outpost that "will stun you" with its "creative preparations" of "exotic", "swooningly delicious" "twists on seafood" and "aloha hospitality" from a "solicitous" staff; the "busy", "happening scene makes it a winner" for some, although sensitive sorts insist "the acoustics could use a bit of tuning . . . down."

Ruth's Chris Steak House

25 | 22 | 24 | $58

7501 W. Sand Lake Rd. (Turkey Lake Rd.), 407-226-3900
Winter Park Village, 610 N. Orlando Ave. (Webster Ave.), Winter Park, 407-622-2444
www.ruthschris.com

"Bring a big appetite and a bigger wallet" to these "class acts" in Dr. Phillips and Winter Park that offer "the juiciest cuts of beef sizzling in butter", "tableside service to rave about" and a "quiet, subdued" setting; while a few feel they've "seen one, seen 'em all", most think these steakhouse "havens" "have got it down to a science", although they view the Sand Lake venue as "vulnerable to Mouseketeers in flip-flops"; N.B. a flagship location is set to open near the chain's new Lake Mary headquarters.

SEASONS 52
25 | 26 | 25 | $39

Plaza Venezia, 7700 W. Sand Lake Rd. (bet. Della Dr. & Dr. Phillips Blvd.), 407-354-5212
The Altamonte Mall, 463 E. Altamonte Dr. (Palm Springs Dr.), Altamonte Springs, 407-767-1252
www.seasons52.com

"You'll feel positively angelic as you devour" the "flavorful but light" seasonal cuisine at these Dr. Phillips and Altamonte Springs "formula restaurants that finally get the equation right": "creative", "guilt-free" New American entrees "each under 475 calories" topped off with "amazing", "shot glass–sized desserts"; tack on a "well-trained staff", a "wonderful wine list" and "sophisticated yet comfortable", "Frank Lloyd Wright–inspired decor", and you have a place that's "always packed", so "good luck getting in (or even near) it."

Shari Sushi Lounge ⬢
22 | 22 | 17 | $40

621 E. Central Blvd. (bet. Eola Dr. & Summerlin Ave.), 407-420-9420; www.sharisushilounge.com

Swimming off with "the 'Most Sophisticated Sushi' award" is this chic but "small" Thornton Park restaurant that raises raw fin fare "to the next level" with its menu of "creative rolls" and sashimi, plus Asian-influenced grill and tempura specialties; enthusiastic surveyors also "come for the eye-candy" crowd and the "great-looking, trendy decor."

TAQUITOS JALISCO
27 | 17 | 22 | $19

MetroWest Village Shopping Ctr., 2419 S. Hiawassee Rd. (Westpointe Blvd.), 407-296-0626
Tri-City Shopping Ctr., 1041 S. Dillard St. (W. Colonial Dr.), Winter Garden, 407-654-0363

At these twin "family restaurants" in MetroWest and Winter Garden, you'll "feel like you're on vacation in Mexico" as you down *delicioso* south-of-the-border eats that are "consistent, authentic" and served with "big smiles"; live mariachi bands play Thursday–Sunday at both locations, so "sip a cold Corona" (or a "great margarita") and enjoy the "comfortable decor", "fun" ambiance and low tabs.

Thai House ⬢
25 | 15 | 22 | $21

2117 E. Colonial Dr. (N. Hillside Ave.), 407-898-0820

Satisfied surveyors "can't wait to get back" to this "consistent" "favorite" located just east of Downtown for its "delicious, wonderfully seasoned, expertly prepared" Thai food made with the "freshest ingredients"; despite unassuming decor, this "not-to-miss restaurant" "exceeds expectations by far" right down to the "professional" service and "downright cheap" charges.

Thai Thani
24 | 21 | 20 | $26

International Plaza, 11025 S. International Dr. (Central Florida Pkwy.), 407-239-9733; www.thaithani.net

"Thai me up and let me stay here" demand devotees who appreciate this sprawling Southeast Asian's "vast selection" of "authentic", "flavorful and bountiful" edibles at "very reasonable" prices; though this "treat" is located "in a strip-mall setting" near the convention center, it's "smartly decorated" with "wonderful, traditional" trimmings that are so elaborate, it's like "walking through the door into a different land."

Todd English's bluezoo

24 | 26 | 23 | $53

Walt Disney World Dolphin, 1500 Epcot Resorts Blvd. (World Dr.),
Lake Buena Vista, 407-934-1111; www.thebluezoo.com
"Todd English outdid himself" with this "classy" Eclectic seafooder
in the Walt Disney World Dolphin hotel, where a "funky but elegant", "under-the-sea" setting that's "more aquarium than zoo" is
the backdrop for "artistic", "out-of-this-world dishes with prices to
match"; most find it "an overall wonderful experience", with an
"excellent, knowledgeable staff" and "fabulous wines", but a "disappointed" few deem the scene "more show than substance."

Venetian Room, The Ⓜ

24 | 22 | 24 | $66

Caribe Royale Orlando, 8101 World Center Dr. (bet. International Dr. &
S. Apopka Vineland Rd.), Lake Buena Vista, 407-238-8060;
www.thevenetianroom.com
"Miss Manners would be at home" at this "fine-dining establishment", a "posh", "classy" Continental "hidden" in Lake Buena
Vista's unassuming Caribe Royale resort and convention center; it's
a copper-domed den of "elegance and decadence", with "lavish
cuisine" and "smart service" that's "second to none", which makes
it some savvy surveyors' culinary equivalent of a "get out of jail
free card", i.e. a "destination to get me out of trouble with the Mrs.!"

VICTORIA & ALBERT'S

27 | 27 | 27 | $89

Disney's Grand Floridian Resort & Spa, 4401 Grand Floridian Way
(bet. Maple Rd. & W. Seven Seas Dr.), Lake Buena Vista, 407-939-3463;
www.disneyworld.com
This jacket-required "oasis of civility" in Disney's Grand Floridian
Resort "really does [try] to spoil you", offering "pricey" six-
course New American meals (with global touches) from "culinary
god" Scott Hunnel that can be "exquisitely matched" with wines
or enjoyed at the "coveted chef's table" (reservable six months in
advance); if a few find it "overhyped", more consider it a "once-
in-a-lifetime experience" complete with "superb service" from a
Victorian-garbed staff and nightly harp music.

Vito's Chop House

25 | 21 | 24 | $50

8633 International Dr. (bet. Austrian Row & Via Mercado),
407-354-2467; www.vitoschophouse.com
An old-timer "in the heart of tourist land" near the convention
center, this chophouse "blows away the other big-name" beef
purveyors by "doing the classics well", offering "succulent
steaks" and seafood plus an "amazingly long", "nicely priced"
wine list to "make any connoisseur quiver"; although a handful of
surveyors suggest it's "solid, but not overly memorable", meat-
mavens maintain that "attentive", "professional" service and a
"cozy" setting are just two more reasons that "Vito's has it all."

WOLFGANG PUCK CAFE

21 | 19 | 18 | $34

Downtown Disney West Side, 1482 E. Buena Vista Dr. (Hotel Plaza Blvd.),
Lake Buena Vista, 407-938-9653; www.wolfgangpuck.com
If you "want variety and quality", "the Puck stops here" praise pals
of this Downtown Disney Californian, a "bright, breezy" culinary
oasis encompassing a "fun downstairs" cafe and sushi bar, a
"more refined" upstairs dining room ("i.e. a thousand less kids"),
plus a quick-service section; still, opponents point to "long lines",
"shaky service" and a "noisy atmosphere" as proof that Wolfgang's
"well-known name is pretty much all he brought to this place."

Palm Beach

TOP FOOD RANKING

Restaurant	Cuisine
27 11 Maple Street	New American
Chez Jean-Pierre	French
Four Seasons	New American
Little Moirs Food Shack	Seafood
26 Kathy's Gazebo	Continental
Cafe Chardonnay	New American
Café Boulud	French
New York Prime	Steakhouse
Le Mistral	French
25 Café L'Europe	Continental

OTHER NOTEWORTHY PLACES

Addison, The	Continental
Cheesecake Factory	American
Houston's	American
Kee Grill	Seafood
Marcello's La Sirena	Italian
Morton's	Steakhouse
P.F. Chang's	Chinese
Spoto's Oyster Bar	Seafood
Ta-boo	Continental/New Amer.
32 East	New American

F	D	S	C

Addison, The   23 | 27 | 22 | $54

2 E. Camino Real (S. Dixie Hwy.), Boca Raton, 561-395-9335;
www.theaddison.com
The epitome of "special-occasion" dining is this "romantic" Boca Raton Continental set in Addison Mizner's restored 1925 office building; though the "consistently good" fare pleases patrons, it's the "stunning" setting enhanced by the "gorgeous courtyard" complete with banyan tree that wins over the hearts of many; surveyors may be split on service (from "excellent" to "erratic"), but the majority concurs that a "memorable" evening's in store.

Café Boulud   26 | 27 | 25 | $71

Brazilian Court Hotel, 301 Australian Ave. (Hibiscus Ave.), 561-655-6060;
www.danielnyc.com
Daniel Boulud's "sophisticated" Palm Beach French (a satellite of the NYC original) in the Brazilian Court Hotel "makes a lasting impression" with "magical" fare paired with "wonderful" wines and "perfect service", and offers a crowd "dripping in diamonds" the option of dining in either the "beautiful outdoor patio" or in the "elegant" dining room; the prices, not surprisingly, are strictly "haute"; N.B. open for brunch on Saturday and Sunday; jackets suggested in season for dinner.

Cafe Chardonnay
26 | 22 | 24 | $52

Garden Square Shoppes, 4533 PGA Blvd. (Military Trail),
Palm Beach Gardens, 561-627-2662; www.cafechardonnay.com
It's "hard to believe" it's in a strip mall, but this Palm Beach Gardens "jewel" defies expectations with "divine" New American food delivered by an "excellent staff", a "stellar wine list" and "pretty decor" that contributes to an overall "unpretentious" ambiance; all in all, it's a "winner", albeit one that comes with a "high price" tag.

CAFÉ L'EUROPE Ⓜ
25 | 27 | 25 | $70

331 S. County Rd. (Brazilian Ave.), 561-655-4020; www.cafeleurope.com
"Even after 25 years", Palm Beach's "grande dame" is still "on top" of her game, offering its "society clientele" "outstanding" Continental food complemented by a "killer" 2,100-label wine list and a "pampering" floor crew who "attend to every detail" in the "best looking dining room" in town; it's "chichi" to the nth degree, so expect to find "unparalleled people-watching" and to catch up on area "drama and gossip"; P.S. "bring your banker" to pay for it.

CHEESECAKE FACTORY ●
20 | 18 | 19 | $26

5530 Glades Rd. (Butts Rd.), Boca Raton, 561-393-0344
Downtown at the Gardens, 11701 Lake Victoria Gardens Ave.
(Gardens Blvd.), Palm Beach Gardens, 561-776-3711
CityPlace, 701 S. Rosemary Ave. (Okeechobee Blvd.),
West Palm Beach, 561-802-3838
www.thecheesecakefactory.com
The "best chain – ever" aver acolytes of these South Florida Traditional Americans (and Palm Beach's Most Popular restaurants) whose "encyclopedic" menus feature "giant-size portions" of everything – from "burgers to Thai" – and the legendary, "unbelievable" namesakes, all served by a "cheerful" staff; sure, "the line goes all the way to I-95" and it's so loud you may want to "bring your megaphone", but the "consistently good", reasonably priced fare and "kid-friendly" credo make it a "winner."

CHEZ JEAN-PIERRE BISTRO Ⓩ
27 | 21 | 25 | $67

132 N. County Rd. (bet. Sunrise & Sunset Aves.), 561-833-1171
"*Chez* incredible!" exclaim fans about the "undisputed champion" of French dining in Palm Beach, a redoubt of "old-time", "magnificent" Gallic dishes ("flawless Dover sole") delivered by "classy", "friendly" servers; owners Nicole and Jean-Pierre Leverrier "take care of their patrons" and see to it that the ambiance is "perfect without being pretentious."

11 MAPLE STREET Ⓜ
27 | 24 | 25 | $53

3224 NE Maple Ave. (11th Ave.), Jensen Beach, 772-334-7714
"It all works" at this Jensen Beach New American (the county's No. 1 ranking for Food) thanks to chef-owner Mike Perrin's "wonderful" cuisine that employs the "freshest ingredients" and includes "imaginative" options for vegetarians; the "unobtrusive" service works its magic in a "beautifully appointed" "old house."

FOUR SEASONS – THE RESTAURANT Ⓜ
27 | 27 | 27 | $73

Four Seasons Resort, 2800 S. Ocean Blvd. (Lake Ave.), 561-533-3750;
www.fourseasons.com
A hotel restaurant to "judge others by", this "pearl" perched oceanside in Palm Beach beckons with "genius"-chef Hubert

Des Marais' "outstanding" New American food that manages to be "comforting and innovative"; the "perfection" trickles down to the "superb" staff, "elegant" setting and nightly live piano – just "break the piggy bank" to foot the bill; N.B. the Food score may not reflect a change in concept – there are now vegetarian, organic and gourmand prix fixe menus.

HOUSTON'S 21 20 21 $32

1900 NW Executive Center Circle (Glades Rd.), Boca Raton, 561-998-0550; www.houstons.com
Floridians fare well at this national chain known for "rock-solid" American food, especially "great burgers" and the now legendary, "fabulous" spinach dip; the "comfortable", "clubby" setting, "consistently good service" and "active bar scene" is a testament to their "popularity" and reason for many to endure "long waits."

KATHY'S GAZEBO CAFE 🚫 26 22 23 $59

4199 N. Federal Hwy. (Spanish River Rd.), Boca Raton, 561-395-6033; www.kathysgazebo.com
"So civilized" and "old-school", this "classy" Boca Continental is still "worth dressing up for" after nearly 25 years in light of the "wonderful" menu featuring time-tested signatures such as "outstanding" Dover sole; though the "treatment" seems "stuffy" to some, and others opine that "reservations need to be honored on time", the majority maintains "you can't find better" in its class – just "bring money, and then bring more money."

KEE GRILL 24 22 21 $42

17940 N. Military Trail (bet. Champion Ave. & Clint Moore Rd.), Boca Raton, 561-995-5044
14020 US 1 (Donald Ross Rd.), Juno Beach, 561-776-1167
"Fabulously fresh fish" paired with "excellent sides" can be had at these Palm Beach County seafooders; the "friendly", "efficient service" (the "check arrives with the coffee – get it?") and "great" "South Pacific"–style setting make waiting in season on "way-too-long lines" a "no-brainer"; N.B. reservations taken at only the Boca location.

Le Mistral 26 19 21 $57

North Beach Plaza, 12189 US 1, Unit 30 (PGA Blvd.), North Palm Beach, 561-622-3009
This little "piece of Provence" has le tout North Palm Beach swooning with delight thanks to "lovingly prepared" classic French dishes served in "romantic" quarters; the "caring" owners and staff "always remember you" and make dining here a "treat"; insider's tip: don't let the "wonderful" summer prix fixe menu blow by you.

LITTLE MOIRS FOOD SHACK 🚫 27 14 20 $27

103 US 1 (E. Indiantown Rd.), Jupiter, 561-741-3626; www.littlemoirsfoodshack.com
Prepare yourself for "funky", "beachy", "chintzy" digs and "some of the best food in the county" at this "secret" Jupiter seafooder where locals in-the-know put up with "terrible waits" and jam into the "small", "noisy" space to get their hands on "fresh", "exciting" fish preparations with "zing"; "slow service" is an afterthought when you consider this "shack" provides a "cheap" ticket to a "great meal."

Marcello's La Sirena
| 25 | 18 | 22 | $55 |

6316 S. Dixie Hwy. (Forest Hill Blvd.), West Palm Beach, 561-585-3128;
www.lasirenaonline.com

This West Palm Beach Italian is "a breath of fresh air" in a sea of "strip plazas", offering food "so delicious you could never produce it at home", a "welcoming" vibe and an "intimate" setting; cognoscenti crow that the "good" Boot-centric vino selections come at "uninflated prices", and even if the "attentive" service "slows down" at times, this "jewel" is on many "repeat-visit" lists.

Morton's, The Steakhouse
| 24 | 21 | 23 | $59 |

Phillips Point Office Bldg., 777 S. Flagler Dr. (Lakeview Ave.),
West Palm Beach, 561-835-9664; www.mortons.com

"Many compete, but few deliver" as well as this "premium" Chicago steakhouse chain, where business types with expense accounts and other carnivores herd in to a typically "clubby" atmosphere for "mouthwatering filets" that require nothing more than "a butter knife", "delicious sides" and "decadent desserts" all served by a "professional" staff; though critics are cowed by "obscene" prices, others are willing to fork over the cash and say it's "worth it."

New York Prime
| 26 | 22 | 22 | $64 |

2350 Executive Center Dr. NW (Glades Rd.), Boca Raton, 561-998-3881;
www.newyorkprime.com

Carnivores "count the ways" they "love" this "cavernous" Boca steakhouse where a "noisy" crowd of "glitterati" and "celebs" "dressed to the nines" wolf down "fabulous" steaks, "delicious sides" and a chocolate cake "to die for"; critics, however, counter that the "wallet-busting" goods are served by a staff that's well aware of "the pecking order."

P.F. CHANG'S CHINA BISTRO
| 21 | 21 | 18 | $29 |

The Gardens, 3101 PGA Blvd. (Campus Dr.), West Palm Beach,
561-691-1610; www.pfchangs.com

Though "hardly authentic", the fare's "reasonably priced" and "consistently delicious" at this "contemporary" Chinese chain servicing South Florida sinophiles who stick out "long waits" for a table; the handful of salty sorts who see "spotty service" and "commercial"-grade food are overruled.

Spoto's Oyster Bar
| 24 | 19 | 22 | $35 |

125 Datura St. (bet. N. Flagler Dr. & S. Narcissus Ave.),
West Palm Beach, 561-835-1828; www.spotos.com

Those who believe in "extraordinary" oysters and fin fare that's "delicious" angle for John Spoto's seafooder/shellfisher near the water in Downtown West Palm; the "knowledgeable" staff guides diners through the "wide variety" of menu options, while the "great" raw bar keeps bivalve backers busy.

Ta-boo
| 22 | 21 | 21 | $49 |

221 Worth Ave. (bet. Hibiscus Ave. & S. County Rd.), 561-835-3500;
www.taboorestaurant.com

This "classy" Worth Avenue "old-timer" is lauded for its "wonderful" Continental–New American fare and "excellent lunches" that are a "tough ticket in season", and for an "attentive staff"; the "sparkling" setting's ready-made for a "beautiful", "dressed-for-a-fashion-show" crowd that picks up on the "delicious conversations" at the other tables; P.S. "beware the man eaters" at the "active bar."

32 East

25 | 20 | 22 | $48

32 E. Atlantic Ave. (bet. SE 1st & Swinton Aves.), Delray Beach, 561-276-7868; www.32east.com
This crowd-"pleaser" on Delray Beach's "hot" Atlantic Avenue "continues to shine" with chef Nick Morfogen's "imaginative", "delicious" New American food, "first-rate service", a "great wine list" and "soothing", wood-appointed quarters suitable for both "romance" and "people-watching"; even those who think the prices are "more NYC" than FLA consider it "fabulous"; P.S. the "happening bar scene" means it "can get loud."

TOP FOOD RANKING

Restaurant	Cuisine
28 Fountain	Continental/New French
Le Bar Lyonnais	French Bistro
Birchrunville Store	French/Italian
Le Bec-Fin	New French
Vetri	Italian
27 Lacroix/Rittenhouse	French
Gilmore's	French
Morimoto	Japanese
Savona	French/Italian
Amada	Spanish/Tapas
Buddakan	Asian
Bluefin	Japanese
Deux Cheminées	French
26 Paloma	French/Mexican
Gayle	New American
Mainland Inn	New American
Striped Bass	Seafood
Blue Sage	Vegetarian
La Bonne Auberge	French
Swann Lounge	New Amer./New French

OTHER NOTEWORTHY PLACES

Alison at Blue Bell	New American
Brasserie Perrier	New French
Dmitri's	Greek/Seafood
General Warren Inne	American
Jake's	New American
L'Angolo	Southern Italian
Little Fish	Seafood
Marigold Kitchen	New American
Melograno	Northern Italian
Nan	French/Thai
Overtures	French/Med.
Pif	French Bistro
Prime Rib	Steakhouse
Shiao Lan Kung	Chinese
Southwark	New American
Sovalo	Californian/Italian
Susanna Foo	Asian/French
Totaro's	Eclectic
Twenty Manning	New American
Washington Square	New American

Alison at Blue Bell ⓈⓂ⊄
26 | 16 | 22 | $44

721 Skippack Pike (Penllyn-Blue Bell Pike), Blue Bell, 215-641-2660;
www.alisonatbluebell.com

There's "no need to schlep to Center City" since "skilled" chef-owner Alison Barshak is "on top of every detail" at her cash-only New American BYO in the Montco burbs; her fan club calls it a "foodie's delight" with "innovative", "Manhattan-quality" eats served in a "warm", "simple" space – just don't mind "being squashed" ("get used to sitting in your neighbor's lap").

Amada
27 | 25 | 23 | $47

217 Chestnut St. (bet. 2nd & 3rd Sts.), 215-625-2450;
www.amadarestaurant.com

Spanish-loving surveyors dip into their bag of superlatives over Jose Garces' Old City venue (this *Survey's* top newcomer), where "magical" justly describes the tapas that are accompanied by "fantastic" sangria, "phenomenal" flamenco dancers (some nights) and "attentive" service; it's the "best thing to happen to Philadelphia in a long time", but it's advised to go early before "noise" rises "above the pain threshold."

BIRCHRUNVILLE STORE CAFE ⓈⓂ⊄
28 | 23 | 26 | $50

1403 Hollow Rd. (Flowing Springs Rd.), Birchrunville, 610-827-9002;
www.birchrunvillestorecafe.com

Bring cash along with your GPS to Francis Trzeciak's "remote", "bare-bones" BYO in an old Chester County "country" store; die-hards know to "reserve" a spot "well in advance" for the "sophisticated" Franco-Italian cuisine prepared with "thought and care", "romantic" atmosphere and servers so "gracious" you "want them as your friends."

Bluefin Ⓢ
27 | 14 | 20 | $34

1017 Germantown Pike (Virginia Rd.), Plymouth Meeting,
610-277-3917; www.sushibluefin.com

Sushi-philes swear "if you aren't going to Morimoto", this "tiny" Japanese BYO in a "slightly dated" Plymouth Meeting strip center is an "excellent" alternative, where the "phenomenal", "amazingly fresh" fare includes rolls that are a "treat for the eyes and taste buds"; a "pleasant" staff helps make up for "modest" decor.

Blue Sage Vegetarian Grille Ⓢ Ⓜ
26 | 14 | 22 | $26

772 Second Street Pike (Street Rd.), Southampton, 215-942-8888;
www.bluesagegrille.com

Come "prepared to wait" – even with "reservations" – for the "ridiculously good" fare at Mike and Holly Jackson's "tiny", Bucks strip-mall vegetarian BYO, where fans forget about "mock" ingredients, "substitutes" and meat, since what they taste is an "amazing creativity with veggies"; who cares if the setting "isn't fancy-schmancy" when "huge" portions can supply you with a "tantalizing" meal the next day?

BRASSERIE PERRIER
26 | 24 | 24 | $57

1619 Walnut St. (bet. 16th & 17th Sts.), 215-568-3000;
www.brasserieperrier.com

Philly's "established boomer crowd" keeps "coming back" to Le Bec-Fin's nearby, "scaled-down" Center City brother "for the rest of us", an art deco–designed destination where Georges Perrier and Chris Scarduzio join forces to deliver "divine" New French cuisine; though the fare's "not cheap", a "professional" staff helps – overall, this one "hits all the right notes"; insider's dish: check out the bar area before "a night on the town."

BUDDAKAN   27 27 23 $53
325 Chestnut St. (bet. 3rd & 4th Sts.), 215-574-9440;
www.buddakan.com
If you want to "impress someone" who's "hard to impress", join the "wait list" for Stephen Starr's "swank", "theatrical" Asian in Old City, a fave of "fashionistas" and "celebs"; it's Philly's Most Popular restaurant thanks to "memorable", "groundbreaking" food served by "solicitous" servers and a "gorgeous" setting that "makes you feel beautiful, even if you think you're not"; as far as scoring a reservation in prime time, try rubbing the "giant" Buddha's belly inside.

Deux Cheminées ⓈⓂ   27 26 26 $80
1221 Locust St. (bet. 12th & 13th Sts.), 215-790-0200;
www.deuxchem.com
Fit for a "17th-century king" is Fritz Blank's "utterly *romantique*" Classic French mainstay in an "elegant" 1875 Center City townhouse; "hedonists" sit down and partake of the "superior", "richly prepared" "haute cuisine" served by an "impeccable" staff "devoid of pretense"; the "seamless experience" is, no doubt, "memorably" expensive; N.B. closed July–August.

Dmitri's   24 13 18 $30
2227 Pine St. (23rd St.), 215-985-3680
795 S. Third St. (Catharine St.), 215-625-0556 Ⓟ
"A shark couldn't get better seafood" than at Dmitri Chimes' "bustling", "no-frills" Greek twins serving the "freshest" grilled calamari, octopus and other bounty of the sea there is; the Queen Village BYO isn't for "claustrophobes", and if you want to "hear your companion" or avoid the "crush", arrive early at both locations.

FOUNTAIN RESTAURANT   28 28 29 $82
Four Seasons Hotel, 1 Logan Sq. (Benjamin Franklin Pkwy.),
215-963-1500; www.fourseasons.com
"As good as it gets" sizes up the winner of Philadelphia's top Food score; the "elite" come to the Four Seasons to "live it up" and find "a treat for all the senses" in an "opulent" setting that showcases Martin Hamann's "divine" New French–Continental cuisine and "formal", yet "low-key" service that gives you the "royal treatment" ("they could serve me Cheerios and I'd think it was the best meal I ever had"); yes, the "shockingly high" tabs may be hard to absorb, but they're easily justified, especially for "expense-account" or "special-occasion" visits; N.B. jacket required.

Gayle Ⓢ   26 19 24 $58
617 S. Third St. (bet. Bainbridge & South Sts.), 215-922-3850;
www.gaylephiladelphia.com
"Go and be adventurous" at former Le Bec-Fin executive chef Daniel Stern's "little" New American off South Street, a "casual" though still upscale newcomer blowing away fans with "knowledgeable" service and "well-executed", "complex" cooking that deftly combines the "experimental" and "classic"; N.B. it's à la carte on Mondays–Wednesdays, but prix fixe only Thursdays–Saturdays.

General Warren Inne | 24 | 23 | 23 | $47 |

General Warren Inne, Old Lancaster Hwy. (Warren Ave.), Malvern,
610-296-3637; www.generalwarren.com

"Bring the parents" for beef Wellington and bananas Foster at
this newly renovated, "elegant" Colonial "hideaway" in Malvern;
"high-quality" Traditional American cookery complements the
"wonderful" service with a "flourish" (i.e. tableside preparations), and those under the spell of the place's "romance" may
want to "book one of the rooms upstairs."

Gilmore's ⑤ Ⓜ | 27 | 23 | 27 | $55 |

133 E. Gay St. (bet. Matlack & Walnut Sts.), West Chester, 610-431-2800;
www.gilmoresrestaurant.com

Peter Gilmore (an alum of Georges Perrier) "amazes" with his
Classic French West Chester BYO widely regarded as the "Le Bec
the of 'burbs'" for its "fantastic" "special-occasion" cuisine
served by an "attitude-free" staff; at 35 seats, scoring a reservation in the the snug, "intimate" quarters means either many
redials or divine intervention.

Jake's | 25 | 21 | 23 | $51 |

4365 Main St. (bet. Grape & Levering Sts.), 215-483-0444;
www.jakesrestaurant.com

"Main Line yuppies" happily "slum it" at Bruce Cooper's "sophisticated" Manayunk New American; it's "the grande dame" of
Main Street with "skillfully prepared", "splurge"-worthy food and
"impeccable" service; the seating's "tight", especially at peak
times, so expect to almost "sit in your neighbor's lap."

La Bonne Auberge Ⓜ | 26 | 27 | 26 | $75 |

Village 2 Apartment Complex, 1 Rittenhouse Circle (River Rd.),
New Hope, 215-862-2462; www.bonneauberge.com

An auberge to remember is Gerard Caronello's "formal", "precious"
French serving up a "romantic" ambiance, "super" food and "super" service to "special-occasion" seekers; the 18th-century
farmhouse setting (within a New Hope apartment complex) evokes
the French "countryside", though "stratospheric" prices bring
everyone back to reality; N.B. dinner only, Thursdays–Sundays.

LACROIX AT THE RITTENHOUSE | 27 | 27 | 27 | $79 |

Rittenhouse Hotel, 210 W. Rittenhouse Sq. (bet. Locust & Walnut Sts.),
215-790-2533; www.lacroixrestaurant.com

For a taste of what "the gods on Olympus eat", there's no better
example than Jean-Marie Lacroix's "dreamy" French extravaganza in the Rittenhouse Hotel; count on "culinary mastery", with
a menu devised of three-, four- and five-course "artfully presented" small plates, a "modern", "tranquil" room overlooking
the Square and "sublime" service; true, you'll have to dip heavily
into your piggy bank, but it's undeniably sure to impress;
N.B. post-*Survey*, Lacroix has yielded the reins to new executive
chef Matt Levin; jacket required at dinner.

L'Angolo Ⓜ | 26 | 15 | 22 | $35 |

1415 W. Porter St. (Broad St.), 215-389-4252

It's "well worth" braving South Philly's "double-parking traps"
and bringing your "best Barolo" to pair with Davide Faenza's
"outstanding" Southern Italian cooking at this "upbeat" BYO trattoria, where the chef's wife, Kathryn, oversees a "charming" floor

crew who "aim to please"; keep in mind, "you may need a shoe-horn to get in", but after all the "amazing" food, "you'll need a wheelbarrow to get out."

LE BAR LYONNAIS ⊠

| 28 | 23 | 25 | $58 |

1523 Walnut St. (bet. 15th & 16th Sts.), 215-567-1000; www.lebecfin.com
"Philly" Georges Perrier's "hidden" Center City "gem" beneath Le Bec-Fin continues to impress gourmets who crave an "inti-mate" meal with "spectacular" French bistro food and "fantas-tic" service but can't fork over a "whole paycheck" at the mother ship upstairs; it's even better when you can visit the bar at peak times and gaze at the "impressive examples of plastic surgery."

LE BEC-FIN ⊠

| 28 | 27 | 27 | $120 |

1523 Walnut St. (bet. 15th & 16th Sts.), 215-567-1000; www.lebecfin.com
Still "the pinnacle" of Philly restaurants is Georges Perrier's "big-bucks" haute Center City French institution that "bows to no other" in its class and is a "must-see" "must-experience" "masterpiece" that's de rigueur "before dying"; indeed, the "magnificent" food (and the "unbelievable" dessert cart), ornate, "beautiful Parisian" setting and "perfect" service from a "fleet" of waiters all leave you as "breathless" as the "sticker-shock"-inducing bill; N.B. jacket required at dinner.

Little Fish Ⓜ

| 24 | 12 | 19 | $35 |

600 Catharine St. (6th St.), 215-413-3464
"Little only describes the size" of John Tiplitz's "quirky", "guppy-sized" BYO seafooder in Queen Village, and afishionados dis-pense with "elbow-room" issues and pack in like "sardines" to sit "almost in the kitchen" for "astonishingly" fresh fare served by a "sweet" staff; P.S. though you'd better "beware of flying pans", this one's a catch if you can get a seat.

Mainland Inn

| 26 | 23 | 25 | $48 |

17 Main St. (Sumneytown Pike), Mainland, 215-256-8500;
www.mainlandinn.org
"Understated" is another name for this central Montco "secret" decorated in "18th-century Americana" that "lives up to its rep" as "one of the best" in the 'burbs with "sublime" New American food and service that makes you "forget about traveling to Center City"; insiders advise if you want to make an impression on some-one, check out the $21.95 Sunday brunch.

Marigold Kitchen ⊠Ⓜ

| 25 | 18 | 22 | $45 |

501 S. 45th St. (Larchwood Ave.), 215-222-3699
Acolytes of "culinary artistry" are all over this "hidden" New American BYO in a touched-up West Philly Victorian, the show-case for chef Michael Solomonov who twirls his "magic wand" over "eccentric", yet "excellent" dishes; many also endorse the service, which is "well-informed" considering what's on the plate "ain't mama's cooking."

Melograno Ⓜ

| 25 | 16 | 20 | $37 |

2201 Spruce St. (22nd St.), 215-875-8116
"Pure joy" sums up this "minimally" decorated yet "inviting" (and "tiny") Tuscan BYO corner bistro, a Fitler Square "treasure" where you must "arrive as soon as it opens" to avoid the crowds who await Gianluca Demontis' "simple" and "beautifully prepared" fare that's "not to be missed" and "warm",

"professional" staff that works the "deafening" room; now, if only they "took reservations."

Morimoto
27 | 27 | 25 | $72

723 Chestnut St. (bet. 7th & 8th Sts.), 215-413-9070;
www.morimotorestaurant.com
Even with '*Iron Chef*' Masaharu Morimoto spending time in the new namesake NYC offshoot, Stephen Starr's "trendy" "neo"-Japanese "masterpiece" in Center City is still a "must visit" for "sublime", "Tokyo-quality" sushi and "exciting" fusion fare in a "surreal" and "seriously sexy" setting complete with "changing mood lights"; "flawless" service is part of an overall experience that feels like "winning the lottery", so it's advised to "splurge" to take advantage of what will be a "memorable" meal ("you won't be sorry, even when you get the bill").

Nan ☒
26 | 16 | 21 | $38

4000 Chestnut St. (40th St.), 215-382-0818; www.nanrestaurant.com
Word is "from the outside, you'd never guess that you're in for one of the best meals" around at "talented" chef-owner Kamol Phutlek's French-Thai BYO, a "jewel" in University City's "lower rent district"; they "get all the courses right" say the amazed when describing the "exceptional" fare, though it also helps when service is this "good."

Overtures Ⓜ
24 | 23 | 23 | $50

609 E. Passyunk Ave. (bet. Bainbridge & South Sts.), 215-627-3455
Peter LamLein continues to create "lovely" music in the kitchen of his "romantic" French-Med BYO off South Street, arguably "Philly's best-kept secret" for "terrific" midweek prix fixes "worthy of your finest wines; it's all complemented by "excellent" service in a "jewel box" of a setting featuring trompe l'oeil paintings and "beautiful" flower arrangements; in other words, "bravo!"

Paloma ☒
26 | 18 | 25 | $49

6516 Castor Ave. (bet. Hellerman St. & Magee Ave.), 215-533-0356
In a "food-starved", "down-at-the-heels" Northeast Philly area resides this "haute" French-Mexican "standout" wowing those who've been to its "relaxing" space for Adan Saavedra's "artistic" presentations backed by "reasonably" priced wines and "excellent" service; for some who're thinking twice about making the trip, consider that food "doesn't get any better than this."

Pif Ⓜ⊄
26 | 15 | 23 | $44

Italian Mkt., 1009 S. Eighth St. (Kimball St.), 215-625-2923
"Oenophiles" "break out their best" bottles for the "superb" food at David Ansill's cash-only, "true" *petit* French bistro BYO near the Italian Market; the strains of Edith Piaf" in the background complete the "Parisian" vibe and "warm" service "makes you want to move in", but just bring more than a few euros to cover somewhat "pricey" tabs.

PRIME RIB
25 | 25 | 24 | $63

Radisson Plaza Warwick Hotel, 1701 Locust St. (17th St.), 215-772-1701;
www.theprimerib.com
Tame the "carnivore in you" at this "old-school" Warwick steakhouse supplying "top-of-the-line" steaks to a well-heeled crowd who dig the "quiet" "Rat Pack"-esque setting and "amazing" piano music (the "crowning touch"); you'll feel like a "royal" sitting

in the "cushy", "thronelike chairs" while "attentive" servers pamper you, and though your "budget will be eaten up quickly" here, it still "doesn't get any better than this"; N.B. jackets required in the main dining room, but upstairs is more casual.

Savona   27 | 26 | 25 | $69
100 Old Gulph Rd. (Rte. 320), Gulph Mills, 610-520-1200;
www.savonarestaurant.com
For a "special occasion" (like "winning the lottery") Main Liners "heartily recommend" this "formal" yet "convivial" "winner" in Gulph Mills for Andrew Masciangelo's "glorious" French-Italian menu, an "incredible" 1,000-label wine list and "romantic" Riviera-style setting; "mind-reading" servers tend to a well-heeled crowd so enthralled they thought they "owned the place."

Shiao Lan Kung ●Ⓜ   25 | 9 | 18 | $22
930 Race St. (bet. 9th & 10th Sts.), 215-928-0282
The salt-baked shrimp is the stuff of "dreams" at this "small" Chinese Chinatown BYO whose looks may be "lacking" but where the "excellent" quality of the food "speaks for itself"; you may have to "wait or share a table with strangers", but it's worth it since "this is the only place" you need to go when in the neighborhood.

Southwark Ⓜ   24 | 20 | 21 | $42
701 S. Fourth St. (Bainbridge St.), 215-238-1888
Sheri Waide's takes on New American at this "warm" Queen Villager "put many NYC restaurants to shame", while the ambiance (abetted by a "beautiful" mahogany bar) satisfies as a "fine-dining" destination or a "neighborhood haunt"; it also gets points for "helpful" servers and an "affordable" wine list – in other words, it's "super in every way."

Sovalo ⑤   25 | 22 | 23 | $43
702 N. Second St. (bet. Brown St. & Fairmount Ave.), 215-413-7770;
www.sovalo.com
Northern Liberties bursts with pride over this "chic" and "charming" Napa-meets-Italy "up-and-comer" on the Second Street strip; it's hard not to "come back" considering the "intensely flavorful" dishes (Italian food has "never been better") under the hand of Joseph Scarpone, and factor in "excellent" service and this "bright spot" is likely to stick around awhile.

Striped Bass   26 | 26 | 24 | $72
1500 Walnut St. (15th St.), 215-732-4444; www.stripedbassrestaurant.com
A "Starr's shining" on this "reincarnated" Center City seafooder, Stephen Starr's "grand" yet "sexy", high-ceilinged "triumph" where the "extraordinary creativity" shows in every one of the "cleverly presented", "intensely flavorful" dishes supported by "crisp" service; it's no surprise then that the room swarms with a "contented", "beautiful" crowd that willingly pays "top dollar" (it *is* in a former bank) for the experience.

Susanna Foo   25 | 24 | 25 | $59
1512 Walnut St. (bet. 15th & 16th Sts.), 215-545-2666;
www.susannafoo.com
"Food is art" at Philly's best-known and best-"loved" French-Asian "Foo-sion" spot, the "calm and classy" salon of celeb chef Susanna Foo, who turns "any ingredient into a masterpiece" on the plate; the staff specializes in "pampering" (perhaps making it

easier to swallow the "exorbitant" prices), and while some "aren't sure what all the hype is about", legions of loyalists say this "gold standard for Chinese food" remains "one of the city's treasures."

Swann Lounge ☪

| 26 | 27 | 27 | $55 |

Four Seasons Hotel, 1 Logan Sq. (Benjamin Franklin Pkwy.), 215-963-1500; www.fourseasons.com

"All the best for a little less" than the Fountain, and "less formal" (but still a picture of "luxury"), this New American–New French at the Four Seasons offers "spectacular" food, whether in the cafe, the "great" bar, or at the "amazing" brunch and buffets or during afternoon tea; P.S. some should go here for a "primer" on service, for "every restaurant should treat its customers this well."

Totaro's ☒

| 26 | 13 | 22 | $49 |

729 E. Hector St. (bet. Righter & Walnut Sts.), Conshohocken, 610-828-9341; www.totaros.com

"Who woulda thunk" something so "plain" on the outside could produce such "great" food? is the first question you'll ask yourself after a meal at this "intimate" Conshy Italian-influenced Eclectic, where "wild game of all sorts" pops up on the "adventurous" menu; insiders know to "head for the happy hour" at the bar, but also advise "don't let the decor fool you – this place isn't cheap."

Twenty Manning

| 21 | 22 | 19 | $43 |

261 S. 20th St. (bet. Locust & Spruce Sts.), 215-731-0900; www.twentymanning.com

Audrey Claire's "snazzy" relative near Rittenhouse Square is as "trendy" as ever; you'll still find Kiong Banh's "artfully prepared" Asian-inflected New American cuisine, "exciting" drinks in the lounge and "plenty of window coverage for the outdoor parade"; in all, it's easy to "impress a date" here even if the bill is more accessible for "BMW" owners.

VETRI ☒

| 28 | 22 | 27 | $78 |

1312 Spruce St. (bet. Broad & 13th Sts.), 215-732-3478; www.vetriristorante.com

"I thought I'd died and gone to Italy" is a common refrain when speaking of "genius" chef Marc Vetri's "rustic" 35-seat Italian in a Center City brownstone; "become the guest who doesn't want to leave" after you sample "wondrous" fare that's the "essence of pleasure" served without "pomp" by the "expert" staff; you'll need to use "speed-dial" on your phone to land a reservation, and sure, it's "costly", but then again, it's a "great use for a home equity loan" since it may be the "best restaurant of its kind in America."

Washington Square

| 20 | 24 | 18 | $50 |

210 W. Washington Sq. (bet. Locust & St. James Sts.), 215-592-7787; www.washingtonsquare-restaurant.com

"Look at all the pretty people" who populate this "ultra-chic" Washington Square New American, part of the Stephen Starr constellation: the "fabulous" Todd Oldham–designed garden is officially "the best setting in town for a drink", while the "interesting" cooking from the kitchen (now under the direction of Christopher Lee) "impress" most of the time but comes with "quite a price tag"; P.S. sightseers get to check out the "Jags and Porsches that clog the street."

Phoenix/Scottsdale

TOP FOOD RANKING

Restaurant	Cuisine
28 Pizzeria Bianco	Pizza
Sea Saw	Japanese
27 Marquesa	Mediterranean
Binkley's	New American
Barrio Café	Mexican
T. Cook's	Mediterranean
Mary Elaine's	New French
Drinkwater's City Hall	Steakhouse
26 Mastro's	Steakhouse
Cyclo	Vietnamese

OTHER NOTEWORTHY PLACES

Eddie V's Edgewater	Seafood/Steakhouse
elements	Asian/New American
Greene House	Californian
Los Sombreros	Mexican
Michael's at the Citadel	New American
P.F. Chang's	Chinese
Roaring Fork	American
Roy's	Hawaii Regional
Trader Vic's	Eclectic
Vincent's on Camelback	New French/SW

F	D	S	C

BARRIO CAFÉ Ⓜ   27 | 17 | 22 | $29

2814 N. 16th St. (Thomas Rd.), Phoenix, 602-636-0240;
www.barriocafe.com
"Come early or late" or "bet on a wait" at this "small", "popular" "gem" dishing "exciting", "nuevo" renditions of Mexican standards that draw crowds unafraid to venture "beyond the burrito"; if the "amazing guacamole" (prepared tableside during dinner) and "scrumptious churros" aren't enough, pros propose that it's best to take the edge off with some "sangria with a hit of Jack Daniel's."

BINKLEY'S RESTAURANT Ⓢ Ⓜ   27 | 20 | 25 | $54

6920 E. Cave Creek Rd. (1/2 mile west of Tom Darlington Dr.),
Cave Creek, 480-437-1072; www.binkleysrestaurant.com
"Fresh", "fabulous" and "fastidiously prepared" cuisine comes to gastronomy starved Cave Creek thanks to chef-owner Kevin Binkley (ex Napa's French Laundry, Inn at Little Washington in VA) and his "sophisticated" "art-filled" New American; indeed, this "rising culinary star" has the "energy" to revise the menu daily and invent "splendid tasting menus" to sate "serious foodies" who make a trip to the man they're dubbing the "Gary Danko of the desert."

Cyclo ⊠ | 26 | 15 | 20 | $18 |
1919 W. Chandler Blvd. (Dobson Rd.), Chandler, 480-963-4490;
www.cycloaz.com
Expect "plenty of sass" and "charm" from "fashionable" proprietor/
menu designer/server Justina Duong, who "makes everyone feel
like a lifelong friend" at her "casual" Vietnamese BYO in a
Chandler strip mall; since the "amazing", reasonably priced food
is as "fresh" and "lovely" as its owner, this "small" "piece of
Saigon" is always "worth the wait."

Drinkwater's City Hall Steakhouse | 27 | 24 | 25 | $54 |
6991 E. Camelback Rd. (Goldwater Blvd.), Scottsdale, 480-941-4700;
www.mastrorestaurants.com
Scottsdale citizens soak up the "dark" and "sexy" atmosphere at
this beloved beefery, whose backers crown it the "king of AZ's
steakhouses"; the "unbeatable" chops are as "juicy" as a scene
that's abetted by "great martinis", live music and a "terrific bar
area" where a "spunky" crowd works off the "huge portions" on the
dance floor; "if you have to go somewhere, make this the place."

Eddie V's Edgewater Grille | 26 | 25 | 24 | $47 |
20715 N. Pima Rd. (E. Thompson Peak Pkwy.), Scottsdale,
480-538-8468; www.eddiev.com
Find some surf on desert turf at this "large", "clubby" seafood-
steak combo in North Scottsdale serving "fresh", "fantastic" sea
fare and "excellent" chops for red-meat mavens; budget-seekers
baited by the "amazing 35-cent oysters" and selected half-price
appetizers at happy hour forsake the "vibrant dining room" for the
"happening" jazz lounge.

elements | 25 | 27 | 24 | $52 |
Sanctuary on Camelback Mountain, 5700 E. McDonald Dr.
(bet. Scottsdale Rd. & Tatum Blvd.), Paradise Valley,
480-607-2300; www.elementsrestaurant.com
"Request a window table at sunset" and treat yourself to a
"breathtaking view" and "romantic" dinner at this "stunning"
Asian–New American tucked away on the northern slope of
Camelback Mountain; the "spectacular architecture" and "contemporary", "Zen-like" decor echo the menu, which offers "divine", "healthy" fare in "artful", "minimalist" presentations; all
things considered, it's certifiably "perfect" for a "special occasion."

Greene House, The | – | – | – | E |
Kierland Commons, 15024 N. Scottsdale Rd. (Greenway), Scottsdale,
480-889-9494; www.foxrestaurantconcepts.com
This new upscale concept brings a decidedly serene vibe to the
popular Kierland Commons shopping center; the restaurant's appeal lies in the Asian sensibility of its bungalow-style, Frank Lloyd
Wright/Craftsman-inspired decor, which in turn informs the simple Californian menu.

Los Sombreros Ⓜ | 25 | 19 | 20 | $28 |
2534 N. Scottsdale Rd. (bet. Oaks St. & Thomas Rd.), Scottsdale,
480-994-1799
Chef-owner Jeff Smedstad turns out "authentic", yet "original"
takes on regional Mexican food so "absolutely amazing" that
many "hate to share" this South Scottsdale eatery with anyone
else, considering it the "best of its kind" in AZ; P.S. since you may

find the "cozy" digs "packed" on any given day, try to score a spot in the "fabulous" patio.

MARQUESA Ⓜ | 27 | 27 | 27 | $59 |

Fairmont Scottsdale Princess, 7575 E. Princess Dr. (bet. Hwy. 101 & N. Scottsdale Rd.), Scottsdale, 480-585-4848; www.fairmont.com/scottsdale

"Absolutely beautiful", this "top-notch" North Scottsdale Mediterranean is a "foodie's delight", "from the imaginative appetizers" to the "exotic" entrees to the "fabulous desserts"; the "flawless" service means that guests are "treated like royalty", resulting in a "truly marvelous experience that makes any meal a special occasion"; of course, it comes with a "big price tag", but otherwise, "what's not to love?" here; P.S. its marketplace-style Sunday brunch, set outside in the courtyard, is "second to none."

MARY ELAINE'S Ⓢ Ⓜ | 27 | 28 | 27 | $82 |

The Phoenician, 6000 E. Camelback Rd. (N. 60th St.), Scottsdale, 480-423-2530; www.thephoenician.com

Setting the standard for a "special-occasion" experience, this "elegant", "ultrafancy" room at The Phoenician is where the city views are "heavenly", the wine list "extraordinary" and Bradford Thompson's "exquisite" New French fare way up there with "the best in the country"; the "unparalleled" service "anticipates every desire", so even though you'll need to bring "buckets of cash", it's "more than worth it"; N.B. jackets required, and summer hours are limited.

MASTRO'S STEAKHOUSE | 26 | 24 | 24 | $59 |

La Mirada, 8852 E. Pinnacle Peak Rd. (N. Pima Rd.), Scottsdale, 480-585-9500; www.mastrorestaurants.com

Meat mavens award this North Scottsdale "paradise" an "A+" for serving up "mouthwatering" steaks, "excellent sides" and a "seafood tower that's not to be missed", while scene-seekers say the "lively bar" (fully stocked with "eye candy") amps up both the "East Coast vibe" and "noise levels"; even the "high rollers" concede it's "expensive", but they, like most, can't help "loving it."

Michael's at the Citadel | 25 | 24 | 24 | $53 |

The Citadel, 8700 E. Pinnacle Peak Rd. (N. Pima Rd.), Scottsdale, 480-515-2575; www.michaelsrestaurant.com

It may be "a bit of a hike", but this "sophisticated" New American in Pinnacle Peak is "well worth it" considering chef Michael DeMaria's "exceptional" cooking and "stunning decor" featuring an indoor waterfall, "lovely fireplace" and patio (complete with tropical plants and fountains); although curmudgeons carp the "big price tag" raises "value-for-money" issues, the majority says it all adds up to a "spectacular" experience.

P.F. CHANG'S CHINA BISTRO | 21 | 20 | 20 | $29 |

Kierland Commons, 7132 E. Greenway Pkwy. (N. Scottsdale Rd.), Scottsdale, 480-367-2999

The Waterfront, 7135 E. Camelback Rd. (Scottsdale Rd.), Scottsdale, 480-949-2610

Chandler Fashion Ctr., 3255 W. Chandler Blvd. (bet. Chandler Villlage Dr. & Rte. 101), Chandler, 480-899-0472

6610 E. Superstition Springs Blvd. (Power Rd.), Mesa, 480-218-4900

16170 N. 83rd Ave. (E. Alameda St.), Peoria, 623-412-3335

(continued)

(continued)

P.F. CHANG'S CHINA BISTRO
740 S. Mill Ave. (E. University Dr.), Tempe, 480-731-4600
www.pfchangs.com
"Wear comfortable shoes" to help cushion the invariably "un-bearable waits" at these "busy" Chinese outposts of a national chain; while purists pan the provisions as "Americanized Chinese", partisans praise the "dependably delicious" fare, singling out the "fabulous lettuce wraps" as edible proof.

PIZZERIA BIANCO 🖼 Ⓜ   28 | 20 | 21 | $25
Heritage Sq., 623 E. Adams St. (N. 7th St.), Phoenix, 602-258-8300;
www.pizzeriabianco.com
"Believe the hype": copping the No. 1 rating for Food in AZ is Chris Bianco's "adorable" "pizza temple" that draws droves of devotees who deem the "outstanding" pies ("they make life worth living") to be "the best in the country"; with all the publicity, expect "mind-numbing waits", but insiders suggest sipping wine at the adjacent Bar Bianco.

Roaring Fork   25 | 24 | 24 | $43
4800 N. Scottsdale Rd. (Chaparral Rd.), Scottsdale, 480-947-0795;
www.roaringfork.com
Locals "love" this Regional American "favorite" where chef-owner Robert McGrath elevates "cowboy cooking" to the level of "fine dining"; that it's known as a "happy-hour" "hangout" (the "great" huckleberry margaritas are the order of the day) helps corral even more fans into its "Western"-decorated digs; P.S. their "big-ass burger" is "legendary."

ROY'S   24 | 22 | 22 | $44
J. W. Marriott Desert Ridge Resort & Spa, 5350 E. Marriott Dr.
(bet. Deer Valley Rd. & Tatum Blvd.), Phoenix, 480-419-7697;
www.roysrestaurant.com
Scottsdale Seville, 7001 N. Scottsdale Rd. (Indian Bend Rd.),
Scottsdale, 480-905-1155; www.roysrestaurant.com
7151 W. Ray Rd. (bet. N. 54th & N. 55th Sts.), Chandler,
480-705-7697; www.roys.com
Fusion fare lands in the desert at Roy Yamaguchi's "gorgeous" trio serving "magical", "cutting-edge" Hawaii Regional food, including "beautifully prepared fish" and downright "sinful desserts"; though some find they "don't compare" to the original locations, most swim with the tide, saying they "meet the highest standards."

SEA SAW   28 | 18 | 25 | $61
7133 E. Stetson Dr. (E. 6th Ave.), Scottsdale, 480-481-9463;
www.seasaw.net
"Take out a loan" if necessary before visiting this spartan, 28-seat "foodie destination" in Oldtown Scottsdale for "astonishing" Japanese tapas and "unsurpassed sushi" (courtesy of "genius" chef Nobuo Fukuda) prepared in "ways you never thought possi-ble"; an "incredible" 2,800-plus-label wine list and the "best sake selection in town" help put it in the "inspirational" category.

T. COOK'S   27 | 28 | 26 | $56
Royal Palms Resort and Spa, 5200 E. Camelback Rd. (bet. N. Arcadia Dr. &
N. 56th St.), Phoenix, 602-808-0766; www.royalpalmshotel.com
"All around", it "doesn't get better" than this "romantic" retreat in the Royal Palms – the Most Popular place in AZ – that "blows

away" admirers with its "beautiful hacienda-style" setting and "luxurious" atmosphere; it's also impossible to overlook the "marvelous" Mediterranean creations and the "professional staff", making a trip here "a must for out-of-town guests" and "lots of locals" alike; N.B. chef Lee Hilson has replaced Gregory Casale.

Trader Vic's   – | – | – | M

Historic Hotel Valley Ho, 6850 E. Main St. (Blvd. on Main Street), Scottsdale, 480-421-7799; www.hotelvalleyho.com

Befitting its home in the newly renovated, retro Hotel Valley Ho is this Downtown Scottsdale Polynesian hang known for its oversized tropical cocktails (the mai tai was invented here) and an Eclectic menu (think Indonesian rack of lamb); though surrounded by sand, this tiki-fied addition is all surf.

Vincent's on Camelback ⊠   26 | 22 | 24 | $58

3930 E. Camelback Rd. (N. 40th St.), Phoenix, 602-224-0225; www.vincentsoncamelback.com

Considered a "classic" by its many fans, this "elegant" Camelback Corridor stalwart still "charms" with Vincent Guerithault's "terrific", "innovative" Gallic interpretation of Southwestern fare and "elegant", "upscale" country French decor; if it's "tired" to a few, this piece of "gastronomic heaven" in the desert remains "at the top" to most.

Portland, OR

TOP FOOD RANKING

Restaurant	Cuisine
27 Paley's Place	Pacific Northwest
Genoa	Italian
Apizza Scholls	Pizza
26 Higgins	Pacific Northwest
Heathman	Pacific Northwest
Joel Palmer House	Pacific Northwest
Alberta St. Oyster Bar	Pacific Northwest
Tabla	Mediterranean
Caffe Mingo	Italian
Nuestra Cocina*	Mexican

OTHER NOTEWORTHY PLACES

Alba	Northern Italian
Andina	Peruvian
Bluehour	Med./New American
clarklewis	New Amer./Pacific NW
Giorgio's	Northern Italian
Murata	Japanese
Olea	Mediterranean
Park Kitchen	New Amer./Pacific NW
3 Doors Down	Mediterranean
Wildwood	Pacific Northwest

F	D	S	C

Alba Osteria & Enoteca Ⓜ

24	19	22	$39

6440 SW Capitol Hwy. (Bertha Blvd.), 503-977-3045; www.albaosteria.com

Set in an old train depot, this "hidden" Northern Italian "bastion" hosts aficionados of Barolos and Barbarescos who swear by the "authentic" (if somewhat obscure in the United States) Piedmontese dishes offered on the "killer" roster, especially the "fantastic" pastas and the "best" sweetbreads; "spot-on" service and a "darling" setting play a large role in the restaurant's winning formula.

Alberta St. Oyster Bar & Grill

26	21	24	$38

2926 NE Alberta St. (29th Ave.), 503-284-9600; www.albertaoyster.com

It may have a plain-Jane name, but this rising "star" is shining in "funky" NE Alberta; beyond the "outstanding variety" of "fresh" oysters is "dangerously delicious" and moderately "pricey" Pacific Northwest creations served by "polished" staffers in a "warm", "stylish" setting, all serving to make this spot a "wonderful addition" to the scene.

---

* Indicates a tie with restaurant above

ANDINA
25 | 24 | 22 | $38 |

*Pennington Bldg., 1314 NW Glisan St. (13th Ave.), 503-228-9535;
www.andinarestaurant.com*

"Imaginative" modern Peruvian cuisine that scales uncharted "culinary heights" distinguishes this "chic", "high-energy", high-ceilinged Pearl District venue; the "extensive" small-plate options make sampling the "sexy" offerings easy, and "pro" service and "fabulous" drinks should help give everyone a reason to come and experience a "hedonistic feast for the senses."

APIZZA SCHOLLS Ⓜ
27 | 13 | 18 | $20 |

*4741 SE Hawthorne Blvd. (bet. 47th & 48th Aves.), 503-233-1286;
www.apizzascholls.com*

Depending on who's talking (or eating), the "best pizza this side of the Mississippi" – or perhaps "this side of Italy" – can be found at this "cramped" Hawthorne pizzeria whose pies leave even a "New Yorker happy"; aside from "long lines", "spacey" service and "strict limitations on the number of toppings" (there are "more regulations than the nastiest divorce settlement"), few dispute there's "sublime" 'za here that's "more for foodies than fratties."

BLUEHOUR
23 | 25 | 22 | $46 |

*Wieden & Kennedy Headquarters, 250 NW 13th Ave. (Everett St.),
503-226-3394; www.bluehouronline.com*

Wear your "Helmut Langs" to this "swanky" Pearl District Med–New American, the "hang of P-Town's who's who" where the "dramatic" interior (complete with soaring drapery) matches the "glam" crowd; it's no surprise that happy hour here is the "best" around, and as far as the food, it's "good", but since the staff supplies as much "eye candy" as the patrons, does it really matter?

Caffe Mingo
26 | 20 | 23 | $33 |

807 NW 21st Ave. (Johnson St.), 503-226-4646

Devotees line NW 21st for this "lively" Nob Hill eatery cranking out "fantastic" "farmhouse" Italian specialties enhanced by a staff that "couldn't be friendlier"; you'll feel like you're eating "in someone's home", especially if you dine at the communal "chef's table" that boasts prime kitchen viewing.

clarklewis Ⓢ
25 | 19 | 19 | $43 |

*Eastbank Commerce Ctr., 1001 SE Water Ave. (bet. Taylor &
Yamhill Sts.), 503-235-2294; www.ripepdx.com*

Chef Morgan Brownlow's cooking seems to defy "physics" marvel gourmets who visit this "minimalist", "dark" (you'll "dine by flashlight") New American–Pacific NW in the industrial Southeast waterfront district; for those who can abide the "uncomfortable chairs" and "noise", the food here "makes every mouthful an epiphany."

GENOA ◑
27 | 19 | 27 | $74 |

*2832 SE Belmont St. (bet. 28th & 29th Aves.), 503-238-1464;
www.genoarestaurant.com*

"Fulfill all your palate's dreams" at this 35-year-old Portland "institution" in Belmont where the "incredible hospitality" complements the "formal" ambiance and "lovingly prepared" Italian fare consisting of three, four or seven course meals; even though it's known as the city's "most expensive" restaurant, it's still, for many, "the most special" and "worth every penny."

Giorgio's Ⓜ　　　　　25 | 22 | 24 | $43
1131 NW Hoyt St. (12th St.), 503-221-1888; www.giorgiospdx.com
The din of "happy diners" bounces off the tile floors of this "elegant", banquette-lined "gem of the Pearl" District; the Northern Italian cuisine (courtesy of Peter Schuh, an alum of NYC's per se) uses French technique to "phenomenal" effect and plays a major part in an overall "wonderful" experience that includes "attentive" yet "subtle" service and an "understated", "warm" ambiance; no question then: it's "one of Portland's best."

HEATHMAN RESTAURANT, THE　　26 | 22 | 24 | $46
The Heathman Hotel, 1001 SW Broadway (Salmon St.), 503-790-7752; www.heathmanhotel.com
"One dines, not eats" at this Downtown Heathman Hotel stalwart for "special occasions" that's perfect either for a "power lunch" or "dress-up dinner"; chef Philippe Boulot's kitchen sends out "superlative" Pacific NW fare infused with "Gallic savoir-faire" while "helpful" service ensures such a smooth ride that any thoughts of "high costs" are quickly erased from memory; P.S. a "great" high tea is served in the adjacent lounge.

HIGGINS RESTAURANT & BAR　　26 | 22 | 25 | $44
(aka Higgins)
1239 SW Broadway (Jefferson St.), 503-222-9070
The bona fide "temple" of Pacific Northwest fare is this Downtown mainstay (Portland's Most Popular) where chef Greg Higgins, an early champion of organic, seasonal and sustainable agriculture, has a knack for turning the "simple things into something extraordinary"; more kudos go to the "laid-back" ambiance, "excellent" service and "impressive" beer and wine lists; P.S. bargain-hunters applaud the "affordable" menu (and the "best" burgers in town") at the adjoining bar.

Joel Palmer House Ⓢ　　　　26 | 23 | 24 | $50
600 Ferry St. (6th St.), Dayton, 503-864-2995; www.joelpalmerhouse.com
"Mushroom maniacs" clear a path to Dayton and end up at this "historic" house in the "country", the showcase of chef Jack Czarnecki, who uses 'shrooms – from matsutakes to morels – and "lovingly weaves" them into Pacific NW dishes; the consensus: for "fun and fungi in the middle of nowhere", it's "fabulous."

Murata　　　　　　　　25 | 17 | 21 | $36
200 SW Market St. (bet. 2nd & 3rd Aves.), 503-227-0080
This Downtown Japanese is well known to most for serving sushi so "absolutely fresh" it must be "illegal"; pros propose you sit at the bar and "watch Mr. Murata work his magic" with raw fare, or bring a crew and settle in to one of the tatami rooms to get a sense of what a "family-run *ryokan*" in Japan must be like.

Nuestra Cocina ⓈⓂ　　　　26 | 20 | 22 | $28
2135 SE Division St. (bet. 21st & 22nd Aves.), 503-232-2135; www.nuestra-cocina.com
When it comes to "fabulous" food to lift you up when the "city's grays" are getting you down, this SE Portland Mexican favorite "takes the cake ("or rather, the flan"); while the "long waits" can grate, the "colorful" mosaic-tiled setting and an "authentic", "no-burrito" Oaxacan-influenced menu compensate.

Olea
| 23 | 23 | 21 | $43 |

1338 NW Hoyt St. (bet. 13th & 14th Aves.), 503-274-0800;
www.olearestaurant.com
Chef Scott Shampine (ex Aqua in SF) brings culinary "sophistication" to the Pearl District with this "buzzy" Mediterranean whose
claim to fame is "exciting" dishes offered in small- and large-
plate formats; the "fantastic", "industrial-chic" room boasts
"sky-high" ceilings and a curved bar at the entrance, the latter
lending the space a "loungey" vibe.

PALEY'S PLACE BISTRO & BAR
| 27 | 22 | 26 | $50 |

1204 NW 21st Ave. (Northrup St.), 503-243-2403; www.paleysplace.net
At this "intimate" "upscale bistro" on Nob Hill's Restaurant Row,
"consummate hostess" Kimberly Paley oversees a staff that
makes you "feel like you have just arrived at their home", while
husband and chef Vitaly puts a French spin on "superb" Pacific
NW food; it seems everyone here has the "perfect touch", so it's no
surprise that its reputation "still holds."

Park Kitchen Ⓢ
| 25 | 19 | 23 | $39 |

422 NW Eighth Ave. (Flanders St.), 503-223-7275; www.parkkitchen.com
Enthusiasts eagerly await whatever surprises chef Scott Dolich has
up his sleeve at this "low-key" bistro at the north end of the Pearl
District; the "intriguing", "clever" New American–Pacific NW food is
ably matched by "engaging" service, and the whole package is
made even more enticing with "cool" decor and sidewalk seating
that "looks out onto the bocce" action.

Tabla Ⓜ
| 26 | 21 | 24 | $35 |

200 NE 28th Ave. (Davis St.), 503-238-3777; www.tabla-restaurant.com
Fans invariably "end up falling in love" with this "hip"
Mediterranean small-plate specialist that "manages to stand
apart" from the other restaurants lining NE 28th Street; the fare is
"worth repeat visits", as are the three-course tasting menu (aka
"the best deal in Portland"), "comfortable" casual vibe and the back
bar, where patrons can watch the drama unfold in the kitchen.

3 Doors Down Café Ⓜ
| 25 | 21 | 23 | $33 |

1429 SE 37th Ave. (Hawthorne Blvd.), 503-236-6886;
www.3doorsdowncafe.com
The meals are "always memorable" for the "crowds" who throng
this "welcoming", no-reservations cafe tucked away on a side
street off Hawthorne Boulevard; the extensive larder of affordable
Mediterranean fare features "marvelous" pastas ("I could eat the
vodka penne with sausage every day") backed by "attentive, unobtrusive" service; P.S. slogging through the "long lines" is now
a bit easier since the owners expanded the lounge area.

WILDWOOD
| 25 | 23 | 23 | $44 |

1221 NW 21st Ave. (Northrup St.), 503-248-9663;
www.wildwoodrestaurant.com
Serving "true" Pacific Northwest fare for more than a decade, this
Nob Hill mainstay, the domain of celebrity chef Corey Schreiber
(one of the founding fathers of the local-sustainable-organic move-
ment) is where the "divine" food still "shines" and where sitting
at the "chef's table" by the wood-burning oven or in the "casual"
dining room is a treat; overall, it's a "must" for anyone wanting to
experience one of the Northwest's gastronomic "treasures."

Salt Lake City & Mountain Resorts

TOP FOOD RANKING

	Restaurant	Cuisine
27	Tree Room	Regional American
	Red Iguana	Mexican
	Mariposa, The	New American
26	Michelangelo	Italian
	Seafood Buffet	Seafood
	Glitretind	New American
	Fresco Italian Cafe	Northern Italian
	Metropolitan	New American
	Martine	Mediterranean
25	Chez Betty	American/Continental

OTHER NOTEWORTHY PLACES

Restaurant	Cuisine
Bambara	New American
Chimayo	Southwestern
Franck's	American/French
Log Haven	New American
Lugano	Northern Italian
Market St. Grill	Seafood
New Yorker Club	American
Pine American	New American
Takashi	Japanese
Wahso	Asian Fusion

F	D	S	C

Bambara

24	25	24	$36

Hotel Monaco, 202 S. Main St. (200 South), 801-363-5454;
www.bambara-slc.com

"Bringing energy and style to Downtown", this "hip", "urban" "favorite" in the "trendy Hotel" Monaco boasts a "busy open kitchen" helmed by "talented chef" Robert Barker, whose "dynamite" New American cuisine "excites foodies' imaginations"; with "swanky decor" and a "hip atmosphere", its "great space" (the historic Continental Bank lobby) is a "nice place to impress your date", but it's "not for a quiet romantic dinner" and "not if you're in a hurry" – so just "sit back, have a drink and take it all in."

Chez Betty

25	18	24	$45

Copper Bottom Inn, 1637 Short Line Rd. (Deer Valley Dr.), Park City,
435-649-8181; www.chezbetty.com

"You can *Betty*" that this "jewel" (named after its resident goldfish) "off Main Street" in Park City's Copper Bottom Inn is "a delight" thanks to its "consistent", "creative kitchen's" "innovative menu" of "delicious" Continental–Traditional American fare; partisans praise the "superb, personal service" from the "warm, friendly" staff and "romantic, cozy, intimate" environs that "feel like an auberge", even if a few feel that the decor "needs updating"; P.S. there's "always at least one delicious vegetarian plate" on offer.

CHIMAYO

24 | 25 | 22 | $43

368 Main St. (4th St.), Park City, 435-649-6222; www.chimayorestaurant.com

"You're immediately engulfed by a ritzy vibe" and "warm ambiance" "reminiscent of Santa Fe in winter" at this Main Street "Park City favorite" where the "charming" decor (recently renovated) and "aromas set the perfect mood"; connoisseurs are "impressed with" the "wonderful flavors" featured in its "expensive" but "unusual spins on traditional Southwestern-style food", which are "innovative without being weird" and include "great wild-game selections" such as "the best elk in town"; all told, it's "a must-visit."

Franck's ⊠

– | – | – | E

6263 S. Holladay Blvd. (bet. Holladay Blvd. & 6200 South), 801-274-6264; www.francksfood.com

In an intimate country cottage set amid towering trees is this Cottonwood newcomer where chef Franck Peissel turns out an idiosyncratic selection of French-American offerings, from the *ménage a foie* (foie gras three ways) to Southern fried chicken; the fire pit on the patio offers a distinctive 'round-the-campfire appeal.

Fresco Italian Cafe

26 | 22 | 24 | $38

1513 S. 1500 East (bet. Emerson & Kensington Aves.), 801-486-1300; www.frescoitaliancafe.com

Adoring *amici* swoon over the "fresh", "tasty Northern Italian" dishes – now overseen by chef Dave Jones (ex Log Haven) – on offer at this "romantic little spot" set in a "secluded former home" "tucked away in a quiet Eastside residential neighborhood"; those who find its "intimate" interior a bit "cramped" say it's "best in summer" when one can dine on the "darling patio" surrounded by "beautiful grounds"; P.S. "the place draws a loyal clientele, so be prepared to wait" – and "make your reservations way in advance."

Glitretind Restaurant

26 | 24 | 26 | $52

Stein Eriksen Lodge, 7700 Stein Way (Royal St.), Deer Valley, 435-645-6455; www.steinlodge.com

Even those who "can't pronounce the name" "love" ascending to the "beautiful alpine setting" of this "Deer Valley treasure" "in the Stein Eriksen Lodge", where a "professional, polished and polite" staff caters to "discerning diners" with "beautifully presented", "manicured meals" of "wonderful, inventive" New American cuisine, accompanied by a "killer wine list" and offered in a "European-feeling" room that's "formal yet comfortable for *après*-ski"; N.B. if it's "pricey" for your pocketbook, "wait for the summer two-for-one coupons."

Log Haven

– | 27 | 23 | $44

6451 E. 3800 South (Wasatch Blvd.), 801-272-8255; www.log-haven.com

"A magical place" "high in the mountains", this "secluded", "rustic cabin" boasts a "beautiful Millcreek Canyon setting" "complete with waterfall"; in summer of 2005, new chef Frank Mendoza introduced his New American menu that makes good use of local fish, game and produce; given his résumé, which includes stints at Metropolitan and San Francisco's La Folie, a visit here should remain an "exceptional experience" "to remember."

Lugano   25 | 19 | 24 | $31 |
3364 S. 2300 East (3300 South), 801-412-9994;
www.luganorestaurant.com
"It's not uncommon to see" "magnificent chef" and owner Gregory Neville "among the tables" of this "cozy, upscale" Northern Italian in Holladay, "working the crowd" and "ensuring diners a quality experience"; devotees declare that his "reasonably priced", "seasonally changing menu" and "attentive", "knowledgeable staff" "deserve the accolades" regularly "piled upon" them, even if the "lively, upbeat atmosphere" can be more than a little "noisy" ("don't expect to hear everything your date says").

MARIPOSA, THE Ⓜ   27 | 25 | 25 | $58 |
Silver Lake Lodge, Deer Valley Resort, 7600 Royal St. (Rte. 224),
Deer Valley, 435-645-6715; www.deervalley.com
Smitten surveyors sum up this "special-occasion" spot in the "world-class Deer Valley" Resort's Silver Lake Lodge as "one of Park City's treasures", touting its "uniformly" "exquisite" New American fare (including a "very good vegetarian tasting menu"), "wonderful wine" list and "consistently superb service"; lauders love the "informal elegance" and "mountain appeal" of its "fabulous" alpine interior, and if you get too "hot sitting next to the fireplace", the signature Chocolate Snowball dessert will cool you off nicely; N.B. open December through mid-April.

MARKET STREET GRILL   24 | 21 | 22 | $30 |
2985 E. Cottonwood Pkwy. (3000 East), 801-942-8860
48 W. Market St. (West Temple St., bet. 300 South & 400 South),
801-322-4668
www.gastronomyinc.com
Collectively ranked Most Popular among Utah restaurants, this "terrific" twosome "sets the standard" for "excellent seafood" with its "expansive" selection of "reasonably priced" "fresh fish" dishes ("start with" the "superior clam chowder" – a "classic favorite"); whether visiting the "fun Downtown" "institution" or its younger sibling "in the suburbs", which "wows" with "great mountain and creek views", expect "friendly service" and a "packed", "noisy", "high-energy" environment; P.S. the "earlybird special is a wondrous thing."

Martine Ⓢ   26 | 23 | 23 | $33 |
22 E. 100 South (bet. Main & State Sts.), 801-363-9328
Happy habitués hail the "innovative menu" of "top-notch" "Mediterranean food with serious influences from Morocco and Spain" (including "inventive tapas") that "leaves diners pleased" at this "well-established Salt Lake classic" set in a "cozy Downtown brownstone"; "romantics" report it's a "great place to bring your main squeeze" thanks to "refined service" from an "attentive staff" and "fine ambiance that feels like a great small restaurant in San Francisco or Boston."

Metropolitan Ⓢ   26 | 25 | 24 | $52 |
173 W. Broadway (300 South, bet. 200 West & West Temple St.),
801-364-3472; www.themetropolitan.com
"Fine-art platings" of "exquisite food" matched with "incredible wine pairings" are the hallmark of this "excellent-albeit-

expensive New American", a "chic" "favorite" whose "cool", "cosmopolitan" interior is manned by "a hip host" and "funky" staffers providing "impeccable service"; contrarians contend it "falls short" of its "pretensions", but acolytes aver it's Downtown's "definition of high-end dining"; P.S. its "casual bistro is an escape to NYC, but at SLC prices."

MICHELANGELO RISTORANTE M   26 | – | 21 | $27 |

Hyland Plaza Mall, 2156 S. Highland Dr. (2100 South), 801-466-0961; www.michelangeloristorante.com

"Excellent risottos and house-made pastas" are among the "outstanding" offerings that "consistently impress" at this "authentic" "little trattoria" "in a hard-to-find" Eastside location; fans "love" that it's manned by "actual Italian waiters" in a new, and comparatively elegant, setting (i.e. the old plastic plants have been exchanged for real ones).

NEW YORKER CLUB ⌧   25 | 24 | 24 | $45 |

60 W. Market St. (West Temple St., bet. 300 South & 400 South), 801-363-0166; www.gastronomyinc.com/ny

The "grand patriarch of Downtown SLC restaurants", this "tasteful, elegant" "classic" is the "always reliable, always appropriate" choice of "well-dressed", "mature" Utahns celebrating "special occasions" and "power brokers" looking to "seal the deal" over "excellent" traditional American fare (including "great steaks" and "to-die-for soufflés") delivered by a "top-notch" staff; some sigh over the "steep prices", but most say it's "a pleasure" ponying up the nominal membership fee to "join the club."

Pine American Restaurant   – | – | – | M |

4760 South 900 E. (4500 South 900 E.), 801-288-2211; www.pinerestaurant.com

Chef-owner Greg Neville (of Lugano fame) goes all-(New) American with his wine-country inspired dishes at this modern, multilevel restaurant/bar; though the deck is an undeniable draw (it overlooks Big Cottonwood Creek and supplies views of the Wasatch Mountains to the east), fans are keyed into the moderately priced light bites and full-fledged savories that are capped by pastry chef Amber Billingsley's sweets.

RED IGUANA, THE   27 | 12 | 20 | $17 |

736 W. North Temple St. (800 West), 801-322-1489; www.rediguana.com

Though the "amazing moles" are "the most flavorful north of the border", you "can't go wrong with any dish" from the "impressive menu" of "authentic Mexican" treats at "this crowded joint" in a "sketchy neighborhood" west of Downtown, where the "friendly waiters" keep the "focus on customer service"; sure, it's a bit of a "dive", and you might have to "wait outside" "on the sidewalk" ("the line often snakes down the block"), but for 20 years now, spicy-food fanatics "have fantasized about" its "fantastic food."

SEAFOOD BUFFET ⌧   26 | 18 | 22 | $56 |

Snow Park Lodge, 2250 Deer Valley Dr. (Mellow Mountain Rd.), Deer Valley, 435-645-6632; www.deervalley.com

"Serious overeaters" "skip the slopes" and simply slalom to this "seafood-aficionados paradise", a "high-end buffet" and bastion of "conspicuous consumption" where the "abundant variety" of "excellent-quality" ocean fare ("incredible fresh fish, oysters, sushi, crab, smoked salmon") and "desserts galore" are an "all-you-can-eat bargain" offered "in a casual atmosphere" that's "great for families and groups"; "pace yourself", though, as "this kind of indulgence requires stamina"; P.S. sadly, it's solely a "ski-season" "event" – "if only it were open year round!"

Takashi ⊠ | – | – | – | M |

18 W. Market St. (West Temple St., bet. 300 South & 400 South), 801-519-9595

Chef Takashi Gibo helms this Japanese showcase where sushi subjects sample his exquisite rolls, small plates and entrees, all served with premium sakes, wines and brews; the enamored crowds haven't subsided since day one, packing into the contemporary, arty Downtown space (once the site of Au Bon Appetit) that features a giant mesh fish by local sculptor Willy Litig.

TREE ROOM | 27 | 27 | 26 | $45 |

Sundance Resort, Scenic Rte. 92 (Hwy. 189), Sundance, 801-223-4200; www.sundanceresort.com

"Even the most sophisticated guests are invariably charmed by" this "special place" "surrounded by the splendor of the Sundance" Resort whose "flawless" Regional American meals have earned it the No. 1 rating for Food among Utah restaurants; "outstanding service" and the "rustic", "romantic", "relaxed ambiance" of its "beautiful" space with "Native Indian art all around" "only enhance" the "absolutely memorable dining experience", which is made even more "magical" by "Robert Redford sightings" – and yes, there's "a tree growing through the dining room."

WAHSO | 25 | 26 | 23 | $48 |

577 Main St. (Heber Ave.), Park City, 435-615-0300; www.wahso.com

Slip into "one of the secluded curtained booths for a nice romantic escape" at this "oh-my-God! good" Asian fusion palace where "the decor is stunning and inventive", the "impeccable" fare features "fabulous flavors and textures", the saketinis and other "cocktails are fantastic" and the staff is "informed, friendly and attentive"; gourmets gush that it's chef-owner "Bill White's best", and the one to "try if you have time for only one Park City restaurant" (though nearby Chimayo is also a "reliable" choice).

San Antonio

TOP FOOD RANKING

	Restaurant	Cuisine
28	Le Rêve	New French
27	Lodge Rest.	New American
26	Korean B.B.Q. House	Korean
	Biga on the Banks	New American
	Bistro Vatel	French
	L'Etoile	French/Seafood
25	Las Canarias	French/Med.
	Francesca's at Sunset	New American
	Fleming's Prime	Steakhouse
	Frederick's	Asian/French
	Silo*	New American

OTHER NOTEWORTHY PLACES

Restaurant	Cuisine
Ácenar	Tex-Mex
Azúca Sabor Latino	Nuevo Latino
Bin 555	New American
Boudro's/Riverwalk	Seafood/Steakhouse
Ciao Lavanderia	Italian
El Mirador	Mexican
Liberty Bar	Eclectic
Paesanos	Italian
Pesca on the River	Seafood
P.F. Chang's	Chinese

F	D	S	C

Ácenar

22	24	20	$27

146 E. Houston St. (Soledad St.), 210-222-2362; www.acenar.com
With "groovy" decor and a "fabulous outdoor patio", this River
Walk Downtowner provides a "swinging atmosphere" to go with
its "va-va-voom" "nuevo Tex-Mex" fare and "killer margaritas";
drama-loving diners urge stop in "before or after the [nearby] theater", though some surveyors warn of "long waits" and "uneven
service" in the "sometimes noisy" dining area; N.B. the street-
level bar, Átomar, is open till 2 AM Fridays and Saturdays.

Azúca Sabor Latino ⌷

22	20	18	$31

713 S. Alamo St. (S. Presa St.), 210-225-5550; www.azuca.net
"Wild, hot and spicy" in more ways than one, this Southtown
Nuevo Latino combines "explosive flavors" (e.g. paella that
"smells and tastes wonderful") with "multifaceted art glass", a
"Havana-romantic feel" and "oh-god" mojitos; weekend revelers
can also rumba to the rhythms of a live tropical orchestra, which
makes the scene "too loud" for some and may explain the sometimes "inattentive" service.

---

* Indicates a tie with restaurant above

BIGA ON THE BANKS
26 | 25 | 26 | $48

203 S. St. Mary's St. (W. Market St.), 210-225-0722; www.biga.com
Foodies are "big on" this "urbane" Downtown dining room, a "modern", "gossamer-curtained" space where "culinary magician" Bruce Auden conjures up "bold", "luscious" Asian-inflected New American cuisine to go with his "excellent" wine list; meanwhile, the "knowledgeable, attentive" servers enable diners to "relax" and enjoy the "fantastic River Walk views."

Bin 555 ●⏹
– | – | – | M

The Shops at Artisans Alley, 555 W. Bitters Rd. (bet. Blanco Rd. & West Ave.), 210-496-0555; www.bin555.com
Jason Dady's New American in Hill Country Village is a more casual version of his first restaurant, The Lodge; this time out he's serving up tony tapas, wood-oven offerings, larger plates with a Mediterranean cast and affordable vintages – all in a sunny yellow (if sometimes noisy) setting tucked away behind an eclectic shopping center; N.B. in a nod to the restaurant's name, the wine list offers 55 choices priced at $55 each.

BISTRO VATEL ⏹
26 | 18 | 23 | $44

218 E. Olmos Dr. (El Prado Dr. W.), 210-828-3141; www.bistrovatel.com
Chef-owner Damien Watel's "delicately delectable", "perfectly prepared French classics" ("outstanding foie gras", "exquisite" seafood) and "great" wine list have elevated his Olmos Park strip-center bistro to "gourmet-haven" status; "twice-a-week" regulars rhapsodize over its "intimate", "truly European" vibe – complete with "flea-market chic" styling – and a "gracious" staff that's "diligent but not overwhelming"; in short, an "unexpected" "gem"; P.S. three-course, $34 prix fixe dinners are such a "bargain" they're practically a "gift."

BOUDRO'S ON THE RIVERWALK
24 | 20 | 21 | $33

421 E. Commerce St. (N. Presa St.), 210-224-8484; www.boudros.com
"One of the few" River Walk restaurants lauded by locals, this "much-talked-about" "haven" "continues to succeed" because of its "excellent regional" (read: Louisianan-Texan) seafood and steaks, bolstered by "awesome guacamole" and "addictive" cactus-pear margaritas; "knowledgeable" staffers can "manage groups big or small", and since there may be "lots of noise" and "very little elbow room" inside, "snag an outdoor table" if weather permits; P.S. "dinner on one of the barges as you float" downstream "is a blast."

Ciao Lavanderia ⏹
21 | 17 | 19 | $26

226 E. Olmos Dr. (El Prado Dr. W.), 210-822-3990
"You'll clean your plate at this renovated washeteria" predict *amici* who chow down on the "tasty", "innovative" and "reasonably priced" petite-portion offerings at chef-owner Damien Watel's "quirky" Olmos Park Italian; the "funky, relaxed atmosphere", fostered by a "casual" yet "attentive" staff, is another reason this place's "hip clientele" considers it such a "likable eatery."

El Mirador
23 | 17 | 20 | $19

722 S. St. Mary's St. (King William St.), 210-225-9444
Probably SA's most widely-written-about Mex – situated, ironically, in the historically German King William area – this almost-40-year-old "institution" is a "must-visit"; the "classic" cuisine (e.g.

"superb", "habit"-forming Saturday soups that'll "cure what ails ya") is a "great value" and proffered by "helpful and courteous" staffers; no wonder "all the locals" ("politicos", "lots of attorneys") gather here for the "latest gossip", especially since a "recent face-lift" has made this "good old" place even "better."

Fleming's Prime Steakhouse & Wine Bar 25 | 23 | 23 | $50
255 E. Basse Rd. (Hwy. 281), 210-824-9463;
www.flemingssteakhouse.com
Contented carnivores have no beef with these "upscale" yet "laid-back" steakhouses, claiming they "do everything well": the "high-quality" rib-eyes are "delicious" and the wine list "extensive", while "cheerful" staffers "make you feel like kings and queens"; though a few find these places "noisy" and "overpriced", most consider this chain a "can't-miss" choice.

Francesca's at Sunset 🗷 Ⓜ 25 | 27 | 27 | $48
Westin La Cantera Hotel, 16441 La Cantera Pkwy. (Fiesta Texas Dr.), 210-558-2442; www.westinlacantera.com
Appropriately "breathtaking" sunset views make this upscale New American in the Westin La Cantera SA's No. 1 for Decor – but surveyors are also gasping over the "spectacular" Southwestern-slanted cuisine (à la Santa Fe's Mark Miller) served up by "knowledgeable" staffers; those who "want to live large" and explore the "extensive" wine list can put off the "long drive home" by staying overnight at the resort.

Frederick's 🗷 25 | 15 | 23 | $44
7701 Broadway St. (Nottingham Pl.), 210-828-9050;
www.fredericksa.com
"Amazing" and "always reliable" French–Asian fusion fare "bursting with flavor" (especially the "extremely well done" seafood) is the forte of this Alamo Heights "fave", "hidden in the back" of a strip center; owner Frederick Costa, who's "always present to ensure things run smoothly", and his "friendly, attentive" staff foster a "pleasant ambiance" despite the place's "cramped confines" and "less-than-inspirational", apparently "improvised decor."

KOREAN B.B.Q. HOUSE 🗷 Ⓜ 26 | 13 | 19 | $22
(aka Go Hyang Jib)
4400 Rittiman Rd. (Melton Dr.), 210-822-8846
"You want ethnic in SA? this is it" assert admirers who adore the "very authentic" Korean barbecue ("the best babyback ribs in Bexar County") and "excellent bulgoki and bibimbop" at this far Eastside eatery, complete with exotic indoor waterfall; the "wonderful owners" and "helpful staffers" help neophytes out with "knowledgeable explanations" of unfamiliar fare.

Las Canarias 25 | 25 | 25 | $48
La Mansion del Rio Hotel, 112 College St. (bet. Navarro & N. St. Mary's Sts.), 210-518-1063; www.lamansion.com
Chef Scott Cohen has turned this "spacious, gracious" venue in the "elegant" La Mansion del Rio Hotel into a "tremendous" dining destination replete with "class and taste"; his "polished", "imaginative" French-Med cuisine, drawing on local ingredients, "lives up to the hype" (the Sunday brunch buffet, in particular, is "unbeatable"), while a crew of "true professionals" helps create a "romantic" ambiance via "impeccable" service and "lovely", "gentle" guitar music on weekends.

LE RÊVE ⍜ Ⓜ

28 | 24 | 27 | $81

The Historic Exchange Bldg., 152 E. Pecan St. (N. St. Mary's St.), 210-212-2221; www.restaurantlereve.com

Now that smitten surveyors have voted it SA's No. 1 for Food, Andrew Weissman's "romantic" Downtown "gem" might as well be renamed Le Rave; this petite New French exhibits its chef-owner's "amazing attention to detail" throughout each "three-hour" dinner – "excellent" prix fixe and tasting menus with "superb" wine pairings are "impeccably" served by a "pampering" staff in a modern room adorned with "lovely, fresh floral arrangements"; a vocal minority sniffs the scene is "beyond snooty", but most find it "the epitome of elegant dining"; N.B. jacket required.

L'Etoile

26 | 19 | 24 | $43

6106 Broadway St. (Normandy Ave.), 210-826-4551; www.letoilesa.com

"It's not called the star for nothing" beam Lone Star Staters who are high on this "comfortable", "quiet and relaxing" Alamo Heights "favorite"; they report its "classic" French seafood is "perfectly prepared" and "artistically presented" by "careful" servers; trendier types declare "it's time for some new recipes" at this "dowdy" spot and detect a soupçon of Gallic "attitude"; P.S. shellfish lovers laud the "wonderful" summer lobster festival.

Liberty Bar

23 | 20 | 21 | $23

328 E. Josephine St. (Ave. A), 210-227-1187; www.liberty-bar.com

Located in North Central San Antonio, the building housing this "funky" "classic" "leans noticeably" to the left, just like much of its "arty" "hipster" clientele; its similarly "unique" Eclectic menu lets you "mix and match" an array of "strictly gourmet" noshes with "awesome homemade bread", "great desserts" and esoteric wines and beers; the "friendly" servers can be "quirky", but this "pure Texas" "charmer" is often "the first place [locals] take visiting foodies."

LODGE RESTAURANT OF CASTLE HILLS, THE ⍜

27 | 26 | 24 | $51

1746 Lockhill Selma Rd. (West Ave.), 210-349-8466; www.thelodgerestaurant.com

It feels like you're spending the evening "at a rich friend's house" when you settle in at this 1929 Castle Hills "converted mansion" where "inventive" chef-owner Jason Dady turns out "expertly prepared" Texas-style New American dishes you can savor à la carte or in various prix fixe configurations, cared for by staffers who manage to be "knowledgeable and attentive" without "smothering"; plan to occupy one of the "quaint", "romantic" small rooms "for hours" enjoying this "pricey" but "fabulous" experience.

PAESANOS

22 | 21 | 20 | $31

555 E. Basse Rd. (Treeline Park), 210-828-5191; www.paesanos.com

PAESANOS RIVERWALK

111 W. Crockett St. (Presa St.), 210-227-2782; www.paesanosriverwalk.com

PAESANOS 1604

3622 Paesanos Pkwy. (NW Military Dr.), 210-493-1604; www.paesanos1604.com

Thanks to its "transcendent" shrimp Paesano, these "lively" Italian "institutions" remain "family favorites" – indeed, they're voted SA's Most Popular; "better service" and a "fun ambiance" impel locals toward the Alamo Quarry Market location – where "boldface" types mingle at the city's "largest sit-down cocktail party" – rather than the "contemporary", "tourist-destination" River Walk outpost (the promising Shavano Park branch opened post-*Survey*); still, a sizable minority charges the "decent" but "dull" fare "has been declining."

Pesca on the River   22 | 22 | 20 | $45

Watermark Hotel & Spa, 212 W. Crockett St. (Navarro St.), 210-396-5817; www.watermarkhotel.com

"Refined", "spacious" and handsome, this seafooder at the Watermark Hotel "has the potential for excellence"; pescavores who feel "the best seat is at the [raw] bar" can slurp "excellent" oysters "from around the world" and sample any of the 75 tequilas on hand, while mellower sorts prefer dining outdoors "along the River Walk" with a glass of wine.

P.F. CHANG'S CHINA BISTRO   22 | 21 | 20 | $25

The Alamo Quarry Mkt., 225 E. Basse Rd. (Hwy. 281), 210-507-1000; www.pfchangs.com

"Always crowded" and "consistent", this "ubiquitous" chain keeps its clientele coming back with "generous portions" of "tasty", "upscale" (if "Americanized") Chinese food and "great wine by the glass", served amid "distinctive" decor; still, even fans grumble about waiting "too long" in "too-noisy" environs for "too-pricey" cuisine that sometimes seems "too formulaic."

Silo   25 | 23 | 23 | $43

1133 Austin Hwy. (Mt. Calvary Dr.), 210-824-8686; www.siloelevatedcuisine.com

This "hip", "minimalist" Terrell Heights showplace provides an "elevated experience" in more ways than one; the dining mezzanine overlooks a "fabulous", "wild and fun" first-floor bar, and the New American fare "hits great heights" as well with "imaginative", "beautifully presented" dishes complemented by "astonishing" wines and served "attentively"; though a few sigh the food's "static" and "pricey", most maintain this eatery is "as close to a sure thing as you can get"; N.B. the kitchen is now under the direction of founding chef Mark Bliss.

San Diego

TOP FOOD RANKING

Restaurant	Cuisine
27 WineSellar & Brasserie	French
Sushi Ota	Japanese
Pamplemousse Grille	French/New Amer.
Arterra	New American
A.R. Valentien	Californian
26 Tapenade	New French
Oceanaire	Seafood
El Bizcocho	French
Donovan's	Steakhouse
Rama	Thai

OTHER NOTEWORTHY PLACES

Azzura Point	Californian
George's at the Cove	Californian
Laurel	French/Med.
Marine Room	New French
Mille Fleurs	New French
Modus	Belgian/French
Ortega's	Mexican
Roppongi	Asian Fusion
Ruth's Chris	Steakhouse
Vivace	Northern Italian

F	D	S	C

ARTERRA 27 | 23 | 24 | $53

San Diego Marriott Del Mar, 11966 El Camino Real (Carmel Valley Rd.), 858-369-6032; www.arterrarestaurant.com

Fans "love Bradley Ogden in any city", and his "not-your-average" Marriott destination near Del Mar confirms it; though gourmets need look no further than the "sublime" New American dishes, most also consider the "excellent" service by "waiters, not surfers", "buzzy" ambiance and "cool, modern" decor to all factor in the success of this "outstanding" venue from one of the West's more prominent chefs.

A.R. VALENTIEN 27 | 27 | 26 | $61

The Lodge at Torrey Pines, 11480 N. Torrey Pines Rd. (Torrey Pines Golf Course), La Jolla, 858-777-6635; www.lodgetorreypines.com

This "genteel" "great getaway" on the Torrey Pines golf course benefits from a "gorgeous" setting, namely the "classic" Craftsman-designed space with "beautiful" views of the pines and the ocean, all supplying an ideal stage for "superb" Californian cuisine (courtesy of chef Jeff Jackson) and service that's "attentive" "from the moment you drive up"; even after the "expensive" tabs arrive, this place is still easy to "love."

Azzura Point Ⓜ   24 | 25 | 23 | $60

Loews Coronado Bay Resort, 4000 Coronado Bay Rd. (Silver Strand Blvd.), Coronado, 619-424-4000; www.loewshotels.com

The "beautiful setting overlooking the bay" and a "gorgeous view of the Downtown skyline" alone justify the "expense" at this Loews Californian; fans enjoy the "accommodating" service and "very good" preparations while pointing to the "relaxing" resort ambiance – you can even "reserve a gondola" and "glide along the canal while you have dessert."

Donovan's Steak & Chop House Ⓩ   26 | 23 | 25 | $60

4340 La Jolla Village Dr. (Genesee Ave.), 877-611-6688; www.donovanssteakhouse.com

"Get your money's worth" of meat and plentiful portions of "test-osterone" at this wood-paneled, "old-school" chophouse in the Golden Triangle; "if you crave outstanding, top-quality beef, this is your place" confirm carnivores who also aver the "extensive" (if "expensive") wine list and "detail"-oriented service make it "the best of the steakhouses" in town.

El Bizcocho   26 | 25 | 25 | $62

Rancho Bernardo Inn, 17550 Bernardo Oaks Dr. (Rancho Bernardo Rd.), Rancho Bernardo, 858-675-8550; www.jcresorts.com

Still as "sturdy" as ever, this mainstay of "special-occasion" dining unites chef Gavin Kaysen's "sumptuous" French fare with "impeccable" service, an "excellent" 1,600 label wine list and an "old-money" formality that has sustained its appeal over the years; the standards here are perhaps as "high" as the bill when it comes, so be sure to bring "someone else to pay"; N.B. the restaurant no longer requires jackets.

GEORGE'S AT THE COVE   25 | 25 | 24 | $53

1250 Prospect St. (bet. Cave St. & Ivanhoe Ave.), La Jolla, 858-454-4244; www.georgesatthecove.com

Once again San Diego's Most Popular restaurant, this "romantic" La Jolla "grande dame" offers ocean views that "take your breath away", Californian food that "has the same effect" and "dignified" servers who cater to a necessarily well-heeled crowd basking in the "beauty" of a setting that includes a rooftop bar as well as the main dining room downstairs; this "not-to-be-missed" experience may be somewhat "touristy", but that's no surprise, since visitors know something "special" when they see it.

Laurel   24 | 24 | 23 | $55

505 Laurel St. (5th Ave.), 619-239-2222; www.laurelrestaurant.com

Stylish sorts show up at this "trendy" Banker's Hill venue near Balboa Park serving "sophisticated", "interesting" French-Mediterranean fare along with an "incomparable" wine list; decorwise, the "hip" *"Alice In Wonderland"*–like setting is either "brilliant" or somewhat "overdone."

MARINE ROOM   24 | 25 | 24 | $60

2000 Spindrift Dr. (Roseland Dr.), La Jolla, 858-459-7222; www.marineroom.com

"The ocean seems to roll right into the dining room" at this "breathtaking" La Jolla Shores landmark that some say is the "best place to take guests from out of town"; chef Bernard Guillas' New French cuisine deftly employs "classic techniques" with "inventive" results, while the "attentive" service makes the clientele feel "pampered"; tip: it's so "romantic" you can "take your date and you're sure to get another one."

Mille Fleurs
| 25 | 25 | 25 | $70 |

Country Squire Courtyard, 6009 Paseo Delicias (Avenida De Acacias), Rancho Santa Fe, 858-756-3085; www.millefleurs.com

"Top host" Bertrand Hug's ab-"fab" New French salon in posh Rancho Santa Fe offers an "elegant" stage for "superb" fare (thanks to chef Martin Woesle) and for the "professional" servers who attend to the "old-money" clientele; sure, the prices are "high" and flip-flop fans find fault in the setting ("stuffy"), but supporters say "if you want to treat yourself right", go here.

Modus ☒ Ⓜ
| ▽ 21 | 23 | 23 | $42 |

2202 Fourth Ave. (Ivy St.), 619-236-8516

This "fantastic" new addition occupies a cool, "sexy" Banker's Hill space that's an easy choice for the area's scenesters; the food also delights, with "terrific" French-Belgian fare (offered until 1 AM at the "attractive" bar) supported by "wonderful" service.

Oceanaire Seafood Room, The
| 26 | 25 | 24 | $55 |

400 J St. (4th Ave.), 619-858-2277; www.theoceanaire.com

"What a place for a date" avow advocates of this "winning" Minneapolis-based seafood chain link and "jewel" in San Diego's Gaslamp Quarter; "bring a life vest because the food will blow you away" say enthusiasts also baited by "exceptional" service and "great" decor done up like a "'30s ocean liner"; ok, it's "pricey", but overall, things are shipshape here.

Ortega's, A Mexican Bistro
| 24 | 20 | 21 | $28 |

141 University Ave. (bet. 1st & 3rd Aves.), 619-692-4200

"*Muy delicioso*" dishes mark the menu of this "gourmet" Hillcrest Mexican celebrated for serving the same "incredible" Baja California-style lobsters and flour tortillas popularized by the original namesake in Puerto Nuevo, Mexico; "exceptionally warm", "rustic" decor lends a welcome "neighborhood" vibe; P.S. it may be "the best bargain in San Diego."

PAMPLEMOUSSE GRILLE
| 27 | 22 | 25 | $61 |

514 Via de la Valle (Hialeah Circle), Solana Beach, 858-792-9090; www.pgrille.com

The "gastronomical equivalent of a Panerai watch" is this Solana Beach "staple for gourmands" opposite the Del Mar Racetrack; there's "no horsing around" though, since chef-owner Jeffrey Strauss' French–New American preparations are "lovingly transformed into art" and partnered with "knowledgeable" service and an "endless" wine list amid an "entertaining", "provincial-France" setting; overall, it's "extra special."

Rama
| 26 | 27 | 23 | $33 |

327 Fourth Ave. (bet. J & K Sts.), 619-501-8424; www.ramarestaurant.com

Like its "trendy, sexy" clientele, this "transporting" Gaslamp Quarter Thai is a "beauty" to behold and features a floor-to-ceiling water wall and "willowy" fabrics – in all a "heavenly" setting for "fresh", "incredibly" good dishes; what's more, you'll be treated like a "special guest" of the staff, which helps you feel as if "you're on the other side of the Pacific."

ROPPONGI
24 22 21 $45

875 Prospect St. (Fay Ave.), La Jolla, 858-551-5252;
www.roppongiusa.com
Asian fusion fans frequent this Downtown La Jolla "favorite"
offering "fabulous" selections on an "interesting" slate; "order
several dishes and share" with "friends", hit the "sake sampler"
or just take in the "trendy" types who simultaneously provide "eye
appeal" and blend right in to the "terrific" feng shui–inspired
space; P.S. it's got the "best happy hour" in the neighborhood.

RUTH'S CHRIS STEAK HOUSE
25 22 24 $59

1355 N. Harbor Dr. (Ash St.), 619-233-1422
11582 El Camino Real (Carmel Valley Rd.), Del Mar, 858-755-1454
www.ruthschris.com
"Nothing beats the sizzling sound" when steak arrives at these
chain chophouses, aka "the kings of coronary clogging" whose
"attentive" staff serves "butterific" beef and "yummy" sides;
Downtown's got the "picture-perfect" view of San Diego Bay while
Del Mar boasts a "sleek" interior; either way, both are "worth the
spike in your cholesterol count" and dent in your wallet.

SUSHI OTA
27 12 19 $40

4529 Mission Bay Dr. (Bunker Hill St.), 858-270-5670; www.sushiota.com
"You know it has to be good when you need a reservation" for a
"storefront" aver amazed fans of this "legendary" Japanese –
what its Pacific Beach "strip-mall" locale lacks in charm is more
than made up for by "incomparable" sushi from "genius" chef-
owner Yukito Ota; it's widely known as "heaven" for raw-fish
purists and "businessmen from Japan", so expect "waits."

Tapenade
26 20 23 $58

7612 Fay Ave. (bet. Kline & Pearl Sts.), La Jolla, 858-551-7500;
www.tapenaderestaurant.com
"Bravo to Jean-Michel Diot" and company for the "excellent" New
French cooking and overall "high standards" at his "upscale" bistro that's La Jolla's answer to "Paris or New York"; it's "always a
treat – and a splurge" coming here, though most maintain it's also
a "deal" considering the quality of the food – besides, you can always capitalize on the "excellent" pre-theater or lunch prix fixes.

Vivace
25 27 26 $60

Four Seasons Resort Aviara, 7100 Four Seasons Point (Aviara Pkwy.),
Carlsbad, 760-603-6800; www.fourseasons.com
Rating high on the "special-occasion" scale, this "elegant"
Carlsbad Northern Italian meets the "high standards" set by the
Four Seasons Resort Aviara, namely "beautiful food in a beautiful
setting" abetted by "excellent" service; it will cost "extra dough",
but it's a small concession considering the payoff.

WINESELLAR & BRASSERIE ⊠ Ⓜ
27 19 26 $59

9550 Waples St. (off Mira Mesa Blvd.), 858-450-9557;
www.winesellar.com
It's "tough to find, but find it" insist oenophiles and gourmets of this
retail store/French brasserie (No. 1 for Food in SD) in an industrial
area of Sorrento Mesa; true, neither the "exceptionally" good
food (served on the second floor) nor "smooth" service is a surprise, but it's the wine that "shines" say those who "explore the
shop" pre- or post-dinner.

San Francisco Bay Area

TOP FOOD RANKING

Restaurant	Cuisine
29 Gary Danko	New American
French Laundry	French/New Amer.
28 Cyrus	New French
Marinus	New French
Chez Panisse	Californian/Med.
Kaygetsu	Japanese
27 Fleur de Lys	Californian/New French
Manresa	New Amer./New French
La Folie	French
Michael Mina	New American
Terra	New American
Ritz-Carlton Din. Rm.	New French
Rivoli	Californian/Med.
Farmhouse Inn	Californian
Sushi Ran	Japanese/Pac. Rim
Le Papillon	New French
Quince	New French
Redd Restaurant	New American
Sierra Mar	Californian
Masa's	New French

OTHER NOTEWORTHY PLACES

Ame	New American
Aqua	Californian/Seafood
Bar Tartine	Californian/Med.
Bistro Jeanty	French Bistro
Boulevard	Californian/French
Canteen	Californian
Chez Panisse Café	Californian/Med.
Coi	Californian/French
Delfina	Northern Italian
Fifth Floor	Cal./New French
Greens	Vegetarian
Jardinière	Californian/French
Lark Creek Inn	American
La Toque	French
Myth	New American
Oliveto Cafe	Italian
Range	New American
Scott Howard	Californian/French
Slanted Door	Vietnamese
Zuni Café	Mediterranean

subscribe to zagat.com

Ame
25 | 25 | 24 | $67

St. Regis Hotel, 689 Mission St. (Third St.), 415-284-4040;
www.amerestaurant.com
Set in the lobby of SoMa's St. Regis Hotel, this "minimalist" yet
"sexy" "Japanese-influenced" New American from Hiro Sone
and Lissa Doumani (St. Helena's Terra) is off to "a promising start";
the "highly imaginative", "beyond-eclectic", seafood-centric
menu "kicks some serious foodie butt" with the "sublime" flavors of
its "exquisite" entrees, enhanced by a "special" wine cellar and
"extensive list" of sakes; service is "attentive", if "inconsistent"
at times (perhaps because "it's still in its early" days).

Aqua
26 | 25 | 25 | $68

252 California St. (bet. Battery & Front Sts.), 415-956-9662;
www.aqua-sf.com
For "flawless fish" worthy of Neptune, plus chef Laurent
Manrique's "flavorful" "foie gras additions", "financial moguls"
and "celebrities" drop anchor at this "stunning, high-ceilinged"
"deep-pocket" "deep-sea" Downtowner; it's a "real dining adventure" with "exquisitely prepared" Cal-seafood with a slight
French influence, "omnipresent" "white-glove service" and a
"resident wine expert to help with the extensive list"; if gripers
find it hard to part with "hard-earned clams" for "crammed"
tables and a "punishing" "noise level", Aqua-nuts concur it "still
delivers one of the most impressive experiences in town."

Bar Tartine Ⓜ
23 | 20 | 20 | $38

561 Valencia St. (17th St.), 415-487-1600
Despite "no sign" ("look for a giant antler light chandelier"), it's
"a mob scene" at this "friendly", "foodie-hipster" haunt that may
be the "best thing to hit the Mission" since their "hugely popular"
Tartine Bakery sibling opened; natch, "it's worth it for the bread
alone" and "desserts are ethereal", but don't miss the "wonderful" small and large plates of "country-style" Cal-Med cuisine
and the "price-conscious" pours; still, a tart-tongued few feel
"service suffers due to their popularity."

Bistro Jeanty
25 | 20 | 23 | $49

6510 Washington St. (Mulberry St.), Yountville, 707-944-0103;
www.bistrojeanty.com
"Berets" off to Monsieur Jeanty's original "oh-so-French bistro"
in "the heart of wine country" in Yountville that's as "unchanging
as the Arc de Triomphe", churning out "spectacular", "stick-to-
the-ribs" "*cuisine grand-mère*" fare ferried by "friendly"
"*garçons*"; the "welcoming" "sit-in-your-neighbor's-lap" experience in a "warm" setting costs less than "other top" spots, and
the large "community table" where "drop-ins" can "get all the
latest vintner dirt" epitomizes *égalité*.

BOULEVARD
27 | 25 | 25 | $62

Audiffred Bldg., 1 Mission St. (Steuart St.), 415-543-6084;
www.boulevardrestaurant.com
"After all these years", this "boisterous", "beautiful" "belle
epoque landmark" with a "classy atmosphere" set in an "enviable"
Embarcadero location with "wonderful Bay views" still "mesmer-
izes" "visiting VIPs", "learned tourists" and "big-blowout" celebrants, delivering "all the trimmings" that more than "live up to
the hype"; the "exquisite experience" of Nancy Oakes' "sublime"

"down-to-earth while out-of-this-world" Cal-French "food artistry" accompanied by "unparalleled wines" "thrills" "each time", while the staff "bends over backwards" "to make you feel rich for a day", regardless of whether you're in "jeans or furs."

Canteen | 25 | 14 | 20 | $42 |

Commodore Hotel, 817 Sutter St. (Jones St.), 415-928-8870
Chef-owner Dennis Leary's 20-seat "sleeper sensation" in the Commodore Hotel is "a silk purse if I ever saw one" marvel those lucky to gain entry to the "quirky", retrofitted "1950s diner" where he prepares a "short, always changing" roster of "clever" Californian cuisine that "matches many multi-stars" "without the pretension"; there's "minimal" decor and "no lingering over dinner", but acolytes love that "the whole operation takes on the aspect of a magic show."

CHEZ PANISSE ⊠ | 28 | 24 | 26 | $76 |

1517 Shattuck Ave. (bet. Cedar & Vine Sts.), Berkeley, 510-548-5525; www.chezpanisse.com
Little wonder it "caused NY foodies to face west", but with "oh-so-much history and aura surrounding" Alice Waters' Cal-Med "mecca" in Berkeley, visitors are "surprised how moved" they are "by the simplicity of it all", from the "wonderful Craftsman home setting" to the "stellar" staff that skips the "hovering and the fluff"; acolytes agree that the daily prix fixe menus "never disappoint", offering "fruits, vegetables, almost any living thing, in fact" "so fresh, perfectly selected" and prepared with such "reverence" that they "taste the way they're meant to."

Chez Panisse Café ⊠ | 27 | 23 | 25 | $48 |

1517 Shattuck Ave. (bet. Cedar & Vine Sts.), Berkeley, 510-548-5049; www.chezpanisse.com
You can get anything you want at this "upstairs annex" of Alice's restaurant, a true "destination" where "urbane" Berkeleyites and "fussier eaters" enjoy the "Chez Panisse experience on their own terms"; exuding a "more casual" "clubhouse" air than the prix fixe "temple downstairs", this "less costly" à la carte cafe offers the "same inventive", "locally grown, ethically conscientious" Cal-Med creations, "so fresh you appreciate each ingredient", served by a "passionate" staff in that "charming Craftsman-design setting" – and it all comes "without the busy signals."

Coi Ⓜ | 27 | 25 | 25 | $108 |

373 Broadway (Montgomery St.), 415-393-9000; www.coirestaurant.com
"Daniel Patterson has done it again" – his "elegant", "intimate" nine-table newcomer Downtown is a "wonderful successor to fabulous Elisabeth Daniel" declare loyalists who laud the "wonderful" wine choices, "pampering service" and "sensational" four- ($75) and nine-course ($105) Californian-French tasting menus; the "extremely fresh", organic ingredients deliver an "intense" "rush of flavors around every turn" – little wonder why it's a "big hit", even with "jaded SF foodies"; P.S. the adjoining "little lounge" serves a more rustic, affordable à la carte menu until midnight.

CYRUS | 28 | 27 | 27 | $98 |

Les Mars Hotel, 29 North St. (Healdsburg Ave.), Healdsburg, 707-433-3311; www.cyrusrestaurant.com
Nick Peyton and chef Douglas Keane, also of Market in St. Helena, deliver "an ultimate gastronomic experience" that's

"as good as it gets for refinement" with "prices to match" at Healdsburg's "phenomenal" "new culinary destination" in Les Mars Hotel; "everything's over-the-top" – from the "dueling" "rolling champagne and caviar carts" and "fabulous" "formal" decor to the "orchestrated" presentation of "flawless" New French "flexible tasting menus" and "stellar wine pairings" – yet you "don't feel like you had to win the lottery to get in."

Delfina
26 | 19 | 22 | $44

3621 18th St. (bet. Dolores & Guerrero Sts.), 415-552-4055; www.delfinasf.com

There's "good-reason" why "celebs" and "San Franciscans fight to get into this tiny", "filled-to-the-rafters", "buzzing" Mission trattoria – namely "incredibly flavorful", "superb", "rustic" Tuscan fare that "surpasses expectations" "served by hot hipster chicks" "with just the right touch of anarchy" and "polish"; "you're pretty much stuck with a 6:30 PM reservation or walk-in luck unless you plan weeks in advance", but there's always the bar, plus the "new pizza cafe attached to the restaurant is also amazing!"

Farmhouse Inn & Restaurant, The
27 | 25 | 26 | $63

Farmhouse Inn, 7871 River Rd. (Wohler Rd.), Forestville, 707-887-3300; www.farmhouseinn.com

"Foodies rejoice at this secluded, intimate" Russian River farmhouse in Forestville, a "must-stop for a romantic evening in wine country" that captures the "essence of Sonoma living"; from the Californian fare "so fresh it just screams farmer's market", "amazing cheese cart" and "well-assembled" vino list spotlighting "local growers" to the "quaint", "definitely country" surroundings with a "sense of home" and a staff that pays "superb attention to little details", "all of the elements fuse into that oh-so-rare special dining experience"; N.B. open for Thursday–Monday dinner only.

Fifth Floor ⌾
25 | 25 | 24 | $83

Hotel Palomar, 12 Fourth St. (Market St.), 415-348-1555; www.fifthfloorrestaurant.com

"Dazzled" diners "would climb to the 50th floor" of SoMa's Hotel Palomar for the "heavenly" Cal–New French gastronomy, now created by chef Melissa Perello, at this "impressive, innovative, expensive" experience; "relax" in a "tiger-striped" "interior that makes you feel sexier", and "spoil" yourself with a "mind-bending wine list" and "impeccable", "seamless service"; sure, prices seem "weighted toward millionaires", but "if it was good enough for Julia Child's 90th birthday", "it's good enough for me"; N.B. renovation plans underway for late 2006.

Fleur de Lys ⌾
27 | 26 | 25 | $88

777 Sutter St. (bet. Jones & Taylor Sts.), 415-673-7779; www.fleurdelyssf.com

For a "fairy-tale" evening, don "party clothes, sashay into this dreamy" Nob Hill "shrine" to "nouvelle cuisine" and "cocoon yourself" in the "opulent", *Arabian Nights*–like" setting with "ambiance out the wazoo"; "eat like a queen" on Hubert Keller's "beyond artistic", "rich" Cal-French prix fixe menus (including a "great vegetarian" option) – "every course, every bite, is truly divine" – as are the "phenomenal wines" – all "flawlessly presented" by a "fantastic" staff that adds to the "exquisite experience"; P.S. "crack open that extra piggy bank – this one will cost you"; N.B. jacket required.

FRENCH LAUNDRY, THE 　　29 | 26 | 28 |$254|
6640 Washington St. (Creek St.), Yountville, 707-944-2380;
www.frenchlaundry.com
"Heaven on earth" gush "gourmands" after "an indulgent five hours" of a "near-religious dining experience" that's "about so much more than eating" and "worth every hundred dollar bill" at Thomas Keller's "outrageously" priced "holy grail of haute" French–New American cuisine "nestled in Yountville"; from the "mind-bending", "sublime" tasting menus and the "phone book-size wine list" to the "impeccable" "staff that treats you like royalty" it's everything it's "hyped up to be" – no wonder "foodies" "would be willing to sell a family member to get a reservation"; N.B. jacket required.

GARY DANKO 　　29 | 26 | 28 |$100|
800 N. Point St. (Hyde St.), 415-749-2060; www.garydanko.com
Gary Danko is "still the king of this town" swoon "blissful" "gastronomes and oenophiles" who once again crown this "elegant" "super-nova"that's No. 1 for Food; "catch a cable car" to Fisherman's Wharf for a "hedonistic evening of pleasure" that begins with "delightful, delicious, de-lovely", "flexible" New American prix fixe menus and culminates with a "cheese cart that's an event in itself"; the "smooth, unpretentious", "telepathic staff" is never "more that an arm's length away" (ditto your "dressed-to-kill" neighbors at "surrounding tables") offering "insightful wine suggestions" – wow, "it's as good as it gets."

Greens 　　23 | 22 | 21 |$40|
Bldg. A, Fort Mason Ctr. (Buchanan St.), 415-771-6222;
www.greensrestaurant.com
"The grandmother of organic vegetarian restaurants" is "still going strong" – where else can vegans and "confirmed carnivores" "graze" "off each others' plates" while "gazing" at "fabulous bridge" and Marina views?; although the "enchanted forest" "warehouse" decor ("complete with tree in the middle") "shrieks 1978", the "knockout veggies" and "stunning wines" reveal what "heights" "alfalfa sprouts" served by "attentive" "hippies" "can rise to", particularly on "amazing prix fixe Saturday nights"; P.S. "you can't beat" the Greens to Go counter for lunch.

Jardinière 　　26 | 26 | 25 |$65|
300 Grove St. (Franklin St.), 415-861-5555; www.jardiniere.com
"*Iron Chef* winner" Traci Des Jardins' "gorgeous circular speakeasy" is the still the "sexiest" dining destination in Hayes Valley for both the "well-heeled" "pre- and post-opera crowd" and the "regular guy splurging"; the "sparkling atmosphere", "exquisite" service and "imaginative, locally grown PC" Cal-French fare makes for a "sumptuous" "experience for all the senses" – especially if you "sit by the art deco"–inspired balcony railing "near the jazz combo" and peer down at the "swells at the bar" below.

Kaygetsu Ⓜ 　　28 | 20 | 26 |$73|
Sharon Hts. Shopping Ctr., 325 Sharon Park Dr. (Sand Hill Rd.),
Menlo Park, 650-234-1084; www.kaygetsu.com
Prized for its "elegant kaiseki meals", a "seasonally changing creative feast for the senses" that "leaves you breathless with its

beauty and quality", this "extraordinary gem" with "amazing service" in a Menlo Park strip mall makes you feel "like you're on the panel of *Iron Chef*"; sure, you'll find some of the most "pristine" sushi on the à la carte menu, but the multicourse tasting menu is where owner "Toshi really works his magic."

La Folie ⑤　　27 | 24 | 26 | $86

2316 Polk St. (bet. Green & Union Sts.), 415-776-5577; www.lafolie.com

"Splurgers are rewarded by the generous spirit" of "genius" chef Roland Passot's "family-run" French on Russian Hill; fans are folie smitten by the "extraordinary", "artistically presented" dishes and "terrific wines", "understated" yet "outstanding" service and "beautiful" space; though a handful huff about ever-"ratcheting-up" prices, others boast it's "worth every penny" for "exquisite" cuisine that rivals "the best in the Bay Area."

Lark Creek Inn, The　　24 | 26 | 24 | $53

234 Magnolia Ave. (Madrone Ave.), Larkspur, 415-924-7766; www.larkcreek.com

"As romantic a setting as you could imagine", this "lovely" Larkspur longtimer is "worth the drive" just for the "charming" converted Victorian digs and "gorgeous surroundings"; but better yet, the "superb", "seasonal" "haute American cuisine", "fine wines" and "divine" desserts including the signature butterscotch pudding are ferried by a "fantastic" staff, and though it's decidedly "pricey" and a few wish Bradley Ogden "would come home", it's still one of the "best" "special-occasion" destinations "north of the Golden Gate Bridge."

La Toque Ⓜ　　26 | 22 | 26 | $102

Rancho Caymus Inn, 1140 Rutherford Rd. (east of Hwy. 29), Rutherford, 707-963-9770; www.latoque.com

"Master chef" Ken Frank's "exquisite", "exciting" French cuisine plus "brilliant" sommelier Scott Tracy's "phenomenal" wine pairings equal an "extraordinary dining experience" that's "worthy of the terrain" at this Rutherford "treasure"; the meal is complemented by "intelligent" service, and the "elegant", "romantic" room is warmed by a "roaring fire"; even if "you'll have to take out a second mortgage" to pay for the prix fixe–only tasting dinner (vino is extra), it's still "considered a bargain" compared with some of its Napa neighbors; N.B. closed Monday and Tuesday.

Le Papillon　　27 | 24 | 27 | $68

410 Saratoga Ave. (Kiely Blvd.), San Jose, 408-296-3730; www.lepapillon.com

"Don't let the neighborhood fool you – walk inside" San Jose's "hideaway" for "gastronomes" and "expense-accounters" and you "feel like you've arrived in Oz" declare the spellbound who deem it "outstanding in every way"; if the "stellar" New French tasting menus "beautifully presented" with "increasingly inspired wine pairings" don't bewitch, the "friendly", "flawless" service that "anticipates your needs" will; sure, it's "sticker-shock" city, but this "old-school" "butterfly just gets better with age."

Manresa Ⓢ Ⓜ　　27 | 24 | 26 | $94

320 Village Ln. (bet. N. Santa Cruz & University Aves.), Los Gatos, 408-354-4330; www.manresarestaurant.com

"Dollars fly from wallets" at this "romantic" "hideaway" in Los Gatos where diners "throw frugality and culinary prejudices to the wind" after indulging in "daring chef" David Kinch's "avant-garde", "physics"-inspired New American–New French tasting menus with "provocative wine pairings"; "no celebrity blarney here" – instead, a "supremely delicious" "spa for your taste buds" that "elicits many wows", though a few cynics quibble about "tight tables" and a "staff that could be more seasoned."

MARINUS   28 | 26 | 27 | $80

Bernardus Lodge, 415 Carmel Valley Rd. (Laureles Grade Rd.), Carmel, 831-658-3500; www.bernardus.com

It's a "longer drive than you might expect" to get to Carmel Valley's "luxurious" Bernardus Lodge in "the middle of nowhere" but "wow!" what an "incredible setting" – this is where "SF foodies visiting the Monterey Peninsula" come to splurge; chef Cal Stamenov's "sublime" derring-do with New French fare "speaks volumes" – pair it with the "tremendous wine list" for a "not-so-cheap thrill" you'll talk about long after dining by the "gorgeous fireplace"; "stroll the grounds before" dinner – or stay overnight – "you won't be sorry."

Masa's ⑤Ⓜ   27 | 24 | 27 | $96

Hotel Vintage Ct., 648 Bush St. (bet. Powell & Stockton Sts.), 415-989-7154; www.masasrestaurant.com

Who woulda thunk the "legacy could have lasted this long" but "even with the round robin" of chefs, this "sophisticated" Downtowner remains the "king of the power dinner" – and with Gregory Short "at the helm", the "divine" New French tasting menus are "nothing short of ecstasy"; what a "rare, fantastic experience" – "every course is first rate" ("loved the little post-meal candy tray"), the "decor is soothing and romantic" and service is "impeccable" – if only "you had a better job to pay for it"; N.B. jacket required.

MICHAEL MINA   27 | 24 | 26 | $105

Westin St. Francis, 335 Powell St. (bet. Geary & Post Sts.), 415-397-9222; www.michaelmina.net

"Mama Mina!", the "Aqua alum's" New American "temple of gastronomy" Downtown is "wickedly expensive" but it "holds its end of the bargain", delivering an "eating extravaganza" that pushes your "wow meter off the scales"; the tasting menu "emphasizing a common ingredient prepared" "three ways" scores an "incredible" trifecta while the "wine tomb" is an "oenophile's paradise" and the service "flawless"; however, the "much-ballyhooed interior is lost on" celebrants who don't want to "shout at their companions" over the din of "tourists squealing in the Westin St. Francis lobby."

Myth ⑤Ⓜ   25 | 25 | 24 | $55

470 Pacific Ave. (bet. Montgomery & Sansome Sts.), 415-677-8986; www.mythsf.com

"The apple doesn't fall far from the tree" laud acolytes who go out on a limb to praise "Danko protégée" Sean O'Brien who "branched out" to this "sleek NYC"-style Downtowner, offering a "happy mixture of good design, fabulous" New American food, a "buzzy" bar, an "inspired wine list" and servers that "have their act down"; if a few are "mythtified" about this "hot reservation", the "sexy sleek" purr "can't wait to find a sugar daddy to take me again" 'cause the "only bigger show in town is Barry Bonds."

Oliveto Cafe & Restaurant 25 | 22 | 22 | $52

5655 College Ave. (Keith St.), Oakland, 510-547-5356; www.oliveto.com

Chef Paul Canales' "handcrafted salumi", "homemade pastas" and "classy, artisanal" Italian fare "regularly anointed with once-in-a-lifetime aceto balsamico and extra virgin olive oil" frenzy the faithful ("any more authentic, artistic and passionate it would be in the Vatican" instead of Oakland); however, heretics eschew "aggressive prices", "limited choices" and service that swings from "cheerful" to "snotty"; P.S. "if you can't get into the posh upstairs, the downstairs cafe" offers "good vino" and "artisanal" pizza and small plates.

Quince 27 | 23 | 25 | $63

1701 Octavia St. (bet. Bush & Pine Sts.), 415-775-8500; www.quincerestaurant.com

"Food is now the drug of choice" at this "tranquil" former "apothecary" in Pac Heights, whose chef-owner "crafts" daily changing New French and "Italian-influenced" dishes "so fresh you feel virtuous eating them" ("don't skip" the "heavenly" homemade pastas) and a "veteran staff" of "pros" "guides you through" the "fantastic wine list"; "good luck getting a reservation" – the 15 "tables are hard to come by" (ditto the "wonderful chef's table") – but the experience rivals the city's "best" "with much less hype."

Range 25 | 21 | 22 | $44

842 Valencia St. (20th St.), 415-282-8283

Even city folk "feel at home on the Range", calling this Mission "hot spot", run by a husband-and-wife team, one of "the best restaurants to open in many moons"; the "exceptional" New American menu "incorporates local organic products" in "exciting flavor" combos, while "inspired" cocktails make it "almost as fun to stop just for a drink" and soak up the "industrial-chic" vibe at the "cool bar" where crowds are "cheek to jowl" every night.

Redd Restaurant ◐ 27 | 21 | 25 | $65

6480 Washington St. (California Dr.), Yountville, 707-944-2222; www.reddnapavalley.com

A "new star has risen in Yountville" attest admiring "tourists", "vintners" and "the Napa chic" awed by (ex Masa's and Auberge du Soleil) chef-owner Richard Reddington's "stylish" New American "masterpiece"; every "divine" dish on his "wine-friendly" à la carte and tasting menus "hits the high notes – very high" and it's all "beautifully presented" by a "flawless" staff; a few find it too "hard edged and noisy", but most give it the green light, insisting the "very architectural", "minimalist" setting allows the "lavish food" "to shine."

Ritz-Carlton Dining Room S M 27 | 27 | 28 | $93

Ritz-Carlton Hotel, 600 Stockton St. (bet. California & Pine Sts.), 415-773-6198; www.ritzcarlton.com

Not just TV fans "cheer" on "*Iron Chef*" Ron Siegel at Nob Hill's "most adult dining room" – "class"-act patrons "dressed for a black-tie event" jest he should "be knighted" for his "dazzling", "sublime" prix fixe menus – it's a "superb showcase of Modern French cuisine" "with Japanese influences"; expect a "sense of luxury not found" elsewhere, from the "fabulous" carts of cheese, champagne, candy and cordials rolled through the "formal" room to the "synchronized" staff – just "prepare to pay" the "price for perfection."

Rivoli　　27 | 23 | 25 | $46 |
1539 Solano Ave. (bet. Neilson St. & Peralta Ave.), Berkeley, 510-526-2542; www.rivolirestaurant.com

Truly the "highlight of Solano Avenue", Wendy and Roscoe's "East Bay find" with "polished service" is "wonderful without being pretentious"; "order anything" from the "innovative, high-caliber" menu "mixing Californian and Mediterranean" flavors and the "astounding wine list" and you'll "go home happy" – especially if you land a "window seat" and watch the nocturnal animals poke about the garden" "in bloom"; just "book ahead" because everyone from "foodies" to "Nobel laureates and world-renowned scientists from UC Berkeley" are in on the "secret."

Scott Howard　　24 | 23 | 22 | $60 |
500 Jackson St. (Montgomery St.), 415-956-7040; www.scotthowardsf.com

A "new star in the gourmet ghetto" Downtown gush gastronomes who applaud this "stylish" Cal-French newcomer; chef/co-owner Scott Howard "puts his heart and soul" into the "out-of-this-world" fare featuring "wild flavors that blend together so subtly and perfectly" – "true foodies shouldn't let another day go without experiencing" the "tantalizing" dishes, or the "imaginative cocktails"; N.B. the menu changed post-*Survey,* with larger portions and a simpler approach.

Sierra Mar　　27 | 28 | 25 | $83 |
Post Ranch Inn, Post Ranch/Hwy. 1 (30 mi. south of Carmel), Big Sur, 831-667-2800

"Words cannot describe" "the experience of dining in God's living room" – the "terrific service" and "epic view" from your "perch" "high on the hills" above the Pacific in Big Sur is almost "too spectacular to recall" the Californian cuisine confirm fklempt foodies who fawn over the "drop-dead gorgeous everything"; tear yourself away from "watching the whale migration below" as a "dreamy mist creeps up the window" and you'll find yourself "dining with multimillionaires" on equally "stunning food" while "sipping" "great wines" from the 1,800-bottle list.

SLANTED DOOR, THE　　25 | 22 | 20 | $45 |
The Embarcadero, 1 Ferry Bldg. (Market St.), 415-861-8032; www.slanteddoor.com

"There's magic happening" at Charles Phan's "urbane Vietnamese standard setter" at the Embarcadero's Ferry Building where fans fawn over "stellar Bay views" while "feasting family-style" on "sublime" Saigon "sensations" as servers "swish by" to make "perfect wine pairings"; a few phos fear "tourists" make even the "shaking beef" "vibrate differently" than in Mission days past, but it's still worth "pushing" through the portals, providing you "can get in" – if not, "graze" in the bar or head "Out the Door for carryout."

Sushi Ran　　27 | 19 | 20 | $47 |
107 Caledonia St. (bet. Pine & Turney Sts.), Sausalito, 415-332-3620; www.sushiran.com

"Run don't walk" to this "higher-class" "nirvana" "tucked away in Sausalito" that feels like a "neighborhood spot" but cranks out "unbelievable" Japanese–Pacific Rim creations "every bit as good as Masa's" for a "buzzy crowd"; expect "more than the usual suspects" – the "sushi chefs take great pride" in "skillfully" presenting raw fish "basics done to perfection" along with "delicious dishes" and "Kobe beef that melts in your mouth" – and "don't be discouraged if you have to sit" in the wine bar next door – it's a "good alternative."

Terra   27 | 24 | 26 | $64

1345 Railroad Ave. (bet. Adams & Hunt Sts.), St. Helena, 707-963-8931; www.terrarestaurant.com

"Hiro is our hero" and he "makes beautiful music" in his St. Helena "hideaway", "blending disparate cuisines" from Northern Italian to Southern French into an "incredible" New American menu offset by "excellent wines" chorus fans of chef Sone; the "complete experience" is orchestrated by a "formal but friendly" staff that "describes every ingredient" in every "revelatory" bite, and it's served in a "gorgeous restored farmhouse" – talk about "romantic"; N.B. the chef and his co-owner wife recently opened Ame in SF.

Zuni Café ●Ⓜ   25 | 20 | 21 | $45

1658 Market St. (bet. Franklin & Gough Sts.), 415-552-2522

Having "defied the odds and lasted as a trendy spot" in a "desolate" Hayes Valley location since 1979, Judy Rodger's "Energizer Bunny" remains the "go-to" "hot spot" for "simple, but right on" "Mediterranean soul food" delivered by a staff that's "gracious, if a bit distracted"; join the "foodies", opera swells and "tourists" slurping "divine oysters" and "delicious drinks" at the "see-and-be-seen bar" or swoop upstairs to the "festive" "jigsaw of rooms" for "legendary" "roast chicken or "the best late-night burger", and you'll see why it's "worthy of all the fuss."

Seattle

TOP FOOD RANKING

	Restaurant	Cuisine
28	Herbfarm, The	New American
	Nishino	Japanese
	Lampreia	New Amer./Pacific NW
	Rover's	New French
	Mistral	New Amer./New French
	Cafe Juanita	Northern Italian
	Lark	New American
	Salumi	Italian
27	Le Gourmand	French
	Shiro's Sushi	Japanese
	Harvest Vine	Spanish/Tapas
	Canlis	Pacific Northwest
26	Campagne	French
	Metropolitan Grill	Steakhouse
	Il Terrazzo Carmine	Italian
	JaK's Grill	Steakhouse
	Seastar	Seafood
	Union Bay Cafe	Pacific Northwest
	La Carta de Oaxaca	Mexican
	Dahlia Lounge	Pacific Northwest

OTHER NOTEWORTHY PLACES

Boat Street Cafe	French Bistro
Carmelita	Vegetarian
Cascadia	New American
Chiso	Japanese
Crush	New American
El Gaucho	Steakhouse
Georgian, The	Pacific Northwest
Green Leaf	Vietnamese
Inn at Langley	Pacific Northwest
Macrina	Bakery
Matt's in the Market	Seafood
Monsoon	Vietnamese
Nell's	New American
Paseo	Caribbean
Russell's	New American
Sitka & Spruce	New American
Toyoda Sushi	Japanese
Union	New American
Volterra	Northern Italian
Wild Ginger	Pacific Rim

Boat Street Cafe ⊠   ▽ 26 | 22 | 24 | $36

3131 Western Ave. (Denny Way), 206-632-4602;
www.boatstreetkitchen.com
Pâtés and poussins rule the roost at this French bistro at the bottom of Queen Anne Hill; the "delicious", "beautifully" conceived fare comes courtesy of chef-owner Renee Erickson and provides a fitting match for the reasonably priced wines and "sweetly understated" decor that's ripe for "intimacy."

CAFE JUANITA Ⓜ   28 | 23 | 27 | $56

9702 NE 120th Pl. (97th St.), Kirkland, 425-823-1505;
www.cafejuanita.com
Habitués say chef-owner Holly Smith's Kirkland Northern Italian hideaway operating in an "intimate" yet "chic" midcentury house serves up "what manna must taste like" considering the "brilliant combinations" of ingredients used in "meticulously prepared" dishes made with locally grown produce and meats; "impeccable" service is part of a package that "regardless of the price" has everyone waiting to "go back."

Campagne   26 | 23 | 24 | $55

Pike Place Mkt., 86 Pine St. (1st Ave.), 206-728-2800;
www.campagnerestaurant.com
The "crème de la crème of market fresh haute cuisine" laud loyal francophiles loyal to this "serene" enclave in the bustling Pike Place Market; chef Daisley Gordon conjures up "magical" country French food while "gracious, unobtrusive" servers glide between the "refined" dining room overlooking the market and the "romantic" summer patio; P.S. penny-pinchers should look out for the "amazing" prix fixe deals along with the less expensive downstairs cafe.

CANLIS ⊠   27 | 27 | 28 | $69

2576 Aurora Ave. N. (Halladay St., south of Aurora Bridge),
206-283-3313; www.canlis.com
"When only the best will do", movers and shakers head for this "old-money" family-owned 56-year-old "classic" with "spectacular views" of Lake Union, "phenomenal", "haute-modern" Pacific NW cuisine, a serene, "modern" space and a "deep" wine list (abetted by a crew of sommeliers) that keeps winning "every award in the book"; a staff that's "discreet" yet "attuned to your every need" also helps neutralize any thoughts about prices here.

Carmelita Ⓜ   25 | 20 | 21 | $35

7314 Greenwood Ave. N. (bet. 73rd & 74th Sts.), 206-706-7703;
www.carmelita.net
"Vegetables have never tasted as good" as they do at this Greenwood vegetarian offering a boldly accented, stylish setting to showcase "complex" dishes that reveal an "attention to flavor and color"; for "some of the tastiest eats" around, even those who "love meat would return in a heartbeat."

Cascadia ⊠   25 | 26 | 25 | $55

2328 First Ave. (bet. Battery & Bell Sts.), 206-448-8884;
www.cascadiarestaurant.com
"Beautiful in every way", chef-owner Kerry Sear's "uptempo" Belltown New American garners accolades for its "exquisite attention to detail" that's evident on all fronts, from the "out-of-this-

world" dishes, "well-chosen" Pacific NW–focused wine list, "attractive" decor featuring a water wall and "top-notch" staff; the $25 prix fixe and vegetarian tasting menus are "dreams come true."

Chiso Restaurant　　　　　　▽ 27 | 21 | 23 | $33 |
3520 Fremont Ave. N. (N. 36th St.), 206-632-3430; www.chisoseattle.com
"The enjoyment here is only limited by my budget" confess admirers of this Fremont Japanese where the "quality, freshness and presentation of sushi is high" while the "excellent" cooked fare puts a twist on classic dishes; the "addition of a liquor license" has helped pump up the "noise" and made it all the more "fun."

Crush ⌧ Ⓜ　　　　　　　25 | 22 | 21 | $56 |
2319 E. Madison St. (23rd Ave.), 206-302-7874;
www.crushonmadison.com
"Serious food lovers" descend on this "super-hot" Capitol Hill New American boasting a "terrific" mix of a "quaint" yet "modern" converted-house setting and "carefully crafted" comestibles that "delight the palate" (thanks to chef Jason Wilson, ex Jeremiah Tower's Stars in Seattle) and "take advantage of fresh, local ingredients"; N.B. small plates are served from 10:30 PM to midnight.

DAHLIA LOUNGE　　　　　26 | 23 | 24 | $47 |
2001 Fourth Ave. (Virginia St.), 206-682-4142;
www.tomdouglas.com
"A jewel in Tom Douglas' crown" and the flagship of the chef's mini-empire, this Pacific Northwest "favorite" of locals and tourists "shoots and scores" with "zippy", "artful food in an arty" crimson-toned space complete with Chinese lanterns, and "attentive, not cloying" service; there's "a lively buzz in the air" along with an abundance of "deliciousness" at the attached bakery.

El Gaucho ❶　　　　　　　25 | 24 | 25 | $65 |
2505 First Ave. (Wall St.), 206-728-1337
2119 Pacific Ave. (S. 21st St.), Tacoma, 253-272-1510
www.elgaucho.com
"Dining is theater" and "swank" is standard at these "retro" steakhouses whose plush booths and banquettes complete the overall "Rat-Pack"-y vibe and ensure a "fabulously decadent" time; the "pro" crew serves up "melt-in-your-mouth" beef and some old-school flourishes – "tableside"-made Caesars and bananas Foster – all for tabs tailored to expense accounts, while the nightly piano provides the crowning touch.

Georgian, The　　　　　　26 | 28 | 27 | $67 |
Fairmont Olympic Hotel, 411 University St. (bet. 4th & 5th Aves.),
206-621-7889; www.fairmont.com/seattle
Epitomizing "timeless beauty", this Downtown Pacific NW hotel "class" act is where "generations of Seattleites" have gathered for "special occasions" or an "upper-class dining fix" in a "high-ceilinged", chandeliered space framed by butter-yellow walls; the "wonderful" food at breafast, lunch and dinner delights, as does the "exceptional" service.

Green Leaf ⌧ Ⓜ　　　　　▽ 24 | 16 | 21 | $15 |
418 Eighth Ave S. (S. Jackson St.), 206-340-1388
"Authentic, delicious" Vietnamese food and the magic combination of "large portions and small prices" have conspired to transform this "small" bamboo-decorated newcomer into a popular choice

for local foodies; hence, it's often "crowded", so it's smart to get there early.

Harvest Vine, The
| 27 | 20 | 22 | $46 |

2701 E. Madison St. (27th Ave.), 206-320-9771; www.harvestvine.com

Lovers of high-end Basque cuisine swoon over the "fresh, intense, complex" creations at chef/co-owner Joseba Jimenez de Jimenez's Madison Park "gastronomic" destination where you can nab a chair at the copper dining bar, swap tapas tips with fellow diners and watch "great dinner theater" while "down-to-earth" staffers cater to you; reservations are recommended for this "taste of San Sebastián", since the "intimate" space seats only 40.

HERBFARM, THE Ⓜ
| 28 | 26 | 28 | $153 |

Willows Lodge, 14590 NE 145th St. (Woodinville-Redmond Rd.), Woodinville, 206-784-2222; www.theherbfarm.com

A "mecca" for "serious diners" from all over the world sums up this New American extravaganza (No. 1 for Food in Seattle) in Woodinville's burgeoning wine country, the showcase for chef Jerry Traunfeld, who seamlessly "weaves herbs" into a "beautiful symphony" – nine courses of "resoundingly excellent" dishes paired with wines and served by a "terrific" staff in a "precious" setting; true, given the "amazing expense", this "event" may need to be reserved for a "financial windfall", but go if you can, for it's likely to be an "unforgettable" experience.

Il Terrazzo Carmine Ⓩ
| 26 | 24 | 26 | $48 |

411 First Ave. S. (bet. Jackson & King Sts.), 206-467-7797

Just "wonderful" is what you'll hear from fans who describe this popular Pioneer Square "treasure" of an Italian which still "charms" comers after 22 years; you can taste the "care in every bite" of the "superb" food brought to table by a "top-notch" staff in a space that exudes "warmth": "is it possible to be in love with a restaurant?"

Inn at Langley Ⓜ
| ▽ 27 | 25 | 27 | $75 |

Inn at Langley, 400 First St. (bet. Anthes & Park Aves.), Langley, 360-221-3033; www.innatlangley.com

"A wonderful part of a great getaway" in Langley, this "grand" multihour event involves Matt Costello's "inventive", "unforgettable" Pacific NW six-course tasting menus bolstered by "local delicacies" – all prepared in the gleaming, stainless-steel kitchen right before patrons' eyes; Japanese antiquities and a river rock fireplace add to the "deluxe" experience, but book ahead, since the restaurant is only open Thursdays–Sundays in the summer, and Fridays–Sundays the rest of the year.

JaK's Grill
| 26 | 17 | 21 | $39 |

4548 California Ave. SW (bet. Alaska & Oregon Sts.), 206-937-7809
3701 NE 45th St. (37th Ave.), 206-985-8545
14 Front St. N. (Sunset Way), Issaquah, 425-837-8834
www.jaksgrill.com

It's all about the "high-quality" beef that's "seared to mouthwatering perfection" at this steakhouse trio where service is "fast and pleasant" and the rooms "noisy"; the combination of "bang-for-the-buck" appeal ("your pocketbook doesn't get à la carte-d to death") and no reservations suggests you should go "early or really late" or expect a wait akin to "an endurance event."

La Carta de Oaxaca ⊠   26 | 19 | 19 | $22
5431 Ballard Ave. NW (22nd Ave.), 206-782-8722
"Like *abuela's* kitchen" describes this "small" Mexican eatery in
quaint Ballard packing in enthusiasts eager to indulge in "heavenly" "authentic" Oaxacan fare; while the servers seem well
practiced in the art of "crowd control", the "super-friendly
bartenders" do their bit too, and help make "the long waits fly by"
with "great" margaritas.

LAMPREIA ⊠   28 | 23 | 25 | $68
2400 First Ave. (Battery St.), 206-443-3301; www.lampreiarestaurant.com
An "amazing dining experience", this "extraordinary" Belltown
Pacific NW–New American is "a place for foodies" to sample
"sublime", "visually stunning" small plates of "art" (conceived
and executed by chef Scott Carsberg, an "uncompromising
genius") while being attended to by "excellent" servers within a
"soothing" room; naturally, it's a "bit pricey", but few mind given
that a meal here "is one you'll never forget."

Lark   28 | 23 | 25 | $49
926 12th Ave. (bet. E. Marion & E. Spring Sts.), 206-323-5275;
www.larkseattle.com
"Seductive" small plates steer devotees to Capitol Hill for this
"temple" of "extraordinary", seasonal New American preparations from chef John Sundstrom; the menu mirrors the rusticated
"elegance" expressed in the small room, where the "good"
service influences the overall effect: "you feel like you're eating
in a friend's house, albeit a friend with amazing talent";
N.B. reservations taken only for parties of six or more.

Le Gourmand ⊠Ⓜ   27 | 24 | 27 | $63
425 NW Market St. (6th Ave.), 206-784-3463
Bruce Naftaly's "fabulous" French food – and fresh ingredients
sourced from his garden – makes "dreamy dinners" happen at
this "pricey", "overlooked" Ballard "hideaway" that keeps gourmands dazzled with a "jewel-box" setting and "sweet" service;
P.S. grab an "incredible drink" and some "fancy snacks" at the
modern, "*très* hip" Sambar cocktail bar next door.

Macrina Bakery & Cafe   25 | 15 | 16 | $17
2408 First Ave. (Battery St.), 206-448-4032
615 W. McGraw St. (6th Ave.), 206-283-5900
www.macrinabakery.com
These "essential" "artisan" bakeries supply not only "amazing"
baked goods (including the "best breads in town"), but also en-
tice as "tasty" stops for breakfast, brunch and lunch; "expect a
line whenever you go", and note that while the settings are "hip",
the spaces seem no bigger than a "closet"; N.B. McGraw Street
is counter service only.

Matt's in the Market ⊠   26 | 17 | 22 | $32
Pike Place Mkt., 94 Pike St. (1st Ave.), 206-467-7909;
www.mattsinthemarket.com
"It's a wonder that they can crank out" all that "terrific" food on
two burners and an oven at this Pike Place Market "cubbyhole"
(23 seats) of a seafooder; it's routinely "packed", but if you can
get in, "sit at the counter" for the "best show" around while being
tended to by "personable" servers.

METROPOLITAN GRILL
26 | 23 | 25 | $57

820 Second Ave. (Marion St.), 206-624-3287;
www.themetropolitangrill.com

"They know how to take care of you" at this "big" and "bustling" Downtown "epitome of a classic steakhouse", "one of the greats" synonymous with "manly" steaks (the "kids' portions are fit for adults"), "classy", "clubby" wine-hued and wood-appointed quarters, a "superb" wine list and martinis, and, of course, "pricey" tabs; it all "sits well with the sports and business set", who help keep the place booked solid.

MISTRAL ⊠
28 | 20 | 26 | $109

113 Blanchard St. (bet. 1st & 2nd Aves.), 206-770-7799;
www.mistralseattle.com

This "star" would shine everywhere – "even in NYC" is the refrain at "amazing" chef-owner William Belickis' Belltown New American–New French, where the "austere" setting provides contrast for the "visual and gustatory" "brilliance" of the dishes and the "warm" service from a staff that seem to move around "effortlessly"; just know you may have to "blow your bank account" for the privilege of dining at "one that's not to be missed."

Monsoon
25 | 20 | 21 | $37

615 19th Ave. E. (bet. Mercer & Roy Sts.), 206-325-2111;
www.monsoonseattle.com

Woks and grills turn out "amazing" upscale Vietnamese cuisine that's ingeniously paired with fine wines at this Capitol Hill staple helmed by siblings Eric and Sophie Banh; the "innovative" menu changes daily, which helps explain why fans swarm the "stark", modern dining room in droves.

Nell's
26 | 19 | 24 | $46

6804 E. Green Lake Way N. (bet. 2nd & 4th Aves.), 206-524-4044;
www.nellsrestaurant.com

"Why would anyone live far from Green Lake" when there's this New American around – the domain of chef-owner Philip Mihalski, who brings an "innovative" awareness to his menu, one from which you can "order anything and it will be excellent"; though some say it's "nondescript", the setting seems suited to "relaxing" repasts.

NISHINO
28 | 21 | 25 | $47

3130 E. Madison St. (bet. 31st & 32nd Aves.), 206-322-5800;
www.nishinorestaurant.com

The fare's so "creative" you'd think "Armani was designing" it at Nobu protégé Tatsu Nishino's "minimalist", "ever-popular" Madison Park Japanese proffering the chefs' "fabulous" handiwork, whether it's "sublime" sushi or "wonderful" cooked dishes; after eating all the goods – and seeing the "pricey" tabs – you're bound to walk out "weak in the knees"; P.S. "take advantage of the omakase option."

Paseo ⊠ Ⓜ ⇗
∇ 28 | 8 | 15 | $12

4225 Fremont Ave. N. (bet. 14th St. & Motor Pl.), 206-545-7440

"Castro would embrace capitalism if he tasted the pork sandwich" at this "funky" Fremonter proffering "fabulous", affordable Caribbean comestibles; some say service can be "brusque", others that it comes with a "smile", but everyone agrees that "takeout is the best plan" given the "quintessentially hole-in-the-wall" digs.

ROVER'S Ⓢ Ⓜ
28 | 25 | 28 | $95

2808 E. Madison St. (28th Ave.), 206-325-7442;
www.rovers-seattle.com

"Superlative" sums up the workings of "Seattle icon" Thierry Rautereau and his Madison Valley cottage where the "incomparable" staff serves New French dishes fit for the most discerning "foodie" (the "vegetarian menu is a testament to excellent eating without meat") and the "intimate" quarters delight; go "if you can afford it", or at least capitalize on the offerings at the Friday lunch.

Russell's Ⓢ Ⓜ
– | – | – | M

3305 Monte Villa Pkwy., Bothell, 425-486-4072

In a stately, renovated Mill Creek barn just minutes from Woodinville's wine country, Russell Lowell has opened this spacious new enterprise; fans will be happy to find the preeminent caterer's signature A-list New American menu, reasonable prices and a wine list to boot.

Salumi Ⓢ Ⓜ
28 | 10 | 17 | $16

309 Third Ave. S. (bet. Jackson & Main Sts.), 206-621-8772;
www.salumicuredmeats.com

"Shoehorn your way in" to this "warm", "authentic" tiny salumeria, Armandino Batali's (Mario's father) veritable "wonderland" for those seeking "incomparable" examples of "Italian charcuterie" and the "best sandwiches in Seattle"; expect "slabs of cured meat" for decor and "long lines" – both part of the one-of-a-kind experience you'll have here.

Seastar Restaurant & Raw Bar
26 | 24 | 24 | $49

205 108th Ave. NE (2nd St.), Bellevue, 425-456-0010;
www.seastarrestaurant.com

If ever there was "a reason to go to the Eastside", this "trendy" Bellevue fisherie provides it on account of "utterly sumptuous" seafood that's "right-off-the-boat fresh", dispensed by an open kitchen with chef John Howie at the helm; sommelier Erik Liedholm's "excellent" wine selections are oenophile-friendly, and "professional" service keeps the ship steady.

Shiro's Sushi
27 | 15 | 22 | $42

2401 Second Ave. (Battery St.), 206-443-9844; www.shiros.com

Despite "minimal" decor, "heaven on earth" can still be found in this Japanese mainstay, the domain of "star"-chef Shiro Kashiba, whose sushi expresses "pristine" "simplicity"; for a "wonderful" experience, fans advise sit at the bar and let the "personable" servers "take care of you" – but arrive early since it fills up fast.

Sitka & Spruce Ⓢ Ⓜ
– | – | – | M

2238 Eastlake Ave. E. (E. Boston & E. Lynn Sts.), 206-324-0662

Seattleites have quickly taken to this Eastlake newcomer that uses wholesome organic ingredients and coaxes them into New American dishes fit for gourmets; a communal table dominates the tiny, quirky space, whose strip-mall surroundings supply an interesting contrast to the vibe inside.

Toyoda Sushi
▽ 27 | 14 | 21 | $28

12543 Lake City Way NE (bet. 125th & 127th Sts.), 206-367-7972

"Better than Tokyo itself for not much yen" say sushi sharks about this "family-owned" "hole-in-the-wall" Lake City spot whose "outside looks" belie the tasty fish inside; the "traditional" offerings are fresh, and the best place to sit is "at the bar" to watch "friendly" Natsuyoshi Toyoda's renowned knife skills; sample the Japanese beer and sake and expect a waiting line; grumblers growl that "ambiance is secondary" to the food and table service "takes a long time."

Union 25 | 21 | 23 | $56

1400 First Ave. (Union St.), 206-838-8000; www.unionseattle.com

"Blissful" dining defines this "pricey" Downtown New American whose chef sources his ingredients locally (and daily) and transforms them into "delicious" dishes geared to palates that pick up on "delicate, subtle" flavors; the modern space seems in union with the food and mood here.

Union Bay Cafe 26 | 22 | 24 | $41

3515 NE 45th St. (bet. Mary Gates Dr. & 36th Ave.), 206-527-8364; www.unionbaycafe.com

For the "ultimate feel-good" dinner, U. of Washington and Laurelhurst locals convene at this "neighborhood" "treasure" still scoring with its savory bounty of Pacific NW preparations, not to mention "surprisingly modest prices"; the "come-as-you-are" vibe seems to suit everyone, as evidenced by the "pleased"-as-can-be clientele.

Volterra ◗ 26 | 22 | 23 | $42

5411 Ballard Ave. NW (22nd Ave.), 206-789-5100; www.volterrarestaurant.com

"*Cucina fantastico*" is another name for chef Don Curtiss' "bold" and "comforting" Northern Italian cooking at this "inviting" room on Ballard's hippest street; service is "good", and thanks perhaps to the tiled floor, the din from happy gourmets is high ("I can't hear you, but this pasta is amazing!").

WILD GINGER 25 | 23 | 22 | $41

1401 Third Ave. (Union St.), 206-623-4450; www.wildginger.net

"Wildly popular" (in fact, Seattle's Most Popular restaurant), this "cavernous", colorful Downtown "landmark" is an "obligatory destination for out-of-towners" and locals, where the "excellent" staff serves "clever" Pacific Rim preparations bound to "tickle the taste buds" in a (not surprisingly) "noisy" setting; P.S. savvy diners say the "satay bar is the place to be."

St. Louis

TOP FOOD RANKING

Restaurant	Cuisine
28 Sidney St. Cafe	New American
Paul Manno's	Southern Italian
27 Tony's	Italian
Trattoria Marcella	Italian
Niche	New American
Al's Restaurant	Seafood/Steakhouse
Dominic's	Italian
Pomme	New Amer./New French
26 Crossing, The	New American
Annie Gunn's	American

OTHER NOTEWORTHY PLACES

Atlas	French/Italian
Chez Leon	French Bistro
1111 Mississippi	Californian/N. Italian
Frazer's	New American
Harvest	New American
King Louie's	New American
Limoncello	Italian
Mira/Roxane	Eclectic
Truffles	New American
Zinnia	New American

F	D	S	C

Al's Restaurant 🅍 🅜   27 | 18 | 26 | $55
1200 N. First St. (Biddle St.), 314-421-6399; www.alsrestaurant.net
Although longtime owner Al Baroni has passed away, this "true St. Louis landmark" ("since 1925") remains "a trip back in time", an Italian-style chophouse featuring "fabulous steaks, veal" and seafood that are "worth" both "the dress code" (jackets required in fall and winter) and the "expense-account" prices; sure, the "tired but nostalgic" Downtown digs "could use some dusting", but given the "fantastic" food and service , most "don't even remember the decor."

ANNIE GUNN'S 🅜   26 | 21 | 23 | $44
16806 Chesterfield Airport Rd. (Baxter Rd.), Chesterfield, 636-532-7684; www.anniegunns.com
One of "the best West County has to offer" is this Traditional American that's "worth the trip" to Chesterfield for "superb steaks" and "top-notch seafood" from chef "Lou Rook, the genius in the kitchen"; it's "pricey but you get what you pay for" – "terrific service", a "casual atmosphere" and a "fantastic wine list" – although a few warn that it's also "crowded", making reservations "a must"; P.S. don't forget to "fill your car up with goodies" from the attached Smoke House Market.

Atlas Restaurant ⊠ Ⓜ
| 26 | 20 | 25 | $35 |

*5513 Pershing Ave. (bet. De Baliviere Ave. & Union Blvd.), 314-367-6800;
www.atlasrestaurantstl.com*

Regulars "hope nobody ever finds out about" Midtown's "true
Paris bistro without the jet lag", where the "honest, uncontrived,
classic" French and Italian dishes are both "toe-curlingly good"
and "a great value"; the seasonal fare (plus a "nice late-night
dessert and coffee menu") is enhanced by "warm", "attentive
owners", a "thoughtful" staff and a "simple", recently "rede-
signed interior that's wonderful" and "much more roomy."

Chez Leon Ⓜ
| 26 | 24 | 24 | $43 |

4580 Laclede Ave. (Euclid Ave.), 314-361-1589; www.chezleon.com

"There's something about it that makes me happy" smile
supporters of this "authentic" Central West End bistro where a
"skillfully executed menu" is paired with "faithfully French decor" that's "so charming, you feel like you're in Paris"; the "lively,
inviting atmosphere" comes complete with "fantastic service",
sidewalk seating and a pianist on Fridays and Sundays, so "order
the Grand Marnier soufflé" and "settle in for the evening";
P.S. the prix fixe menu is a "great value."

Crossing, The ⊠
| 26 | 20 | 24 | $47 |

*7823 Forsyth Blvd. (Central Ave.), Clayton, 314-721-7375;
www.thecrossingstl.com*

Chef-owner Jim Fiala delivers one of "the finest dining experiences in St. Louis" at this Clayton New American offering a "continually updated" selection of "innovative, delicious" dishes
"with French and Italian influences" ("the tasting menu with wine
flights is the way to go"); "unmemorable decor" gives nitpickers
pause, but most agree it's an "intimate", "charming environment"
with "seamless" "service to match", hence fans "never come
away with anything but a giant smile."

Dominic's ⊠
| 27 | 23 | 26 | $52 |

*5101 Wilson Ave. (Hereford St.), 314-771-1632;
www.dominicsrestaurant.com*

"Old-world charm meets fine Italian cuisine" at this "all-around
wonderful", family-owned "classic" that's "a must on the Hill" for its
"outstanding, authentic" fare and "extremely attentive", "personal
tableside service"; entering the "dimly lit, romantic" space is
"like stepping back in time", and its "elegant", "classy" decor
makes it a "favorite" "for special occasions and business dinners."

1111 MISSISSIPPI ⊠
| 25 | 25 | 23 | $37 |

1111 Mississippi Ave. (Chouteau Ave.), 314-241-9999; www.1111-m.com

"A cornerstone in the Lafayette Square revival", this "trendy" spot
set in a "renovated warehouse" offers an "interesting menu" of
Tuscan-Californian cuisine "with an emphasis on fresh provisions",
"variety and quality" but "without pretension"; the "multilevel interior" can get "noisy, but who cares" counter fans who focus
instead on the "meticulous service", "superbly cultivated wine
list" and patio seating; P.S. the "gooey butter cake is a must-try!"

Frazer's ⊠
| 24 | 19 | 22 | $30 |

1811 Pestalozzi St. (Lemp Ave.), 314-773-8646; www.frazergoodeats.com

"Continuing to subtly impress, year after year", this "funky" New
American in Benton Park (just west of Anheuser-Busch) is "con-

sidered a local treasure" for its pairing of "refined" New Orleans–influenced cuisine with a "casual atmosphere" whose "warmth sets it apart"; it's the type of "sophisticated yet comfortable" spot "where you can take a first date", and outdoor seating plus a "striking new bar/lounge" "add a level of interest."

Harvest ⓜ
25 | 23 | 24 | $45

1059 S. Big Bend Blvd. (Clayton Rd.), Richmond Heights, 314-645-3522; www.harveststlouis.com

This "fabulous" Richmond Heights restaurant is "worth checking out every few months" for some of "the most creative cooking in St. Louis" courtesy of a "seasonally changing menu" that "incorporates regional, market-ready ingredients" into "adventurous takes on [New] American cuisine"; the "cozy", "rustic atmosphere" and "wonderful service" are "exceeded only by the wine list", although a few sweet tooths find "the bread pudding alone" reason enough to go.

King Louie's ⓢⓜ
25 | 24 | 24 | $41

3800 Chouteau Ave. (39th St.), 314-865-3662; www.kinglouies.com

"You may wonder what part of town you're going to" – recent road work has made this Midtown New American even more "difficult to find" – but "a pilgrimage here is a necessary part of any foodie's existence"; a "terrific", "seasonally changing menu" that "uses local ingredients" is served in the "sophisticated" interior or out on an "awesome patio" where everything "is cooked on the grill or in the brick oven"; "overall, it's a lovely experience" that's "costly but worth it."

Limoncello Italian Cafe
– | – | – | E

7927 Forsyth Blvd. (Central Ave.), Clayton, 314-862-0550; www.limoncelloitaliancafe.com

After shuttering his eponymous West County ristorante, owner Benedetto Buzzetta headed to the heart of Clayton to open this upscale yet warm and comfortable cafe where wife Lia whips up a wide variety of Italian fare, both classic and modern; it's already buzzing with political types from the county courthouse across the street as well as fans of the proprietor's former venture.

Mira
– | – | – | E

12 N. Meramec Ave. (Forsyth Blvd.), Clayton, 314-721-6472

Roxane ⓓ

12 N. Meramec Ave. (Forsyth Blvd.), Clayton, 314-721-7700 www.mirastl.com

Returning to the site of his original Clayton restaurant (the erstwhile Café Mira), chef-owner Mike Johnson brings two very different dining experiences to one address; they may share a roof, but the classy, upscale bistro, Mira, caters to a mature crowd with its imaginative Eclectic fusion cuisine, while Roxane offers light fare in a funky, loungelike atmosphere; the twosome sees eye-to-eye, however, when it comes to patio seating and a menu of desserts from pastry chef Carolyn Downs.

NICHE ⓢⓜ
27 | 25 | 24 | $40

1831 Sidney St. (I-55), 314-773-7755; www.nichestlouis.com

"Bringing great food and an enjoyable ambiance together", this "welcome newcomer" in Benton Park offers a "short" "but top-notch" menu of "flawless", "cutting-edge" New American cuisine in a "sleek, modern" setting that "makes you feel chic";

meanwhile, "outstanding service" and a "fabulous value" of a three-course $30 prix fixe meal "makes it a delight on every visit"; N.B. a late-night dessert and wine menu is served until 1:30 AM on Fridays and Saturdays.

PAUL MANNO'S ⊠ 28 | 18 | 24 | $39

75 Forum Shopping Ctr. (Woodsmill Rd.), Chesterfield, 314-878-1274
"Skip the Hill" and head to this veteran Italian "hidden" in a Chesterfield strip mall, where the "marvelous", "authentic" Sicilian fare is "just like mama used to make, because mama is still in the kitchen"; an "attentive staff" provides "impeccable service", while owner Paul Manno "loves to make his customers happy"; but a "small" dining room means you "sometimes have to wait" and then "eat elbow-to-elbow" – so do yourself a favor and "don't tell anyone."

Pomme ⊠ Ⓜ 27 | 22 | 25 | $44

40 N. Central Ave. (bet. Forsyth Blvd. & Maryland Ave.), Clayton, 314-727-4141; www.pommerestaurant.com
For "inventive cuisine that's always satisfying" and "executed with care", take a detour to this "intimate" Clayton venue where chef-owner Bryan Carr delivers "big flavor" via "fresh, innovative, seasonal" New French–New American cuisine that "uses only the best ingredients"; it's "great for a date or quiet dinner", with a "comfortable atmosphere" that's enhanced by "attentive service" and a "thoughtful wine list"; nevertheless, a handful harrumph about portions that are "modest given the prices."

SIDNEY STREET CAFE ⊠ Ⓜ 28 | 23 | 26 | $43

2000 Sidney St. (Salena St.), 314-771-5777; www.sidneystreetcafe.com
Rated No. 1 for Food and Popularity in St. Louis, this Benton Park "standard for others to follow" is a "perennial favorite" proffering a "superb", "inventive" array of "universally wonderful" New American cuisine; the "friendly", "knowledgeable" servers recite "from chalkboard menus" "with appetizing flair", while the "inviting" and "romantic atmosphere" proves "perfect for business, dates or special occasions"; nevertheless, "for such fine dining", regulars recommend "calling weeks in advance for a reservation."

TONY'S ⊠ 27 | 24 | 27 | $62

410 Market St. (bet. B'way & 4th St.), 314-231-7007; www.tonysstlouis.com
It's "still the best special-occasion restaurant in St. Louis" sigh supporters of this Downtown "treasure" that "lives up to its reputation" via "impeccable" Italian cuisine and "professional servers" who "anticipate your every need"; an "elegant ambiance" and "attention to detail" make this "a class act" for most, although modernists maintain it can be "a bit old-fashioned" (jackets are required) and cite "high prices."

TRATTORIA MARCELLA ⊠ Ⓜ 27 | 20 | 25 | $36

3600 Watson Rd. (Pernod Ave.), 314-352-7706; www.trattoriamarcella.com
"Sometimes the labor of love that goes into a restaurant is so palpable you can taste it in the food" fawn fans of this "vibrant", "convivial" South Side Italian where "always remarkable", "reasonably priced" fare ("risotto to dream about") is served by a "friendly, gracious staff"; "now that they've expanded, you can

get a seat" in the still-"cramped" space, although a nostalgic few feel it "lost a little of its ambiance" in the process.

Truffles ⊠ 23 | 22 | 23 | $46 |
9202 Clayton Rd. (Price Rd.), Ladue, 314-567-9100;
www.trufflesinladue.com
Since chef Mark Serice (ex Brennan's in New Orleans) "relocated here post-Katrina", things "have gotten really interesting" at this Ladue standby: the new toque "has breathed life into the kitchen", "adding Cajun flair" to an already "inspiring" New American menu; the "exceptional wine list" and "warm", "personable service" have stayed the same, however, as has a "lovely", "classy atmosphere" that seems "a little stodgy" to some.

Zinnia Ⓜ 24 | 18 | 23 | $38 |
7491 Big Bend Blvd. (Shrewsbury Ave.), Webster Groves,
314-962-0572; www.zinnia-stl.com
"The purple exterior may have you wondering what you're getting yourself into", but this "favorite" set in a "charming converted gas station" is "a Webster Groves gem" whose chef-owner "David Guempel has it and has had it for years", whipping up "creative, seasonal" New American meals; and whether you're relaxing in the "intimate" dining room or out on the "fabulous" patio, you'll find the same "attentive staff" and "welcoming" ambiance.

Tampa/Sarasota

TOP FOOD RANKING

	Restaurant	Cuisine
28	Cafe Ponte	New American
27	Restaurant B.T.	French/Vietnamese
	Beach Bistro	Floridian
	SideBern's	New American
26	Mise en Place	New American
	Black Pearl	New American
	Pane Rustica	Bakery/Eclectic
	Roy's	Hawaii Regional
	Bern's	Steakhouse
	Armani's	Northern Italian

OTHER NOTEWORTHY PLACES

Restaurant	Cuisine
Bijou Café	Continental
Cevíche	Spanish/Tapas
Columbia	Cuban/Spanish
Euphemia Haye	Eclectic
Fred's	New American
Marchand's	Mediterranean
Michael's On East	New American
Ophelia's	Eclectic
Salt Rock Grill	Seafood
Six Tables	Contin./New French

	F	D	S	C

Armani's ⬧   26 | 26 | 26 | $62
Grand Hyatt Tampa Bay, 2900 Bayport Dr., 14th fl. (Hwy. 60), Tampa, 813-207-6800; www.armanisrestaurant.com
"High-end and high up" on the 14th floor of the Grand Hyatt, Tampa's "venerable" "special-occasion place" pairs a "killer view" of the bay ("Giorgio would totally appreciate" it) with "consistent", "top-notch" Northern Italian cuisine, including a "fabulous antipasti bar" and a "tasting menu that shouldn't be missed"; it "drips with romance" and enough "suave sophistication" to satisfy even those who grumble about "pricey tabs" and "snooty" servers.

BEACH BISTRO   27 | 22 | 27 | $63
6600 Gulf Dr. (66th St.), Holmes Beach, 941-778-6444; www.beachbistro.com
"Setting the standard for fine dining on Florida's west coast" is this "consistent" Anna Maria Island "winner", a "beautiful little gem" that "foodies love" for its "knowledgeable staff" ("a well-oiled machine"), "pricey", "world-class" Floridian cuisine and "awesome wine selections"; although some make note of the "tight quarters", it's located "literally on the beach" with "magnificent views of the sunset."

BERN'S STEAK HOUSE
26 | 20 | 26 | $63

1208 S. Howard Ave. (bet. Marjory Ave. & Watrous St.), Tampa, 813-251-2421; www.bernssteakhouse.com

"Take your chains, I'll take Bern's" aver acolytes of this "independent, locally owned" "Tampa landmark" (voted Most Popular on the Gulf Coast) that pairs its "pricey" "melt-in-your-mouth steaks" and vegetables "straight from their own farm" with an "encyclopedic wine list"; although nitpickers insist the "gaudy" "bordello decor" "needs a revamp", an "exceptional" staff and a "unique", "don't-miss" upstairs dessert room compensate; P.S. "insider tip: the kitchen/wine cellar tour is amazing."

BIJOU CAFÉ
25 | 23 | 25 | $50

1287 First St. (Pineapple Ave.), Sarasota, 941-366-8111

"As the name suggests, this is Sarasota's jewel", a "classy" Downtown "standby" that's "beloved by gourmets" for its "consistent" if "costly" Continental cuisine; the recently expanded setting in a "former gas station" now has a "warm", "dignified ambiance" that's matched by a "professional staff" that quipsters say wins "top service in a service station" honors, especially for its ability to get "opera buffs" "out in time for the curtain"; P.S. the "valet makes parking easy."

Black Pearl
26 | 21 | 26 | $49

315 Main St. (Broadway St.), Dunedin, 727-734-3463; www.theblackpearlofdunedin.com

This "wonderful" "surprise" in "charming", small-town Dunedin is "worth driving to" for its "satisfying" menu of "inventive" New American dishes "cooked to perfection"; the "quiet, dark, intimate setting" is "very romantic" and enhanced by "attentive" servers who "could not be better", leading regulars to recommend you "make a reservation" in advance, since it's as "popular" as it is "small."

CAFE PONTE ⊠Ⓜ
28 | 23 | 25 | $47

Icot Ctr., 13505 Icot Blvd. (Ulmerton Rd.), Clearwater, 727-538-5768; www.cafeponte.com

Rated No. 1 for Food on the Gulf Coast, this "smart, stylish" gastronomic "gem" in Clearwater has foodies singing the praises of "gifted" chef-owner Christopher Ponte, who delivers "quality for the price" via "playful presentations" of "exquisite" New American cuisine; "don't be fooled" by the "strip-mall setting" – "everything is top-notch" here, including the "attentive" staff – but do keep in mind that "reservations are a must" to experience one of these "magical, memorable meals."

Cevíche Tapas Bar & Restaurant ●
25 | 22 | 21 | $32

10 Beach Dr. (Central Ave.), St. Petersburg, 727-209-2302 Ⓜ
Bayshore Royal, 2109 Bayshore Blvd. (S. Howard Ave.), Tampa, 813-250-0203
www.cevichetapas.com

With a "cozy", "seductive atmosphere", this "Tampa favorite" is "wonderful for a first date" fueled by "creative, tasty" Spanish "finger food" and "superb sangria"; the newer St. Petersburg location boasts the same "excellent variety" of tapas, along with a "beautiful interior and trendy scene", so sit "on the patio and people-watch" or "wander downstairs to listen" to live music in the basement bar.

COLUMBIA

20 | 21 | 20 | $35

1241 Gulf Blvd. (½ mi. south of Sand Key Bridge), Clearwater, 727-596-8400
411 St. Armands Circle (Blvd. of the Presidents), Sarasota, 941-388-3987
St. Petersburg Pier, 800 Second Ave. (Beach Dr.), St. Petersburg, 727-822-8000
2117 E. Seventh Ave. (bet. 21st & 22nd Sts.), Ybor City, 813-248-4961
www.columbiarestaurant.com

"One of Florida's oldest and finest", this "enormous" Ybor City Cuban-Spanish ("the original" in a statewide chain) is "a real classic" that gets the nod as a "great place to take visitors" for "authentic food", "ambrosial sangria" and "flamenco dancers that stomp it up inches from your table"; the signature "1905 salad is worth the trip" to any of the four locations, but the patio at the Sarasota branch is an added treat "for watching the shoppers" "on beautiful St. Armands Circle."

Euphemia Haye

26 | 22 | 23 | $56

5540 Gulf of Mexico Dr. (Gulf Bay Rd.), Longboat Key, 941-383-3633;
www.euphemiahaye.com

A "romantic atmosphere and superb service contribute to the longevity" of Longboat Key's 26-year-old "favorite" for "gourmet, Southern-influenced" Eclectic fare that's "pricey" but "consistently excellent"; "few first-time visitors can find" this "charming", "out-of-the-way place", but once they do, they agree that a post-meal trip upstairs to The HayeLoft is "a must" "for outstanding and very generous" "desserts, coffee and jazz."

Fred's

21 | 21 | 20 | $43

1917 S. Osprey Ave. (bet. Hillview & Hyde Park Sts.), Sarasota, 941-364-5811; www.epicureanlife.com

The anchor of Sarasota's "trendy" Southside Village, this "jumping" "alfresco favorite" is an "'in' spot for foodies", who appreciate its "unique" New American comfort food (the "best chicken pot pie ever"); it's "the place to be seen", a "sophisticated" setting for enjoying "well-made cocktails" and a "superb wine list", but quiet types note that "noise from the bar can stifle conversation"; N.B. a Lakewood Ranch location is set to open soon.

Marchand's Bar & Grill

24 | 25 | 25 | $47

Renaissance Vinoy Resort & Golf Club, 501 Fifth Ave. NE (Beach Dr.), St. Petersburg, 727-894-1000; www.vinoyrenaissanceresort.com

"You can feel the excitement of the Roaring '20s as you sample Med dishes "prepared with skill" at this "elegant", "historically preserved" restaurant in the Renaissance Vinoy Resort; the "swanky atmosphere" is "perfect for breakfast with clients, lunch with colleagues or drinks with old friends", and given a "most accommodating staff", live jazz and a "legendary Sunday brunch", some even go so far as to call it "the premier dining experience in St. Pete."

Michael's On East 🖾

24 | 24 | 23 | $55

1212 East Ave. S. (Bahia Vista St.), Sarasota, 941-366-0007;
www.bestfood.com

Suitable for either "a very special occasion" or a "power lunch", Sarasota's "feast at East" is a "consistent leader", proffering "gourmet" New American fare that remains "heavenly" despite a "revolving door for chefs in recent years"; though it's "a bit pricey" to some, acolytes aver you'll be as "pleased" as the "local dignitaries" and "beautiful people" who come here for "well-versed" service, a "clubby atmosphere" and a 350-bottle "wine cellar that's tops in the area."

MISE EN PLACE 🖼 Ⓜ   26 | 22 | 24 | $49
442 W. Kennedy Blvd. (Grand Central Pl.), Tampa, 813-254-5373;
www.miseonline.com

For over two decades, this "gem" blessed with "beautiful views of the University of Tampa" has been the stage on which chef/co-owner Marty Blitz "shines as always", "dazzling the palates" of area foodies with a "creative, changing menu" of New American cuisine that utilizes "fresh, local ingredients" in "unexpected" "flavor combinations"; "understated", "modern" decor and "friendly" service add to the "spectacular" experience.

Ophelia's on the Bay   24 | 26 | 23 | $54
9105 Midnight Pass Rd. (south of Turtle Beach), Siesta Key,
941-349-2212; www.opheliasonthebay.net

"You can't eat atmosphere", but fortunately the "terrific" Eclectic cuisine matches the ambiance at this "intimate, elegant" Siesta Key "favorite" whose "creative", "pricey" seafood "tends to the exotic"; its "romantic" bayside patio has "candlelight, tropical breezes" and the same "attentive service" as the dining room, so "sit outside on a special night" to watch "the setting sun paint mangroves across the water" – be assured you'll "remember it for a long time."

Pane Rustica Ⓜ   26 | 18 | 18 | $22
3225 S. MacDill Ave. (Bay to Bay Blvd.), Tampa, 813-902-8828;
www.panerustica.com

Long known as a "delightful", counter-service spot "packed at lunchtime" with fans of its "delicious sandwiches", "great bread and pastries" made on-site and "crisp", wood-fired pizza ("a religious experience"), this "old standby" in South Tampa "has now added a casual fine dining menu" featuring Italian-tinged Eclectic fare; with a "warm, inviting" setting and "aim-to-please owners" and staff, devotees decree that, "dollar for dollar, it's the best meal in town."

RESTAURANT B.T. 🖼   27 | 24 | 24 | $44
1633 W. Snow Ave. (S. Rome Ave.), Tampa, 813-258-1916;
www.restaurantbt.com

At this ambitious "oasis" in the middle of "trendy" Old Hyde Park Village, "incredibly talented" and "demanding chef-owner" B.T. Nguyen-Batley "expects only the best", and her "continually innovative" French-Vietnamese fusion fare has "an uncanny flair for pleasing both the taste buds and the eyes"; "sophisticated", "minimalist decor" and a "hip staff" draw "a well-groomed South Tampa clientele", as does a "hot bar scene" fueled by "amazing", "exotic drinks."

ROY'S   26 | 23 | 24 | $51
Promenade at Bonita Bay, 26831 S. Bay Dr. (Tamiami Trail S.),
Bonita Springs, 239-498-7697
4342 W. Boy Scout Blvd. (bet. Lois Ave. & Westshore Blvd.),
Tampa, 813-873-7697
www.roysrestaurant.com

They "may be part of a chain, but don't tell that to the food" at Roy Yamaguchi's "lively", "loud" links in Bonita Springs and Tampa, where "presentation and inventive sauces are the hallmarks" of the "exotic", "unbelievably delicious" Hawaii Regional seafood dishes that can be followed up with "don't-miss" desserts like the signature "luscious lava cake"; the "pricey" duo proves equally "great for family and business" occasions with its "eager servers" and "fantastic wine selection"; N.B. a Sarasota offshoot is set to open soon.

Salt Rock Grill | 24 | 25 | 22 | $42 |

19325 Gulf Blvd. (¼ mi. north of Park Blvd.), Indian Shores, 727-593-7625; www.saltrockgrill.com

This "always jumping" Indian Shores seafooder sporting "spectacular views of the Intracoastal Waterway" is "popular" for its "updated Florida classics" and "tender, juicy steaks" "cooked on a wood-burning grill" and paired with "great wine cellar selections"; the bi-level dining room can get "incredibly noisy on a busy night" – "brush up on your sign language" – but the outdoor deck proves "a quieter alternative"; note: there's also "a fantastic bargain" of an early-bird menu.

SIDEBERN'S Ⓩ | 27 | 25 | 24 | $53 |

2208 W. Morrison Ave. (S. Howard Ave.), Tampa, 813-258-2233; www.bernssteakhouse.com

At "stately" Bern's Steak House's "trendy", "energetic" little sister, "young Tampa flirts and feeds" on chef-partner Jeannie Pierola's "must-try" dim sum and "pricey", "inventive" New American entrees and desserts that "combine the best of the old world with new-world sensibilities" and "international ingredients"; meanwhile, "top-notch service" and an attached wine store (sample from the "excellent choices" for a small corkage fee) make it even more of "a joy to visit."

Six Tables Ⓜ | 25 | 19 | 26 | $66 |

1153 Main St. (Pinehurst Rd.), Dunedin, 727-736-8821
The Peninsula Inn & Spa, 2937 Beach Blvd. (54th St.), Gulfport, 727-346-9800
118 W. Bay Dr. (west of RR tracks), Largo, 727-518-1123
4267 Henderson Blvd. (south of JFK Blvd.), Tampa, 813-207-0527
www.sixtables.com

"There's nothing else like" these "unique" "concept restaurants" from founder Roland Levi (the toque at the original Dunedin location) that "really do have only six tables" each and offer a "pricey but exquisite" prix fixe sextet of New French–Continental courses; the "attention to detail" at these "special-occasion favorites" includes a discussion "with the chef before your meal" ("call in advance" for special dietary needs), and a "quiet, romantic", one-room setting that will make you feel "like you're eating in someone's fancy home."

Tucson

TOP FOOD RANKING

Restaurant	Cuisine
28 Dish, The	New American
26 Vivace	Northern Italian
Grill at Hacienda del Sol	New American
Le Rendez-Vous	French
Cafe Poca Cosa	Mexican
25 Ventana Room	New American
Feast	Eclectic
Janos	Southwestern
24 Beyond Bread	Bakery/Cafe
Wildflower	New American

OTHER NOTEWORTHY PLACES

Acacia	New American
Bistro Zin	New American
Bluefin	Seafood
Cuvée World Bistro	Eclectic
J Bar	Nuevo Latino
McMahon's Prime	Steakhouse
Montana Avenue	New American
Neo of Melaka	Malaysian
Primo	Mediterranean
Terra Cotta	Southwestern

	F	D	S	C

Acacia — 23 | 24 | 23 | $46
St. Philip's Plaza, 4340 N. Campbell Ave. (E. River Rd.), 520-232-0101;
www.acaciatucson.com
With "brilliant" cuisine via chef-owner Albert Hall (formerly of Hacienda del Sol), this New American in a "peaceful haven" in St. Philip's Plaza is "one of the best" Tucson has to offer; though the "stunning", "superbly lit" interior (featuring "colorful paintings and sculptures") "raises the decor bar a notch", fans are just as apt to opt for "terrific patio dining under the trees" where they may catch some "fabulous" live jazz that's playing Fridays–Sundays.

Beyond Bread — 24 | 15 | 19 | $11
Monterey Vlg., 6260 E. Speedway Blvd. (Wilmot Rd.),
520-747-7477
3026 N. Campbell Ave. (Blacklidge Dr.), 520-322-9965
www.beyondbread.com
"Knead we say more?" for "fabulous", "freshly baked" goods, these Tucson bakery/cafes go "above and beyond" the call of duty by purveying "amazing" breads, sandwiches and pastries to those who "plan their day around" visits there; P.S. they're "popular", so arrive as early as you can.

Bistro Zin ❶
24 | 22 | 22 | $39

1865 E. River Rd. (Campbell Ave.), 520-299-7799;
www.foxrc.com

So "very NYC", this "cramped", "stylish" New American bistro
(aka "Bistro Din") is a second home to the "young and beautiful"
who drop by for "delicious" French-inspired comestibles including "sinful desserts"; the bigger draw, however, may be the
"wonderful" wine selection (with an "extensive" by-the-glass
options), where grape groupies can choose from 25+ flights.

Bluefin
– | – | – | E

Casas Adobes Plaza, 7053 N. Oracle Rd. (W. Giaconda Way),
520-531-8500; www.bluefinseafoodbistro.com

With its brick walls, winding staircase and wrought iron balcony,
this modern, sultry seafooder (from the owners of Kingfisher)
channels New Orleans, right down to the live jazz on the weekends; meanwhile, the menu covers all the fishy bases, including
Parmesan-crusted scallops, wild salmon and trout (served on
Sunday–Thursday nights).

CAFE POCA COSA ⑤
26 | – | 22 | $28

100 E. Pennington St. (Scott Ave.), 520-622-6400

"Bring an open mind and empty stomach" to Suzana Davila's
"frantically" paced Downtown "must-visit" Mexican (Tucson's
Most Popular restaurant) where the "exciting" food blends the
"homestyle" with the "innovative"; the daily-changing menu
showcasing a slew of "interesting moles" helps make a meal
here "magical"; N.B. they are now in sleeker digs featuring an
appropriately swanky bar area.

Cuvée World Bistro ⑤
23 | 21 | 21 | $34

Rancho Ctr., 3352 E. Speedway Blvd. (bet. Alvernon Way &
Country Club Blvd.), 520-881-7577; www.cuveebistro.com

"A real find", this "trendy" Midtown bistro from chef-owner
Mitch Levy lures locals with "terrific" temptations in the way of
"artistically presented" Eclectic eats and a "friendly staff" that
makes everyone "feel at home" – even those who "dine alone";
the "great wine list" (and wine pairings with each course) makes
it a "treat."

DISH, THE ⑤ Ⓜ
28 | 20 | 26 | $44

3200 E. Speedway Blvd. (Country Club Rd.), 520-326-1714;
www.dishbistro.com

"Reservations are a must" at this "tiny", "romantic" "hideaway"
that's ranked No. 1 for Food in Tucson – no surprise, considering
each "fabulous" course on its New American menu is a "treasure"; a "discreet" atmosphere enhanced by a "wonderful staff"
helps ensure an "exceptional evening" at the town's "best-kept
secret"; P.S. being hitched to the Rum Runner wine shop has its
advantages, namely "unlimited wine potential."

Feast Ⓜ
25 | 16 | 20 | $24

4122 E. Speedway Blvd. (bet. Alvernon Way & Columbus Blvd.),
520-326-9363; www.eatatfeast.com

Although slightly roomier, it's still tough to get a seat at this re-
vered, no-reservations take-out destination, a "festive" Eclectic
bistro perpetually "packed" with loyalists who can't get enough
of "happy chef" Doug Levy's "inventive", "vegetarian-friendly"

preparations that many maintain are "heaven on a plate"; what's more, the "fantastic wine wall" along with the "casual" atmosphere complete with communal table makes it feel like you're in "San Francisco."

GRILL AT HACIENDA DEL SOL | 26 | 27 | 25 | $55 |
Hacienda del Sol, 5601 N. Hacienda del Sol (bet. E. River Rd. & E. Sunrise Dr.), 520-529-3500; www.haciendadelsol.com
A "romantic" representative of "quintessential old Arizona", this perennially popular New American, situated in a "historic" "resort to the golden-age Hollywood crowd", cops the top Decor rating in Tucson for its "beautiful" interior and "stunning" setting that boasts "magnificent city views" and an enviable perch for catching a "great sunset"; if the "divine" food appears a little "pricey", save this "star in the desert" for "those special nights when only the best will do."

JANOS ⑤ | 25 | 25 | 25 | $63 |
Westin La Paloma, 3770 E. Sunrise Dr. (bet. N. Campbell Ave. & N. Swan Rd.), 520-615-6100; www.janos.com
Dinner at this "top-notch" hotel restaurant in the foothills is always "an event", thanks to its "guru", chef-owner Janos Wilder, whose "superb", "cutting-edge" French-inspired Southwestern cooking gets "extra points" for using "local ingredients"; although a few lament prices "in orbit", most insist that the "wild man" and his "special-occasion" place deserve their reputation as one of the "Southwest's best"; P.S. the wine list is "a feast in itself."

J Bar ⑤ | 23 | 21 | 21 | $34 |
Westin La Paloma, 3770 E. Sunrise Dr. (bet. N. Campbell Ave. & N. Swan Rd.), 520-615-6100; www.janos.com
"Can't afford Janos?" try its "trendy" "little brother" next door, a "lively" Nuevo Latino offshoot where "every bite" from the open kitchen "amazes", making it for some "as good as its relative" at a "fraction of the cost"; supporters who "love that happy hour" rave about "out-of-sight" margaritas and add that the "cool view" from the balcony makes this "hipster" a "wonderful place to hang."

LE RENDEZ-VOUS Ⓜ | 26 | 17 | 20 | $45 |
3844 E. Ft. Lowell Rd. (N. Alvernon Way), 520-323-7373; www.lerendez-vous.com
"By all means the place to go" for the closest thing to a "trip to France", this "favorite" offers a "delicious" lineup of "rich", "old-time" Gallic classics; while a finicky faction suggests the decor "needs a face-lift", fawning Francophiles shrug *c'est la vie* and testify that "amazing sauces" and a "to-die-for Grand Marnier soufflé" help turn this place into "a must."

McMahon's Prime Steakhouse | 23 | 24 | 22 | $51 |
2959 N. Swan Rd. (bet. E. Ft. Lowell Rd. & E. Glenn St.), 520-327-2333; www.metrorestaurants.com
This "clubby", "traditional" steakhouse turns out "fabulous" "melt-in-your-mouth" meat in portions so "overly generous" that they give new meaning to "diet-busting" fare; if the price rubs some the wrong way (it's a "budget breaker"), others factor in the "fantastic wine selection" and "top-notch cigar bar" and agree it's perfect for "expense-account dining."

Montana Avenue
–   –   –   M

6390 E. Grant Rd. (Wilmot Rd.), 520-298-2020; www.foxrc.com
Sam Fox, the restaurateur of Bistro Zin and Wildflower, has
opened this trendy Midtown New American whose open kitchen
turns out Californian-Southwest preparations, while the muted
tones of the space (graced with wooden beams) supplies a thoroughly chic, Zen-like air; the buzz (and noise) is noticeable here,
as evidenced by the trendy types who swarm.

Neo of Melaka
–   –   –   M

1765 E. River Rd. (Campbell Ave.), 520-299-7815;
www.neomelaka.com
It's a tossup which gets more notice at this Midtown Malaysian
neophyte: the exposed ductwork and antique wood carvings of
the modern decor, or the fare, which melds flavors from China,
India and the Middle East; count on the staff to explain unfamiliar dishes, and if there's a wait to get a table, pass your time by
checking out all the duded-up local foodies.

Primo
–   –   –   E

JW Marriott Starr Pass Resort & Spa, 3800 Starr Pass Blvd.
(bet. Deer Bend Ct. & Players Club Dr.), 520-791-6071;
www.primotucson.com
Chef Melissa Kelly brings the Mediterranean to the desert in the
form of this new addition in Tucson's latest resort, the JW
Marriott Starr Pass; France, Italy and Spain are all represented
on the moderately expensive menu, while the warm setting offers
two distinct experiences: hip and casual near the sleek bar area,
and more formal in the main dining room.

TERRA COTTA
22   23   21 $37

3500 E. Sunrise Dr. (Campo Abierto), 520-577-8100;
www.dineterracotta.com
This Southwestern "mainstay" is "better than ever", still serving
up a combo of "fantastic" standards (the garlic custard appetizer
is "sensuous") and newer items in a dramatic Southwestern–
style building; if the disaffected denounce "uneven" food and
service, others are glad to have this place around.

Ventana Room ⌧ Ⓜ
25   26   25 $65

Loews Ventana Canyon Resort, 7000 N. Resort Dr. (N. Kolb Rd.),
520-299-2020; www.ventanaroom.com
It's "no contest" crow culinary cognoscenti who put this
altogether "spectacular" New American hotel restaurant in the
foothills at the "top of the heap" for its "breathtaking views",
"impeccable service" and "artful presentations" of "fabulous"
food; sure, it may be a little "stodgy" (as well as "expensive"),
but that's part and parcel of a "first-class" experience;
N.B. jackets required.

VIVACE ⌧
26   23   24 $41

St. Philip's Plaza, 4310 N. Campbell Ave. (River Rd.),
520-795-7221
"Memorable" in more than a few ways, this "charming" Tucson
Northern Italian is considered an "all-around" winner by locals
who point to chef-owner Daniel Scordato's "creative cooking"
driven by the "finest", "freshest" ingredients; indeed, many marvel at "reasonable prices" given the "excellent quality" of the

dishes (served by the "responsive staff"); P.S. alfresco dining in the "pretty courtyard" complete with fountain is "a plus."

WILDFLOWER   24 | 21 | 22 | $33 |
Casas Adobes Plaza, 7037 N. Oracle Rd. (W. Ina Rd.), 520-219-4230; www.foxrestaurantconcepts.com

It's not just the "yuppie flock" that flies to this perennially "popular", "ultratrendy" New American, which "overcomes its strip-mall locale" with an "unbeatable combination" of "excellent", "unique" food and a "snappy", "modern" setting that features a "relaxing patio"; insiders insist it's "especially good for lunch" when the "energetic staff" is less "flustered."

Washington, DC

TOP FOOD RANKING

	Restaurant	Cuisine
29	Inn at Little Washington	New American
28	Makoto	Japanese
	Maestro	Italian
	Citronelle	New French
	Marcel's	Belgian
27	Eve	New American
	2941	New American
	Ray's the Steaks	Steakhouse
	L'Auberge Chez François	French
	Obelisk	Italian
	Gerard's Place	New French
	Le Paradou	New French
	Prime Rib	Steakhouse
	Seasons	New American
26	CityZen	New American
	Kinkead's	Seafood
	Palena	New American
	Tosca	Northern Italian
	Thai Square	Thai
	La Bergerie	French

OTHER NOTEWORTHY PLACES

Bis	French Bistro
BlackSalt	New Amer./Seafood
Black's Bar & Kitchen	New American
Blue Duck Tavern	New American
Bread Line	Bakery/Cafe
Café Atlántico/Minibar	Nuevo Latino
Cashion's Eat Place	New American
DC Coast	New American
Equinox	New American
IndeBleu	French/Indian
Indigo Landing	New American
Jaleo	Spanish/Tapas
Pizzeria Paradiso	Pizza
Rasika	Indian
1789	New American
Taberna del Alabardero	Spanish/Tapas
TenPenh	Pan-Asian
2 Amys	Pizza
Vidalia	New American
Zaytinya	Med./Middle-Eastern

Bis
24 | 22 | 22 | $51

Hotel George, 15 E St. NW (bet. N. Capitol St. & New Jersey Ave.), 202-661-2700; www.bistrobis.com

"All the cosmos align" at this "minimalist" Capitol Hill French bistro with "subdued lighting, plenty of Olympians lobbying Congress" and an "inventive, comforting" menu that includes a "fabulous frisée salad and a primo wine list"; then there's the "happening" bar, "fun and efficient service" and the anticipation that "you never know who you'll see" during any given "power lunch" or "pricey" dinner.

BlackSalt Ⓜ
26 | 20 | 21 | $53

4883 MacArthur Blvd. NW (U St.), 202-342-9101

The Black restaurant family's latest "winner", a fin-fare-focused New American in the Palisades, earns praise for "sophisticated and assured" creations that "explode with taste", along with a wine list of "exceptionally well-valued gems"; if you can't snag a table in the "minimalist", "noisy" dining room or the unreserved cafe, go for a "drink at the great bar", down a couple of "fresh" oysters and then pick up some "pristine" fish to cook at home.

Black's Bar & Kitchen
23 | – | 20 | $43

7750 Woodmont Ave. (bet. Cheltenham Dr. & Old Georgetown Rd.), Bethesda, MD, 301-652-6278; www.blacksbarandkitchen.com

Bethesda's "go-to place" for "terrific seafood", a "fantastic raw bar" and "plenty of choices for meat eaters" on its New American menu recently reopened after a $2.5-million floor-to-ceiling renovation; the restaurant family behind Addie's, Black Market and BlackSalt went for a contemporary setting with lots of light, glass bifold doors, a black pebble patio with a reflecting pool and cherry-red tile lining an open kitchen; expect new small plates plus meat and game prepared on a hardwood grill.

Blue Duck Tavern
– | – | – | E

Park Hyatt Hotel, 1201 24th St. NW (M St.), 202-419-6755; www.parkwashington.hyatt.com

Chef Brian McBride returns to this West End hotel dining room (he was the toque at Melrose, its predecessor), where he's crafting upscale, regional New American cuisine at a cobalt-blue, state-of-the-art, wood-burning Molteni range using innovative techniques and artisanal ingredients; diners get to watch the action since the open kitchen is set in the midst of designer Tony Chi's eye-popping dining room, which incorporates handcrafted furnishings and raw materials like wood and burlap for a look of edgy rusticity.

Bread Line Ⓩ
24 | 10 | 15 | $13

1751 Pennsylvania Ave. NW (bet. 17th & 18th Sts.), 202-822-8900

"Absolutely the best" carb-based lunch in town keeps this "wonderful" "industrial bakery/cafe", "just steps from the White House", jammed; luckily, the "long lines move quickly", and loyalists, including the WH press corps, are "rewarded with the freshest most flavorful sandwiches" on "terrific, crunchy" artisan bread, "amazing salads" and "don't-miss" fries.

Café Atlántico/Minibar
25 | 22 | 22 | $49

405 Eighth St. NW (bet. D & E Sts.), 202-393-0812; www.cafeatlantico.com

"Phenomenal" mojitos and "mouthwatering" guacamole made tableside kick start a "mini-vacation" on this Penn Quarterite's "three levels of Caribbean fun"; its Nuevo Latino kitchen "makes cutting-edge food deliciously edible"; at its six-seat, reservations-only Minibar – an "interactive carnival" of "art and chemistry" – "daring types" test their "bravado" on 30-plus bite-size "creations."

Cashion's Eat Place Ⓜ | 25 | 21 | 22 | $46 |
1819 Columbia Rd. NW (bet. Biltmore St. & Mintwood Pl.), 202-797-1819; www.cashionseatplace.com
"Exquisitely talented" chef Ann Cashion gives a "down-home" (Southern) spin to the "amazingly creative" "ever-changing" seasonal menu at her "vibrant" Adams Morgan New American, where a "seashell"-shaped room with high ceilings and a "sophisticated" yet "unpretentious" staff contributes to "the best date place in town", plus they whip up one of the tastiest brunches "you'll ever hope to find"; P.S. there's "people-watching" at the sidewalk tables.

CITRONELLE | 28 | 25 | 26 | $88 |
(aka Michel Richard's Citronelle)
Latham Hotel, 3000 M St. NW (30th St.), 202-625-2150; www.citronelledc.com
Georgetown's "Washington monument" for "visiting dignitaries" is chef-owner Michel Richard's "extraordinary" New French, where "sterling ingredients, a sure hand and a dollop of whimsy" (try the "breakfast" dessert, a "masterwork of trompe l'oeil") make it "the best DC has to offer"; get a table near the see-in kitchen to watch the "fun", then relax in the "lovely" modern space and be "spoiled" by an "impeccable" staff; P.S. "take a full wallet" since the lofty prices match the "high caliber."

CityZen Ⓢ Ⓜ | 26 | 26 | 25 | $100 |
Mandarin Oriental, 1330 Maryland Ave. SW (bet. 12th & 14th Sts.), 202-787-6006; www.cityzenrestaurant.com
For "New York chic" in a "government town" head to this New American "extravaganza" in the "plush" Mandarin Oriental in SW; its "sleek" look, with an open kitchen, a wall of flames in the bar and lots of steel, leather and wood, suits the "fashionable" enthusiasts of its "glorious" tasting menus, "attractive wine list" and "creative" details like the "fantastic mini–Parker House rolls"; add in a "personable" staff and you might want to save this "flawless operation" "for birthdays and anniversaries."

DC Coast Ⓢ | 24 | 23 | 22 | $51 |
Tower Bldg., 1401 K St. NW (14th St.), 202-216-5988; www.dccoast.com
What makes this Downtown New American a "surefire winner" is its yin-yang blend of contrasts: the "outstanding" cooking, focused on "wonderful fish", is both "adventurous and comforting", its "delightful deco" look is "both classic and modern" and it serves a "great power lunch without the stuffiness"; although the "space is acoustically challenged" ("upstairs is quieter and has a view"), many find the buzz "energizing" at "cocktail hour."

Equinox | 25 | 20 | 23 | $63 |
818 Connecticut Ave. NW (bet. H & I Sts.), 202-331-8118; www.equinoxrestaurant.com
Todd and Ellen Gray's "wonderful" Golden Triangle New American near the Oval Office rings "superb" to its many fans who fawn over the "highly innovative" tasting menus full of "exquisite delights" and "local flavors" paired with "tastefully chosen" wines (there are à la carte selections as well); the service is "at-

tentive without being intrusive", and even if a few faultfinders want an "update" of the "ho-hum" decor, others find it amenable for "quiet" conversation; P.S. for a less-expensive option, try a "power lunch" instead.

Eve, Restaurant Ⓢ 27 24 25 $71
(aka Eve)
110 S. Pitt St. (bet. King & Prince Sts.), Alexandria, VA, 703-706-0450; www.restauranteve.com
"Save the superlatives" for this Old Town New American "foodie paradise", where Irish-born chef-owner Cathal Armstrong's "creative insights into flavors" transform "interesting ingredients" (tripe as well as foie gras) into "mind-blowing" meals with "memorable" matches of wine; "knowledgeable" staffers "treat you like VIPs" and you can choose among its "romantic bistro", "happening bar" or tasting room where the "beautiful dance of waiters" is "worth every penny"; since "none of the many faces of Eve disappoint", she's a "tough" reservation.

Gerard's Place Ⓢ 27 21 24 $75
915 15th St. NW (bet. I & K Sts.), 202-737-4445
"Ooh-la-la" – it's like "dining in an intimate chef-owned restaurant in France" at this New French Downtown "hideaway" enthuse local bec fins; N.B. while the recent departure of eponymous chef Gerard Panguad (he now teaches at the L'Academie de Cuisine in Gaithersburg, MD) may put the Food score in question, his experienced team (including co-founder Michelle Panguad) continues to offer "more affordable" multicourse dinners and à la carte midday selections.

IndeBleu 23 25 21 $62
707 G St. NW (bet. 7th & 8th Sts.), 202-333-2538; www.bleu.com
"Swanky hipsters" say this "ultrachic" Penn Quarter Indo-French via chef Vikram Garg "does Washington proud"; the "glamorous" space – including a "sleek, sexy" "sybarite's heaven" of a bar/lounge and a "light and airy" dining room with a chef's table that "merry-go-rounds into the kitchen" – makes them feel "like A-listers", and the "hints of India in the French fare" are "distinctive and special"; add to that the seemingly "choreographed" service in which four-to-eight waiters simultaneously "whisk off the covers of your entrees", and most have a "truly 'ta-da' experience."

Indigo Landing – – – E
1 Marina Dr. (George Washington Memorial Pkwy.), Alexandria, VA, 703-548-0001; www.indigolanding.com
This posh regional New American mines coastal South Carolina's rich culinary traditions in a picturesque, naturalistic setting overlooking the Potomac River in Alexandria; the nautically themed dining room offers sweeping views of DC, as well as a menu that mixes down-home and luxury ingredients; there's also a bar/lounge and a 100-seat veranda for balmy nights.

INN AT LITTLE WASHINGTON 29 28 28 $141
The Inn at Little Washington, 309 Middle St. (Warren Ave.), Washington, VA, 540-675-3800; www.theinnatlittlewashington.com
"Heaven on earth" is found in the Virginia countryside at this "mecca of fine dining" that's No. 1 for Food; its loyalists find a "gourmand's paradise" featuring the "best" New American cuisine, a setting that's a "treat for the eyes" and "choreographed"

"masterful service" that makes you "feel coddled from the moment" you pull in; everything from the "exquisite" amuse-bouche to the "hilarious" "cow-shaped mooing cheese cart" "exceeds expectations" – but, of course, "perfection doesn't come cheap."

JALEO | 23 | 20 | 19 | $33 |

480 Seventh St. NW (E St.), 202-628-7949 ●
2250A Crystal Dr. (23rd St. S.), Arlington, VA, 703-413-8181
7271 Woodmont Ave. (Elm St.), Bethesda, MD, 301-913-0003
www.jaleo.com

Invite your amigos to "nibble the evening away" on "tantalizing", "imaginative" yet "authentic" Spanish tapas with "never-ending sangria to wash it all down" at these "crowd-pleasers" in DC, Bethesda and Crystal City; they're a "loud", "chaotic" "fiesta", especially if there's flamenco dancing, and they're among the "few places where 'small plate' does not equal 'large bill'"; P.S. expect "waits" since no reservations are taken past 6:30 PM.

KINKEAD'S | 26 | 21 | 24 | $59 |

2000 Pennsylvania Ave. NW (I St.), 202-296-7700; www.kinkead.com

"The perfect catch" for "seafood-inside-the-Beltway power dining", Bob Kinkead's Foggy Bottom "classic", DC's Most Popular, "easily holds its own with newer pretenders to the throne", serving "glistening" fin fare "inventively prepared" in "classy" quarters filled with "celebs and politicos"; it has a "can't-miss location" – a "short walk from the White House" and an "easy trip" to the Kennedy Center – and while the service is generally "meticulous", it's probably "best enjoyed in the company of a VIP."

La Bergerie | 26 | 22 | 25 | $55 |

218 N. Lee St. (bet. Cameron & Queen Sts.), Alexandria, VA,
703-683-1007; www.labergerie.com

"C'est magnifique" declare devotees of this "charming" Old Town boîte serving "classic" French fare in a "splendid" setting with "fresh flowers and cozy banquettes" that's perfect for a "long romantic lunch"; it's "worth absolutely every penny of the bankroll you'll need" – from the "amazing Caesar salad, prepared tableside" to the "must-order" quenelles to the "best dessert soufflé in town", all served by a "super solicitous staff"; P.S. don't miss the "bargain" prix fixe lunch.

L'Auberge Chez François Ⓜ | 27 | 26 | 27 | $75 |

332 Springvale Rd. (Beach Mill Rd.), Great Falls, VA, 703-759-3800;
www.laubergechezfrancois.com

Generations of "special occasions" are made "memorable" at this "universally beloved" "rustic" Alsatian in a "magical" country setting in Great Falls that "transports" you to "pastoral" France; the "excellent" French fare is served by a staff that makes you "feel loved and taken care of" whether you're enjoying the "fireplace warmth" in winter or the garden "on a lovely summer night", so overall many find it a "top-value" choice.

Le Paradou Ⓢ | 27 | 25 | 24 | $89 |

678 Indiana Ave. NW (bet. 6th & 7th Sts.), 202-347-6780;
www.leparadou.net

"Brilliant" chef Yannick Cam "has done it again" at this "unique and exquisite" New French Penn Quarter eatery that's risen to DC's "top echelon"; the "out-of-this-world" tasting menu can be paired with bottles from an "amazing wine bible" in a "sublime setting" (notable art, fiber optic ceiling lights), presided over by "professional" (if sometimes "haughty") help; devotees are surprised it's "easy to get into", but that's probably because a meal ends up costing "more than your mortgage payment."

MAESTRO 🏢Ⓜ   28 | 27 | 28 | $114

Ritz-Carlton Tysons Corner, 1700 Tysons Blvd. (International Dr.), McLean, VA, 703-821-1515; www.maestrorestaurant.com

A "fabulous experience" awaits at this luxurious Italian in the Tysons Corner Ritz-Carlton, where the "tasting menus" are "works of art", the "skilled" sommelier is worthy of "trust" and the rest of the "incredibly attentive and welcoming" staff will make "you feel like a celebrity"; "soft lighting and subtle music" melt away stress, and if you sit by the open kitchen and watch the "concentrated creativity" of "genius" chef Fabio Trabocchi and his crew "plate food using tweezers", you'll get "an immediate appreciation" of why this one ranks so high.

MAKOTO Ⓜ   28 | 21 | 27 | $65

4822 MacArthur Blvd. NW (U St.), 202-298-6866

"Take off your shoes" and time travel "back to the 19th century" when you enter this "shoebox"-size Palisades eatery, reminiscent of a Kyoto *ryokan* (rustic inn) that feels "more Japanese than today's Japan"; its highlights include "exquisite", "authentic" omakase meals that are "almost too pretty to eat" and "witty sushi chefs" who create "a wonderful meal at the bar"; it's just the "horrendously uncomfortable" box seats that annoy.

MARCEL'S   28 | 24 | 27 | $73

2401 Pennsylvania Ave. NW (24th St.), 202-296-1166; www.marcelsdc.com

"A class act" from the "exquisitely prepared" French-inflected Belgian fare to the "first-rate" staff to the "door-to-door" sedan service to the Kennedy Center, this West End fine-dining venue oozes ambiance; chef-owner Robert Wiedmaier's cooking, including a "wonderful" pre-theater prix fixe, "makes your heart sing" (and the cash register ring) with selections like the "best boudin blanc (sausage) in the city"; but lovers beware, when it gets "loud" it's "not the place for intimacy."

Obelisk 🏢Ⓜ   27 | 20 | 25 | $73

2029 P St. NW (bet. 20th & 21st Sts.), 202-872-1180

"Fanatic" chef-owner Peter Pastan "keeps you focused on the finest Italian in the city" at his "intimate" Dupont Circle space; connoisseurs swear his daily changing prix fixe menu "could pass a blind taste test" with Italy's "best", and the "unique" dishes are "prepared and served by people who clearly respect food" and want to "take very good care of you"; just remember to reserve "well in advance" if you want to "spend an evening with your true love" in this 30-seat room.

Palena 🏢   26 | 22 | 22 | $57

3529 Connecticut Ave. NW (bet. Ordway & Porter Sts.), 202-537-9250; www.palenarestaurant.com

Have "a night to remember" with "all-around excellence in food, wine and service" at this "casual" Cleveland Park New American, "whether supping in the bar"/cafe or dining in the "quieter and more romantic" formal space in back; "if you can get reservations", you'll be amazed at chef-owner Frank Ruta's "superbly prepared" "twists on classics" and his "ambitious" "attention to detail" from the "house-cured" charcuterie to the "produce from his garden."

Pizzeria Paradiso | 24 | 15 | 18 | $23 |

3282 M St. NW (bet. 32nd & 33rd Sts.), 202-337-1245
2029 P St. NW (bet. 20th & 21st Sts.), 202-223-1245
www.eatyourpizza.com

It's "pizza nirvana" at these "dressed-down" Dupont Circle and Georgetown eateries where the "slightly chewy" yet "crisp" wood-oven-baked pies come topped with the "very freshest ingredients", accompanied by "wonderful salads" and "rustic wines by the tumbler"; since they're "always bustling" with a "lock on fun with style", you should "get there early and be prepared to wait"; N.B. the Georgetown branch's cozy basement is now a birreria with 90-plus brews from around the world.

PRIME RIB | 27 | 24 | 26 | $62 |

2020 K St. NW (bet. 20th & 21st Sts.), 202-466-8811;
www.theprimerib.com

"Classy, swanky and all dressed up", this black-lacquered "old-fashioned supper club" in Golden Triangle is the quintessential spot to celebrate anniversaries or the "close of a big deal" over "massive cuts of buttery, beefy, masculine prime rib", the "most succulent" crab and "perfect" martinis brought to table by "impeccable" tuxedoed waiters; it's still a "powerhouse scene" in DC where "high-profile politicians" "wine and dine", but even sentimentalists think the leopard-print rug should "be retired to a '70s time capsule."

Rasika | 26 | 26 | 23 | $46 |

633 D St. NW (bet. 6th & 7th Sts.), 202-637-1222;
www.rasikarestaurant.com

Here's a "hip and happening" Penn Quarter Indian that's in a "class by itself" say its sophisticated fans; expect a "sexy" setting, "exemplary service" and "unique" subcontinental tapas influenced by street cooking (you "must have" the "crispy" deep-fried spinach appetizer) and "innovative and thoughtful wine pairings that work well with the dynamic range" of "fabulous flavors"; indeed, from the "killer" cocktails to the "delectable dishes fit for the maharajah", they "seem to be doing everything right."

Ray's The Steaks Ⓜ | 27 | 10 | 22 | $43 |

Colonial Village, 1725 Wilson Blvd. (Rhodes St.), Arlington, VA,
703-841-7297

Chef-owner/butcher Michael Landrum (Ray) is "a genius with a side of cow" – and the "no-frills ambiance" at his "bare-bones" eatery "buried" in an Arlington strip mall near the Courthouse metro "keeps the price down" for "some of the best red meat you'll eat anywhere", "cooked to perfection" and complemented by a "thoughtful gently priced wine list"; so even if you're "crammed" in, many say this one "easily outshines the big chains"; P.S. "come early" – they don't take reservations.

Seasons | 27 | 25 | 27 | $64 |

Four Seasons Hotel, 2800 Pennsylvania Ave. NW (28th St.),
202-944-2000; www.fourseasons.com

The Georgetown Four Seasons' "elegant" "high standards pay off" at its New American where the "out-of-this-world" fare, "quiet ambiance, terrific service and tables spaced so that you're not afraid to tell the person you're with what you're thinking about" draw a "diplomatic and senior policy crowd"; it's "*the* business hotel in DC", so "having breakfast anywhere else before you've been elected (or after you've been impeached) is just plain silly", plus there's a "mind-boggling" Sunday brunch.

1789   26 | 25 | 25 | $61

1226 36th St. NW (Prospect St.), 202-965-1789;
www.1789restaurant.com
"Everything" about this "elegant" Georgetowner "screams quality and class": the "excellent" seasonal New American fare, the "impeccable" service and the "classic" Federal period dining rooms favored for "romance" "by the fireplace"; the recent departure of longtime chef Ris Lacoste concerned loyalists, but early reports say her replacement, Nathan Beauchamp (ex Restaurant Eve), has been able to "liven up the menu while still keeping true to the standards."

Taberna del Alabardero ⊠   24 | 24 | 23 | $59

1776 I St. NW (18th St.), 202-429-2200; www.alabardero.com
You'll "feel like you're blocks from the Puerta del Sol, rather than the White House" at this "sumptuously decorated" bastion of "old-world Madrid" near the World Bank, where the "excellent", "authentic" blend of "modern cuisine with Spanish tradition" means there are even some "Ferran Adrià–like" items (i.e. frozen olive oil) to try; "dress well" and experience "wonderfully civilized" cosseting that makes "special occasions" "*muy romantico*", or for a "far less expensive evening out", try the bar's half-price happy-hour tapas.

TENPENH ⊠   24 | 24 | 23 | $48

1001 Pennsylvania Ave. NW (10th St.), 202-393-4500; www.tenpenh.com
"Everyone looks beautiful" at this Downtown Asian and "the food is just as pretty"; a "killer menu of tongue-tingling favorites" from chef Jeff Tunks "pushes the Pan-Asian envelope without straying into truly rebellious territory", and the "dramatic, colorful atmosphere" is as "stylish" as its crowd; even though pensive types pout it "gets really loud" and the "tables are too close together", seasoned vets say the "biggest problem will be getting past the appetizers" – they're the "winners."

Thai Square   26 | 10 | 18 | $22

3217 Columbia Pike (S. Highland St.), Arlington, VA, 703-685-7040;
www.thaisquarerestaurant.com
"Hot means hot for a change" at this "authentic" Arlington "hole-in-the-wall" "where Thais go for Thai food"; it "doesn't put on airs, decorwise", the "space is cramped" and service can be "surly" – but "in terms of pricing and quality" "no other place can match" the "exciting blend of texture and flavors" in the "simply wonderful" dishes.

Tosca ⊠   26 | 23 | 25 | $59

1112 F St. NW (bet. 11th & 12th Sts.), 202-367-1990; www.toscadc.com
Celebrated for "inventive modern interpretations of Northern Italian", this "understated and elegant" Penn Quarterite is set in a "serene, monochromatic" space that's usually "buzzing with 'heavy hitters'"; it "always lives up" to "expectations of the highest quality in food and service" with "amazing dishes and beautiful

presentations", but it can be a "somewhat expensive date" unless you opt for the "absolute steal" $32 pre-theater three-course dinner.

2941 Restaurant | 27 | 28 | 25 | $77 |

2941 Fairview Park Dr. (Arlington Blvd.), Falls Church, VA, 703-270-1500; www.2941.com

"Manhattan meets the Beltway in this surprisingly sophisticated suburban enclave" set in a Falls Church office park, where "wonderful" French-inflected New American is served in "gorgeous" tall-windowed dining rooms overlooking koi ponds and waterfalls; chef-owner Jonathan Krinn "architects flavors masterfully", pairs them "excellently" with wines and has them served by a "gracious, pampering" staff; but with all those "generous" end-of-meal goodies (chocolates, cotton candy), you'll wonder "does 2941 refer to the bill or the calories from the extra desserts?"

2 Amys | 25 | 15 | 18 | $23 |

3715 Macomb St. NW (Wisconsin Ave.), 202-885-5700; www.2amyspizza.com

"Divine wood-fired pizza" ("the only ones in town that come close to the true Italian" variety), "inspired" antipasto, "wonderful modestly priced wine" and "perhaps a too child-friendly" vibe at this Cleveland Park "hot spot" beget "long waits" and a "noisy" "stroller-set" atmosphere during prime time; its black-and-white-tile decor is "a little spartan, as befits a Neapolitan pizzeria" – but this one is certified by the Italian pie-makers association and the pedigree shows in the "amazing" output.

Vidalia | 26 | 22 | 24 | $58 |

1990 M St. NW (bet. 19th & 20th Sts. NW), 202-659-1990; www.vidaliadc.com

"It has its off nights, but when it's 'on'", this Golden Triangle "destination" "really delivers" via a "delicious, innovative" New American menu with "an upscale Southern touch"; the "ambrosial fare" is served by a "gracious" staff that provides "VIP treatment" and "excellent wine matches" in a "lovely" underground setting "made brighter" by a "beautiful remodeling"; there's also a "stylish bar" suitable for sampling small plates or one of the 40 "well-researched" vinos by the glass.

ZAYTINYA ◐ | 25 | 25 | 20 | $39 |

Pepco Bldg., 701 Ninth St. NW (G St.), 202-638-0800; www.zaytinya.com

"Stunning, sleek white walls provide a dramatic background for a buzzing crowd" at this "fabulous" "fast-paced" Penn Quarter "meze heaven" where an "epic menu" of Middle-Eastern/ Mediterranean (Turkish, Greek and Lebanese) "unique" small plates encourages "sharing", and a "knowledgeable staff keeps it from being overwhelming"; its "divine" "big city atmosphere" (one of the "best-looking restaurants in town"), "excellent" prices and "great service" make "tables hard to come by."

Westchester/ Hudson River Valley

TOP FOOD RANKING

Restaurant	Cuisine
29 Freelance Café	New American
Xaviar's at Piermont	New American
27 Rest. X & Bully Boy Bar	New American
Blue Hill/Stone Barns	New American
Buffet de la Gare	French
Il Cenàcolo	Northern Italian
La Panetière	French
26 Escoffier	French
Zephs'	Eclectic/New Amer.
La Crémaillère	French
Coromandel	Indian
Ocean House	New England/Seafood
Il Barilotto	Italian
L'Europe	Continental
Arch	Eclectic
Johnny's Pizzeria	Italian/Pizza
Wasabi*	Japanese
Iron Horse Grill	New American
Busy Bee	New American
Azuma Sushi	Japanese

OTHER NOTEWORTHY PLACES

Aberdeen	Chinese/Cantonese
Bear Cafe	New American
Cafe Mezé	Mediterranean
Caterina de Medici	Italian
Crabtree's Kittle House	New American
DePuy Canal House	New American
Equus	French/New Amer.
French Corner	French
Harvest on Hudson	Mediterranean
Koo	Japanese
Old Drovers	American
Plates	New American
Relish	American/Eclectic
Serevan	Mediterranean
Sonora	Nuevo Latino
Sterling Inn	French/New Amer.
Sushi Nanase	Japanese
Swoon Kitchenbar	New American
Terrapin	New American
Valley at the Garrison	New American

* Indicates tie with restaurant above

Aberdeen
25 | 17 | 22 | $27

Marriott Residence Inn, 3 Barker Ave. (Cottage Pl.), White Plains, 914-288-0188

It's as "close to China as you can get" declare devotees of this "authentic, refined" White Plains Cantonese "jewel" in the Marriott Residence Inn, which features "fresh" seafood live from the tanks (including some "unusual" choices) and "amazing dim sum" deemed "on a par with" what you'd find in "NYC's Chinatown"; "courteous", "knowledgeable" service and digs considered "more comfortable than the old Harrison location" make it "not your usual Sunday night" option; N.B. dim sum is served at lunch only.

Arch ⓜ
26 | 25 | 26 | $66

1296 Rte. 22 (end of I-684), Brewster, 845-279-5011; www.archrestaurant.com

"If you want to be pampered", head up the "winding road" to this "charming" Brewster "hideaway" and dine on "superb" Eclectic cuisine in "tastefully decorated" rooms; surveyors swoon it's the "epitome of elegance", with service "so refined you almost don't know it's there", so although it's "expensive", most agree it's more than "worth the price" (and "the hike"); N.B. jackets preferred at dinner.

Azuma Sushi ⓜ
26 | 13 | 19 | $41

219 E. Hartsdale Ave. (Bronx River Pkwy.), Hartsdale, 914-725-0660

"Can't pass through Hartsdale without stopping" at this "superlative" Japanese sushi "classic" declare devotees of its "pristine" raw selections that make a "wonderful" but "expensive addiction"; "cramped" quarters and "cranky" service turn off a few sensitive sorts, but most don't mind much considering the "out-of-this-world" "quality."

Bear Cafe
25 | 23 | 23 | $41

295 Tinker St./Rte. 212 (2 mi. west of Rte. 375), Bearsville, 845-679-5555; www.bearcafe.com

"Bravo!" cheer those bullish on the "top-notch" New American fare and "appealing" "streamside setting" that have helped this "intimate", "country-style" "staple" near Woodstock in Bearsville "stand the test of time"; the "accommodating staffers" serve "current and past hippies", "weekenders" and a sprinkling of celebs, and the "fun bar scene" means that there's "always a buzz" – and "reservations are a must."

BLUE HILL AT STONE BARNS ⓜ
27 | 28 | 26 | $76

Stone Barns Center for Food & Agriculture, 630 Bedford Rd. (Lake Rd.), Pocantico Hills, 914-366-9600; www.bluehillstonebarns.com

"Manhattan dining meets the countryside" at this "sublime" New American from Dan Barber and family (of NYC's Blue Hill), which is blessed with a "magical" converted Norman-style barn setting amid a "working farm"/educational center in the Rockefeller State Park in Pocantico Hills; the "fresh, local" ingredients give the "superb" cuisine "a whole new dimension", while the "warmly elegant" decor and "incredibly knowledgeable staff" complete the "culinary nights to remember" (not to mention Sunday brunches); P.S. call "far in advance" to "snare a reservation" and then "arrive early to walk the grounds."

BUFFET DE LA GARE ☒Ⓜ   27 | 22 | 26 | $58

155 Southside Ave. (Spring St.), Hastings-on-Hudson, 914-478-1671
A "beautifully romantic" "visit to a special place in France" is the feeling at this "*magnifique*" bistro that's located "near the train station" in Hastings, but in spirit is "as close to Paris (without the attitude)" as you can get; a "confident, sure-footed" staff "from heaven" delivers "first-rate" cassoulet and other classics, inspiring groupies to gush "it doesn't get much better than this"; N.B. a post-*Survey* change in ownership puts the ratings in question.

Busy Bee Cafe ☒   26 | 16 | 21 | $35

138 South Ave. (Reade Pl.), Poughkeepsie, 845-452-6800
"Don't judge a book by its cover", because contrary to appearances this New American in a "former deli" tucked among family homes in Poughkeepsie is a "great little bistro" serving "scrumptious" meals to "knock your socks off"; "thoughtful service" adds to the overall "good vibe", which recently got even better thanks to a post-*Survey* renovation adding some much-needed elbow room.

Cafe Mezé   24 | 19 | 21 | $46

20 N. Central Ave. (Hartsdale Ave.), Hartsdale, 914-428-2400;
www.cafemeze.com
"Creative" chef Mark Filippo "always has something new and inventive on the menu" at this "top-notch" Hartsdale Mediterranean housed in a "boxy building that hides its pretty interior"; simply "delicious" dishes (the artichoke ravioli and grilled octopus are "particularly recommended") and an "excellent family of waiters" make it "another Livanos family triumph", even if a few curmudgeons crab it's "too loud" during "crowded times."

Caterina de Medici ☒   26 | 25 | 23 | $47

Colavita Center for Italian Food and Wine, Culinary Institute of America,
1946 Campus Dr. (Rte. 9), Hyde Park, 845-471-6608; www.ciachef.edu
"It's all terrific" declare disciples of the "mouthwatering" preparations by CIA chefs-to-be at this reservations-required Hyde Park Italian, housed in a "magnificent" space that looks like a "bright Tuscan villa" – albeit one with Venetian glass chandeliers and "de Medici crests hidden everywhere"; although the student staff sometimes "isn't polished", it "makes up for it with enthusiasm", contributing to a dining experience that all in all is deemed "elegant and relaxing at the same time"; N.B. the Al Forno room offers more casual meals overlooking the kitchen.

Coromandel   26 | 16 | 21 | $31

30 Division St. (bet. Huguenot & Main Sts.), New Rochelle,
914-235-8390; www.coromandelcuisine.com
"Long live India!" declare devotees of this "superb" subcontinental known for its "innovative" cuisine, giving patrons the chance to "discover taste buds they never knew they had"; with "service that could not be friendlier or faster" and a "bargain lunch buffet", you "feel like you could be in London, New Delhi or Midtown."

CRABTREE'S KITTLE HOUSE   25 | 25 | 24 | $56

Crabtree's Kittle House Inn, 11 Kittle Rd. (Rte. 117), Chappaqua,
914-666-8044; www.kittlehouse.com
"You'll feel like landed gentry" at this "beautiful, old-school" institution in Chappaqua that "captures the eloquence of rustic dining" – and nabs the Most Popular ranking in Westchester/HRV –

with "artfully prepared" New American cuisine "fit for a president" ("it's a fave of Bill Clinton", who lives nearby), "an exhaustive" wine list boasting some 6,000 labels and a "gorgeous", truly "romantic" "country setting"; in sum, it's a "wonderful place to take out-of-town guests", "impress the in-laws" or enjoy a "celebratory meal."

DePuy Canal House Ⓜ   23 | 26 | 22 | $62
1315 Rte. 213 (Lucas Tpke.), High Falls, 845-687-7700; www.depuycanalhouse.net
"One of the original homes of New American cuisine", this "gorgeous", "very romantic" High Falls Colonial stone building serves as the perfect backdrop for "hot dates, anniversaries" and everything in between; chef-owner John Novi's menu is always "full of surprises" with "exotic flavors" making for some "unforgettable dinners", so go ahead and "splurge" – it's "a wonderful adventure."

Equus   26 | 29 | 25 | $70
Castle on the Hudson, 400 Benedict Ave. (bet. Maple St. & Martling Ave.), Tarrytown, 914-631-3646; www.castleonthehudson.com
A "glorious" "hilltop location" in Tarrytown is the "stunning" "baronial setting" for this jackets-required French–New American housed in a turreted palace replete with "romantic corners for quiet, intimate meals"; sure, the "incredible" cuisine and "no-detail-overlooked" "formal" service comes with a "hefty price tag", but how else are you going to know "what it's like to eat in a castle?"; P.S. in summer, the "terrace and gardens" are "magnificent."

Escoffier, The Ⓢ Ⓜ   26 | 25 | 24 | $56
Culinary Institute of America, 1946 Campus Dr. (Rte. 9), Hyde Park, 845-471-6608; www.ciachef.edu
"Lovely high French" cuisine "served with style" "the classic way" in the "most elegant room" makes this CIA standout "the star of the Hyde Park school's marvelous restaurants" rave reviewers, noting that desserts prepared tableside "are a great show" too; "cheap it's not", but it's perfect for "special moments" – or get a seat overlooking the kitchen to witness "the wonders of the culinary world"; P.S. remember to "plan ahead", because "reservations are hard to come by."

FREELANCE CAFÉ & WINE BAR ⊅   29 | 20 | 26 | $45
506 Piermont Ave. (Ash St.), Piermont, 845-365-3250; www.xaviars.com
"Deee-lightful" coo the "cosmopolitan" cognoscenti who collect at Xaviar's "superb" sister in Piermont, which was voted No. 1 for Food in Westchester/HRV thanks to its "coconut shrimp that dreams are made of" and other "exquisite" New American offerings; it's more "affordable" than next door (though still "not for a freelancer's budget"), and "you've gotta love" "gracious" maitre d' Ned Kelly, who sets the tone for the "excellent service" in its "minimalist" space; yes, the no-reservations policy means the "lines" practically "start forming at the crack of dawn", but to most it's "worth it" for such "out-of-this-world" dining.

French Corner Ⓜ   24 | 23 | 22 | $47
3407 Cooper St./Rte. 213 W. (Rte. 209), Stone Ridge, 845-687-0810; www.frcorner.com
"Skillful and knowledgeable" chef-owner Jacques Qualin makes "good use of local ingredients" to create "delicious Regional French cuisine" at this Stone Ridge entry; a few antique touches add to the chic interior, and though some find the "Manhattan

"prices" a tad too steep for the area, the "$25 prix fixe is a bargain" in any town.

HARVEST ON HUDSON   22 | 26 | 20 | $48

1 River St. (¼ mi. north of Hastings-on-Hudson RR), Hastings-on-Hudson, 914-478-2800; www.harvest2000.com

Savor the smell of the "inviting fireplace" as you "watch the Hudson River float by" at this "gorgeous" Hastings Med, whose "picturesque views of the Palisades" and "Napa Valley feel" captivate visitors as much as the "delicious" dishes "made with ingredients from on-premises gardens"; some say the kitchen "doesn't match the extraordinary setting", and there are a few complaints that the service "needs polishing", but most don't notice because "on a clear night" it's hard to find a more "enchanting" locale.

Il Barilotto   26 | 22 | 23 | $44

1113 Main St. (North St.), Fishkill, 845-897-4300

"Another crowd-pleaser" from Eduardo Lauria, this "first-rate", "posher" sister to Fishkill's Aroma Osteria draws raves with "sophisticated" Italian fare, so when ordering "be a bit adventurous – you won't be disappointed"; the dining room housed in a 19th-century brick building is deemed "handsome", the list of Italian boutique wines "awesome" and the staff "professional and accommodating", so the only drawback is "it can get noisy."

Il Cenàcolo   27 | 21 | 25 | $56

228 S. Plank Rd./Rte. 52 (Rte. 300), Newburgh, 845-564-4494

"Phenomenal" cooking that "explodes with complex flavors", plus a "list of specials a mile long (forget about the menu)", make this Northern Italian "the epitome of fine dining" in "gritty Newburgh" – or "anywhere"; the simple decor is enhanced by a "fantastic array of antipasti" on display, and other pluses include a "thoughtful and kind staff" and an "excellent wine selection"; yes, meals here cost "a pretty penny", but "hoo, boy are they good!"

Iron Horse Grill ⊠   26 | 21 | 24 | $53

20 Wheeler Ave. (Manville Rd.), Pleasantville, 914-741-0717; www.ironhorsegrill.com

"I don't have to go to NYC anymore!" shout devotees of this "exquisite" Pleasantville New American, where "passionate" chef-owner Philip McGrath "is a genius" who "greets you as you come in" to partake of his "sublime" "seasonal" cuisine; a "confident staff" and "intimate" "restored train station" setting are other reasons this is a "winner" worth "splurging on."

Johnny's Pizzeria ⊠ M ≠   26 | 9 | 15 | $17

Lincoln Plaza, 30 W. Lincoln Ave. (bet. N. 7th Ave. & Rochelle Terrace), Mt. Vernon, 914-668-1957

There are "no slices" to be had at this Mt. Vernon Italian, "but that's ok because" the "melt-in-your-mouth", "world-class pizza" "is so light and thin" "you can almost eat a whole pie by yourself"; never mind if "parking is next to impossible" and the rest of the menu's only "ordinary", just focus on that "best-in-the-county" house specialty – "yum!"

Koo   24 | 20 | 20 | $51

17 Purdy Ave. (2nd St.), Rye, 914-921-9888; www.koorestaurant.com

"Young", "cool and cosmopolitan" Rye residents suffering "Nobu withdrawal" make a beeline for this "amazing" nouveau

Japanese, whose "innovative", "eclectic" cuisine is tailor-made for the "sophisticated palate" and comes via an "attentive", "welcoming" staff; you may "need a second mortgage to pay the bill", but after a couple of pours from the "top-quality" sake list, you won't notice the "NYC prices."

La Crémaillère Ⓜ 26 | 26 | 26 | $68

46 Bedford-Banksville Rd. (Round House Rd.), Bedford, 914-234-9647; www.cremaillere.com

"Tucked in the backwoods of Bedford" is the Meyzen family's "first-class", "wonderful retreat" where you "wait for the waiters to lift the lids" to experience "the art of French cooking" at its "finest"; "charming decor", an "astonishing" wine list (some 14,000 bottles) and servers "that treat you like an old, valued friend" make it a fitting "place to get engaged"; N.B. jackets required.

LA PANETIÈRE 27 | 26 | 26 | $70

530 Milton Rd. (Oakland Beach Ave.), Rye, 914-967-8140; www.lapanetiere.com

"You don't have to wait to get into heaven" when this "first-class" French housed in an "elegant" Rye "mansion" awaits; here, "sublime meals" backed by an "impeccable" wine cellar are presented amid "stunning" environs by a staff that "treats you royally", adding up to a guaranteed "evening to remember" (owner Jacques Loupiac "never disappoints"); surveyors suggest "don't just save this for a special occasion" – though you may want to "win the lottery" or take out "a loan" first; N.B. jackets required.

L'Europe Restaurant Ⓜ 26 | 22 | 25 | $60

407 Smith Ridge Rd./Rte. 123 (Tommys Ln.), South Salem, 914-533-2570; www.leuroperestaurant.com

"Refinement lives" at this South Salem "sit-up-straight" "bastion of Continental cuisine" where a "courteous" staff presents a "fabulous", "rarely changing" menu along the lines of venison, rack of lamb and "fabulous soufflés that are not to be missed"; fittingly, the "beautiful setting" and "precise", "old-world" service (not to mention the "pricey"-but-"worth-it" tab) make you "feel like you're in Europe."

Ocean House ⓈⓂ 26 | 19 | 21 | $38

49 N. Riverside Ave. (Rte. 9A), Croton-on-Hudson, 914-271-0702

This "simple and delicious" New England "gem" of a fish house hidden in a "tiny" ("only 19 seats") Croton "converted diner" is "run by a couple who really care"; from the "oysters that sparkle" to the "excellent chowder", everything's "unbelievably good", but the "no-reservations policy" has some asking "have they heard of winter on the Hudson?" – it's way too "cold" to "stand outside waiting for a table."

Old Drovers Inn 24 | 26 | 23 | $57

Old Drovers Inn, 196 E. Duncan Hill Rd. (Rte. 22), Dover Plains, 845-832-9311; www.olddroversinn.com

It's "heaven" rhapsodize reviewers of this 18th-century Dutchess County inn "dripping with history", where "low ceilings with hand-cut beams" and a "huge stone fireplace" form a "charming" backdrop for Traditional American fare from a new chef (post-*Survey*) who has added a few contemporary flourishes (think boneless quail over wild mushroom risotto); an extensive wine list and an "efficient" staff further enhance the "special and memorable" experience, which, no surprise, does not "come cheap."

Plates Ⓜ   24 | 19 | 21 | $49
121 Myrtle Blvd. (off Chatsworth Ave.), Larchmont, 914-834-1244; www.platesonthepark.com
"Terrific" plate-cleaning fare from a "creative chef" makes this Larchmont New American a "special place" that's "sophisticated without being precious"; there are "growing pains with respect to service" ("uneven"), but nonetheless most find it possesses "all the right elements"; P.S. sensitive ears will appreciate that an acoustic ceiling was added post-*Survey* to address complaints of "loud" "noise levels."

Relish   26 | 15 | 23 | $44
4 Depot Sq. (Main St.), Sparkill, 845-398-2747; www.relishsparkill.com
"Rockland County residents can be smug" about this "first-rate" relative newcomer to "the wilderness" of Sparkill, where an "off-beat", "skillfully prepared" American-Eclectic menu, "loyal to organic" ingredients, results in "outstanding flavors"; "an inspired, reasonable wine list", "great hospitality" and "funny '50s decor that's funky but appropriate" also make the place "worth every bit of time you spend finding it."

RESTAURANT X & BULLY BOY BAR Ⓜ   27 | 26 | 25 | $54
117 Rte. 303 (bet. Lake Rd. & Rte. 9W), Congers, 845-268-6555; www.xaviars.com
From the "delectable" savory dishes and "desserts almost too beautiful to eat" to the "fabulous wine cellar" and "gracious" staff, "everything's simply marvelous" gush gourmands of Peter Kelly's New American in Congers that's "more relaxed" than his flagship Xaviar's; its three rooms are "hip but homey", "especially when the fire is lit", and even the duck pond is rated "romantic", so "splurge", or go for the "excellent" $20.06 prix fixe lunch, because "these people really know how to run a restaurant."

Serevan   – | – | – | E
6 Autumn Ln./Rte. 44 (west of Rte. 22), Amenia, 845-373-9800; www.serevan.com
Armenian chef-owner Serge Madikians has locals swooning at this Dutchess County Med newcomer, where a weekly changing menu offers dishes like couscous-crusted halibut and Moroccan crêpes, reflecting the chef's heritage as well as his time with some top Manhattan toques; pared-down elegance in the sage-and-slate-blue room puts the food center stage, while an open kitchen adds a dash of drama.

Sonora   25 | 23 | 22 | $46
179 Rectory St. (Willett Ave.), Port Chester, 914-933-0200; www.sonorany.com
"No need to go to the city for diversity" of flavor when right in Port Chester there's this Nuevo Latino and its "creative chef", Rafael Palomino, who "excels" at "delicious", "definitive" cooking, including a "wide variety" of "excellent tapas"; equally "vibrant" is the "wonderful decor" and "noisy", "festive" atmosphere, overseen by a "helpful" staff – in short, it lives up to "the rave reviews"; P.S. don't miss the "wonderful" tropical cocktails.

Sterling Inn, The Ⓜ
| – | – | – | E |

1279 North Ave. (Northfield Rd.), New Rochelle, 914-636-2400; www.thesterlinginnrestaurant.com

With Aureole and Lespinasse among the notches on his résumé, chef Sterling Smith should win a following at this new upscale New American–French in the Wykagyl section of New Rochelle; expect à la carte offerings of classics with surprise ingredients (like a beet-based dessert) and inventive preparations (lamb timbale, lobster borscht).

Sushi Nanase
| – | – | – | VE |

522 Mamaroneck Ave. (DeKalb Ave.), White Plains, 914-285-5351; www.sushinanase.com

Don't expect California rolls and other Americanized sushi at this big-ticket White Plains raw-fish shrine where master Yoshimichi Takeda, previously at Masa and Nobu, lords over the *oh toro* and orange clam; imports from Japan, soy sauce from scratch and an impressive sake list lend a taste of Tokyo and an anti-typical suburban sushi joint feel.

Swoon Kitchenbar
| ▽ 26 | 23 | 18 | $36 |

340 Warren St. (bet. S. 3rd & N. 4th Sts.), Hudson, 518-822-8938; www.swoonkitchenbar.com

"A winner!" exclaim enthusiasts of this New American that's the "first really ambitious upscale eatery in Hudson"; chef-owner Jeffrey Gimmel's "delicious" menu "is inventive" but "casual", just like the "elegant and original" bistro-style interior, with its tin ceilings, silver columns, earth tones and plentiful plants; add "well-chosen wines" and "drop-dead desserts", and even though "service is a bit spotty", this is the "new jewel on the antiques Riviera."

Terrapin
| 24 | 24 | 20 | $42 |

6426 Montgomery St. (bet. Chestnut & Livingston Sts.), Rhinebeck, 845-876-3330; www.terrapinrestaurant.com

Really "two fabulous restaurants in one", chef-owner Josh Kroner's "striking" Rhinebeck New American offers a "dramatic" fine-dining room with a mezzanine and "divine" decor as well as a "casual, less-expensive" bistro-bar; as befits the converted church setting, both offer "heavenly meals and sinful desserts", with a few signatures appearing on both "imaginative" menus; the staff sometimes enters "the *Twilight Zone*" on weekends when it gets "hectic", but at least "they try hard."

Valley Restaurant at the Garrison
| 25 | 25 | 20 | $58 |

Garrison Resort, 2015 Rte. 9 (Snake Hill Rd.), Garrison, 845-424-2339; www.thegarrison.com

This "brilliant" two-year-old has "nailed it" by "pairing a light, welcoming interior with the Garrison golf club's gorgeous vistas"; its "delicious" New American cuisine that "changes to reflect local produce" (as well as what's available in the kitchen garden visible from the dining balcony) is equally "impressive", and though it's still "a work in progress", repasts here are "a great treat" that rank among "the Valley's best."

Wasabi
| 26 | 25 | 23 | $44 |

110 Main St. (Park St.), Nyack, 845-358-7977; www.wasabichi9.com

"Nobu, watch out" – chef-owner Doug Nguyen "has scored big" with this Rockland Japanese serving "interesting combos" of "impeccable sushi and sashimi" as well as "fabulous" "culinary adventures" like "outrageous sushi pizza" and "divine grilled yellowtail cheeks", all looking like "works of art"; "hip", "modern" decor (complete with wasabi-hued walls) gives a "cosmopolitan feel" to the "glamorous Zen scene", and even though it's a bit "heavy on the purse" for "locals' budgets", it's "worth it."

XAVIAR'S AT PIERMONT ⌂   29 | 25 | 28 | $73

506 Piermont Ave. (Ash St.), Piermont, 845-359-7007; www.xaviars.com
"Please let the food in heaven be like this" sigh the sated at "virtuoso" chef Peter Kelly's "magical" Piermont "gem", where "exquisite" New American fare, "phenomenal waiters", "beautiful china and glassware" and a "romantic", "intimate", "simple yet elegant" dining room make it "the best on the planet, down to the last detail"; even though the $70 prix fixe ($35 at lunch) may mean you'll have to "save up, you'll be glad you did" – it's "worth every red cent"; N.B. don't forget, it's cash only.

Zephs'   26 | 18 | 24 | $48

638 Central Ave. (bet. Nelson Ave. & Water St.), Peekskill, 914-736-2159
"More people should know about this" "exceptional", "off-the-beaten-path but well-worth-finding" Peekskill New American–Eclectic where the "gracious service" from a "friendly staff" headed by "wonderful host Michael" Zeph is only topped by the "unending appeal" of his "creative" sister Vicky's "short" but "sophisticated" "seasonal" menu, which features "delightful couplings of flavors and ingredients"; even most who fault the "nondescript room" concede it's offset by the "charming" "old-mill" location, thereby ensuring a "first-rate experience."

Indexes

CUISINES BY AREA

Atlanta
American (New)
Aria
Bacchanalia
BluePointe
Canoe
dick and harry's
Muss & Turner's
Park 75
Quinones
Rathbun's
Rest. Eugene
Asian
BluePointe
Sia's
Californian
Woodfire Grill
Continental
Ecco
Pano's & Paul's
Delis
Muss & Turner's
European
Seeger's
French
Floataway Cafe
Joël
French (New)
Ritz Buckhead Din. Rm.
Greek
Kyma
Indian
Madras Saravana
Italian
(N=Northern)
di Paolo (N)
Floataway Cafe
La Grotta (N)
La Tavola
Sotto Sotto (N)
Japanese
(* sushi specialist)
Hashiguchi*
MF Sushibar*
Taka*
Mediterranean
Ritz Buckhead Din. Rm.
Pan-Latin
Tierra
Seafood
Atlanta Fish
Chops/Lobster Bar
dick and harry's

Small Plates
Ecco (Continental)
Southern
South City Kitchen
Watershed
Wisteria
Southwestern
Nava
Sia's
Steakhouses
Bone's
Chops/Lobster Bar
McKendrick's Steak
New York Prime
Thai
Nan Thai
Tamarind
Vegetarian
Madras Saravana
Vietnamese
Nam

Atlantic City
Chinese
P.F. Chang's
Suilan
French
Suilan
Italian
Capriccio
Chef Vola's
Mia
Ombra
Mediterranean
Mia
Sandwiches
White House
Seafood
Dock's Oyster
Steakhouses
Bobby Flay Steak
Brighton Steak

Austin
American (New)
Café/Four Seasons
Driskill Grill
Hudson's
Jeffrey's
Mirabelle
Starlite
Wink
Zoot
Asian
Bistro 88

Barbecue
 Salt Lick
European
 Bistro 88
French
 Aquarelle
Italian
(N=Northern)
 La Traviata
 Siena (N)
 Vespaio
Japanese
(* sushi specialist)
 Musashino Sushi*
 Uchi*
Mediterranean
 Fino
Mexican
 Fonda San Miguel
Seafood
 Eddie V's
Small Plates
 Fino (Mediterranean)
Steakhouses
 Eddie V's
Tex-Mex
 Chuy's

Baltimore/Annapolis

Afghan
 Helmand
American (New)
 Charleston
 Corks
 Hampton's
 Linwoods
 Paul's Homewood
 Peter's Inn
 Saffron
American (Traditional)
 Clyde's
French
 Tersiguel's
Greek
 Paul's Homewood
 Samos
Hamburgers
 Clyde's
Italian
(N=Northern)
 Boccaccio (N)
Japanese
(* sushi specialist)
 Joss Cafe/Sushi*
 Sushi Sono*
Mexican
 Mari Luna Mexican

Pub Food
 Clyde's
Seafood
 McCormick & Schmick's
Small Plates
 Charleston (New American)
Steakhouses
 Lewnes' Steak
 Prime Rib
 Ruth's Chris
Thai
 Lemongrass

Boston

Afghan
 Helmand
American (New)
 Franklin
 Hamersley's Bistro
 Harvest
 Icarus
 Meritage
 Salts
 Troquet
 UpStairs on the Sq.
Asian Fusion
 Blue Ginger
 Restaurant L
Barbecue
 East Coast Grill
Continental
 Locke-Ober
Eclectic
 EVOO
French
 Mistral
 No. 9 Park
French (Bistro)
 Coriander Bistro
 Craigie St. Bistrot
 Hamersley's Bistro
 Petit Robert Bistro
 Pigalle
 Troquet
French (New)
 Aujourd'hui
 Clio/Uni
 L'Espalier
 Radius
Indian
 Tamarind Bay
Italian
(N=Northern; S=Southern)
 Carmen
 Grotto
 Il Capriccio (N)
 No. 9 Park

Sage (N)
Saporito's (N)
Taranta (S)
Japanese
(* sushi specialist)
Oishii*
Mediterranean
Mistral
Oleana
Rendezvous
Rialto
Peruvian
Taranta
Seafood
B&G Oysters
East Coast Grill
Legal Sea Foods
Neptune Oyster
Small Plates
(See also Spanish tapas
specialist)
Meritage (New American)
Spanish
(* tapas specialist)
Dalí Restaurant*
Toro*

Charlotte

American (New)
Barrington's
Bonterra Dining/Wine
Carpe Diem
Sonoma
Californian
Sonoma
Continental
McNinch House
Eclectic
Noble's
French
Lulu
Patou
French (New)
Zebra Rest.
Greek
ilios noche
Italian
(N=Northern)
ilios noche
Luce
Toscana (N)
Volare
Japanese
(* sushi specialist)
Nikko*
Rest. i*

Mediterranean
Lulu
Seafood
McIntosh's
Upstream
Steakhouses
McIntosh's
Mickey & Mooch
Palm
Sullivan's

Chicago

American (New)
Alinea
Blackbird
Charlie Trotter's
Courtright's
mk
Naha
North Pond
Schwa
Seasons
Spring
Vie
American (Traditional)
Wildfire
Asian
Mulan
French (Bistro)
Barrington Bistro
French (New)
Ambria
Avenues
Carlos'
Everest
Le Français
Les Nomades
NoMI
Oceanique
one sixtyblue
Ritz-Carlton Din. Rm.
Tallgrass
Tru
Italian
Spiaggia
Japanese
(* sushi specialist)
Heat*
Japonais*
Mirai Sushi*
Mediterranean
Avec
Naha
Mexican
Frontera Grill
Topolobampo

Pan-Asian
Shanghai Terrace
Pizza
Lou Malnati Pizza
Seafood
Avenues
Oceanique
Spring
Small Plates
Avec (Mediterranean)
Green Zebra (Vegetarian)
Steakhouses
Chicago Chop Hse.
Gibsons Steak
Morton's Steak
Wildfire
Thai
Arun's
Vegetarian
Green Zebra

Cincinnati

American (New)
Palace, The
Palomino
Asian Fusion
Beluga
Bakeries
BonBonerie
Barbecue
Montgomery Inn
Chinese
China Gourmet
Continental
Palace, The
Dessert
BonBonerie
Eclectic
Daveed's at 934
Nectar
Sturkey's
French
JeanRo
Pho Paris
French (New)
Jean-Robert at Pigall's
Indian
Cumin
Italian
(N=Northern)
Boca
Nicola's (N)
Mediterranean
Palomino
Pizza
Dewey's Pizza

Seafood
South Beach Grill
Steakhouses
Jeff Ruby's Steak
Morton's Steak
Precinct, The
South Beach Grill
Tearooms
BonBonerie
Vietnamese
Pho Paris

Cleveland

American (New)
Fahrenheit
fire
Lolita
One Walnut
Three Birds
American (Traditional)
Flying Fig
Brazilian
Sergio's Saravá
Cambodian
Phnom Penh
Continental
Baricelli Inn
Johnny's Bar
Eclectic
Flying Fig
French
Chez François
Classics
Sans Souci
Italian
(N=Northern)
Battuto
Giovanni's (N)
Johnny's Bar (N)
Vivo (N)
Mediterranean
Lolita
Sans Souci
Seafood
Blue Point Grille
Parallax
Small Plates
Sergio's Saravá (Brazilian)
Steakhouses
Hyde Park Prime
Red/Steakhouse

Connecticut

American (New)
Ann Howard
Bonda
Bricco

Carole Peck's
Jeffrey's
Max Downtown
Mayflower Inn & Spa
Métro Bis
Rebeccas
American (Traditional)
City Limits Diner
Coffee Shops/Diners
City Limits Diner
Continental
Jeffrey's
French
Bernard's
Da Pietro's
Jean-Louis
L'Escale
Ondine
Rest. du Village
French (Bistro)
Cafe Routier
Le Petit Cafe
Union League
French (New)
Cavey's
La Colline Verte
Thomas Henkelmann
Indian
Coromandel
Italian
(N=Northern)
Bravo Bravo
Cavey's (N)
Da Pietro's (N)
Peppercorn's Grill
Piccolo Arancio
Valbella (N)
Japanese
(sushi specialist)*
Mako of Japan*
Malaysian
Bentara
Nuevo Latino
Roomba
Pan-Asian
Ching's Table
Pan-Latin
Isla Montecristi
Pizza
Frank Pepe
Frank Pepe's Spot
Sally's Apizza
Seafood
Max's Oyster Bar
Ocean 211

Spanish
(tapas specialist)*
Barcelona*
Ibiza
Meigas*
Steakhouses
Max Downtown

Dallas/Ft. Worth
American (New)
Aurora
Cafe Aspen
Craft Dallas
Goodhues Wood Fired
Grape
Hibiscus
Iris
Local
Lola
Mercury Grill
Nana
62 Main
Standard
York Street
American (Traditional)
French Room
Barbecue
Angelo's Barbecue
Brazilian
Texas de Brazil
Eclectic
Abacus
French
French Room
Lavendou
Saint-Emilion
Italian
(N=Northern)
Bice
Modo Mio (N)
Japanese
(sushi specialist)*
Nobu Dallas*
Steel*
Tei Tei Robata Bar*
Teppo*
Pan-Latin
La Duni Latin
Peruvian
Nobu Dallas
Seafood
Café Pacific
Oceanaire
Southwestern
Bonnell's
Lonesome Dove

Mansion/Turtle Creek
Reata
Steakhouses
Al Biernat's
Capital Grille
Del Frisco's
Pappas Bros.
Texas de Brazil
Tex-Mex
Joe T. Garcia's
Mi Cocina
Thai
Chow Thai
Vietnamese
Steel

Denver Area & Mountain Resorts

American (New)
Flagstaff House
Highland's Garden
John's
Kevin Taylor
Keystone Ranch
Mel's Rest./Bar
Mizuna
Montagna
Opus
Potager
Q's
Six89 Kitchen/Wine
Solera Rest./Wine
Sweet Basil
Syzygy
240 Union
American (Regional)
Grouse Mountain Grill
Piñons
Steuben's
American (Traditional)
Alpenglow Stube
Asian
Zengo
Brazilian
Cafe Brazil
Colombian
Cafe Brazil
Eclectic
Flagstaff House
Kitchen, The
French
L'Atelier
Left Bank
French (Bistro)
Z Cuisine Bistrot
French (New)
La Tour

German
Alpenglow Stube
Indian
India's
Italian
(N=Northern)
Barolo Grill (N)
Frasca (N)
Full Moon Grill (N)
Luca d'Italia
Japanese
(* sushi specialist)
Matsuhisa*
Sushi Den*
Sushi Sasa*
Mediterranean
rioja
Nuevo Latino
Zengo
Seafood
240 Union
Small Plates
rioja (Mediterranean)
Steakhouses
Capital Grille
Del Frisco's
Morton's Steak
Vietnamese
New Saigon

Detroit

American (New)
Beverly Hills Grill
Five Lakes Grill
Seldom Blues
West End Grill
American (Traditional)
Opus One
Rugby Grille
Sweet Georgia Brown
Continental
Lark, The
Opus One
Rugby Grille
Delis
Zingerman's Deli
Eclectic
Traffic Jam & Snug
French
Tribute
French (New)
Cafe Bon Homme
Italian
Bacco
Il Posto
Rist. Café Cortina

Japanese
(* sushi specialist)
   Oslo Sushi Bar*
Seafood
   Coach Insignia
   Common Grill
   No. VI Chop Hse.
Steakhouses
   Coach Insignia
   No. VI Chop Hse.
   Rochester Chop Hse.

Ft. Lauderdale

American (New)
   Cafe Maxx
   Sunfish
   3030 Ocean
American (Traditional)
   Blue Moon Fish
   Cheesecake Factory
   Houston's
Brazilian
   Chima Brazilian
Chinese
   Silver Pond
Eclectic
   Cafe Maxx
   Eduardo/San Angel
Floribbean
   Johnny V's
Floridian
   Mark's Las Olas
Italian
(N=Northern)
   Cafe Martorano
   Cafe Vico
   Casa D'Angelo (N)
   Josef's (N)
Japanese
   Galanga
Mediterranean
   La Brochette
Mexican
   Eduardo/San Angel
Pizza
   Anthony's Pizza
Seafood
   Blue Moon Fish
   Sunfish
   3030 Ocean
Southwestern
   Canyon
Steakhouses
   Chima Brazilian
   Ruth's Chris
Thai
   Galanga

Honolulu

American (Traditional)
   Orchids
Asian Fusion
   Indigo
French
   Michel's
French (New)
   Chef Mavro
   La Mer
Greek
   Olive Tree Café
Hawaii Regional
   Alan Wong's
   Chef Mavro
   Pineapple Room
   Roy's
   Roy's Ko Olina
Italian
   town
Japanese
(* sushi specialist)
   Sansei*
Mediterranean
   Olive Tree Café
Pacific Rim
   Bali by the Sea
   Hoku's
   L'Uraku
   Sansei
   3660 on the Rise
Seafood
   Duke's Canoe Club
   Sansei
Steakhouses
   d.k Steak House
   Hy's Steak House
   Ruth's Chris

Houston

American (New)
   Artista
   Backstreet Café
   benjy's
   Gravitas
   Mark's American
   Mockingbird Bistro
   Rainbow Lodge
   Remington
   Shade
   t'afia
Asian Fusion
   Bank by Jean-Georges
Brazilian
   Fogo de Chão

Continental
  Charivari
  Tony's
Creole
  Brennan's
Eclectic
  Shade
French
  Chez Nous
French (Bistro)
  Bistro Moderne
French (New)
  Bank by Jean-Georges
Indian
  Indika
  Kiran's
Italian
  Carrabba's Italian
  Da Marco
  Frenchie's
  La Griglia
  Quattro
Mediterranean
  Ibiza
Mexican
  Hugo's
  Otilia's
Nuevo Latino
  Julia's Bistro
Seafood
  Goode Co. Seafood
  Pesce
  Rainbow Lodge
  Tony Mandola's
South American
  Américas
  Cafe Red Onion
  Churrascos
Southwestern
  Brennan's
  Cafe Annie
Spanish
  Ibiza
Steakhouses
  Capital Grille
  Churrascos
  Fleming's Prime
  Fogo de Chão
  Pappas Bros.
  Strip House
  Vic & Anthony's

Kansas City
American (New)
  American Rest.
  Bluestem
  Café Sebastienne

Circe
40 Sardines
1924 Main
Starker's Reserve
zin
American (Traditional)
  Room 39
  Stroud's
Barbecue
  Danny Edwards'
  Fiorella's Jack Stack
  Oklahoma Joe's
Eclectic
  Grand St. Cafe
French
  Tatsu's
French (Bistro)
  Café Maison
  Le Fou Frog
Italian
(N=Northern)
  Lidia's (N)
Seafood
  McCormick & Schmick's
Steakhouses
  Plaza III

Las Vegas
American (New)
  Aureole
  Bradley Ogden
  Medici Café
  MIX
  Rosemary's
  Sterling Brunch
Cajun
  Emeril's
Californian
  NOBHILL
Creole
  Commander's Palace
  Emeril's
Eclectic
  Buffet at Bellagio
  Todd's Unique Dining
French
  Alex
  André's
  Eiffel Tower
  MIX
  Pamplemousse
French (Bistro)
  Bouchon
  Daniel Boulud
French (New)
  Alizé
  Daniel Boulud

Fleur de Lys
Guy Savoy
Joël Robuchon
L'Atelier
Le Cirque
Picasso

Italian
(N=Northern)
Gaetano's (N)
Osteria del Circo (N)
Valentino

Japanese
(* sushi specialist)
Nobu*
Okada*

Mediterranean
Alex

Peruvian
Nobu

Seafood
Craftsteak
Emeril's
Michael Mina
NOBHILL
Seablue

Small Plates
(See also Spanish tapas specialist)
Rosemary's (New American)

Southwestern
Mesa Grill

Spanish
(* tapas specialist)
Firefly*

Steakhouses
Capital Grille
Craftsteak
Delmonico Steak
Prime Steak
Steak House
SW Steak

Thai
Lotus of Siam

Long Island

American (New)
Barney's
Chachama Grill
Coolfish
Della Femina
Mill River Inn
On 3
Panama Hatties
Piccolo
Plaza Cafe
Polo
Starr Boggs

American (Traditional)
American Hotel
Cheesecake Factory

Chinese
Orient

Dessert
Cheesecake Factory

Eclectic
Frisky Oyster
La Plage
Maroni Cuisine
Mill River Inn
Mirko's

French
American Hotel
Barney's
Le Soir
Mirabelle
Stone Creek

French (Bistro)
Kitchen à Bistro

French (New)
Louis XVI

Italian
(N=Northern)
Dario's (N)
Da Ugo (N)
Harvest on Ft. Pond (N)
Il Mulino NY (N)
La Piccola Liguria (N)
Maroni Cuisine
Mio (N)
Nick & Toni's
Piccolo
Rialto (N)
Robert's
Trattoria Diane (N)

Japanese
(* sushi specialist)
Kotobuki*

Mediterranean
Harvest on Ft. Pond
Nick & Toni's
Stone Creek

Seafood
Coolfish
Kitchen à Bistro
Palm
Plaza Cafe
Starr Boggs
Tellers Chophouse

Steakhouses
Bryant/Cooper
Jimmy Hays
Palm
Peter Luger
Tellers Chophouse

Thai
Siam Lotus

Los Angeles
American (New)
Belvedere, The
BLD
Grace
Josie
Mélisse
Providence
Saddle Peak
American (Traditional)
Cheesecake Factory
Grill on Alley
Asian
Chaya Brasserie
Chinois on Main
Californian
A.O.C.
Café Bizou
Campanile
Derek's
Hotel Bel-Air
JiRaffe
Leila's
Spago
Chinese
Yujean Kang's
Delis
Brent's Deli
Dessert
Cheesecake Factory
Eclectic
Chaya Brasserie
Depot, The
French
A.O.C.
Derek's
Hotel Bel-Air
Mélisse
Shiro
French (Bistro)
Café Bizou
Frenchy's Bistro
Mimosa
French (New)
La Cachette
Italian
Angelini Osteria
Capo
Piccolo
Valentino
Japanese
(sushi specialist)*
Hamasaku*
Hump, The*

Katsu-ya*
Matsuhisa*
Mori Sushi*
Nobu Malibu*
Shiro
Sushi Nozawa*
Jewish
Brent's Deli
Mediterranean
Campanile
Christine
Pacific Rim
Christine
Seafood
Water Grill
Small Plates
A.O.C. (Californian/French)
Steakhouses
Cut
Saddle Peak

Miami
American (New)
Mark's South Beach
Nemo
North One 10
Talula
Wish
American (Traditional)
Cheesecake Factory
Houston's
Asian
Azul
Brazilian
SushiSamba
Caribbean
Off the Grille
Cuban
Versailles
Eclectic
Vix
French (New)
Palme d'Or
Pascal's on Ponce
Haitian
TapTap
Italian
(N=Northern)
Casa Tua (N)
Escopazzo
Osteria del Teatro (N)
Romeo's Cafe (N)
Timo
Japanese
(sushi specialist)*
Matsuri*
Nobu Miami Beach

Shoji*
SushiSamba*
Toni's Sushi*
Mediterranean
Azul
Michy's
Timo
New World
Chef Allen's
Norman's
Ortanique on Mile
Nuevo Latino
Cacao
Pan-Asian
Lan
Pacific Time
Pan-Latin
Jaguar
Peruvian
Francesco
Nobu Miami Beach
SushiSamba
Seafood
AltaMar
Francesco
Joe's Stone Crab
La Dorada
Prime One Twelve
River Oyster Bar
Spanish
La Dorada
Steakhouses
Capital Grille
Prime One Twelve
Thai
Tamarind

Milwaukee

American (New)
Bacchus
Barossa
Immigrant Room
Sanford
American (Traditional)
Riversite, The
Asian
Roots
Sake Tumi
Californian
Roots
Chinese
P.F. Chang's
French
Coquette Cafe
Lake Park Bistro

Indian
Dancing Ganesha
Saffron Indian
Italian
(N=Northern)
Maggiano's
Osteria del Mondo (N)
Sandwiches
Potbelly Sandwich
Seafood
River Lane Inn
Steakhouses
Eddie Martini's
5 O'Clock Club
Mr. B's: Steak
Thai
Singha Thai

Minneapolis/St. Paul

American (New)
Alma
Bayport Cookery
Cue
Five
Levain
Lucia's
20.21
Zander Cafe
American (Regional)
Dakota Jazz
American (Traditional)
St. Paul Grill
Eclectic
Cosmos
112 Eatery
French (Bistro)
Vincent
French (New)
La Belle Vie
Italian
(N=Northern)
D'Amico Cucina (N)
Ristorante Luci
Zelo
Mediterranean
La Belle Vie
Seafood
Oceanaire
Spanish
(tapas specialist)*
Solera*
Steakhouses
Manny's

New Jersey

American (New)
  Amanda's
  Bernards Inn
  Blu
  CulinAriane
  David Burke Fromagerie
  Dining Room
  Frog & Peach
  Nicholas
  Pluckemin Inn
  Rosemary & Sage
  Saddle River Inn
  Whispers
American (Traditional)
  Latour
  Perryville Inn
  Washington Inn
Cuban
  La Isla
Eclectic
  Anthony David's
  Cafe Matisse
  Cafe Panache
  Gables
French
  Chez Catherine
  Ixora
  Latour
  Saddle River Inn
  Siri's Thai French
  Zoe's
French (New)
  Origin
  Rat's
  Ryland Inn
  Serenade
  Stage House
Italian
(N=Northern; S=Southern)
  Anthony David's (N)
  Augustino's (S)
  Fascino
  Giumarello's
  Scalini Fedeli (N)
Japanese
(* sushi specialist)
  Ixora*
  Sagami*
Mediterranean
  Hamilton's Grill
Pan-Latin
  Zafra
Pizza
  DeLorenzo's

Portuguese
  Bistro Olé
Seafood
  Blu
  Blue Point
South American
  Cucharamama
Spanish
  Bistro Olé
Thai
  Origin
  Siri's Thai French

New Orleans

American (New)
  Bayona
  Dakota
  Herbsaint
  Iris
  New Orleans Grill
  Pelican Club
  Stella!
Cajun
  Cochon
  K-Paul's
Chinese
  Nine Roses
Contemporary Louisiana
  Brigtsen's
  Dakota
  Emeril's
  Herbsaint
  La Petite Grocery
  NOLA
  Peristyle
  Ralph's on Park
  Upperline
Continental
  August
  Cuvée
  Rib Room
Creole
  Antoine's
  Arnaud's
  Brennan's
  Broussard's
  Café Adelaide
  Clancy's
  Cuvée
  Dick & Jenny's
  Galatoire's
  Jacques-Imo's Cafe
  Muriel's Jackson Square
  NOLA
  Ralph's on Park
  Upperline
  Vizard's on the Avenue

French
 Antoine's
 Brennan's
 Broussard's
 Clancy's
 Dick & Jenny's
 Galatoire's
 La Provence
 Peristyle
French (Bistro)
 Alberta
 Café Degas
 La Petite Grocery
 Lilette
French (New)
 August
 Herbsaint
Italian
(S=Southern)
 Irene's Cuisine (S)
 Mosca's
Mediterranean
 Vizard's on the Avenue
Seafood
 Arnaud's
 RioMar
Soul Food
 Jacques-Imo's Cafe
Spanish
(tapas specialist)*
 Lola's
 RioMar*
Steakhouses
 Dickie Brennan's
 Rib Room
Vietnamese
 Nine Roses

New York City

American (New)
 Annisa
 Aureole
 Blue Hill
 Eleven Madison
 Gotham B&G
 Gramercy Tavern
 Grocery, The
 Modern, The
 per se
 River Café
 Saul
 Telepan
 Union Sq. Cafe
 Veritas
American (Traditional)
 Tavern on Green
 21 Club

Asian Fusion
 Buddakan
 Buddha Bar
Austrian
 Danube
Chinese
(dim sum specialist)*
 Oriental Garden*
 Shun Lee Palace
Continental
 Four Seasons
Delis
 Carnegie Deli
French
 Café Boulud
 Café des Artistes
 Chanterelle
 La Grenouille
 Modern, The
 per se
 Picholine
French (Brasserie)
 Balthazar
French (New)
 Alain Ducasse
 Bouley
 Daniel
 Jean Georges
 Le Bernardin
Greek
 Milos
Indian
 dévi
Italian
 Babbo
 Del Posto
 Il Mulino
 Roberto's
Japanese
(sushi specialist)*
 Masa*
 Morimoto
 Nobu*
 Sushi of Gari*
 Sushi Seki*
 Sushi Yasuda*
 Tomoe Sushi*
Jewish
 Carnegie Deli
Mediterranean
 Picholine
Seafood
 Le Bernardin
 Milos
 Oriental Garden
Southeast Asian
 Spice Market

Steakhouses
Palm
Peter Luger
Thai
Sripraphai

Orange County, CA
American (New)
Ramos House
Stonehill Tavern
American (Traditional)
Cheesecake Factory
Houston's
Asian Fusion
Roy's
Californian
Cafe Zoolu
Napa Rose
Studio
Caribbean
Golden Truffle
Chinese
P.F. Chang's
Continental
Hobbit, The
Dessert
Cheesecake Factory
French
Basilic
Golden Truffle
Hobbit, The
Pinot Provence
Tradition/Pascal
French (New)
Studio
Hawaii Regional
Roy's
Italian
Antonello
Japanese
(* sushi specialist)
Bluefin*
Seafood
Blue Coral
Tabu Grill
Steakhouses
Mastro's Steak
Ruth's Chris
Tabu Grill
Swiss
Basilic

Orlando
African
Boma
Jiko/Cooking Place

American (New)
Boheme, The
Doc's Rest.
Flying Fish Café
Hue
Primo
Seasons 52
Victoria & Albert's
American (Traditional)
Boma
Asian
Emeril's Tchoup Chop
Asian Fusion
Hue
Californian
California Grill
Wolfgang Puck Cafe
Contemporary Louisiana
Emeril's Orlando
Continental
Café de France
Chatham's Place
Venetian Room
Creole
Emeril's Orlando
Delis
Antonio's Cafe
Eclectic
Blue Bistro & Grill
K Rest./Wine Bar
Todd English's bluezoo
European
Chef Justin's
Floribbean
Chef Justin's
French
Le Coq au Vin
French (Bistro)
Café de France
Chez Vincent
Hawaii Regional
Roy's Orlando
Italian
Antonio's Cafe
Antonio's La Fiamma
Christini's Rist. Italiano
Enzo's/Lake
Primo
Japanese
(* sushi specialist)
Amura*
Shari Sushi*
Mexican
Taquitos Jalisco
New World
Norman's

Polynesian
Emeril's Tchoup Chop
Sandwiches
Antonio's Cafe
Seafood
Flying Fish Café
MoonFish
Roy's Orlando
Todd English's bluezoo
Steakhouses
Del Frisco's
Fleming's Prime
Kres Chophouse
MoonFish
Palm
Ruth's Chris
Vito's Chop Hse.
Thai
Thai House
Thai Thani

Palm Beach

American (New)
Cafe Chardonnay
11 Maple St.
Four Seasons
Ta-boo
32 East
American (Traditional)
Cheesecake Factory
Houston's
Chinese
P.F. Chang's
Continental
Addison
Café L'Europe
Kathy's Gazebo
Ta-boo
French
Café Boulud
Chez Jean-Pierre
Le Mistral
Italian
Marcello's La Sirena
Seafood
Kee Grill
Little Moirs
Spoto's Oyster
Steakhouses
Morton's Steak
New York Prime

Philadelphia

American (New)
Alison/Blue Bell
Gayle
Jake's
Mainland Inn
Marigold Kitchen
Southwark
Swann Lounge
Twenty Manning
Washington Square
American (Traditional)
General Warren
Asian
Buddakan
Susanna Foo
Twenty Manning
Californian
Sovalo
Chinese
Shiao Lan Kung
Continental
Fountain
Eclectic
Totaro's
French
Birchrunville Store
Deux Cheminées
Gilmore's
La Bonne Auberge
Lacroix/Rittenhouse
Nan
Overtures
Paloma
Savona
Susanna Foo
French (Bistro)
Le Bar Lyonnais
Pif
French (New)
Brasserie Perrier
Fountain
Le Bec-Fin
Swann Lounge
Greek
Dmitri's
Italian
(N=Northern; S=Southern)
Birchrunville Store
L'Angolo (S)
Melograno (N)
Savona
Sovalo
Vetri
Japanese
(* sushi specialist)
Bluefin*
Morimoto
Mediterranean
Overtures
Mexican
Paloma

Seafood
  Dmitri's
  Little Fish
  Striped Bass
Small Plates
(See also Spanish tapas specialist)
  Lacroix/Rittenhouse (French)
Spanish
(* tapas specialist)
  Amada*
Steakhouses
  Prime Rib
Thai
  Nan
Vegetarian
  Blue Sage

Phoenix/Scottsdale

American (New)
  Binkley's Restaurant
  elements
  Michael's at Citadel
American (Regional)
  Roaring Fork
Asian
  elements
Asian Fusion
  Roy's
Californian
  Greene House
Chinese
  P.F. Chang's
Eclectic
  Trader Vic's
French (New)
  Mary Elaine's
  Vincent's on Camelback
Hawaii Regional
  Roy's
Italian
(N=Northern)
  Pizzeria Bianco (N)
Japanese
  Roy's
  Sea Saw
Mediterranean
  Marquesa
  T. Cook's
Mexican
  Barrio Café
  Los Sombreros
Pizza
  Pizzeria Bianco
Seafood
  Eddie V's Edgewater

Southwestern
  Vincent's on Camelback
Steakhouses
  Drinkwater's City Hall
  Eddie V's Edgewater
  Mastro's
Vietnamese
  Cyclo

Portland, OR

American (New)
  Bluehour
  clarklewis
  Park Kitchen
French
  Heathman
  Paley's Place
Italian
(N=Northern)
  Alba Osteria & Enoteca (N)
  Caffe Mingo
  Genoa
  Giorgio's (N)
Japanese
(* sushi specialist)
  Murata*
Mediterranean
  Bluehour
  Olea
  Tabla
  3 Doors Down
Mexican
  Nuestra Cocina
Pacific Northwest
  Alberta St. Oyster
  clarklewis
  Heathman
  Higgins
  Joel Palmer
  Paley's Place
  Park Kitchen
  Wildwood
Peruvian
  Andina
Pizza
  Apizza Scholls

Salt Lake City & Mountain Resorts

American (New)
  Bambara
  Glitretind
  Log Haven
  Mariposa, The
  Metropolitan
  Pine American

Cuisines by Area

American (Regional)
Tree Room
American (Traditional)
Chez Betty
Franck's
New Yorker Club
Asian Fusion
Wahso
Continental
Chez Betty
French
Franck's
Italian
(N=Northern)
Fresco Italian Cafe (N)
Lugano (N)
Michelangelo
Japanese
(* sushi specialist)
Takashi*
Mediterranean
Martine
Mexican
Red Iguana
Seafood
Market St. Grill
Seafood Buffet
Small Plates
Takashi (Japanese)
Southwestern
Chimayo

San Antonio
American (New)
Biga on the Banks
Bin 555
Francesca's at Sunset
Lodge Rest.
Silo
Asian
Frederick's
Chinese
P.F. Chang's
Eclectic
Liberty Bar
French
Bistro Vatel
Frederick's
Las Canarias
L'Etoile
French (New)
Le Rêve
Italian
Ciao Lavanderia
Paesanos

Korean
(* barbecue specialist)
Korean B.B.Q. House*
Mediterranean
Las Canarias
Mexican
El Mirador
Nuevo Latino
Azúca Sabor Latino
Seafood
Boudro's/Riverwalk
L'Etoile
Pesca on the River
Southwestern
Francesca's at Sunset
Steakhouses
Boudro's/Riverwalk
Fleming's Prime
Tex-Mex
Ácenar

San Diego
American (New)
Arterra
Pamplemousse Grille
Asian Fusion
Roppongi
Californian
A.R. Valentien
Azzura Point
George's at Cove
French
El Bizcocho
Laurel
Modus
Pamplemousse Grille
French (Brasserie)
WineSellar & Brasserie
French (New)
Marine Room
Mille Fleurs
Tapenade
Italian
(N=Northern)
Vivace (N)
Japanese
(* sushi specialist)
Sushi Ota*
Mediterranean
Laurel
Mexican
Ortega's
Seafood
Oceanaire Seafood
Steakhouses
Donovan's
Ruth's Chris

Thai
  Rama

San Francisco Bay Area
American (New)
  Ame
  Boulevard
  French Laundry
  Gary Danko
  Manresa
  Michael Mina
  Myth
  Range
  Redd Restaurant
  Terra
American (Traditional)
  Lark Creek Inn
Californian
  Aqua
  Bar Tartine
  Boulevard
  Canteen
  Chez Panisse
  Chez Panisse Café
  Coi
  Farmhouse Inn
  Fleur de Lys
  Jardinière
  Rivoli
  Scott Howard
  Sierra Mar
French
  Boulevard
  Coi
  French Laundry
  Jardinière
  La Folie
  La Toque
  Scott Howard
French (Bistro)
  Bistro Jeanty
French (New)
  Cyrus
  Fifth Floor
  Fleur de Lys
  Le Papillon
  Manresa
  Marinus
  Masa's
  Quince
  Ritz-Carlton Din. Rm.
Italian
(N=Northern)
  Delfina (N)
  Oliveto
  Quince

Japanese
(sushi specialist)*
  Kaygetsu*
  Sushi Ran*
Mediterranean
  Bar Tartine
  Chez Panisse
  Chez Panisse Café
  Rivoli
  Zuni Café
Pacific Rim
  Sushi Ran
Seafood
  Aqua
Vegetarian
  Fleur de Lys
  French Laundry
  Greens
Vietnamese
  Slanted Door

Seattle
American (New)
  Cascadia
  Crush
  Herbfarm
  Lampreia
  Lark
  Mistral
  Nell's
  Russell's
  Sitka & Spruce
  Union
  Union Bay Cafe
Bakeries
  Macrina Bakery
Caribbean
  Paseo
Dessert
  Macrina Bakery
French
  Campagne
  Georgian
  Le Gourmand
French (Bistro)
  Boat St. Cafe
French (New)
  Mistral
  Rover's
Italian
(N=Northern)
  Boat St. Cafe
  Cafe Juanita (N)
  Il Terrazzo Carmine
  Salumi
  Volterra (N)

Japanese
(* sushi specialist)
  Chiso*
  Nishino*
  Shiro's Sushi*
  Toyoda Sushi*
Mediterranean
  Carmelita
Mexican
  La Carta de Oaxaca
Pacific Northwest
  Canlis
  Dahlia Lounge
  Georgian
  Herbfarm
  Inn at Langley
  Lampreia
  Matt's in Market
  Nell's
  Union Bay Cafe
Pacific Rim
  Wild Ginger
Sandwiches
  Salumi
Seafood
  Canlis
  Matt's in Market
  Seastar
Spanish
(* tapas specialist)
  Harvest Vine*
Steakhouses
  El Gaucho
  JaK's Grill
  Metropolitan Grill
Vegetarian
  Carmelita
Vietnamese
  Green Leaf
  Monsoon

St. Louis

American (New)
  Crossing
  Frazer's
  Harvest
  King Louie's
  Niche
  Pomme
  Sidney St. Cafe
  Truffles
  Zinnia
American (Traditional)
  Annie Gunn's
Californian
  1111 Mississippi

Dessert
  Mira/Roxane
Eclectic
  Mira/Roxane
French
  Atlas
French (Bistro)
  Chez Leon
French (New)
  Pomme
Italian
(N=Northern; S=Southern)
  Atlas
  Dominic's
  1111 Mississippi (N)
  Limoncello Italian
  Paul Manno's (S)
  Tony's
  Tratt. Marcella
Seafood
  Al's Rest.
Steakhouses
  Al's Rest.

Tampa/Sarasota

American (New)
  Black Pearl
  Cafe Ponte
  Fred's
  Michael's On East
  Mise en Place
  SideBern's
Bakeries
  Pane Rustica
Continental
  Bijou Café
  Six Tables
Cuban
  Columbia
Eclectic
  Euphemia Haye
  Ophelia's on Bay
  Pane Rustica
Floridian
  Beach Bistro
French
  Restaurant B.T.
French (New)
  Six Tables
Hawaii Regional
  Roy's
Italian
(N=Northern)
  Armani's (N)
Mediterranean
  Marchand's B&G

Pizza
Pane Rustica
Sandwiches
Pane Rustica
Seafood
Roy's
Salt Rock Grill
Spanish
(* tapas specialist)
Cevíche Tapas*
Columbia
Steakhouses
Bern's
Vietnamese
Restaurant B.T.

Tucson

American (New)
Acacia
Bistro Zin
Dish, The
Grill/Hacienda del Sol
Montana Avenue
Ventana Room
Wildflower
American (Regional)
Montana Avenue
Bakeries
Beyond Bread
Eclectic
Cuvée World Bistro
Feast
French
Le Rendez-Vous
Italian
(N=Northern)
Vivace (N)
Malaysian
Neo of Melaka
Mediterranean
Primo
Mexican
Cafe Poca Cosa
Nuevo Latino
J Bar
Sandwiches
Beyond Bread
Seafood
Bluefin
Southwestern
Janos
Terra Cotta
Steakhouses
McMahon's Prime

Washington, DC

American (New)
BlackSalt
Black's Bar
Blue Duck Tavern
Cashion's Eat Place
CityZen
DC Coast
Equinox
Eve
Indigo Landing
Inn/Little Washington
Palena
Seasons
1789
2941 Restaurant
Vidalia
Bakeries
Bread Line
Belgian
Marcel's
French
IndeBleu
La Bergerie
L'Auberge/François
French (Bistro)
Bis
French (New)
Citronelle
Gerard's Place
Le Paradou
Indian
IndeBleu
Rasika
Italian
(N=Northern)
Maestro
Obelisk
Tosca (N)
Japanese
Makoto
Mediterranean
Zaytinya
Middle Eastern
Zaytinya
Nuevo Latino
Café Atlántico
Pan-Asian
TenPenh
Pizza
Pizzeria Paradiso
2 Amys
Seafood
BlackSalt
Black's Bar
DC Coast
Kinkead's

Small Plates
(See also Spanish tapas
specialist)
   Zaytinya (Middle Eastern)
Southern
   Vidalia
Spanish
(* tapas specialist)
   Jaleo*
   Taberna/Alabardero*
Steakhouses
   Prime Rib
   Ray's The Steaks
Thai
   Thai Square

Westchester/
Hudson River Valley

American (New)
   Bear Cafe
   Blue Hill/Stone Barns
   Busy Bee
   Crabtree's Kittle Hse.
   DePuy Canal House
   Equus
   Freelance Café
   Iron Horse Grill
   Plates
   Rest. X/Bully Boy Bar
   Sterling Inn
   Swoon Kitchenbar
   Terrapin
   Valley Rest./Garrison
   Xaviar's/Piermont
   Zephs'
American (Traditional)
   Old Drovers Inn
   Relish
Chinese
(* dim sum specialist)
   Aberdeen*

Continental
   L'Europe
Eclectic
   Arch
   Relish
   Zephs'
French
   Buffet de la Gare
   Equus
   Escoffier
   French Corner
   La Crémaillère
   La Panetière
   Sterling Inn
Indian
   Coromandel
Italian
(N=Northern)
   Caterina de Medici
   Il Barilotto
   Il Cenàcolo (N)
   Johnny's Pizzeria
Japanese
(* sushi specialist)
   Azuma Sushi*
   Koo*
   Sushi Nanase*
   Wasabi*
Mediterranean
   Cafe Mezé
   Harvest on Hudson
   Serevan
New England
   Ocean House
Nuevo Latino
   Sonora
Pizza
   Johnny's Pizzeria
Seafood
   Ocean House

AREA ABBREVIATIONS

AC	Atlantic City	MI	Miami
AT	Atlanta	MN	Minneapolis/St. Paul
AU	Austin	MW	Milwaukee
BA	Baltimore/Annapolis	NJ	New Jersey
BO	Boston	NO	New Orleans
CH	Chicago	NY	New York City
CI	Cincinnati	OC	Orange County, CA
CL	Cleveland	OR	Orlando
CR	Charlotte	PB	Palm Beach
CT	Connecticut	PH	Philadelphia
DF	Dallas/Ft. Worth	PO	Portland, OR
DC	Washington, DC	PS	Phoenix/Scottsdale
DE	Denver Area	SA	San Antonio
DT	Detroit	SC	Salt Lake City Area
FL	Ft. Lauderdale	SD	San Diego
HO	Honolulu	SE	Seattle
HS	Houston	SF	San Francisco Area
KC	Kansas City	SL	St. Louis
LA	Los Angeles	TB	Tampa/Sarasota
LI	Long Island	TC	Tucson
LV	Las Vegas	WH	Westchester/Hudson

ALPHABETICAL PAGE INDEX

Abacus, DF 78
Aberdeen, WH 291
Acacia, TC 276
Ácenar, SA.............. 239
Addison, The, PB 212
Alain Ducasse, NY 189
Alan Wong's, HO......... 105
Alba Osteria & Enoteca, PO .. 230
Alberta, NO 180
Alberta St. Oyster Bar, PO.... 230
Al Biernat's, DF........... 78
Alex, LV 125
Alinea, CH 50
Alison at Blue Bell, PH...... 218
Alizé, LV 125
Alma, MN............... 166
Alpenglow Stube, DE....... 88
Al's Restaurant, SL........ 266
AltaMar, MI 154
Amada, PH.............. 218
Amanda's, NJ 172
Ambria, CH............. 50
Ame, SF 249
American Hotel, LI 135
American Rest., KC 119
Américas, HS 111
Amura, OR 204
Andina, PO.............. 231
André's, LV.............. 125
Angelini Osteria, LA 144
Angelo's Barbecue, DF 78
Ann Howard Apricots, CT ... 70
Annie Gunn's, SL.......... 266
Annisa, NY.............. 189
Anthony David's, NJ....... 172
Anthony's Pizza, FL........ 101
Antoine's, NO 180
Antonello, OC 198

Antonio's Cafe & Deli, OR .. 204
Antonio's La Fiamma, OR 204
A.O.C., LA.............. 144
Apizza Scholls, PO........ 231
Aqua, SF 249
Aquarelle, AU 25
Arch, WH 291
Aria, AT 15
Armani's, TB 271
Arnaud's, NO........... 180
Arterra, SD 244
Artista, HS 111
Arun's, CH 50
A.R. Valentien, SD 244
Atlanta Fish Market, AT..... 15
Atlas Restaurant, SL....... 267
August, NO 180
Augustino's, NJ 172
Aujourd'hui, BO 36
Aureole, LV 125
Aureole, NY............. 189
Aurora, DF.............. 78
Avec, CH 50
Avenues, CH 50
Azúca Sabor Latino, SA ... 239
Azul, MI 154
Azuma Sushi, WH......... 291
Azzura Point, SD.......... 245
Babbo, NY 189
Bacchanalia, AT.......... 15
Bacchus, MW 161
Bacco, DT 96
Backstreet Café, HS 111
Bali by the Sea, HO 105
Balthazar, NY 189
Bambara, SC........... 234
B&G Oysters, BO 36
Bank by Jean-Georges, HS.. 111

Alphabetical Page Index

Barcelona, CT	70	Boat Street Cafe, SE	259
Baricelli Inn, CL	64	Bobby Flay Steak, AC	23
Barney's, LI	135	Boca, CI	59
Barolo Grill, DE	88	Boccaccio, BA	30
Barossa, MW	161	Boheme, The, OR	204
Barrington Country Bistro, CH	51	Boma, OR	205
Barrington's, CR	44	BonBonerie, CI	60
Barrio Café, PS	225	Bonda, CT	70
Bar Tartine, SF	249	Bone's Restaurant, AT	15
Basilic, OC	198	Bonnell's, DF	79
Battuto Restaurant, CL	64	Bonterra Dining, CR	44
Bayona, NO	180	Bouchon, LV	125
Bayport Cookery, MN	166	Boudro's Riverwalk, SA	240
Beach Bistro, TB	271	Boulevard, SF	249
Bear Cafe, WH	291	Bouley, NY	190
Beluga, CI	59	Bradley Ogden, LV	126
Belvedere, The, LA	144	Brasserie Perrier, PH	218
benjy's, HS	111	Bravo Bravo, CT	70
Bentara, CT	70	Bread Line, DC	282
Bernard's, CT	70	Brennan's, NO	180
Bernards Inn, NJ	172	Brennan's of Houston, HS	112
Bern's Steak House, TB	272	Brent's Deli, LA	144
Beverly Hills Grill, DT	96	Bricco, CT	71
Beyond Bread, TC	276	Brighton Steakhouse, AC	23
Bice, DF	78	Brigtsen's, NO	181
Biga on the Banks, SA	240	Broussard's, NO	181
Bijou Café, TB	272	Bryant & Cooper, LI	135
Bin 555, SA	240	Buddakan, NY	190
Binkley's, PS	225	Buddakan, PH	219
Birchrunville Store, PH	218	Buddha Bar, NY	190
Bis, DC	282	Buffet at Bellagio, LV	126
Bistro 88, AU	25	Buffet de la Gare, WH	292
Bistro Jeanty, SF	249	Busy Bee Cafe, WH	292
Bistro Moderne, HS	111	Cacao, MI	154
Bistro Olé, NJ	172	Café Adelaide, NO	181
Bistro Vatel, SA	240	Cafe Annie, HS	112
Bistro Zin, TC	277	Cafe Aspen, DF	79
Blackbird, CH	51	Café Atlántico/Minibar, DC	282
Black Pearl, TB	272	Café Four Seasons, AU	26
BlackSalt, DC	282	Café Bizou, LA	145
Black's Bar, DC	282	Cafe Bon Homme, DT	97
BLD, LA	144	Café Boulud, NY	190
Blu, NJ	172	Café Boulud, PB	212
Blue Bistro & Grill, OR	204	Cafe Brazil, DE	88
Blue Coral, OC	199	Cafe Chardonnay, PB	213
Blue Duck Tavern, DC	282	Café de France, OR	205
Blue Ginger, BO	36	Café Degas, NO	181
Blue Hill, NY	189	Café des Artistes, NY	190
Blue Hill/Stone Barns, WH	291	Cafe Juanita, SE	259
Blue Moon Fish Co., FL	101	Café L'Europe, PB	213
Blue Point Grill, NJ	172	Café Maison, KC	120
Blue Point Grille, CL	65	Cafe Martorano, FL	102
Blue Sage, PH	218	Cafe Matisse, NJ	173
Bluefin, OC	199	Cafe Maxx, FL	102
Bluefin, PH	218	Café Mezé, WH	292
Bluefin, TC	277	Café Pacific, DF	79
Bluehour, PO	231	Cafe Panache, NJ	173
BluePointe, AT	15	Cafe Poca Cosa, TC	277
Bluestem, KC	119	Cafe Ponte, TB	272

Cafe Red Onion, HS 112
Cafe Routier, CT 71
Café Sebastienne, KC 120
Cafe Vico, FL 102
Cafe Zoolu, OC 199
Caffe Mingo, PO 231
California Grill, OR 205
Campagne, SE 259
Campanile, LA 145
Canlis, SE 259
Canoe, AT 16
Canteen, SF 250
Canyon, FL 102
Capital Grille, DE 88
Capital Grille, DF 79
Capital Grille, HS 112
Capital Grille, LV 126
Capital Grille, MI 154
Capo, LA 145
Capriccio, AC 23
Carlos', CH 51
Carmelita, SE 259
Carmen, BO 36
Carnegie Deli, NY 190
Carole Peck's, CT 71
Carpe Diem, CR 45
Carrabba's Italian, HS 112
Casa D'Angelo, FL 102
Casa Tua, MI 154
Cascadia, SE 259
Cashion's Eat Place, DC 283
Caterina de Medici, WH . . . 292
Cavey's, CT 71
Ceviche Tapas Bar, TB 272
Chachama Grill, LI 135
Chanterelle, NY 191
Charivari, HS 113
Charleston, BA 30
Charlie Trotter's, CH 51
Chatham's Place, OR 205
Chaya Brasserie, LA 145
Cheesecake Factory, FL . . . 102
Cheesecake Factory, LA . . . 145
Cheesecake Factory, LI 135
Cheesecake Factory, MI . . . 154
Cheesecake Factory, OC . . . 199
Cheesecake Factory, PB . . . 213
Chef Allen's, MI 155
Chef Justin's, OR 205
Chef Mavro, HO 106
Chef Vola's, AC 23
Chez Betty, SC 234
Chez Catherine, NJ 173
Chez François, CL 65
Chez Jean-Pierre, PB 213
Chez Leon, SL 267
Chez Nous, HS 113
Chez Panisse, SF 250
Chez Panisse Café, SF 250
Chez Vincent, OR 206
Chicago Chop House, CH . . . 51
Chima Brazilian, FL 103
Chimayo, SC 235
China Gourmet, CI 60
Ching's Table, CT 71
Chinois on Main, LA 146
Chiso Restaurant, SE 260
Chops/Lobster Bar, AT 16
Chow Thai Addison, DF 79
Chow Thai Pacific Rim, DF . . 79
Christine, LA 146
Christini's Ristorante, OR . . 206
Churrascos, HS 113
Chuy's, AU 26
Ciao Lavanderia, SA 240
Circe, KC 120
Citronelle, DC 283
City Limits Diner, CT 72
CityZen, DC 283
Clancy's, NO 181
clarklewis, PO 231
Classics, CL 65
Clio/Uni, BO 36
Clyde's, BA 31
Coach Insignia, DT 97
Cochon, NO 182
Coi, SF 250
Columbia, TB 273
Commander's Palace, LV . . 126
Common Grill, The, DT 97
Coolfish, LI 135
Coquette Cafe, MW 162
Coriander Bistro, BO 37
Corks, BA 31
Coromandel, CT 72
Coromandel, WH 292
Cosmos, MN 167
Courtright's, CH 52
Crabtree's Hse., WH 292
Craft Dallas, DF 80
Craftsteak, LV 126
Craigie Street Bistrot, BO . . . 37
Crossing, The, SL 267
Crush, SE 260
Cucharamama, NJ 173
Cue, MN 167
CulinAriane, NJ 173
Cumin, CI 60
Cut, LA 146
Cuvée, NO 182
Cuvée World Bistro, TC 277
Cyclo, PS 226
Cyrus, SF 250
Dahlia Lounge, SE 260
Dakota, NO 182
Dakota Jazz, MN 167
Dalí Restaurant, BO 37
Da Marco, HS 113

D'Amico Cucina, MN.......167
Dancing Ganesha, MW 162
Daniel Boulud Brasserie, LV ...127
Daniel, NY................191
Danny Edwards, KC.......120
Danube, NY...............191
Da Pietro's, CT............72
Dario's, LI...............136
Da Ugo, LI................136
Daveed's at 934, CI 60
David Burke Fromagerie, NJ ..173
DC Coast, DC 283
Delfina, SF...............251
Del Frisco's, DE...........88
Del Frisco's, DF............80
Del Frisco's, OR 206
Della Femina, LI..........136
Delmonico Steak, LV......127
DeLorenzo's, NJ..........174
Del Posto, NY 191
Depot, LA 146
DePuy Canal House, WH ..293
Derek's, LA...............147
Deux Cheminées, PH......219
dévi, NY.................191
Dewey's Pizza, CI..........60
dick and harry's, AT.........16
Dick & Jenny's, NO 182
Dickie Brennan's, NO 182
Dining Room, NJ..........174
di Paolo, AT...............16
Dish, TC.................277
d.k Steak House, HO......106
Dmitri's, PH..............219
Dock's Oyster House, AC ...24
Doc's Restaurant, OR 206
Dominic's, SL.............267
Donovan's, SD 245
Drinkwater's, PS 226
Driskill Grill, AU...........26
Duke's Canoe Club, HO.....106
East Coast Grill, BO 37
Ecco, AT 16
Eddie Martini's, MW 162
Eddie V's, AU..............26
Eddie V's, PS.............226
Eduardo de San Angel, FL ..103
Eiffel Tower, LV...........127
El Bizcocho, SD 245
elements, PS 226
1111 Mississippi, SL 267
Eleven Madison Park, NY...191
11 Maple Street, PB 213
El Gaucho, SE............260
El Mirador, SA 240
Emeril's, NO 182
Emeril's New Orleans, LV....127
Emeril's Orlando, OR 206
Emeril's Tchoup Chop, OR...207

Enzo's On The Lake, OR 207
Equinox, DC 283
Equus, WH 293
Escoffier, The, WH........293
Escopazzo, MI 155
Euphemia Haye, TB........273
Everest, CH...............52
Eve, Restaurant, DC 284
EVOO, BO 37
Fahrenheit, CL 65
Farmhouse Inn, SF 251
Fascino, NJ 174
Feast, TC................277
Fifth Floor, SF 251
Fino, AU 26
Fiorella's Jack Stack, KC ...120
fire, CL..................65
Firefly, LV 128
Five, MN 167
Five Lakes Grill, DT 97
5 O'Clock Club, MW 162
Flagstaff House, DE.........89
Fleming's Prime, HS 114
Fleming's Prime, OR 207
Fleming's Prime, SA 241
Fleur de Lys, LV 128
Fleur de Lys, SF 251
Floataway Cafe, AT 17
Flying Fig, CL............66
Flying Fish Café, OR 207
Fogo de Chão, HS 114
Fonda San Miguel, AU 27
40 Sardines, KC 120
Fountain Restaurant, PH ..219
Four Seasons, NY 192
Four Seasons, PB 213
Francesca's at Sunset, SA ...241
Francesco, MI 155
Franck's, SC 235
Franklin Café, BO.........38
Frank Pepe Pizzeria, CT ...72
Frank Pepe's The Spot, CT...72
Frasca Food/Wine, DE 89
Frazer's, SL..............267
Frederick's, SA...........241
Fred's, TB...............273
Freelance Café, WH 293
French Corner, WH 293
Frenchie's, HS 114
French Laundry, SF........252
French Room, DF..........80
Frenchy's Bistro, LA 147
Fresco Italian Cafe, SC.....235
Frisky Oyster, LI 136
Frog and the Peach, NJ 174
Frontera Grill, CH.........52
Full Moon Grill, DE........89
Gables, NJ 174
Gaetano's, LV............128

Galanga, FL 103
Galatoire's, NO 183
Gary Danko, SF 252
Gayle, PH 219
General Warren Inne, PH . . 220
Genoa, PO 231
George's at the Cove, SD . . . 245
Georgian, SE 260
Gerard's Place, DC 284
Gibsons Steakhouse, CH 52
Gilmore's, PH 220
Giorgio's, PO 232
Giovanni's, CL 66
Giumarello's, NJ 174
Glitretind, SC 235
Golden Truffle, OC 199
Goode Co. Seafood, HS 114
Goodhues Grill, DF 80
Gotham Bar & Grill, NY 192
Grace, LA 147
Gramercy Tavern, NY 192
Grand St. Cafe, KC 121
Grape, DF 80
Gravitas, HS 114
Greene House, PS 226
Green Leaf, SE 260
Greens, SF 252
Green Zebra, CH 52
Grill/Hacienda del Sol, TC . . . 278
Grill on the Alley, LA 147
Grocery, NY 192
Grotto, BO 38
Grouse Mountain Grill, DE . . . 89
Guy Savoy, Restaurant, LV . . . 128
Hamasaku, LA 147
Hamersley's Bistro, BO 38
Hamilton's Grill Room, NJ . . 175
Hampton's, BA 31
Harvest, BO 38
Harvest, SL 268
Harvest on Fort Pond, LI . . . 136
Harvest on Hudson, WH . . . 294
Harvest Vine, SE 261
Hashiguchi, AT 17
Heat, CH 53
Heathman, PO 232
Helmand, BA 31
Helmand, BO 38
Herbfarm, SE 261
Herbsaint, NO 183
Hibiscus, DF 81
Higgins, PO 232
Highland's Garden, DE 89
Hobbit, OC 200
Hoku's, HO 106
Hotel Bel-Air, LA 148
Houston's, FL 103
Houston's, MI 155
Houston's, OC 200
Houston's, PB 214
Hudson's on the Bend, AU . . 27
Hue – A Restaurant, OR . . . 207
Hugo's, HS 115
Hump, LA 148
Hyde Park Prime, CL 66
Hy's Steak House, HO 106
Ibiza, CT 72
Ibiza, HS 115
Icarus, BO 39
Il Barilotto, WH 294
Il Capriccio, BO 39
Il Cenàcolo, WH 294
ilios noche, CR 45
Il Mulino, NY 192
Il Mulino New York, LI 137
Il Posto Ristorante, DT 97
Il Terrazzo Carmine, SE 261
Immigrant Room, MW 162
IndeBleu, DC 284
India's, DE 90
Indigo, HO 107
Indigo Landing, DC 284
Indika, HS 115
Inn at Langley, SE 261
Inn/Little Washington, DC . . . 284
Irene's Cuisine, NO 183
Iris, DF 81
Iris, NO 183
Iron Horse Grill, WH 294
Isla Montecristi, CT 73
Ixora, NJ 175
Jacques-Imo's Cafe, NO . . . 183
Jaguar, MI 155
Jake's, PH 220
JaK's Grill, SE 261
Jaleo, DC 285
Janos, TC 278
Japonais, CH 53
Jardinière, SF 252
J Bar, TC 278
Jean Georges, NY 193
Jean-Louis, CT 73
JeanRo, CI 61
Jean-Robert at Pigall's, CI . . 61
Jeffrey's, AU 27
Jeffrey's, CT 73
Jeff Ruby's, CI 61
Jiko, OR 208
Jimmy Hays, LI 137
JiRaffe, LA 148
Joël, AT 17
Joel Palmer House, PO 232
Joël Robuchon, LV 128
Joe's Stone Crab, MI 156
Joe T. Garcia's, DF 81
Johnny's Bar, CL 66
Johnny's Pizzeria, WH 294
Johnny V's, FL 103

Alphabetical Page Index

John's, DE	90	Latour, NJ	175
Josef's, FL	103	La Traviata, AU	27
Josie, LA	148	L'Auberge, DC	285
Joss Cafe, BA	31	Laurel, SD	245
Julia's Bistro, HS	115	Lavendou, DF	81
Kathy's Gazebo, PB	214	L'Escale, CT	73
Katsu-ya, LA	148	L'Espalier, BO	39
Kaygetsu, SF	252	L'Etoile, SA	242
Kee Grill, PB	214	L'Europe, WH	295
Kevin Taylor, DE	90	L'Uraku, HO	107
Keystone Ranch, DE	90	Le Bar Lyonnais, PH	221
King Louie's, SL	268	Le Bec-Fin, PH	221
Kinkead's, DC	285	Le Bernardin, NY	193
Kiran's, HS	115	Le Cirque, LV	129
Kitchen, DE	90	Le Coq au Vin, OR	208
Kitchen à Bistro, LI	137	Le Fou Frog, KC	121
Koo, WH	294	Le Français, CH	53
Korean B.B.Q. House, SA	241	Left Bank, DE	91
Kotobuki, LI	137	Legal Sea Foods, BO	39
K-Paul's, NO	184	Le Gourmand, SE	262
Kres Chophouse, OR	208	Leila's, LA	149
K Restaurant, OR	208	Le Mistral, PB	214
Kyma, AT	17	Lemongrass, BA	31
La Belle Vie, MN	167	Le Papillon, SF	253
La Bergerie, DC	285	Le Paradou, DC	285
La Bonne Auberge, PH	220	Le Petit Cafe, CT	73
La Brochette Bistro, FL	104	Le Rendez-Vous, TC	278
La Cachette, LA	149	Le Rêve, SA	242
La Carta de Oaxaca, SE	262	Les Nomades, CH	53
La Colline Verte, CT	73	Le Soir, LI	138
La Crémaillère, WH	295	Levain, MN	168
Lacroix, PH	220	Lewnes' Steakhouse, BA	32
La Dorada, MI	156	Liberty Bar, SA	242
La Duni, DF	81	Lidia's, KC	121
La Duni Latin Kitchen, DF	81	Lilette, NO	184
La Folie, SF	253	Limoncello Italian, SL	268
La Grenouille, NY	193	Linwoods, BA	32
La Griglia, HS	115	Little Fish, PH	221
La Grotta, AT	17	Little Moirs, PB	214
La Isla, NJ	175	Local, DF	82
Lake Park Bistro, MW	163	Locke-Ober, BO	40
La Mer, HO	107	Lodge, SA	242
Lampreia, SE	262	Log Haven, SC	235
Lan, MI	156	Lola, DF	82
L'Angolo, PH	220	Lola's, NO	184
La Panetière, WH	295	Lolita, CL	66
La Petite Grocery, NO	184	Lonesome Dove, DF	82
La Piccola Liguria, LI	137	Los Sombreros, PS	226
La Plage, LI	138	Lotus of Siam, LV	129
La Provence, NO	184	Louis XVI, LI	138
Lark, SE	262	Lou Malnati's, CH	53
Lark, DT	98	Luca d'Italia, DE	91
Lark Creek Inn, SF	253	Luce, CR	45
Las Canarias, SA	241	Lucia's, MN	168
La Tavola, AT	18	Lugano, SC	236
L'Atelier Joël Robuchon, LV	129	Lulu, CR	45
L'Atelier, DE	91	Macrina Bakery, SE	262
La Toque, SF	253	Madras Saravana, AT	18
La Tour, DE	91	Maestro, DC	286

Maggiano's, MW	163	Michel's, HO	107
Mainland Inn, PH	221	Michy's, MI	156
Mako of Japan, CT	74	Mickey & Mooch, CR	46
Makoto, DC	286	Mille Fleurs, SD	246
Manny's Steakhouse, MN	168	Mill River Inn, LI	138
Manresa, SF	253	Milos, Estiatorio, NY	193
Mansion /Turtle Creek, DF	82	Mimosa, LA	149
Marcello's La Sirena, PB	215	Mio, LI	138
Marcel's, DC	286	Mira, SL	268
Marchand's, TB	273	Mirabelle, AU	27
Marigold Kitchen, PH	221	Mirabelle, LI	139
Mari Luna Mexican, BA	32	Mirai Sushi, CH	54
Marine Room, SD	245	Mirko's, LI	139
Marinus, SF	254	Mise en Place, TB	274
Mariposa, The, SC	236	Mistral, BO	40
Mark's American, HS	116	Mistral, SE	263
Mark's Las Olas, FL	104	Mix, LV	130
Mark's South Beach, MI	156	Mizuna, DE	92
Market Street Grill, SC	236	mk, CH	54
Maroni Cuisine, LI	138	Mockingbird Bistro, HS	116
Marquesa, PS	227	Modern, NY	193
Martine, SC	236	Modo Mio, DF	83
Mary Elaine's, PS	227	Modus, SD	246
Masa, NY	193	Monsoon, SE	263
Masa's, SF	254	Montagna, DE	92
Mastro's, OC	200	Montana Avenue, TC	279
Mastro's, PS	227	Montgomery Inn, CI	61
Matsuhisa, DE	91	MoonFish Restaurant, OR	208
Matsuhisa, LA	149	Morimoto, NY	194
Matsuri, MI	156	Morimoto, PH	222
Matt's in the Market, SE	262	Mori Sushi, LA	150
Max Downtown, CT	74	Morton's, CH	54
Max's Oyster Bar, CT	74	Morton's, CI	62
Mayflower, CT	74	Morton's, DE	92
McCormick & Schmick's, BA	32	Morton's, PB	215
McCormick & Schmick's, KC	121	Mosca's, NO	184
McIntosh's Steaks, CR	45	Mr. B's: Steakhouse, MW	163
McKendrick's Steak, AT	18	Mulan, CH	55
McMahon's Prime, TC	278	Murata, PO	232
McNinch House, CR	45	Muriel's Jackson Sq., NO	185
Medici Café, LV	129	Musashino Sushi, AU	28
Meigas, CT	74	Muss & Turner's, AT	18
Mélisse, LA	149	Myth, SF	254
Melograno, PH	221	Naha, CH	55
Mel's Restaurant, DE	92	Nam, AT	19
Mercury Grill, DF	82	Nan, PH	222
Meritage, BO	40	Nana, DF	83
Mesa Grill, LV	129	Nan Thai, AT	19
Métro Bis, CT	75	Napa Rose, OC	200
Metropolitan Grill, SE	263	Nava, AT	19
Metropolitan, SC	236	Nectar, CI	62
MF Sushibar, AT	18	Nell's, SE	263
Mi Cocina, DF	83	Nemo, MI	157
Mia, AC	24	Neo of Melaka, TC	279
Michael Mina, LV	130	Neptune Oyster, BO	40
Michael Mina, SF	254	New Orleans Grill, NO	185
Michael's at the Citadel, PS	227	New Saigon, DE	92
Michael's On East, TB	273	New Yorker Club, SC	237
Michelangelo, SC	237	New York Prime, AT	19

Alphabetical Page Index

New York Prime, PB	215	Osteria del Teatro, MI	158
Niche, SL	268	Otilia's, HS	116
Nicholas, NJ	175	Overtures, PH	222
Nick & Toni's, LI	139	Pacific Time, MI	158
Nicola's, CI	62	Paesanos, SA	242
Nikko, CR	46	Paesanos Riverwalk, SA	242
Nine Roses, NO	185	Paesanos 1604, SA	242
1924 Main, KC	121	Palace, CI	62
Nishino, SE	263	Palena, DC	286
Nobhill, LV	130	Paley's Place, PO	233
Noble's, CR	46	Palm, CR	46
Nobu, LV	130	Palm, LI	140
Nobu, NY	194	Palm, NY	194
Nobu Dallas, DF	83	Palm, OR	209
Nobu Malibu, LA	150	Palme d'Or, MI	158
Nobu Miami Beach, MI	157	Paloma, PH	222
NOLA, NO	185	Palomino, CI	62
NoMI, CH	55	Pamplemousse, LV	131
No. 9 Park, BO	40	Pamplemousse Grille, SD	246
Norman's, MI	157	Panama Hatties, LI	140
Norman's, OR	209	Pane Rustica, TB	274
North One 10, MI	157	Pano's & Paul's, AT	19
North Pond, CH	55	Pappas Bros., DF	84
No. VI Chop House, DT	98	Pappas Bros., HS	116
Nuestra Cocina, PO	232	Parallax Restaurant, CL	67
Obelisk, DC	286	Park Kitchen, PO	233
Oceanaire Seafood, DF	84	Park 75, AT	20
Oceanaire Seafood, MN	168	Pascal's on Ponce, MI	158
Oceanaire Seafood, SD	246	Paseo, SE	263
Ocean House, WH	295	Patou, CR	46
Oceanique, CH	55	Paul Manno's, SL	269
Ocean 211, CT	75	Paul's Homewood, BA	32
Off the Grille Bistro, MI	157	Pelican Club, NO	185
Oishii, BO	41	Peppercorn's Grill, CT	75
Okada, LV	130	per se, NY	194
Oklahoma Joe's, KC	122	Peristyle, NO	185
Old Drovers Inn, WH	295	Perryville Inn, NJ	176
Olea, PO	233	Pesca on the River, SA	243
Oleana, BO	41	Pesce, HS	116
Oliveto Cafe, SF	255	Peter Luger, LI	140
Olive Tree Café, HO	107	Peter Luger, NY	195
Ombra, AC	24	Peter's Inn, BA	33
Ondine, CT	75	Petit Robert Bistro, BO	41
one sixtyblue, CH	56	P.F. Chang's, AC	24
One Walnut, CL	67	P.F. Chang's, MW	163
112 Eatery, MN	168	P.F. Chang's, OC	200
On 3, LI	139	P.F. Chang's, PB	215
Ophelia's on the Bay, TB	274	P.F. Chang's, PS	227
Opus, DE	93	P.F. Chang's, SA	243
Opus One, DT	98	Phnom Penh, CL	67
Orchids, HO	107	Pho Paris, CI	63
Orient, LI	139	Picasso, LV	131
Oriental Garden, NY	194	Piccolo, LA	150
Origin, NJ	175	Piccolo, LI	140
Ortanique, MI	157	Piccolo Arancio, CT	75
Ortega's, SD	246	Picholine, NY	195
Oslo Sushi Bar, DT	98	Pif, PH	222
Osteria del Circo, LV	131	Pigalle, BO	41
Osteria del Mondo, MW	163	Pine American, SC	237

Pineapple Room, HO	108	Ritz-Carlton Din. Rm., SF	255
Piñons, DE	93	River Café, NY	195
Pinot Provence, OC	201	River Lane Inn, MW	164
Pizzeria Bianco, PS	228	River Oyster Bar, MI	158
Pizzeria Paradiso, DC	287	Riversite, MW	164
Plates, WH	296	Rivoli, SF	256
Plaza Cafe, LI	140	Roaring Fork, PS	228
Plaza III, KC	122	Roberto's, NY	195
Pluckemin Inn, NJ	176	Robert's, LI	141
Polo Restaurant, LI	141	Rochester Chop House, DT	99
Pomme, SL	269	Romeo's Cafe, MI	159
Potager, DE	93	Roomba, CT	76
Potbelly Sandwich, MW	164	Room 39, KC	122
Precinct, CI	63	Roots Restaurant, MW	164
Prime One Twelve, MI	158	Roppongi, SD	247
Prime Rib, BA	33	Rosemary's, LV	131
Prime Rib, DC	287	Rosemary and Sage, NJ	176
Prime Rib, PH	222	Rover's, SE	264
Prime Steakhouse, LV	131	Roxane, SL	268
Primo, OR	209	Roy's, HO	108
Primo, TC	279	Roy's, OC	201
Q's, DE	93	Roy's, PS	228
Quattro, HS	117	Roy's, TB	274
Quince, SF	255	Roy's Ko Olina, HO	108
Quinones Room, AT	20	Roy's Orlando, OR	209
Radius, BO	41	Rugby Grille, DT	99
Rainbow Lodge, HS	117	Russell's, SE	264
Ralph's on the Park, NO	186	Ruth's Chris, BA	33
Rama, SD	246	Ruth's Chris, FL	104
Ramos House Café, OC	201	Ruth's Chris, HO	108
Range, SF	255	Ruth's Chris, OC	201
Rasika, DC	287	Ruth's Chris, OR	209
Rathbun's, AT	20	Ruth's Chris, SD	247
Rat's, NJ	176	Ryland Inn, NJ	176
Ray's The Steaks, DC	287	Saddle Peak Lodge, LA	150
Reata, DF	84	Saddle River Inn, NJ	177
Rebeccas, CT	75	Saffron, BA	33
Redd Restaurant, SF	255	Saffron Indian Bistro, MW	164
Red Iguana, SC	237	Sagami, NJ	177
Red the Steakhouse, CL	67	Sage, BO	42
Relish, WH	296	Saint-Emilion, DF	84
Remington, HS	117	Sake Tumi, MW	164
Rendezvous, BO	42	Sally's Apizza, CT	76
Restaurant B.T., TB	274	Salt Lick 360, AU	28
Restaurant du Village, CT	76	Salt Rock Grill, TB	275
Restaurant Eugene, AT	20	Salts, BO	42
Restaurant i, CR	47	Salumi, SE	264
Restaurant L, BO	42	Samos, BA	33
Restaurant X, WH	296	Sanford, MW	165
Rialto, BO	42	Sansei Seafood, HO	108
Rialto, LI	141	Sans Souci, CL	67
Rib Room, NO	186	Saporito's, BO	43
rioja, DE	93	Saul, NY	195
RioMar, NO	186	Savona, PH	223
Ristorante Café Cortina, DT	98	Scalini Fedeli, NJ	177
Ristorante Luci, MN	169	Schwa, CH	56
Ritz-Carlton Buckhead, AT	20	Scott Howard, SF	256
Ritz-Carlton Din. Rm., CH	56	Seablue, LV	132
		Seafood Buffet, SC	237

Alphabetical Page Index

Sea Saw, PS 228
Seasons, CH 56
Seasons, DC 287
Seasons 52, OR 210
Seastar, SE 264
Seeger's, AT 21
Seldom Blues, DT 99
Serenade, NJ 177
Serevan, WH 296
Sergio's Saravá, CL 68
1789, DC 288
Shade, HS 117
Shanghai Terrace, CH 57
Shari Sushi Lounge, OR 210
Shiao Lan Kung, PH 223
Shiro, LA 151
Shiro's Sushi, SE 264
Shoji, MI 159
Shun Lee Palace, NY 195
Sia's, AT 21
Siam Lotus Thai, LI 141
SideBern's, TB 275
Sidney Street Cafe, SL 269
Siena, AU 28
Sierra Mar, SF 256
Silo, SA 243
Silver Pond, FL 104
Singha Thai, MW 165
Singha Thai II, MW 165
Siri's Thai, NJ 177
Sitka & Spruce, SE 264
Six89 Kitchen, DE 94
Six Tables, TB 275
62 Main Restaurant, DF 84
Slanted Door, SF 256
Solera, MN 169
Solera Restaurant, DE 94
Sonoma Modern, CR 47
Sonora, WH 296
Sotto Sotto, AT 21
South Beach Grill, CI 63
South City Kitchen, AT 21
Southwark, PH 223
Sovalo, PH 223
Spago, LA 151
Spiaggia, CH 57
Spice Market, NY 196
Spoto's Oyster Bar, PB 215
Spring, CH 57
Sripraphai, NY 196
Stage House, NJ 177
Standard, DF 85
Starker's Reserve, KC 122
Starlite, AU 28
Starr Boggs, LI 141
Steak House, LV 132
Steel, DF 85
Stella!, NO 186
Sterling Brunch, LV 132

Sterling Inn, WH 297
Steuben's, DE 94
Stone Creek Inn, LI 141
Stonehill Tavern, OC 201
St. Paul Grill, MN 169
Striped Bass, PH 223
Strip House, HS 117
Stroud's, KC 122
Studio, OC 202
Sturkey's, CI 63
Suilan, AC 24
Sullivan's, CR 47
Sunfish Grill, FL 104
Susanna Foo, PH 223
Sushi Den, DE 94
Sushi Nanase, WH 297
Sushi Nozawa, LA 151
Sushi of Gari, NY 196
Sushi Ota, SD 247
Sushi Ran, SF 256
SushiSamba, MI 159
Sushi Sasa, DE 94
Sushi Seki, NY 196
Sushi Sono, BA 34
Sushi Yasuda, NY 196
Swann Lounge, PH 224
Sweet Basil, DE 95
Sweet Georgia Brown, DT . . .99
Swoon Kitchenbar, WH 297
SW Steakhouse, LV 132
Syzygy, DE 95
Taberna/Alabardero, DC 288
Tabla, PO 233
Ta-boo, PB 215
Tabu Grill, OC 202
t'afia, HS 117
Taka, AT 21
Takashi, SC 238
Tallgrass, CH 57
Talula, MI 159
Tamarind, AT 22
Tamarind, MI 159
Tamarind Bay, BO 43
Tapenade, SD 247
TapTap Haitian, MI 159
Taquitos Jalisco, OR 210
Taranta, BO 43
Tatsu's, KC 123
Tavern on the Green, NY . . .196
T. Cook's, PS 228
Tei Tei Robata Bar, DF 85
Telepan, NY 197
Tellers American, LI 142
TenPenh, DC 288
Teppo Yakitori, DF 85
Terra, SF 257
Terra Cotta, TC 279
Terrapin, WH 297
Tersiguel's, BA 34

subscribe to zagat.com

Texas de Brazil, DF 85
Thai House, OR 210
Thai Square, DC 288
Thai Thani, OR 210
3660 on the Rise, HO 109
3030 Ocean, FL 104
32 East, PB 216
Thomas Henkelmann, CT 76
Three Birds, CL 68
3 Doors Down Café, PO 233
Tierra, AT 22
Timo, MI 160
Todd English's bluezoo, OR . . . 211
Todd's Unique Dining, LV . . . 132
Tomoe Sushi, NY 197
Toni's Sushi Bar, MI 160
Tony Mandola's, HS 118
Tony's, HS 118
Tony's, SL 269
Topolobampo, CH 57
Toro, BO 43
Tosca, DC 288
Toscana, CR 47
Totaro's, PH 224
town, HO 109
Toyoda Sushi, SE 264
Trader Vic's, PS 229
Tradition by Pascal, OC 202
Traffic Jam & Snug, DT 99
Trattoria Diane, LI 142
Trattoria Marcella, SL 269
Tree Room, SC 238
Tribute, DT 100
Troquet, BO 43
Tru, CH 58
Truffles, SL 270
Twenty Manning, PH 224
2941 Restaurant, DC 289
21 Club, NY 197
20.21, MN 169
2 Amys, DC 289
240 Union, DE 95
Uchi, AU 28
Union, SE 265
Union Bay Cafe, SE 265
Union League Cafe, CT 76
Union Square Cafe, NY 197
Upperline, NO 186
UpStairs on the Square, BO . . 43
Upstream, CR 47
Valbella, CT 76
Valentino, LA 151
Valentino Las Vegas, LV . . . 133
Valley at the Garrison, WH . . . 297
Venetian Room, OR 211

Ventana Room, TC 279
Veritas, NY 197
Versailles, MI 160
Vespaio, AU 29
Vetri, PH 224
Vic & Anthony's, HS 118
Victoria & Albert's, OR 211
Vidalia, DC 289
Vie, CH 58
Vincent, MN 169
Vincent's on Camelback, PS . . 229
Vito's Chop House, OR 211
Vivace, SD 247
Vivace, TC 279
Vivo, CL 68
Vix, MI 160
Vizard's on the Avenue, NO . . 187
Volare, CR 47
Volterra, SE 265
Wahso, SC 238
Wasabi, WH 297
Washington Inn, NJ 178
Washington Square, PH . . . 224
Water Grill, LA 151
Watershed, AT 22
West End Grill, DT 100
Whispers, NJ 178
White House, AC 24
Wildfire, CH 58
Wildflower, TC 280
Wild Ginger, SE 265
Wildwood, PO 233
WineSellar, SD 247
Wink, AU 29
Wish, MI 160
Wisteria, AT 22
Wolfgang Puck Cafe, OR . . . 211
Woodfire Grill, AT 22
Xaviar's at Piermont, WH . . . 298
York Street Restaurant, DF . . 86
Yujean Kang's, LA 152
Zafra, NJ 178
Zander Cafe, MN 170
Zaytinya, DC 289
Z Cuisine, DE 95
Zebra Restaurant, CR 48
Zelo, MN 170
Zengo, DE 95
Zephs', WH 298
zin, KC 123
Zingerman's, DT 100
Zinnia, SL 270
Zoe's by the Lake, NJ 178
Zoot, AU 29
Zuni Café, SF 257

Wine Vintage Chart

This chart, based on our 0 to 30 scale, is designed to help you select wine. The ratings (by **Howard Stravitz**, a law professor at the University of South Carolina) reflect the vintage quality and the wine's readiness to drink. We exclude the 1987, 1991–1993 vintages because they are not that good. A dash indicates the wine is either past its peak or too young to rate.

	'86	'88	'89	'90	'94	'95	'96	'97	'98	'99	'00	'01	'02	'03	'04	'05
WHITES																
French:																
Alsace	–	–	26	26	25	24	24	23	26	24	26	27	25	22	24	25
Burgundy	25	–	23	22	–	28	27	24	23	26	25	24	27	23	25	26
Loire Valley	–	–	–	–	–	–	–	–	–	–	24	25	26	23	24	25
Champagne	25	24	26	29	–	26	27	24	23	24	24	22	26	–	–	–
Sauternes	28	29	25	28	–	21	23	25	23	24	24	28	25	26	21	26
German:	–	25	26	27	24	23	26	25	26	23	21	29	27	25	26	26
Austrian:																
Grüner Velt./Riesling	–	–	–	–	25	21	28	28	27	22	23	24	26	26	26	26
California:																
Chardonnay	–	–	–	–	–	–	–	–	–	24	23	26	26	27	28	29
Sauvignon Blanc	–	–	–	–	–	–	–	–	–	–	27	28	26	27	26	–
REDS																
French:																
Bordeaux	25	23	25	29	22	26	25	23	25	24	29	26	24	25	23	27
Burgundy	–	–	24	26	–	26	27	26	22	27	22	24	27	24	24	25
Rhône	–	26	28	28	24	26	22	24	27	26	27	26	–	25	24	–
Beaujolais	–	–	–	–	–	–	–	–	–	–	24	–	23	27	23	28
California:																
Cab./Merlot	–	–	–	28	29	27	25	28	23	26	22	27	26	25	24	24
Pinot Noir	–	–	–	–	–	–	–	24	23	24	23	27	28	26	23	–
Zinfandel	–	–	–	–	–	–	–	–	–	–	–	25	23	27	22	–
Oregon:																
Pinot Noir	–	–	–	–	–	–	–	–	–	–	–	26	27	24	25	–
Italian:																
Tuscany	–	–	–	25	22	24	20	29	24	27	24	26	20	–	–	–
Piedmont	–	–	27	27	–	23	26	27	26	25	28	27	20	–	–	–
Spanish:																
Rioja	–	–	–	–	26	26	24	25	22	25	24	27	20	24	25	–
Ribera del Duero/Priorat	–	–	–	–	26	26	27	25	24	25	24	27	20	24	26	–
Australian:																
Shiraz/Cab.	–	–	–	24	26	23	26	28	24	24	27	27	25	26	–	–